BEYOND THE RULING CLASS

Suzanne Keller

BEYOND THE RULING CLASS

Strategic Elites in Modern Society

RANDOM HOUSE △ NEW YORK

SECOND PRINTING

 Published in New York by Random House, Inc., and simultaneously in Toronto, Canada, by Random House of Canada, Limited.
Library of Congress Catalog Card Number: 63–8270
Manufactured in the United States of America by H. Wolff, New York.

To the Memory of A.R.

ACKNOWLEDGMENTS

▲

As regards this book, my most immediate debt, both intellectual and personal, is to Charles Page, who taught me, by his own example, the meaning of the phrase "an infinite capacity for taking pains." His help and advice extended far beyond editorial criticism as he prodded me to rethink, revise, and rethink again numerous theoretical issues. I drew freely on his knowledge and suggestions, occasionally balked at his criticism, and always marvelled at his generosity of spirit.

Intellectual growth is stimulated by great teachers or great adversaries. I consider myself fortunate to have had the former. To Robert K. Merton I owe more than I can express. The impact of his lectures, altogether magical in memory, grows rather than diminishes with each passing year. It was a challenge and a joy to learn from him.

To Paul F. Lazarsfeld, a brilliant and provocative presence in the classroom, I owe whatever sensitivity and appreciation I have for the science of social science.

An earlier teacher, Phillip Weintraub of Hunter College, first aroused my interest in sociology and to him I am still grateful.

Of all the friends I would like to thank, Marisa Zavalloni deserves special mention for her intellectual and moral support in all kinds of weather.

My thanks to Charles D. Lieber, Leonore C. Hauck, and Judith Hillery of Random House for editorial assistance with the manuscript.

S. K.

CONTENTS

BEYOND THE RULING CLASS

1. INTRODUCTION

The existence and persistence of influential minorities is one of the constant characteristics of organized social life. Whether a community is small or large, rich or poor, simple or complex, it always sets some of its members apart as very important, very powerful, or very prominent. The notion of a stratum elevated above the mass of men may prompt approval, indifference, or despair, but regardless of how men feel about it, the fact remains that their lives, fortunes, and fate are and have long been dependent on what a small number of men in high places think and do.

A great deal has been said about this fact of social life, but men do not know nearly enough about this minority who in every epoch and generation play a large role in shaping the future—by the laws they pass, the books they write, the wars they win or lose, and by the passions that stir them to action. Like a secret society, those at the top rarely reveal the inner workings of their worlds. There are, of course, eyewitness accounts, inevitable letters to mistresses, diaries written early in life and memoirs at its close, but these bear the same relation to a sociology of elites as a compendium of patients' symptoms bears to medicine—they contain some raw material but material that is of little value unless it is classified and organized, so that the general may be distinguished from the particular, and the universal from the temporary and idiosyncratic.

Great difficulties face the investigator who wishes to move from anecdote and ideology to testable theory in this field. The subject has been studied by so many different disciplines in different epochs, each using its own terminology and orientation, that it is next to impossible to develop a comparative perspective of the many accumulated insights. It is not easy to be sure of what we "know" about the "managers of collective life" when we meet them in so many different guises—as noble warriors praying to the gods for yet another victory in war, as Oriental potentates clothed in terrible splendor, or as priests jealously guarding their rituals. Moreover, each writer seems to start afresh without recourse to earlier relevant work, and more often than not, fine theoretical insights are blended with ideological and partisan argument, parading as impartial analysis. Objective analysis itself requires at least as a starting point an inventory of relevant concepts and a systematic overview of empirical materials. This is impossible without some explicit theoretical framework. Such a framework is proposed in this book. It is presented in the hope of clarifying the historical development of elites as well as their current role in industrial societies.

Elites defined

Some of the writings in this field suggest that elites are as old as recorded history; others, that they are as new as the machine age—depending on the definitions employed or implied by different authors. At the start, therefore, it is necessary to establish the definition to be used throughout this study. Here the term *elites*[1] refers first of all to a minority of individuals designated to serve a collectivity in a socially valued way. Elites are effective and responsible minorities—effective as regards the performance of activities of interest and concern to others to whom these elites are responsive. Socially significant elites are ultimately responsible for the realization of major social goals and for the continuity of the social order. Continuity, as used here, implies contributing to an ongoing social process, and while not synonymous with survival includes the possibility of decline.

Social leadership is one of the sustaining forces of organized society. After a given population has reached a certain size, the satisfaction of its material and spiritual needs demands some sort of organization and the establishment of precise rules and roles supported by a system of beliefs. Once so organized, responsibility for the common life devolves not on all but only on some of the members, principally on its chiefs, gods, and rulers, that is, particular elites.

In periods of rapid social change, the outline of these elites against a shifting background is sharply visible. In periods of relative stability, these elites are merged with the objects, habits, and manners of their age. The timeless, functional aspects of their roles is therefore apparent primarily during periods of social transition or crisis.

Two main perspectives characterize past studies of elites—the moral and the functional. The first concentrates on the moral excellence of individuals, the second on the functional role of a stratum. Both, however, start from the existence of a group of people set apart from the rest by a distinctive set of duties and rewards. One accounts for the existence of elite groups in terms of the superiority of given individuals, the other, in terms of the social function of a class or group. The moral approach easily degenerates into mysticism, the functional approach, into tautology.

In this book we shall attempt to reconcile the two. We shall try to keep the functions of elites separate from the success or failure of individuals in fulfilling these functions.

The concept of elites is particularly useful in clarifying major features of modern industrial societies. It is becoming increasingly evident that these cannot be effectively analyzed with such concepts as ruling class, castes, and aristocracies—although all of these tap a part, as we shall see, of what is meant by elites. Because of the characteristics of industrial societies, the social significance of elites is growing, as is the difference between them and ruling classes. One of the striking trends in these societies is not, as many would suppose, toward a decline of elite groups, but toward their proliferation, greater variety, and more extensive powers. As societies become occupationally and economically more differentiated, elites become ever more important both as guardians and creators of collective values, and as managers of collective aims and ambitions. Men should understand the causes of this great change, for the accompanying impact will transform their own and their children's lives.

Influential theories of elites

Elites are a fascinating area of study appealing to diverse types of thinkers. The result has been an abundance of insight alongside of a poverty of concepts and theories. There is no substantial agreement on most aspects of the problem, although there are many arguments over terms and intentions. Essential questions as to how many elites there are, why they emerge, and how they survive, are raised in prefatory remarks only to be later ignored. Such writings as do deal with these matters nearly all refer back to Pareto or Mosca as if the mere invoking of these names were enough to insure safe passage across uncharted intellectual territory.

The writers to be dealt with briefly in this chapter are not exhaustive but representative of the best work done on the general question of the relationship between elites and society. These writers fall into two main groups: those selecting a single elite—usually the political elite—as socially decisive, and here Aristotle, Pareto, and Mosca come to mind; and those who insist that a number of elites coexist, sharing power, responsibilities, and rewards. Here belong such writers as Saint-Simon, Karl Mannheim, and Raymond Aron. Despite the variety, not to say the confusion, in the terms and concepts used, each of these writers has added something to the general understanding of the phenomenon, though none has painted the entire canvas.

ARISTOTLE

Aristotle's purpose in writing the *Politics* was to halt the decline of the ancient city-state by devising a blueprint for a new and better one. His review of the various constitutions of the Greek city-states was an attempt to discover what type of constitution is best adapted to different historical, social, and moral conditions.

Aristotle concentrated on the nature and purposes both of the state and the men selected to serve it. In his view, the state had a function beyond that of preventing crime or regulating exchange. Like Plato, he saw the state as an instrument designed to fulfill collective ends and to serve communal needs, for the state exists, he stressed, not for the sake of life in general but of the good life.[2] In order to fulfill its major mission, it needs extraordinary men, men of virtue and excellence, who value justice and the common interest above private gain. Naturally such men must be wealthy because without wealth no man has the leisure to rule well (and, presumably, the state could not pay them adequately).

As a model of how to begin the study of elites this conception serves rather well, provided one does not define Aristotle's conception of the state too narrowly. His leaders are not merely the political elite but all those whose actions and efforts are oriented to safeguarding and promoting the interests of the community. In this respect they resemble the aggregate of political, economic, moral, and cultural leaders of our own day. But they also remind us of earlier times when a few individuals assumed all or most of these communal responsibilities. In addition, and this is most important, Aristotle approached the entire question of communal leadership from the point of view of the function this leadership served. He did not make the mistake, frequently made by later scholars, of equating the purposes of men seeking to attain positions of leadership with the actual social functions of these positions.

Aristotle also distinguished between general social functions and particular social machinery for fulfilling these functions. In order to achieve such broad communal goals as coordinating conflicting interests, defending territorial boundaries, and allocating rewards and punishments, he reasoned, communities must develop specialized machinery or institutions. The state is an example of such an institution, the government being its dynamic aspect. Whether the state develops into a monarchy, tyranny, or democracy depends on particular social and historical conditions, but that it will assume one of these forms can be predicted from a knowledge of social organization. Irrespective of the form of government that develops, an elite must emerge to carry on the affairs of the state, for elites, Aristotle argued, are more permanent than particular institutional arrangements. The elite of skilled specialists who are at the same time virtuous men should be responsible for the moral and material welfare of the community.

Aristotle thus linked elites to both the moral and material needs of the community. Unlike many later writers, he did not single out one or the other aspect as basic: he conceived of a single group fulfilling both functions. This conception was plausible at a time when the various community functions were still largely undifferentiated. But while Aristotle's own community differs significantly from modern industrial societies, his insistence that communal leaders have both moral and material responsibilities is one of the guiding ideas of the subsequent analysis in this book.

It is a long historical jump from Aristotle to Saint-Simon. However, these two thinkers exhibit a theoretical affinity in their appreciation of the crucial role played by elites in human society.

SAINT-SIMON

Nineteenth-century Europe and America produced many utopian visions of the social order,[3] one of which was held by a French nobleman, Claude Henri de Rouvroy, Count of Saint-Simon, who anticipated some of the major developments of modern times and whose interest in elites was lifelong. All of Saint-Simon's work, most of it published between 1802 and 1825, deals in one way or another with the problem of how industrial society is to be organized, a question that preoccupied many thinkers of the day. The unforeseen changes brought about by the arrival of the machine age had resulted in a series of new social problems pressing for solution.

The social equality anticipated by prophets of the French Revolution was not nearly the panacea that earlier writers had thought it would be; new types of inequalities emerged as rapidly as some of the older ones vanished. This led to a reappraisal of the question of equality in human affairs and to some highly novel theories, one of which formed the basis of Saint-Simon's theory of elites. Saint-Simon believed that the good society is based upon man's natural capacities, and these capacities, physiologists had taught him, were highly unequal. Utilizing the classification of individuals developed by Bichat, he divided society into three mutually exclusive social classes which, he argued, perform distinctive social functions.[4] These three functions, each requiring special personnel, include the planning of social action—the intelligence function; the carrying out of essential industrial work—the motor function; and fulfillment of the spiritual needs of human beings—the sensory function. The members of each class would be functional specialists. Within each class those individuals who naturally excelled others belonged to one of Saint-Simon's three *elites*—the scientists, economic organizers, or cultural-religious leaders.

Revolutionary in Saint-Simon's thought was his anticipation of the crucial importance of industrial producers, an elite group which he viewed as holding a more strategic position in the new social order than had the political leaders of old. In his view, industry and science were to dominate social life and therefore had to be "socialized," that is, their activities had to be carried out for the public good and under public surveillance. In fact, in industrial society, "politics" would consist of the science of production, and only those who "actively participate in the economic life" would have the right to vote. As Durkheim noted, this view stands in direct contrast to that of the classical economists who sought to keep politics and economics separate.[5]

Another prominent characteristic of Saint-Simon's work is his preoccupation with the moral regeneration of the new society. Observing the spiritual malaise resulting from the simultaneous pull of the opposing doctrines of feudalism and industrialism, Saint-Simon urged that men must choose one or the other lest the social order itself perish. Industrialism as the force of the future was viewed as an appropriate basis for such regeneration. Industrial organization itself should be perfected, he argued, and all social activities subordinated to industrial activities. Saint-Simon was an advocate of a directed or a managed equilibrium (though he did not use these terms), for to him society was necessarily a hierarchical system, to be supervised by those at the top. At one stage he thought of the leading industrialists themselves as the appropriate supervisors, but later he seemed to favor setting apart a special group of what amounted to high priests preaching the gospel of industrialism. These later exaggerations should not obscure his earlier insights. He understood, perhaps more fully than most later writers, that the problems of social organization are multidimensional, and require not only efficient administrators but also ideals and larger purposes to which these administrators may be committed.

By rejecting the model of a single dominant political elite and by substituting for it the industrial elite, Saint-Simon anticipated, even while he exaggerated, a number of modern tendencies. The reign of force, for example, was over; the arbitrary despotism of the past would now be supplanted by a reasonable supervision by men of skill and experience. Knowledge, merit, and skill were to be the new forces of social control.[6] In other words, he foresaw the rise of administration as distinct from government, a distinction which Marx would make so much of some years later. The reign of enlightened self-interest had begun.

A serious source of ambiguity in Saint-Simon's work concerns his treatment of social classes and their relationship to elites. Originally, he had stated that the population henceforth was to be divided into three social classes, each of which was to perform a major social function and each of which would be headed by an elite. Later he makes frequent references to the two classes of rich and poor without indicating whether these groups develop within or between or parallel to the original three classes. Saint-Simon implies that the new social order will not disrupt the distinction between rich and poor of the old order. At one point he even advises the rich, in the interest of the new morality, to give away their surplus wealth to the poor, implying that the abuses of class inequalities may be eliminated without doing away with the classes which gave rise to them. On the other hand, he also seems to imply that elites will be linked to specific social functions and will therefore be independent of the rich and poor. These ideas were never made explicit, but Saint-Simon is the first major social analyst to suggest that class divisions are not intrinsically connected with the presence or absence of elites. This was an extraordinary insight in his own day—one neglected by all but a few modern students of social structure.[7]

Saint-Simon, more clearly than Aristotle, understood the interconnection between elites and social functions and tried to work out a theoretical scheme to explain this relationship. He also understood that the functions performed by elites are related to the moral order, although in some unspecified way. Finally, he underlined the distinction between elites and social classes, a distinction, however, which he frequently ignored. His work influenced a number of important thinkers, among them, Vilfredo Pareto and Gaetano Mosca.

PARETO AND MOSCA

The views of these two Italian early twentieth-century contemporaries are by no means identical. That they expressed similar ideas about the nature and role of elites in society, however, perhaps justifies bringing together the discussion of these ideas in the present context.[8]

Pareto, to whom the term "elite" owes much of its current popularity, was aware that in principle there are as many elites as there are different occupational groups, but his writings as well as Mosca's concentrate on the political and governing elite because of its historical and social importance. Their insistence that political elites are constant elements in societies was as much the result of their review of selected historical evidence as of their polemics against Marx. If political elites are inevitable, they seem to say, how can a classless society be established? Like Aristotle, they expect the political elite always to be drawn from the wealthier classes, thus implying that as long as there are political elites there must be classes of wealth. In short, rather than satisfactorily answering Marx, they further obfuscated effective social analysis by failing to distinguish between the function of elites and their recruitment.

The chief dialectical principle for Pareto and Mosca is not the Marxist struggle of the economically deprived against the privileged, but the conflict between two minorities: those who hold and those who seek political office. Pareto saw this conflict as a struggle between representatives of two types of social character, the lions and the foxes; Mosca assigned key significance to the skillful utilization of political formulas by those in power. But both writers, in Machiavellian fashion, emphasized the importance of correct strategy for the maintenance of power, and both underscored the importance of traditional and nonrational forces in communal life. Consequently their conceptions often have been considered cynical or antidemocratic, an interpretation which rests on a misconception of their aims. For these writers were fundamentally concerned with the reasons for minority rule, concluding that such rule is a permanent (although a nonrational) feature of organized social life.

Their explanations are less cogent than their observations, however, for in both cases elements of human nature were used to account for social arrangements. Yet Pareto and Mosca were also aware that this kind of reductionism did not solve the problem they posed. If human nature is to be held responsible for the rule of minorities over majorities, why do these minorities take so many different forms? What accounts for the historical variety of elite types—the Chinese literati, the Turkish warriors, the Venetian merchants, the British manufacturers?

Neither Pareto nor Mosca solved the problem of the relationship between elites and social classes. They seemed to realize in principle that the two were separate entities, but confounded them in practice. Characteristically, Mosca writes: In "fairly populous societies that have attained a certain level of civilization *ruling classes* do not justify their power exclusively by de facto possession of it. . . . So if a society is deeply imbued with the Christian spirit, *the political class* will govern by the will of the sovereign." [9] Pareto, fully aware that different pyramids of talent require different types of men at the top (a Saint Francis of Assisi as distinct from a Krupp, is one of his examples), argued that because the class of superior inviduals in most societies is usually also the richest, wealth and power must go hand in hand. Despite many qualifications he maintained this position throughout his writings. The difficulty faced by Pareto and Mosca stems from their failure to distinguish between the members of an elite who are rich and the rich who may be part of an elite. That the members of a political elite, for example, are rich, does not mean that wealth is the basis of this elite—its members may be rich because they have been rewarded for political services, or because they have managed to marry into wealth.

The analysis of Pareto and Mosca faces another difficulty. Neither writer systematically developed a notion of the political elite as a specialized group responsible for a particular institutional sector. Had they done so they would have noted a striking feature of their own contemporary Italian society, namely the coexistence of an upper class in charge of business, a political elite directing affairs of state, and a cultural elite in charge of leisure and the arts.

The first group consisted predominantly of men who earned their wealth through entrepreneurial activities, the second of individuals elected to office, and the third of aristocrats with the leisure and the taste for the arts.[10]

Both Pareto and Mosca refer to a ruling elite which performs important social functions and represents some of the central values of society, but they did not go much beyond Aristotle's remarks on these points. Exploitation of the ruled by the rulers was considered inevitable, as was the "circulation of the elites" (a conception to be considered later). Both assumed that the existing elite is composed of the "best" people—best, that is, in terms of the values of the society at a given time.

The work of Pareto and Mosca is useful for a study of elites today chiefly because these writers presented some interesting hypotheses and raised fundamental questions about social structure and social control. But these are clearly pioneer statements and should not be taken, as unfortunately they sometimes are, as definitive formulations or reliable conclusions. Perhaps their chief contribution is the insistence that a ruling class or elite is an inevitable feature of complex societies and not, as Marx argued, a passing phase in human history. This insistence has led some scholars to examine more carefully a phenomenon to which the fate of humanity is presumably eternally linked.

KARL MANNHEIM

Karl Mannheim, one of the most imaginative of social analysts, is best known for his contributions to the sociology of knowledge and his strong advocacy of social planning within the framework of political democracy. Although he did not pursue the subject very far on his own, Mannheim also made several notable contributions to the study of elites. Unfortunately, his ideas generally have been neglected by present-day students of elites. In his most ambitious work, *Man and Society in an Age of Reconstruction* (1946), Mannheim notes that elites have proliferated rather than declined with the advance of industrial society. He distinguishes between two fundamentally different types of elites: an integrative elite composed of political and organization leaders; and a sublimative elite made up of moral-religious, aesthetic, and intellectual leaders.[11] The principal function of the first type of elite is the integration of a great number of individual wills; the second type, to sublimate the psychic energies of a people. Mannheim argues that people should not use all their psychic energies in the material struggle for existence, but should channel them into contemplation and reflection, and thereby discover means to alleviate that struggle. In the long run, moral survival is seen as a compeer to physical survival. Whereas the integrative elite works through formal political organizations, the sublimative elite works through more informal channels such as groups, cliques, and coteries. Its aims are to develop socially productive outlets for the hopes, fears, and thwarted desires of individuals, by forming their tastes, by encouraging thoughtful critical discussion on timely issues, and by stimulating the development of original perspectives and interests.

Mannheim is very explicit on this point: elites have functions to perform for the collectivity and it is the nature of these functions rather than the motives of power-hungry individuals that determines the kinds of elites that arise. In short, Mannheim sees elites as part of a system of collective relationships and necessities. This conception provides a theoretical basis for the study of several critical questions: Which elites are particularly important, and why, at a given period in a society's development? How many elites are there in this period, and why? Which elites hold the spotlight in the short-run, which in the long-run, and why?

Mannheim also suggests that elites constitute a system of interdependent parts, each participating in the "body politic"—and here he invests an old term with new meaning. "By 'body politic' we shall . . . understand all groups and leaders who play an active role in the organization of society. They may be self-appointed entrepreneurs, or elected magistrates, high trade-union functionaries or feudal lords of the past. Our concept comprises those political elements par excellence that concentrate in their hands administrative functions, military power, and social leadership." [12] This "body politic" increases in size and scope as industrialism advances. To the dichotomy of state and society, there now is added economy and society, culture and society, army and society, and the academy and society. Each constitutes a center of control, and is partly autonomous and partly bound to the whole. Each is commanded and represented by leading individuals, specializing in economic, cultural, military, and intellectual functions.

Mannheim posed fundamental problems of social analysis by raising these distinctions, but he did not systematically explore them. Like most of his predecessors, he fails to distinguish between elites and ruling classes—he deals with each in a different part of his work, and nowhere does he reconcile the separate discussions. For example, in his essay on the ruling classes of the United States and the Soviet Union,[13] he makes no reference to the elites of either society, and his treatment of elites includes no reference to the class system. Perhaps this feature of his work rests on a sound basis for, as much of the evidence to be presented illustrates, these two aspects of the social order are indeed distinct and independent phenomena. Mannheim, however, nowhere indicates why this must be so.

His essay on power contains important insights into the problems with which this study is concerned. He postulates that "no society can exist without some form of power" and asks what kind of power prevails in given situations. In pursuing this question, Mannheim draws three distinctions: between personal and institutional power; between functional and arbitrary power; and between functional and communal power—conceptual distinctions that have close similarities. Personal power is essentially that exercised by the stronger individual for his own benefit, whereas institutional power is that exercised by individuals on behalf of a collectivity through specified and legitimate social channels. Functional power, in contrast to communal power, is anchored to specialized associations and institutions. Personal power, being based on individual superiority, is arbitrary. Elites, in Mannheim's view, exercise *functional* and *institutional* power.

Contrary to the Marxists and the "Machiavellians" referred to earlier, Mannheim believes the replacement of personal and arbitrary power by functional and institutional power to be a major social trend in modern times. That is, although power and rule by the powerful are inevitable and even necessary features of any society, increasingly, power is being exercised within the context of specific institutions and hence is more legitimate and limited.

Unfortunately, Mannheim does not match his originality and keen awareness of many of the complexities of social arrangements with a thorough and systematic development of his ideas. Many of his most suggestive insights are presented in isolated phrases and paragraphs, and one must reinterpret much of his work, if it is to be effectively exploited. Nevertheless, his writings do contain one of the most important contributions to the analysis of elites in the present century.

Mannheim was a member of a transitional generation of scholars whose works form a bridge between an older (and largely European) generation of philosophical students of social structure and social change and younger writers today (largely American) whose theoretical efforts are grounded in empirical studies. In this respect, and with particular reference to the analysis of patterns of power, Mannheim may be grouped with such scholars as Robert M. MacIver,[14] Robert S. Lynd,[15] Harold D. Lasswell, and Raymond Aron; C. Wright Mills,[16] Daniel Bell,[17] and William Kornhauser[18] represent the younger generation. Of all these contributions, those of Lasswell and Aron are especially relevant to the present discussion.

HAROLD LASSWELL

Lasswell and some of his younger colleagues have made the only attempt to date to conduct comprehensive empirical studies of political elites on a world scale.[19] But the importance of this effort has not been matched by its results; the investigations of various international elites lack historical perspective as well as theoretical depth. On these counts, they do not approach Lasswell's early work on elites, particularly his application of selected concepts from the newer psychological disciplines to the study of elites in *Politics, Who Gets What, When, and How* (1936)[20]—a provocative if somewhat uneven book, with a bit of the quality of a "how to get to the top" manual. There and elsewhere[21] Lasswell is clearly more interested in ascertaining what channels are open for those aspiring to elite positions and what rewards await those who succeed than in the social and cultural circumstances underlying the existence of these positions.

It is never clear, either in Lasswell's early or later work, whether he is primarily concerned with political elites—as the titles of several of his works suggest—or with all types. He never meets the question since he defines elites in socio-psychological rather than in sociological and historical terms. Elites, he tells us, are those who "get the most of what there is to get," and three things worth getting are deference, income, and safety. A single elite may monopolize all three types of reward or several coexisting elites may share them. Lasswell also refers to a "ruling elite" without indicating, however, whether there are subordinate or merely competing elites.

Perhaps Lasswell's most telling observations concern the role of various skills, personality attributes, attitudes, and symbols in the struggle for attaining and maintaining elite status. The social and psychological significance of specific attributes reflects particular historical and social conditions, with symbol manipulation becoming gradually more important in the modern era. Lasswell tends to view the elites of a given epoch as possessing similar skills and values—a conception that plays down or precludes the recognition of the coexistence of elites in a single society with widely divergent or antithetical interests, skills, and values. Such variation among elites as he does find he attributes to socio-psychological factors. But although Lasswell adds little theoretical clarification to the principal problems considered in this study, his concern with the socio-psychological traits of elites, as in the case of Pareto, is stimulating and should be integrated with a more historical and sociological approach.

RAYMOND ARON

The writings of Raymond Aron, the French sociologist and journalist, combine the author's skills as a social theorist and his keen interest in contemporary politics. Of his extensive publications, "Social Structure and the Ruling Class" (1950)[22] is especially relevant to the study of elites.

In this article, Aron analyzes developments in modern France in the light of two theories of power: the Marxist theory of class conflict and the conception of a classless society; and the Paretoan theory of elites and the inevitability of minority rule. Aron raises—though he does not succeed in answering—the fundamental question about the relation between these two theories. More important, he seeks the interconnections between the two sets of empirical facts in social life upon which these contrasting theories rest. "What," he asks, "is the relation between social differentiation and political hierarchy in modern societies?"[23] What, in short, is the relation between economic and political power, between social classes and political elites? To answer this question, he presents data on the structure of the French economy, the distribution of national income, and the changes in the constitution and recruitment of the political elite. These empirical data support his arguments that, judging from the political influence of mass leaders, the working class has increased its political power, while, due to the particular problems confronting French industry in the postwar period, the economic power and well-being of the working class have been relatively reduced. In documenting these paradoxical trends, Aron makes a significant contribution to the analysis of elites, one that should discourage, if not prevent, the equation of political and economic hierarchies in industrial societies. Elites and social classes, as we shall try to show in a later section, are distinct dimensions of the social order. Among contemporary writers, Aron was the first to stress the theoretical and practical importance of this distinction.

A second important insight is Aron's stress on the role of compatibility and cohesion among the political elite of a nation. In this regard the French political leaders in the 1950's were particularly vulnerable—they lacked "unity of opinion and action on essential points" primarily because one group (the Communists in the National Assembly), in its fundamental opposition to the rest, caused a serious split within the ranks of this elite. Moreover, the shifting status of different subtypes—for example, the lesser importance of lawyers, the greater importance of party officials and trade union leaders—led to instability in patterns of recruitment in some sectors and to excessive stability in others. Social class and elite hierarchies are thus seen to play very different roles in the life of society. Knowing the characteristics of one is no certain guide to the traits and functions of the other.

Aron defines the elite primarily in political terms, but his analysis may be applied more broadly. He is especially interested in the role of conflicting perspectives among subgroups within elites arising from incompatible visions of the future. Such conflicts and disharmonies are not peculiar to France, of course, but

reflect complexities and strains in modern industrial societies; unless they are checked, they may become a threat to national survival. This requires a deeper understanding of the role of elites

in modern societies, an objective that Aron has furthered by his own efforts in this direction.

Questions and pitfalls in the study of elites

What can we learn from these various discussions of elites? Clearly, they pose several significant questions. If elites have social functions, as Aristotle and Saint-Simon asserted, how can we ascertain these functions without making either *a priori* assumptions or *ex post facto* deductions? If elites serve to fulfill moral ends, how are their moral roles linked to their functional roles? If the two roles are incompatible, what are the social consequences? Some writers contend that elites have become more accessible with the advance of industrialism, that the patterns of recruitment are not fixed but reflect in some degree major social changes.[24] If this is so, what determines prevalent patterns of selection? What are the links, if any, between these patterns and the functional and moral responsibilities of elites? If, as many writers have claimed, elites are inevitable and indispensable features of any society, why are they alternately vilified or idolized? Is Mannheim's suggestion that there are only two main types of elites ("integrative" and "sublimative") consistent with such empirical evidence as is available—itself inconsistent—about how many elites exist within a given society at a given time? If elites and social classes are not identical, as several scholars imply, what is the nature of their interrelationship? If there are "ruling" elites, can we locate subordinate elites and specify their functions?

In attempting to answer such questions it becomes clear that innumerable historical illustrations, intriguing as they are, are not adequate substitutes for a systematic and comprehensive theory. To be sure, their observations and insights, if organized and tested for consistencies and contradictions, should be very useful in developing such a theory. But one should not simply seek to document or dismiss their assertions.

These assertions—and the reasoning supporting them—are often marked by boldness and originality. Generally, however, these writers display the same theoretical flaw: that of concentrating on one or at most two types of elites, and overemphasizing these particular elites to the exclusion of other types. The few recent studies of cultural and artistic leaders—such as Leo Rosten's *Washington Correspondents,* a classic of its kind, and the numerous works on celebrities and the world of high society—are primarily descriptive, and their findings have not been integrated with discussions of elites in general or of political and economic elites in particular. Nor have patterns of different kinds and degrees of power and influence been carefully delineated. This overemphasis and neglect have resulted in considerable confusion as to the part played by different types of elites in the control and development of the social order.

Such confusion has been compounded by several common pitfalls in the study of elites, especially the following: (1) *Failure to distinguish between different types of elites.* Whereas all elites are important in some social and psychological contexts, only some are important for society as a whole. These must somehow be distinguished from the rest. There is, in effect, a hierarchy among elites; some elites are more elite than others. Beauty queens, criminal masterminds, champion bridge players, and master chefs all hold top rank in certain pyramids of talent or power, but not all are equally significant in the life of society. Certain elites may arouse momentary attention, but only certain leadership groups have a general and sustained social impact. The latter elites are the principal concern of this study—those whose judgments, decisions, and actions have important and determinable consequences for many members of society. We refer to these groups as *strategic elites,* distinguishing them from segmental elites. Strategic elites, in our view, comprise not only political, economic, and military leaders, but also moral, cultural, and scientific ones. Whether or not an elite is counted as strategic does not depend on its specific activities but on the scope of its activities, that is, on how many members of society it directly impinges upon and in what respects.

(2) *Failure to distinguish between the motives of individuals seeking access to an elite and the role of that elite in the life of society.* It often appears as if the subjective desires of individuals for wealth, fame, or power account for the existence of elite positions that provide such rewards. But as Merton reminds us, "The subjective disposition may coincide with the objective con-

sequence, but again, it may not. The two vary independently." [25] An individual may understandably aspire to becoming a leader in the world of big business in order to amass wealth. But from this one can hardly conclude that the major social task of the business elite is the accumulation of wealth. Even if this were the main private motive of every individual member of the business elite, it would not describe their collective responsibilities of directing the economic affairs of society in accord with prevailing standards and values. This is only an instance of the general consideration: the social tasks of any elite cannot be ascertained merely by inquiring into the aims, aspirations, and purposes of its members.[26]

In fact, in trying to utilize the majority of theoretical discussions of elites, one is struck by their ambiguity and the universality of their propositions. Consider Durkheim's complaint voiced in his second preface to the *L'Annee Sociologique:*

> . . . religious, juridical, moral, and economic facts must all be treated in conformance with their nature as social facts. Whether describing or explaining them, one must relate them to a particular milieu, to a definite type of society; . . . The majority of these sciences are still closed to this approach. The science of religion speaks in the most general terms of religious beliefs and practices, as if these were not related to any social system. The laws of political economy are of so general a nature that they are independent of all conditions of time and place, are disconnected from any collective form; exchange, production, value, and so on, are seen as products of very simple forces common to all mankind.[27]

Elites, too, have usually been discussed in this general way "as if these were not related to any social system." In this work we hope to remedy this situation by focusing on *strategic* elites in industrial societies. Any theoretical propositions that will be developed will therefore apply above all to these, and especially to the United States, other elites in other times and places being referred to primarily for comparative and illustrative purposes.

(3) *Failure to distinguish between the objective social responsibilities of elites and the subjective rewards accruing to their individual members.* The frame of reference of an individual trying to scale the heights is quite different from that of an observer seeking to analyze what heights may be scaled and why. The so-

ciologist has as one of his prime tasks the clarification of these two dimensions—the objective duties assigned to particular social positions, and the inducements attached to them so as to attract qualified and interested individuals. To ascertain why some individuals are wealthy, powerful, or very important, it will not be sufficient to examine only their individual desires and intentions. One must also look at the social structure—at certain features of the objective social milieu in which some tasks and positions are rewarded by wealth, power, or renown while others are not. Unless and until the objective and subjective dimensions of the problem are clearly distinguished, studies of elites are bound to be ambiguous on this point. Indeed not all strategic elites do receive impressive material rewards—one need only think of priestly or artistic elites. Thus, to define elites only in terms of conspicuous material attainments would mean omitting some elites and including some nonelite elements. Such ambiguity, we propose, can be avoided.

Plan of this book

The main assumption of this work is that the destinies of industrial societies depend upon the actions and ideas of their *strategic* elites. As societies have become more differentiated and centralized, these elites have multiplied rather than decreased, and have become ever more essential. So, too, has the need to master the principles of their growth and development. To this end, a careful and sustained examination of a variety of strategic elites is required, preferably as they coexist within a given society during a specific epoch, plus a consideration of their historical origins and their processes of formation and decline.

Accordingly, the plan of this book may be divided into four parts. The first part seeks to determine the anatomy of strategic elites; the second, the functions of these elites; the third, the recruitment of strategic elites; and fourth, their survival. Each part corresponds to a series of questions which may be summarized as follows:

1. How many strategic elites are there, and how and why did they emerge?
2. What, specifically, are their social responsibilities?

3. Who can gain access to them, and what rewards and obligations await those who do?
4. How, and why, do strategic elites survive and perish?

One of the first tasks, therefore, is to discover how strategic elites emerged. Here it is well to follow Durkheim who distinguished among three separate elements: the antecedent cause, the concomitant cause, and the current function. Accordingly, Chapter 2 deals with the historical antecedents of strategic elites, specifically with aristocracies, ruling castes, and ruling classes and their interrelationships. In one sense, strategic elites exist today because ruling castes and classes existed yesterday; they did not develop *sui generis*. On the other hand, they are not to be reduced to these historically antecedent groups, but must be analyzed as separate and independent phenomena. Chapter 3 considers the concomitant causes, or the concurrent social forces that underlie the expansion and proliferation of strategic elites. Four processes are seen as crucial in this development—the growth of population, the growth of the division of labor, the growth of formal organizations, and the growth of moral diversity. Instead of a single, uniform, if not united, ruling elite, it appears increasingly that a series of independent yet interdependent strategic elites are emerging who must communicate and cooperate with each other yet differentiate themselves. Karl Mannheim was the first to observe this, but neither he nor his followers systematically explored its rationale or its implications.

In Chapter 4, the functions of strategic elites in industrial societies are discussed in light of the Parsonian theory of social systems. Although Parsons does not deal with strategic elites as such, his structural-functional theory of the dimensions of social action is indispensable for an analysis of them. Strategic elites, in our view, consist of the minority of individuals responsible for keeping the organized system, society, in working order, functioning so as to meet and surpass the perennial collective crises that occur. This minority may occupy formal social positions, it may be concentrated in one or a series of centers, it may perform passably, poorly, or superbly well; whichever, strategic elites do exist and persist because of and to the extent that they perform certain crucial social functions. This minority of key individuals, moreover, is distinguished by the fact that it is in their roles rather than as total personalities that we usually encounter them. Only a part of their persons is being socially utilized. This, incidentally, has always been true—what do we know, after all, of Alexander, or Cyrus, or Solon but the political, military, or legal acts they left behind? If history is the record of the leading rather than the supporting players, it is also a record not primarily of the people but of the parts they played. These parts, in turn, have social functions. Thus it is not individuals but collectivities that create these elites, and it is as collectivities, not as heroic leaders, that we must study them.[28]

This insistence that we seek the rationale for the existence of strategic elites in historical antecedents, concomitant forces, and social functions will enable us to avoid certain pitfalls such as trying to explain characteristic actions, decisions, and indecisions in terms of the motives and drives of individuals alone. In line with this, one must guard against inferring the social significance of various elites from the nature of the rewards available to individual members. How well or how poorly elites are rewarded for their performances is a separate issue, in principle, from why they are rewarded at all. Schumpeter saw quite clearly that function and motivation must be distinguished, although he was referring to social classes rather than to strategic elites. "Every class," he writes, ". . . has a definite function, which it must fulfill according to its whole concept and orientation, and which it actually does discharge as a class and through the class conduct of its members. Moreover, the position of each class in the total national structure depends, on the one hand, on the significance that is attributed to that function, and, on the other hand, on the degree to which that class successfully performs the function." [29] The destiny of a class is not identical with that of the individuals within it. This, as we shall see, is even more true for strategic elites.

In Chapters 4 and 5, the social functions of strategic elites will be related to Parsons' theory of the major dimensions of social systems, and four types of strategic elites will be theoretically derived. These types in turn will be subdivided according to whether they specialize in external or internal system problems, and to whether they are primarily instrumental or symbolic in their orientations and impact. Selected empirical evidence will be used to substantiate or challenge these theoretical propositions.

Chapter 6 deals with the relationship between strategic elites and the moral order, with particular reference to Durkheim's theory of the "collective conscience" in primitive and in advanced societies. Chapter 7 deals with problems of moral cohesion, patterns of communication, and differentiated moral behavior among these elites.

So far nothing has been said of patterns of recruitment, responsibilities, and incentives, suggesting that these are separate questions from those of the functional and moral significance of strategic elites. Chapter 8 proposes a framework for organizing the various unintegrated propositions on equality and aristocracy, and on open and closed societies. Chapter 9 reviews the evidence on the recruitment and selection of the strategic elites of the United States in the twentieth century. Chapter 10 discusses the rise and fall of elites with particular reference to strategic elites. Chapter 11, the conclusion, summarizes the main points of the book and links them, in a general way, to some of the key issues of the present and the future.

Notes

1. The term "elite" derives from the Latin word *eligere,* meaning "to choose." In common usage the word refers to "the choice part" or to "the flower" of a nation, culture, age group, and also to persons occupying high social positions. Initially the term referred to "the choice part or flower of" goods offered for sale and so signified objects worthy of choice. By the eighteenth century, French usage of the word had widened to include distinction in other fields. In social science, the emphasis has shifted from that of choiceness to eminence. The most general meaning is that of a group of persons who in any society hold positions of eminence. Frequently a particular field of eminence is selected, such as politics. *International Social Science Bulletin* 3 (1955), p. 474. See also Otto Stammer, "Das Elitenproblem in der Modernen Demokratie," in *Schmollers Jahrbuch* 71 (1951), Heft 5. Amitai Etzioni defines elites as "groups of actors who have power," thus also emphasizing the political aspect of the problem. Etzioni, *A Comparative*

Analysis of Complex Organizations (1961), Chap. v, p. 89. For numerous other definitions of the term, see R. Treves (ed.), *Le Elites Politiche,* Atti del Quarto Congresso Mondiale di Sociologia (1961).

2. Aristotle, *Politics* (1941), p. 1189.
3. For one of the best sociological examinations of a number of such utopias, including the utopian element in Marxist thought, see Karl Mannheim, *Ideology and Utopia* (1949), esp. pp. 173-236.
4. See, Count Henri de Saint-Simon, *Oeuvres Choisis,* Tome Premier, (1839)—a collection of his major work. See also the two excellent books on his theories and on the cultural and social milieu in which he worked: Emile Durkheim, *Socialism and Saint-Simon* (1958), and F. E. Manuel, *The New World of H. Saint-Simon* (1956).
5. Emile Durkheim, *Socialism and Saint-Simon, op. cit.,* pp. 136-7.
6. Saint-Simon's exact words are: ". . . here it is not the strongest who control but those most capable in science or industry. They are not summoned to office because they have the power to exercise their will but because they know more than others, and consequently their functions do not consist in saying what they want, but what they know." Quoted in Durkheim, *Socialism and Saint-Simon, op. cit.,* p. 150.
7. C. Wright Mills, in *The Power Elite* (1956), expresses a similar view today—esp. in Chap. xii.
8. Vilfredo Pareto, *The Mind and Society,* ed. by Arthur Livingston, 4 vols. (1935), and *Systemes Socialistes,* Vol. I (1902), Part 1. Gaetano Mosca, *The Ruling Class* (1939). A good secondary source is James M. Burnham, *The Machiavellians: Defenders of Freedom* (1943).
9. Gaetano Mosca, *The Ruling Class, op. cit.,* p. 70. Underscoring supplied. See also the excellent book by James H. Meisel, *The Myth of the Ruling Class* (1962).
10. Pareto, to be sure, found counterparts to his political elites in the economic sphere when he likened the lions to rentiers and the foxes to speculators, but he did not delineate these types clearly. One is never quite sure whether he is referring to politicians who also speculate in securities, or who only collaborate with those who do. Parsons, in his exposition of Pareto, is much more convincing on this point. See Talcott Parsons, *The Structure of Social Action* (1949), pp. 288-93.
11. Karl Mannheim, *Man and Society in an Age of Reconstruction* (1946), Part V.
12. Karl Mannheim, "On Power—A Chapter in Political Sociology," in *Freedom, Power, and Democratic Planning* (1950), pp. 41-76.
13. Karl Mannheim, "The Ruling Class in Capitalist and Communist Society," in *Freedom, Power, and Democratic Planning* (1950), pp. 77-106.
14. See Robert M. MacIver, *The Web of Government* (1947), esp. Chaps. i, iii, v, vi.
15. Robert S. Lynd, "Power in American Society as Resource and Problem," in Arthur Kornhauser (ed.), *Problems of Power in American Democracy* (1957), pp. 1-45.
16. C. Wright Mills, *The Power Elite, op. cit.* This controversial portrayal of the current American economic, military, and political elites is weakened by conceptual confusion of power, authority, and influence; and, as many critics have noted, by "lively" but distressing rhetoric.

17. See Daniel Bell, *The End of Ideology* (1960), esp. Chap. iii which contains a critique of Mills' *The Power Elite.*
18. See William A. Kornhauser, *The Politics of Mass Society* (1959). Although this sugggestive work is largely concerned with the sources and composition of "mass movements," questions of power and elites are discussed.
19. See Harold D. Lasswell, Daniel Lerner, and C. E. Rothwell, *The Comparative Study of Elites* (1952), an introduction and bibliography for an outline of their program and for references to specific studies in the series. See also a critical review of the series by Ralph Gilbert Ross, "The Methodology of Politics," *Public Opinion Quarterly* (Spring 1952), pp. 27-32.
20. Harold D. Lasswell, *Politics, Who Gets What, When, and How* (1936).
21. See, for example, Harold D. Lasswell and Abraham Kaplan, *Power and Society* (1950), esp. Introduction and Chap. v on "Power."
22. Raymond Aron, "Social Structure and the Ruling Class," *The British Journal of Sociology* I (1950), pp. 1-16.
23. *Ibid.*, p. 2.
24. The question of accessibility is an important matter discussed by William Kornhauser in *The Politics of Mass Society, op. cit.*, esp. pp. 51-60.
25. Robert K. Merton, *Social Theory and Social Structure* (1957), p. 25.
26. Dr. Juan Linz draws a similar distinction when he suggests that one has to "distinguish the term elite applied to a group of persons, families or strata formed by specific individuals, from the term elite applied to positions from which certain issues are decided." He furthermore suggests that the study of elite positions is in principle separate from a study of their incumbents. In fact, discrepancies between the two can only be discovered by keeping them conceptually distinct. Juan Linz, *Political Elites,* Informal Discussion Meeting on Political Sociology, Fourth World Congress of Sociology (1959).
27. Emile Durkheim, in Kurt Wolff (ed.), *From Emile Durkheim, 1858-1917, A Collection of Essays, with Translations and a Bibliography* (1960), p. 349.
28. Thus the point made by Arthur Schlesinger in a recent article that a democracy "involves a functional need for strong leadership" is well taken despite the writer's tendency to misinterpret Weber's theory of charisma. See Arthur Schlesinger, "On Heroic Leadership," *Encounter* (December 1960), pp. 3-11. Elite roles and elite incumbents must be kept distinct for there is no one-to-one correspondence between them. Elite role "x" for example may be exercised by a number of different individuals, each contributing a part to the role. Conversely, a specific individual may exercise more than one elite role and thus appear in several elite positions. This is why there may be no consensus among the members of a community as to who is politically, economically, or socially powerful. People may be better able to indicate the important elite roles rather than elite individuals in their communities.
29. Joseph Schumpeter, *Imperialism and Social Classes* (1955), p. 137. In recent writings on the problem of elites there is a clear awareness that the functional and the moral roles played by elites must be carefully distinguished. Since these two are interrelated, however, they should also be integrated with one another. Unfortunately, no one has as

yet succeeded in doing so. See, for example, Michalina Clifford-Vaughan, "Some French Concepts of Elites," *The British Journal of Sociology,* XI (December 1960), 4, 319-32; Urs Jaeggi, *Die gesellschaftliche Elite* (1960); Renzo Sereno, *The Rulers* (1962). If the effort at integrating these two dimensions fails, there is a tendency to fall back on earlier conceptualizations of the problem. Jaeggi, for instance, after suggesting a three-fold classification of elites—of power, value, and function—finally seems to rely solely on the definition that stresses the power aspect. Sereno, who is closer to a theoretical solution, favors abandoning the elite concept entirely, replacing it by the older and vaguer concept of the rulers. A provocative recent attempt to clarify the conceptual aspects of the problem focuses on elites as ideal-type representatives of the industrial social order. According to the author, elites are experts engaged in specialized activities, embodying such seminal values as material achievement and progress, and recruited on the basis of individual merit and recognition. Not only is this definition too global, but it also fails to keep recruitment analytically distinct from function. And, although the author, following Saint-Simon and Mannheim in particular, insists that elites derive their social significance from the performance of social functions, he does not specify these functions very clearly. His classification of two main types of elites—of achievement and of leisure—does not seem to go beyond Mannheim's distinction between integrative and sublimative elites. At times, one suspects that the author confounds functions with specialized activities, hence his all-encompassing definition of elites (p. 71) and his neglect of the principle of differentiation and rank-order among elites. Hans P. Dreitzel, *Elite Begriff und Sozialstruktur* (1962). See also, the book review by Kurt P. Mayer in the *American Journal of Sociology,* LXVIII, No. v (March 1963) 600-601.

2. STRATEGIC ELITES: HISTORICAL ANTECEDENTS

▲

It is profitable to examine the origins and backgrounds of current institutions, even if these origins are remote and shrouded in myth. Strategic elites exist today because something gave birth to them, something that resembles them, yet is also different. The ruins of dead civilizations and the pasts of living ones are replete with a family of institutions with whom these elites are frequently confused—ruling castes, aristocracies, high estates, and ruling classes. Since the past is always with us, enriching and confusing the present, elites may be expected to reflect their historical affinity to these groups. As Schumpeter has reminded us, "Every social situation is the heritage of preceding situations and takes over from them not only their cultures, their dispositions, and their 'spirit,' but also elements of their social structure and concentration of power." "Social classes," he adds, "coexisting at any given time, bear the marks of different centuries on their brow." [1] An examination of the origins of strategic elites thus compels us to probe into the origins of social classes with which such elites are frequently and understandably interchanged. Closer scrutiny suggests that strategic elites are a crystallization, a further development, of ruling classes. Thus they may be considered not as functional equivalents but as structural alternatives of ruling classes and ruling castes, representing a more specialized and advanced form of social leadership.

Types of social core groups

In this sense, of course, strategic elites are as old as the first organized human societies, all of which had their leading minorities of priests, elders, warrior kings, or legendary sages and heroes—agents for and symbols of the common life. Societies might be expected to vary considerably in how they arrange to select, train, and reward these leading minorities, but in practice only a few methods have been utilized. These appear in widely dispersed times and places suggesting that they are deeply linked to the objective features of social organization. Recruitment through heredity is perhaps the most familiar one. But co-optation or appointment from the top—as in the Roman Catholic Church and increasingly in modern bureaucracies—election, as of Western political leaders or the heads of the armed forces in ancient Greece, and selection by lot or rote, are other important ones. Social leadership may thus be divided into five principal types.

RULING CASTE

Here one stratum performs what are considered the most important social tasks, recruits its personnel through biological reproduction, and ranks highest in prestige. The ruling caste is set apart by religion, kinship, language, territorial residence, economic standing, and occupational activities. India is the most enduring example of such recruitment. Social control is enforced by religious ritual rather than by means of a centralized body of law, and the state is either nonexistent or plays a minor role in the life of society. Individuals enter the ruling caste through birth and leave it through death. The chief characteristics of caste systems—their rigidity and permanence—can be traced to how the ruling caste is recruited and maintained.

ARISTOCRACY

Here a single stratum also monopolizes the key social functions, and is composed of families bound by kinship and wealth, but lacks the occupational specialization of caste systems. Traditionally, aristocracy has preferred the occupations of politics and war, but these are not assigned through heredity. Aristocracies represent a minority set above and apart from the rest of the population, with a special code of honor, etiquette, and outlook. Wealth is associated with aristocratic status but does not lead to it. As de Tocqueville observed: "An aristocratic body is composed of a certain number of citizens who, without being very removed from the mass of the people, are nevertheless permanently stationed above them; a body which is easy to touch and difficult to strike. . . . Aristocratic institutions cannot exist without laying down the inequality of men as a fundamental principle." [2]

Aristocracies are more inclusive than castes, while occupationally less specialized; they resemble an amalgam of castes, the rituals and endogamous restrictions of which have broken down due to the expansion of the group and the more varied tasks confronting it.

The members of aristocracies must work, but they must not work for a living, and rents are the economic basis of all aristocracies, "which need a gentlemanly and unearned income for their existence." [3] Land has often been considered the basis of aristocracy because, of all the forms of privilege that help create and maintain it, land is the most enduring.[4]

In no industrial society does a governing aristocracy of birth and leisure persist, though traces of it linger in the social order.

THE FIRST ESTATE

This concept refers to a legally defined stratum in a politically centralized society. Access to it is not only through birth but also through the performance of deeds, purchase, ennoblement, and intermarriage—thus estate status can be lost and acquired. Estates are often confused with castes though in some ways they represent an opposite type of leadership because of the role played by law and the centralized state. Again, the members of the first estate perform all or most key social functions, an exception of which in Western Europe was at one time the clergy. In the West the system of estates has been historically no less decisive than that of castes.[5]

RULING CLASS

This form of social leadership also consists of a single stratum in charge of various key social functions. It is recruited in several different ways and although heredity continues to provide access to this class it no longer justifies such access. Lineage is no longer the operative factor but property and wealth, whether ascribed or achieved. Although this need not be the case, historically, ruling classes have derived their main justification from economic, not political, power.

STRATEGIC ELITES

In this type of social leadership, several social strata supply personnel to leading social positions. Social functions are elaborated and specialized, and those in charge of these functions are recruited in a way adapted to their tasks. Merit regardless of other attributes —sex, race, class, religion, or even age—is the predominant justification for attaining elite positions or elite status. The notion of all-round excellence or over-all superiority is gone. Strategic elites are specialists in excellence. Selection on the basis of individual competence implies dismissal for incompetence, and this principle links modern elites to the primitive institution of chiefship, where the chief—be he priest, king, or warrior—may be killed if he fails to bring about the desired end: peace, the harvest, or health. Along with this specialization, diversity, and impermanence of elites, new problems arise—those of cohesion and unity, morale, balance, and a new type of interdependence at the top. No single elite can outrank all others because no one elite knows enough about the specialized work of the others.

As Sorokin has pointed out, the upper and the lower castes, estates, and classes "are superior or inferior not on a single basis but on a multiple basis," the number of bases being related directly to the rigidity and exclusiveness of the stratum. The caste system is thus at one end of a continuum, elites at the other. Castes differ from each other with respect to almost every attribute; classes differ mainly in economic standing and occupational activity, whereas elites are to be distinguished largely on the basis of occupation. Thus what Sorokin calls the "actual sky line of the total stratification" is most diversified in societies with strategic elites.[6]

Most discussions of ruling castes, ruling classes, and elites fail to distinguish between two dimensions: the processes leading to the development of a core group responsible for performing the leading social functions, and the reservoir from which this core group is recruited. These two dimensions are often used interchangeably because it is difficult to separate them historically; the two dimensions shade off into one another. The functions, attributes, and rewards of core groups are sociologically, and therefore conceptually, hard to distinguish. An aristocrat, for example, was a leading politician, born of an ancient and noble family, and possessed wealth. Thus his function (political responsibility) readily became merged with his mode of recruitment (kinship and lineage) and his manner of reward (wealth and an elegant style of life). Since most politicians were then to the manor born, it might readily be assumed that noble birth was indispensable for the exercise of political leadership. This mode of reasoning applies to all such examples. When these elements were fused, in fact, they were not analytically distinguished. In complex industrial societies, however, these elements are no longer fused, and as industrialism develops the distinction between them widens.

The rise of social core groups and social classes

A frequent source of confusion has been for social core groups to be considered interchangeable with social classes. But though the two are related they are by no means identical. The origin of strategic elites (as of all types of ruling groups) lies in the heterogeneity of the community—in age, sex, ethnicity, skills, strength, and the like. The origin of social classes lies in the social division of labor.

Just as the owl of Minerva flies only at dusk, awareness of unity comes only when that unity has been broken. Even without attributing to primitive societies a perfect harmony and homogeneity, it is evident that their relatively small degree of differentiation separates them sharply from the occupationally and technologically more advanced communities. And it is this internal differentiation that permits the rise of strategic elites—where it is slight, elites are few in number and comprehensive in scope; where it is extensive, elites are many and specialized. The tremendous variety of cultures and social structures should not obscure a fundamental similarity in the patterns with which societies have responded to the facts of growth and diversity. We could trace a similar course at a time when neither social classes nor extensive social differentiation existed, and when strategic elites were but single chiefs, groups of elders, or high priests performing their functions sporadically and on a temporary basis. At some later time, perhaps a hundred years, or a thousand, or only a few decades, the population increased, a variety of occupations emerged, social classes arose, and the minorities in charge of social leadership became more numerous, more extensive, and more enduring. The organized boundaries of society no longer coincided with its numerical boundaries; society became separate from the total membership, as well as longer-lived. Once a certain degree of social differentiation was reached, the emergence of a social center, a core, a fulcrum, existing apart from and above the community, sacred and exalted, was inevitable. This core symbolized at once the most precarious and the most exalted aspects of organized social existence.

Strategic elites and social classes must therefore be considered as twin-born, but not identical. The development of social classes and of a social core, though related in complicated ways, are not interchangeable. So, for example, there is a close association between the existence of social classes and the existence of a state, but each is a separate consequence of a series of social developments. To that extent each is an independent occurrence.[7] The dividing of a population into occupations, castes, guilds, or classes is paralleled by its unification around a symbolic center. The shape of this center is determined by the complexity and variety of the whole—the more varied and complex the totality, the more varied and complex the social center.

Thus, while the emergence of social classes divides a society, the development of its center integrates it and puts it together once more. In this way, the society can act in concert even though its various parts are not identical or coequal. With this two-fold development, new and perplexing questions arise: Who is to participate in this center? How large should this group be? How long should given individuals participate? How should they be rewarded? The fate of many societies has hung on the ways in which these questions were answered.

Two historical illustrations

Societies as far apart in time as ancient Mesopotamia and ancient Greece provide apt illustrations of the social processes involved in the development of social classes and elite groups. In Athens the oscillation of birth and wealth as criteria in the recruitment of elites can be traced from the days of Homer through Solon to Pericles. At the beginning of its recorded history, Greece was undergoing a transition between the clan and the class system, the development of the polis and that of social classes going hand in hand. A religious caste seems to have ruled for some time after the old clan organization disintegrated, but gradually it gave way to a powerful aristocracy of birth and wealth. In the sixth century B.C., Solon broke the aristocracy's power by granting the *clients,* a special class of servants, political rights. These revolutionary developments occurred within the framework of the old order and were often unnoticed by those living through them. In fact, the clan designations and the old religious rituals continued to exist far into the classical age, surviving as long as Greece itself survived. After Solon, the fortunes of the aristocracy continued to decline until the reforms of Cleisthenes who, in granting the *clients* moral equality, dealt aristocracy its death blow. Wealth now replaced birth as the criterion for access into the social core group, and territorial proximity replaced extended kinship ties as the basis of social cohesion. The wealthiest members of the society had sole access to the governing and military positions of the polis. However, as de Coulanges remarks, this aristocracy of wealth was far less stable and enduring than the aristocracy of birth had been.[8] In his view, wealth could never attain the quasi-sanctity that birth could and did: "In the presence of wealth, the most ordinary sentiment is not respect, it is envy. The political inequality that resulted from difference of fortunes soon appeared to be an iniquity and men strove to abolish it." [9] By the time of the classical fifth century, Athens had almost abolished the rule of wealth and henceforth was essentially governed by its adult male citizens convening, monthly, in the Assembly. Since this body was too large to attend to all the details of administration, a number of smaller bodies, such as the Council of 500 chosen by lot, and an inner council of fifty men, ten from each tribe, and the nine archons (mere shades of their former powerful selves) were created. Only one vital group escaped selection by lot—the ten commanders of the armed forces, or *strategoi,* who were elected annually. But while re-election was permissible and frequent, it was not uncommon for the general of one year to be the private soldier of the next. Of all the powerful positions in the polis, this was the most strategic. But ultimately it was the Assembly that made the key decisions—hence its historical reputation for direct democracy. Women, slaves, and foreigners could not participate in the deliberations of the Assembly, but nearly all male citizens did. Public issues soon became a part of everyday life.

Less than a century later this society, the polis, was in its death gasp: its very success had doomed it. Comparing the Athens of Pericles with that of Demosthenes, Kitto concludes:

> The leading figures of the Assembly are no longer the responsible officers of state too. Still less are the responsible officers of state also commanders in the field. Certainly the separation of these functions is not absolute. . . . [but professional specialization has appeared.] The polis was made for the amateur. Its ideal was that every citizen (more or less, according as the polis was democratic or oligarchic) should play his part in all of its many activities. . . . It implies a respect for the wholeness or the oneness of life, and a consequent dislike of specialization. It implies an efficiency which exists not in one department of life, but in life itself.
>
> But this amateur conception implies also that life, besides being whole, is also simple. If one man in his time is to play all parts, these parts must not be too difficult for the ordinary man to learn. And this is where the polis broke down. . . .[10]

In Athens, as in other Greek cities, the vicissitudes of birth, wealth, or individual achievement as criteria of recruitment can be traced almost as clearly as they can in modern times. First came the priests, followed by the rule of Eupatrids or nobles, who in turn made way for the reign of the entire adult male population, still formally restricted by sex, age, and citizenship, and informally, by wealth, social contacts, and education—a sequence applicable to the history of the West since the Middle Ages. As in the West, the struggle for political equality was followed by the struggle for economic equality. Similar tendencies can be observed in ancient Rome, Egypt, China, and Mesopotamia.

In describing the cities of Mesopotamia in the fourth millennium B.C., Frankfort points out a fact, often overlooked when discussing the centralized patrimonial administrations of the ancient Near

East, that "in principle all members of the community were equal [for] all received rations as well as allotments to support themselves; all worked on the Common and on the canals and dikes. There was no leisure class. Likewise there were no serfs." [11] The community was both occupationally divided and stratified in terms of class. Originally, however, political authority rested with all the citizens, again suggesting that the dichotomy between rich and poor and between politically free and unfree refers to two separate and potentially independent phenomena. The community (resembling the ancient polis) was divided into two basic units—the temple communities or religious-economic units, each under a specific deity, and the political community consisting of an Assembly guided by a group of elders. "Thus the early Mesopotamian cities resembled those of Greece, of the Hanseatic League, of Renaissance Italy, in many respects. In all these cases we meet local autonomy, the assumption that every citizen is concerned with the common weal, and a small group of influential men who deal with current affairs and sometimes impose an oppressive oligarchy upon the mass of the people." [12] Initially the sovereign power resided in the equalitarian Assembly whose deliberations and decisions required not a majority but unanimity. In times of crisis when speedy decisions were imperative, the Mesopotamian cities put themselves into the hands of a dictator, but once the emergency had passed power reverted to the Assembly. "Threat of an emergency was never absent once the cities flourished and increased in number," and thus the need for efficient social leadership eventually became permanent. Unfortunately, the oppressive qualities of this leadership also became permanent. When Sargon of Akkad established the State by subjugating the cities in 2300 B.C., he proclaimed himself "king of the Four Quarters of the World." [13]

Mesopotamia managed to establish a definite social core or leadership group, but it failed to develop consistent principles of recruitment. The "city ruler in Mesopotamia did not derive his position from any innate superiority or right of birth. He acted either on behalf of the assembly, or as a steward of the real sovereign, the city god. In theology, personal rule was sanctioned by a doctrine of divine election which remained the foundation of kingship down to the end of the Assyrian empire." The theory of kingship as a sign of divine favor prevented the secure establishment of a secular dynasty, and the monarchy therefore failed to become an instrument of unity as it did in Egypt.[14]

These two cases illustrate the principle that the structure of a core group should not be equated with the structure of a caste or class system. No more rigid and all-powerful monarchy existed than the Egyptian, and yet there was no caste system in Egypt; except for the pharaohs, men of humble origins could rise to the highest posts. At the same time "not a single Egyptian was, in our sense of the word, free. No individual could call in question a hierarchy of authority which culminated in a living god." [15]

These early historical instances should also dispel the notion that open class societies are creations of the West or of the industrial revolution. Upward and downward mobility have existed since social classes came into being; they characterize various epochs of the same society, and the same stages of development in different ones. Vertical social mobility, in fact, is most widespread in periods of social transition—whether the transition ushers in despotism or liberty.

Origins of social classes

In all ancient civilizations in which systems of class stratification developed, counterparts to modern strategic elites also evolved. But although these two go hand in hand historically, they should, for reasons noted earlier, be discussed separately. We shall begin with social class.

It is difficult to reconstruct how or when social classes emerged in history. One fact is certain: contrary to a frequently made claim, social classes are not universal—societies have existed and do exist without them. This being so, one can envisage a future classless society, although not a future without some forms of hierarchical differentiation. That societies otherwise quite different from each other have all contained an element of hierarchical differentiation is due to the fact that most of these societies entered recorded history at roughly the same stage of social development. Ancient Greece first appeared on the historical stage when its clan organization was dying and its class system was being born. The same is true for most of the other known ancient civilizations. The transition from clan organization (based on blood ties) to class organizations (based on occupational specialization) was a long and painful one—as transitional periods often are. And although the basis of these two systems differs, they resemble each other because the later system is built upon the earlier one, as Durkheim made clear.

> No doubt when this new organization begins to appear, it tries to utilize the existing organization and assimilate it. The way in which functions are divided thus follows, as faithfully as possible, the way in which society is already divided. The segments, or at least the groups of segments, united by special affinities become organs.[16]

Durkheim goes on to remark that the new organization, while it develops in response to new and unforeseen needs of social organization, nevertheless appropriates for itself certain of the functional arrangements developed within clan society. In clan society, occupational divisions, to the extent that they exist at all, are hereditary. Blacksmiths, flute players, and priests are born to their tasks. The class society that takes over once the clan society grows too small and inadequate for the needs of a growing population also takes over this particular way of organizing occupations. "Classes and castes," Durkheim observes, "probably have no other origin nor any other nature: they arise from the multitude of occupational organizations born amidst the pre-existing familial organization." [17] The division of labor is thus responsible for the growth and development of social classes. At first this division proceeds within the clan framework, but when this becomes too confining a new framework of social classes comes into being.

The division of labor is able to expand under one or both of two sets of conditions: a surplus of food leaves a portion of the community free to perform other tasks which in turn create the basis for further growth and expansion; or, as in the case of Mesopotamia, the climate is such that little time need be spent on farming, and workers can perform other types of labor. No matter how this division of labor evolves, once it is established, further and more varied social development is assured. Gradually, as the community surpasses a given level of size and growth of facilities, broad social strata appear, differentiated by work and style of life. Some societies never develop to that point; others, notably advanced industrial societies, are showing signs of going beyond it.

These socially, economically, and occupationally differentiated broad strata come to be known as social classes.

Initially, the rise of social classes helped solve two pressing problems: how to retain the advantages of the division of labor to assure a supply of adequately motivated and trained people for different tasks; and how to secure the integration of an increasingly diversified society. According to Fahlbeck, there are only four basic classes: priests, warriors (the nobility), free citizens (burghers and peasants), and unfree citizens or slaves. Later, a fifth class, that of free labor, appears.[18] Since the heterogeneity of the expanding community was likewise relatively slight, the complexity of the social core group was small.

Fahlbeck, in contrast to writers who see no connection between the two, considers the emergence of slavery as equal in importance to the emergence of the ruling priestly or warrior class. In his view the highest classes could not have emerged without the lowest. Just as the warrior class made possible the sustained defense of the community, and the political class made possible its continuous administration, slavery made possible continuous and specialized economic activity. Slaves, in contrast to the working citizens of nonstratified societies, worked not primarily for themselves nor for their kin but for special groups within the larger community—the very ones who had been assigned the specialized activities of warfare, religion, or political administration. Thus from the first, a reciprocal relationship existed between the highest and the lowest class. Occupational specialization by social class thereby contributed to the development of civilization. In nonstratified societies, such specialization is minimal or rare. The division of labor is primarily one of sex and age, while the differences in types of work are variations on a theme rather than radically divergent. Should a surplus exist in such societies, people can take life easier for a while. In societies with incipient class systems, however, a surplus is continually being created. Some members of the community are constantly engaged in producing it, others, constantly exempt. No matter how this process came about, its advantages must have been quite apparent. Time and energies were concentrated, skills perfected, and opportunities for survival multiplied. In nonstratified societies leisure is generally used to probe more deeply into culture—through artistic, magical, religious, and recreational activities. In expanding class societies leisure is used to make possible further expansion. The highest and the lowest classes help to ensure this expansion, each drawing its personnel from a larger pool of relatively unspecialized intermediate strata or from foreigners.

Although the origin of classes in the division of labor is fairly clear, we do not know why such stratified communities became organized into socially superior and inferior, not parallel, layers. Ultimately, this development, rather than occupational specialization as such, is responsible for the undesirable features of class systems —inequality in moral dignity and material privileges. But while the source of this inequality is obscure, all stratified communities distinguish between clean and unclean occupations, with priests sanctifying this distinction. Priests and warriors became the highest class, slaves the lowest. A parallel distinction emerged between rich and poor, so that the lowest and unclean class also became the poorest, the highest and clean class, the richest. The lowest class, lacking even the right of possession of their persons, can never, *as a class,* become rich. Individuals may enter or leave it but the characteristics of the class prevail. Initially, then, poverty and wealth are consequences of the distinction between clean and unclean work, but once in existence they become a major cause of perpetuating the wealth of the one class and the poverty of the other.

Originally, the organization of society into social classes was materially and morally beneficial, though not to all parts of society equally, in the sense that it made possible cultural innovation and elaboration on an extensive scale. Social classes, consisting of superimposed strata divided by types of work and types of wealth, were associated with material progress.

Without exception, however, all communities that reached this phase of social organization stigmatized one portion of hard-working community members as morally inferior to the rest. Why this is so seems to be related not to the development of social classes, but to the growth of the social core group which is responsible for offsetting the divisive impact of these classes. Initially, the lower classes had one main function—to perform certain kinds of specialized work—whereas the higher classes had two: to perform different occupational tasks and to prevent the fragmentation of the now occupationally divided community which threatened social survival. The classes that contributed both their work and symbolic unity to the collectivity became everywhere morally superior to other classes. The slaves—whose economic contribution to the community was enormous—occupied everywhere the lowest social status because they lacked this symbolic power: dispersed, disorganized, they were only individually accountable to temples, as in Mesopotamia; to royal storehouses, as in Egypt; or to patrimonial estates, as in Greece, Rome, and Western Europe in the Middle Ages. What the slaves lacked as a class, the higher occupational groups gained—organized power on behalf of the community and control of the source of supplies for physical survival.

The prestige occupations in these early times differed in detail but not in general function or purpose from those of today. Prestige occupations are those most closely linked to the symbolic survival of society, to the maintenance and creation of moral rules and rights that make contiguous but otherwise disconnected individuals a cohesive force. Ultimately, society is primarily a symbolic entity. This helps to explain the otherwise puzzling fact that in all class-stratified societies up to the time of the industrial revolution, social evaluation of economic activities was extremely low. Economic activity was closely related to material needs and could be performed in widely dispersed settings by thousands of independent units: thus its impact on the whole community was indirect. With the industrial revolution, however, the centralization and organization of economic activity increased, as did its symbolic influence, a fact which Saint-Simon was among the first to recognize and emphasize. Long before this development the contribution of the higher classes to the symbolic rather than to the material survival of the society was recognized by Aristotle who justified their greater privileges on this basis:

> States . . . are composed not of one but of many elements. One element is the food producing class, who are called husbandmen; a second, the class of mechanics who practice the arts without which a city cannot exist; of these arts some are absolutely necessary, others contribute to luxury or to the grace of life. The third class is that of traders, and by traders I mean those who are engaged in buying and selling, whether in commerce or in retail trade. A fourth class is that of the serfs or laborers. The warriors make up the fifth class, and they are as necessary as any of the others, if the country is not to be the slave of every invader. . . . Hence we see that this subject,

> though ingeniously, has not been satisfactorily treated in the *Republic*. . . . Yet even among his [Socrates'] four original citizens . . . there must be someone who will dispense justice and determine what is just. And as the soul may be said to be more truly part of an animal than the body, so *the higher parts of the state,* that is to say, the warrior class, the class engaged in the administration of justice, and that engaged in deliberation, which is the special business of political common sense—these *are more essential to the state than the parts which minister to the necessaries of life.*[19]

The higher classes were able to emerge in ancient societies because they were exempt from agricultural work. Subsequently, however, they became paradoxically both superior to and completely dependent on those who performed such work. They naturally tended, therefore, to seek as tight a control over their material source of supplies as possible. What is striking is not the exertion of power by the higher classes but the inability on the part of the lower or working classes who remained separated, divided, and unorganized to claim some of this power for themselves.

Once the organization of society into socially inferior and superior, and occupationally specialized classes takes root, this pattern can continue for a long time. Depending in large part upon the available supply of personnel, the class system will be tight and hereditary—closed—or loose and open to individual achievement. The ebb and flow of individuals who earn or inherit their positions is one of the constants of class-stratified societies, as demographic and technological changes can heighten or lessen the rigidity of the stratification ladder. Once the hierarchy of positions and their rewards has been firmly established those in the high positions seek to retain them, principally for their own kin, whereas those in the low positions strive to abandon them. Unless there is considerable influx of foreign populations, lower class members are often chained to their tasks by heredity, ritual, or force. Yet, there is always some individual mobility between classes although this does not alter the characteristics or the rank order of these class positions.

To say that social classes are initially useful to the communities in which they develop does not mean that they are entirely or even generally advantageous. Their very existence means that some groups are excluded from the better things of life. Whatever the virtues and desires of their individual members, they suffer deprivation as a class. The persistence of social classes—probably a phenomenon of less duration than is often thought, since classes develop at relatively late stages of social growth—has not been the consequence of any increase in human happiness or contentment, but rather because class-stratified societies have been bigger, stronger, and more resourceful than non-class-stratified societies.

The perpetuation of social classes

The rise of social classes is thus paralleled by the rise of a social core or center. Classes grow out of the social division of labor; the social core grows out of the various subdivisions of the expanded and stratified community, and the dichotomy between its management and the total membership. Wherever there exists a large and occupationally diversified community, we must expect to find both social classes and some variant of strategic elites, the two being interdependent. The affinity between the two becomes stronger as a result of the role played by kinship in the survival of both. Kinship leads to an intimate and sustained connection between the propertied class and the strategic elites. In principle these two need not be connected, but once property, obligations, and privileges are passed on from one generation to the next, some classes will be permanently favored, others permanently deprived.

Social stress on biological relatedness accounts for the more or less permanent nature of the hierarchically organized division of labor. The inequalities and advantages thereby transmitted become the justification for the social superiority of the higher classes and the social inferiority of the lower. Whereas, in principle, a caste system is strictly hereditary, especially at its highest and lowest strata, each caste separated from the others by religious rituals, commensality, and marriage rules, a class system is only partly hereditary, transmitting not so much a specific and exclusive right to an occupation as the means and facilities for access to certain social positions. Social classes would exist even without the presence of a hierarchy[20] perpetuated from generation to generation, but these two elements are precisely those usually considered to be most oppressive. If the members of each generation gained their social positions through individual effort alone, there would still be social classes, but they would not be recruited on the basis of birth. How did this linkage between the stratification of social positions and kinship come about?

More than twenty years ago Paul Kirchoff [21] attempted to account for the curious phenomenon that some societies in world history discovered the principle of growth, differentiation, and expansion, while others did not. He found his answer in the type of social organization that preceded the emergence of social class, namely the clan. Clans, which exist in the majority of preliterate societies today, are of two main types. One is based on biological kinship and the economic and cultural cooperation of all its members. This type, Kirchoff describes as *unilateral* (since it traces its origins to a common ancestor), *egalitarian* (since all work for all), and *exogamous* (because of the taboo on intra-clan marriage). Whatever its many advantages—extensive cooperation, social solidarity, and equality—its framework is too rigid to allow for the development of higher forms of cooperation which permit further expansion. This type is found today in technologically stagnant parts of the world.

The second type of clan presents a strikingly different picture. Wherever it occurs, it continues developing and growing: its presence is reported in the earliest records of Western civilization and, generally, in societies where social classes are beginning to emerge. This type is less understood because, as Kirchoff argues, it was long considered to be only a variant of the unilateral, egalitarian, and exogamous clan. Actually, it is a distinctive branch of the clan tree. In both types social organization is based on descent, but they differ in how that descent is woven into the fabric of social life.

"What matters in the one is the relationship *through* either men or women (according to the customs of the tribe), irrespective of the nearness of such relationships to the other members of the group or some ancestor—whereas, on the contrary, in the other type it is precisely the *nearness* of relationship to the common ancestor of the group which matters." [22] The first of the two principles thus results in a clan where all have equal standing in the group, whereas the second results in a clan in which the opposite holds true:

> The second principle results in a group in which every single member, except brothers or sisters, has a different standing: the concept

of the *degree of relationship* leads to *different degrees of membership* in the clan. In other words, some are members to a higher degree than others.[23]

Consequently, contrasting kinds of biological relatedness develop: the closer the relationship, the higher the status of the individual clan members; the more distant the relationship, the lower his status. A core group thus arises—the *aristoi*—composed of the nearest descendants of the common ancestor of the clan. Exogamy is rejected by the core group in favor of close in-group marriage. The distinction between a noble core and the rest of the membership runs through all clans of this second type. Moreover, its internal structure, marriage patterns, and system of social differentiation distinguish it sharply from the first.

In the second type of clan, all central economic, social, and religious functions are reserved for the noble core. And there emerges a circle of blood relations, often composed of high chiefs and slaves. At some point, therefore, a tension develops between two kinds of loyalties: to one's relatives, whether rich and powerful or poor and weak; and to one's social peers, even though they are not kin. Gradually a split occurs betwen those socially and often geographically close, but biologically unrelated, and those who are biologically related but socially distant. Eventually, this split breaks down the clan system, and the struggles between groups of kin are transformed into struggles between social classes. This represents the end of one phase in human history and the beginnings of another—one encountered when we first come upon the Greeks, the Germans, and the Romans.

Before clan organization collapsed, the noble core or aristoi for a time were able to utilize it for their own benefit, as whatever benefited themselves also served the community as a whole—their own prosperity implying communal prosperity. But, eventually, this led to the growth of differential advantages for the core and to the subsequent neglect of the rest of the community, greatly encouraging the shift from clan to class organization. In the first type of clan, such differential advantages of any scale were impossible since individuals shared equally of whatever the community possessed; in the second type institutionalized social inequality was almost inevitable. The first type of clan could not grow, the second could not last. With the rise of social classes, differential privileges and responsibilities become a distinctive characteristic of human societies.

The transmission of privileges from the core group of one generation to that of another constitutes the most objectionable features of class stratification. It is this that is most readily abused when men exploit their positions on behalf of their children, wives, and close kin. A core group related by blood and wealth constitutes what in modern times has been called a *ruling class.*

The ruling class: Marx and Engels

Social scientists often view the phenomenon of social class largely through the eyes of the German expatriate, Karl Marx, and the Manchester manufacturer, Friedrich Engels. To this day, their vivid, partisan, eyewitness account of a society in the making, their sweeping view of humanity, their single-mindedness, and the inner coherence of their analysis are compelling and provocative. The range of their interests, impressive enough in their own day, strikes those reared in an age of specialization as extraordinary: the origin and fate of social classes, politics, revolution, and social change, literature and science, philosophy and the arts. Their theory of social class, the particular aspect of their work of interest in the pages to follow, has been highly influential among students of the social order even though it is an admixture of sound and unsound, essential and superfluous elements. If, as has often been observed, they exaggerated the determinant role of the economic element in social life in their published work, they were more than occasionally troubled by this exaggeration in their private correspondence.

That Marx should have stressed the economic factor is not too surprising in view of the historical epoch in which he was living. But that current Marxists continue to do so suggests an un-Marxist reluctance to face up to accumulated evidence. Marx, after all, hoped to "lay bare the economic law of motion of modern society," which might in itself constitute adequate justification for his overemphasis. His preoccupation with economic man was shared by other thinkers, among them Adam Smith and Saint-Simon, whose writings strongly impressed and influenced Marx's own formulations.

Early in the nineteenth century, Europe underwent a revolution that was to transform a large part of the world as only two other revolutions had done in recorded history—the Neolithic and Urban revolutions of thousands of years before. To these was now added the Industrial Revolution.

The Western world was convulsed by the disorder and terror, mingled with hope, that accompanied the decay of an old era and the birth of a new. Ties of kinships narrowed and weakened, old standards crumbled and new ones struggled to take root. Many feared for the survival of a society split into segments, pitting groups against groups and classes against castes. The struggle of individuals for wealth and of groups for power keynoted the age, setting rural townsmen against urban burghers, peasants against tradesmen, and artisans against mechanics.

Amidst these deep and unnerving rifts, men were caught between the promise of what they were about to gain and what they had irretrievably lost. The twin impulses of hope and nostalgia appear in the writings of Marx as in those of Hegel, Burke, and Saint-Simon before him, and of Durkheim, Toennies, and Weber after him. Marx clearly reveals this tension. Despite his persuasive belief in man's capacity for rational mastery of the world, his message was messianic. He wrote of a golden future, but it was a golden past that he had in mind. Marx deplored the existence, under capitalism, of what he called the illusory community, one existing above and beyond the individuals that composed it. And of the many villains playing their parts in his version of this drama, the exploitative tactics of the ruling class had top billing.

Marx's description of the role and character of the emerging bourgeoisie was both a contribution and a disservice to elite theory: a contribution because no more vivid picture exists of a group newly risen to unprecedented economic power, greedy for more and different kinds of power; a disservice because by focusing on what he viewed as the ruling class of the new era, he distorted the importance and influence of the bourgeoisie. Yet Marx was keenly aware that the bourgeoisie was but one among several elites with whom it had to share power and without whom it could not have survived. Having observed the rise of a semi-autonomous economic sector from local to national and finally to international importance, Marx concluded that its representatives would henceforth—until the "ultimate revolution"—dominate the entire political, military, and cultural life of society. The bourgeoisie would control not only the state, the army, and foreign affairs, but also the artistic and emotional outlook of the age. Yet this notion of an all-embracing ruling class seems to have been borrowed from another time and place: the court society that flourished during feudalism and which did indeed appear to have an overwhelming influence on the ideas, ideals, morals, and manners of the day. The image of the aristocratic court swept from power by the French Revolution provided the model used by Marx for his analysis of the aims and ultimate designs of this newly risen class of economic producers. Such a model, not surprisingly, proved to be inadequate for this task.

It is hardly accidental that Marx, whose analysis of capitalism was heavily indebted to a theory of social stratification, should have written so little of a theoretical nature about social classes as such. His brilliant political studies are demonstrations rather than analyses of classes in action. Only suggestive fragments of a theory of social classes remain. In these Marx is extremely contradictory, and on the very same point: the autonomy of the capitalist ruling class, which he perceives as supremely powerful and, alternately, as not powerful enough.

What, specifically, does Marx mean by ruling class? In the *German Ideology*[24] he describes it as the "ruling material force of society," the "class which has the means of production at its disposal," the class that controls the state which in fact enables it to rule, and the class that determines the leading ideas of the time, for these are "nothing more than the ideal expression of the dominant material relationships grasped as ideas." Marx viewed the minority whose decisions determined economic production as also shaping the distribution of property, of political power, and of intellectual and artistic creativity. At best this highly simplified view characterizes specific stages of economic development and therefore should more properly be considered as describing a temporary regularity rather than a permanent law.[25] In addition, Marx does not define the boundaries of the ruling class with any degree of consistency: in some passages it comprises all groups having decision-making powers in society; in others only the group of capitalist producers. Here the ruling class is seen to be unified, there internally divided and alienated.[26]

Part of the difficulty lies in Marx's inability to reconcile two contradictory explanations of the origin of social classes.[27] He sees social classes growing out of the social division of labor, and also out of the unequal distribution of property. The division of labor is also considered responsible for the disappearance of the true community and for the rise of alienation. Marx is thus forced into the position of attributing singular advantages to feudal society, which are quite incompatible with his political ideas. In *estate* societies, he argues, individuals were freer than they are under capitalism because "a nobleman always remains a nobleman, a commoner, a commoner";[28] individuals knew who they were and where they belonged. Only with the rise of capitalism and the shift from estates to classes do men become specialized and fragmented.[29]

Marx's second explanation of the origin of social classes reverts back to Rousseau who saw all social evils as stemming from the existence of private property. Adam Smith's stress on the social division of labor and Rousseau's plea for the abolition of private property are joined in Marx. When Marx refers to the three main social classes as consisting of capitalists, landowners, and laborers, he is using the division of labor theory; when he refers to those who own property as distinct from those who do not, he is referring to the private property theory. He never managed to reconcile the two.

Marx and Engels, as their correspondence clearly reveals, were aware of the theoretical gaps in their thoughts on these matters.[30] Their difficulties were due not only to their two-fold explanation of the origin of social classes but also to their contradictory image of the ruling class, that is, of the bourgeoisie. They clung to the idea that a single class dominated society in all significant spheres, and that by locating the source of domination and exploitation in this one class these could be abolished by the abolition of the class itself. Yet they also stressed the primacy of economic over other types of social activities, and in this context clearly implied domination by an economic elite. They seem to have been of two minds, alternately treating the bourgeoisie as an all-powerful ruling class, or as one of several powerful ruling groups. In their day such a confusion may best be understood as reflecting the fact that the bourgeoisie, while pursuing its economic mission, was also trying to gain a foothold in many other spheres. Its members were often ruthless and callous, at times intoxicated by their newly won prominence, and frequently indifferent to their larger social responsibilities. Understandably, Marx and Engels fastened on their faults while ignoring such virtues as they may have possessed. But while they contributed to our understanding of the social role of the bourgeoisie, they confounded its real economic powers with its larger and more illusory ambitions. Nor did they systematically distinguish between the elite of entrepreneurs and the entire stratum of capitalists, probably because such an elite was only emerging. Had they lived long enough they might have seen that they were recording the rise of a highly specialized, not a comprehensive, elite. Ultimately, this elite would cease to create and accumulate wealth for its own sake, and would be compelled to assume larger social responsibilities, thereby transforming its social role, its public image, and its public style. The current intermeshing of business, politics, and culture not only bears witness to the sheer power of business over society—for it occurs in capitalist as well as in noncapitalist industrial societies—but in some measure it is also a sign of society's considerable power over business. Marx saw only the first steps of this development. Today the latter is sharply at odds with his forecast of the future, although Marxism itself contributed to bringing about the change.

Like Marx himself, neither the Marxists who followed him nor the anti-Marxists who attacked him have used the term ruling class consistently and unequivocally.[31] The members of the ruling class have been identified as at least six different groups: those deriving profits from the ownership of the means of production; families and individuals whose control of the means of production allow them to dominate the population; men of the state apparatus; any and all groups that exploit others; all who are exempt from productive labor; and those linked by property, kinship, and inheritance, who also govern, and whose interests and ideas prevail in social life.

Most of these so-called definitions are either tautological, as when the ruling class is said to consist of those who dominate the population, or so inclusive that the very rich, the owners of the means of production who may not be very rich, and the holders of high political office are all put under the same rubric.[32]

A difficulty common to the six definitions just cited is the failure to distinguish between individuals who actually hold office, command armies, and organize production, and the larger stratum from which they are recruited. This combines our notion of *elites* as experts with ultimate responsibilities in given spheres with that of *class*—a larger group characterized by certain types of economic activities and culture patterns.

The conceptual vagueness of Marx and Engels on this score reflects the fact that they were observing a transitional period, marked by the rise of a new elite, the decline of old estates, and the realignment and emergence of classes. This vagueness has been continued —and exacerbated—by later-day Marxists. A. Bauer, for example, in suggesting that the traditional classification of societies according to their forms of government should be replaced by one resting on the "activity engaged in by their ruling class," provides examples that fit no existing usage of the term. Entire occupational strata are accorded the status of ruling class: professional soldiers in Sparta, priests in ancient Jerusalem and in seventeenth-century Geneva, bankers and merchants in Venice, and artisans in Athens, Florence, and the medieval communes.[33]

Bukharin accepts the more traditional Marxist connotation of the term but adds some new elements. He sees that ruling classes may perform an essential social service but quickly adds that such services disguise sinister motives. The "existence of generally useful functions on the part of the state," he writes, "does not alter the pure class character of the state authority. The ruling class is obliged to resort to all kinds of generally useful enterprises *in order to* maintain its ability to exploit the masses, extend its field of exploitation, and secure the 'normal' working of this exploitation."[34] The crucial phrase is "in order to," which implies a sequence of cause and effect that makes the useful functions performed by ruling classes mere by-products of other, more fundamental designs, hypocritically masking the true or real motives. Accepting the fact that the pharaohs and great landlords of ancient Egypt performed certain essential community services in regulating the course of rivers and in constructing huge projects, Bukharin nevertheless concludes: "The Pharaonic state did not, however, maintain these constructions for the purpose of averting hardships for the starving, or subserving the general weal, but merely because they were a necessary condition for the process of production, which was simultaneously a process of exploitation. *Class advantage was the basic impulse in this activity.*" [35] No evidence accompanies this assertion.

Trotsky, too, struggles manfully with the ruling class concept but is unable to adhere consistently to original Marxist usage; his additions and adaptations implicitly alter the meaning of the original. He writes that the ruling class succeeds in "putting over its economic and political forms upon the whole of society as the only forms possible" by "swerving the governmental course in its favor," but one is at a loss to know which of the two he is casting in the crucial role: the ruling class's relation to the means of production, or its relation to the government. If the answer is both, how is this to be reconciled with his traditional Marxist view that the government is only the executive committee of the ruling class and not something possessing sufficient autonomy to have to "be swerved in its favor"? [36] Trotsky, well aware of the problem, repeatedly asks himself whether his theory of the "phenomenon of 'dual power' contradicts the Marxian theory of the state." He finally decides that it does not, that it is simply a more complicated version of Marx's original formulation.

In most Marxist discussions of class relations, the term ruling class connotes both an observed phenomenon and a value judgment. The existence of an upper class, often used interchangeably with ruling class—an observable phenomenon—can be empirically determined by taking that stratum of people whose amount and source of income, economic opportunities on the market, and role in the production process is roughly similar and high. The value judgment enters whenever the term ruling is automatically equated with exploitative rather than with directing. In a society stratified by wealth one may anticipate the existence of rich and poor individuals. In a society in which wealth may be acquired, moreover, the rich will comprise a social class rather than a hereditary aristocracy. From this it does not automatically follow that this class must exploit the rest nor that it will dominate society in all respects. If the ruling ideas of an age are the ideas of the ruling class, how can one account for the fact that literature, philosophy, and the arts—surely reservoirs for such ideas—are more often than not opposed to conformity, established opinion, and safe beliefs? The ruling class may try to dominate the other classes, of course, but this is not to say that it will succeed.

The ruling class and strategic elites

The bourgeoisie, though powerful, never succeeded in making its power hereditary as did the aristocracies of old. As Marx himself realized, this class was no more and no less than a part of the ruling circles. Comparing the bourgeoisie with the feudal master class, Schumpeter observes:

> The bourgeoisie did not simply supplant the sovereign, nor did it make him its leader, as did the nobility. It merely wrested a portion of his power from him and for the rest submitted to him. It did not take over from the sovereign the state as an abstract form of organization. The state remained a special social power, confronting the bourgeoisie.[37]

In fact, a major difference between the bourgeoisie and the feudal master class was that the latter was once the supreme pinnacle of a uniformly constructed social pyramid—the bourgeoisie, never. Under feudalism, individuals typically could neither acquire nor lose their social status; under capitalism they could do both.

The bourgeoisie was but one ruling element in a society undergoing rapid and profound social changes. Its major responsibility was to direct the economic affairs of this society—to manage property, produce wealth, employ labor, and exchange products. To the extent that it dominated other spheres as well, this resulted from a temporary contagion of its newly won prestige. Although in the early stages of development, the bourgeoisie resembled a social class more than a specialized strategic elite—being dispersed rather than concentrated, being linked to kinship and wealth rather than primarily to skill—its ultimate destiny was to become a strategic elite.

The rise of this group to the rank of strategic elites marks a significant change from the age-old rule of the trinity of priest, king, and warrior. As is true of all elites in the process of formation, its initial recruits were often humble men, highly ambitious for worldly success, and highly mobile, geographically.[38] Before the industrial revolution, economic activities had been subordinate in importance to religious, military, political, and cultural activities. The economic elite, the richest merchants and traders, were merely rich and had no great social power or influence. Their activities had an obvious effect *within* society, but not on its organization and collective undertakings. In the countries where industrialism first took hold, the bourgeoisie threatened to but did not succeed in establishing itself as a permanent ruling class, principally because the function of ruling the society had become extremely complex. In advanced industrial societies the ruling class concept no longer adequately describes the character of the social core group.

That these matters cannot be handled by means of the traditional conceptual tools has resulted in considerable confusion in the literature. Some reject the very notion of a ruling group; others see all types as simply variants of a single one. Still others try, generally unsuccessfully, to integrate old concepts with new empirical observations. Dahrendorf, as the following excerpts from his writings show, clearly belongs to the third group:

> Ruling groups are, in the first place, no more than ruling groups within defined associations. In theory there can be as many competing, conflicting, or coexisting dominating conflict groups in a society as there are associations.[39]

> Delegation of authority in industry, in the state, and in other associations make possible in industrial societies dominating groups which are no longer small minorities but which in size hardly fall short of subjected groups.[40]

> Who, then, constitutes the ruling class of post-capitalist society? . . . those positions [at] the top of the pyramid of authority in the polity . . . It is admittedly not sufficient to identify a ruling class solely in terms of a governmental elite, but it is necessary to think of this elite in the first place, and never to lose sight of its paramount position in the authority structure of the state. . . . Of course this insistence on governmental elites as the core of the ruling class must be truly shocking to anybody thinking in Marxian terms, or, more generally, in terms of the traditional concept of class. . . . In abstract, therefore, the ruling political class of post-capitalist society consists of the administrative staff of the state, the governmental elite at its head,

> and those interested parties which are represented by the governmental elite.[41]

Dahrendorf thus uses the term ruling class to refer to at least three different groups: (1) to the heads of specific associations which would result in as many ruling classes as there are associations, recalling a warning by Franz Neumann, that "a concept that is boundless cannot be rationally defined";[42] (2) to practically all bureaucrats, both those formulating and those executing policies; and (3) to the governmental elite. So powerful is the spell of the past that even when a concept is patently unsuitable—in this case too narrow to include all of the relevant reality—it is nevertheless retained, although altered, if not distorted, in the process.[43]

Bukharin, with particular reference to working-class leadership, likewise distinguishes between a class, its leading representatives, the party, and, within the party, the individual leaders. He attributes the necessity for a party to the absence of equality and uniformity within the ranks of the working class. The party is the "thing that best expresses the interests of the class," the head of the class, "the most advanced, best schooled, most united segment." But even this vanguard is not uniform, and this necessitates the "formation of more or less stable groups of individual 'leaders' and the emergence of a 'permanent organization of leadership.' "[44]

G. D. H. Cole comes very close to seeing the real point of the distinction when he remarks that although elite and ruling class seem to resemble each other there are some important differences between the two concepts, chief among these being the fact that elites are "in essence constituted on a basis of some sort of personal capacity. . . ."

> Accordingly, in repudiating the identification of the elite with a "ruling class" [one] cannot discard altogether the need to pay attention to the role of certain elites as leaders of classes and exponents of class attitudes, as promoters of "class consciousness" and as opponents of the claims of rival classes. Not all elites rest on a class basis, but some do. . . .[45]

Cole is not content merely to enumerate different kinds of elites. He seeks also to assess and evaluate their impact on society and to distinguish the elites that significantly affect the functioning of the social system from those that do not.

There are, then, several essential distinctions between elites and ruling classes: a ruling class is more diffuse, more permanent, and therefore more difficult to delimit than strategic elites. Its membership is less voluntary, the scope of its activities is wider and less specialized, and its members share not only their occupational and functional positions but also more general habits, customs, and culture. Strategic elites may be thought of as further differentiations of a ruling class, a differentiation necessitated by the growth in size and complexity of advanced industrial societies. In such societies, trained experts are increasingly in demand in all spheres, including those involved with social leadership and the core functions.

In principle there can be only one ruling class in a society, but there must be a number of strategic elites. Any single strategic elite is probably numerically smaller than a ruling class as a whole. Because of the differentiation of tasks, strategic elites are less likely to become despotic than a ruling class. And since an individual cannot occupy an elite position in more than one social sector simultaneously, each strategic elite tends toward structural and functional autonomy.

Another important distinction concerns the modes of recruitment. A ruling class consists of groups of families who have more or less monopolized access to the most important elite positions of society and who are able to transmit their rewards and opportunities to their descendants, thereby dominating society in the present as well as in the future. Strategic elites are composed of individuals selected on the basis of individual motivation and capacity. Since such capacities and motivations may be distributed throughout the social structure, the recruitment of strategic elites is not confined to any specific group or class.

This may account for their members' propensity for hard work. Aristocracies valued leisure—working, so it appeared, out of desire rather than necessity. Members of a ruling class worked hard to make their fortunes, but having made them they sought to imitate the aristocracy in a show of leisure. Strategic elites work because they must, because their entire fate depends upon it. "This generation," said Nehru, "is sentenced to hard labor." The same may be said of all strategic elites today. Corporation executives work harder and longer than factory workers, and the President of the United States would currently receive much overtime pay in industry. Increasingly, leisure is becoming a prerogative of the working class. Full-time devotion to a task, long characteristic of artists, scientists, and professors, is now extending to members of all strategic elites. These elites are not likely, therefore, to become a leisure class in Veblen's sense.

In sum, strategic elites differ from a ruling class in their manner of recruitment, internal organization, and degree of specialization. Strategic elites have existed in some form in every organized human society; ruling classes have not and need not. A society may thus have strategic elites without having a ruling class. The following chart compares the differences between strategic elites and a ruling class side by side:

Comparative Criterion	*Ruling Class*	*Strategic Elites*
Number	One	Several
Size	Large	Small, concentrated
Duration	Longer-lived	Short
Modes of Entry	Birth and wealth	Expert skill
Modes of Exit	Loss of wealth	Incompetence
Scope of Authority	Diffuse and wide	Special and limited
Cultural Bonds	Schooling, background	No specifiable ones
Accessibility	Relatively closed	Relatively open

In short, the emergence and organization of strategic elites is related to but not identical with the emergence and organization of social classes. Their interrelationship is a continual source of confusion because, historically, strategic elites were often recruited from one or another social class whose general social rank was high. In view of their link to the core values of the social system, strategic elites occupied a high social status irrespective of the material wealth or genuine achievements of their members. Since they were often recruited from the upper class, these two types of ranking easily became confused and viewed as interchangeable. Moreover, the high status of the one reflected on that of the other. Thus if the stratum of landowners typically supplied the majority of leading politicians, thinkers, generals, and artists, some of their glamour and prestige became attached to them and merged with their economic powers and privileges. In turn, the leading statesmen and artists stood to gain from the economic power of the stratum from which they originated. As long as the social core group was principally recruited from a small exclusive circle tied by economic position and kinship—that is, from an upper class—it was difficult, if not impossible, to distinguish between the strategic elites and the class that supplied most of their membership. This was even more true if class background rather than social functions was used to justify the holding of strategic elite positions in society. Yet analytically, though not historically, strategic elites and social classes, function and recruitment, are and must be kept quite distinct.

In this age of specialization the core group of society itself becomes specialized. But this specialization does not of itself imply that social class no longer plays a significant role in recruitment, selection, and opportunity. The growth of a managerial elite in business, for example, has often been used as proof of the decline of social class factors in its recruitment and perpetuation, whereas no such conclusion automatically follows. Even Parsons occasionally argues in this manner:

> Ours is not an unstratified society, and shows no signs of becoming one; but it is definitely *not* aristocratic society in the traditional European sense. For a brief historical moment American capitalism appeared to be creating a new Schumpeterian "ruling class" of family dynasties founded by the "captains of industry." But this moment passed early in the present century, and the trend since then is clear —the *occupational manager,* not the lineage-based owner, is the key figure in the American economic structure.[46]

The emergence of professional managers, however, is no proof that class control over property has ceased. It would be surprising if it already had. One needs also to know whether these professional managers have been largely drawn from the ranks of previous "lineage-based owners" or any other segments of the upper class; whether the managers pursue their policies with an eye to pleasing the largest shareholders; and whether they share the ideologies of the nineteenth-century entrepreneurs by defending the same fundamental beliefs of laissez faire, private property, and private profits.[47]

The study of strategic elites must keep three factors separate and distinct. The first refers to the duties, responsibilities, and tasks of these elites. (A later chapter will show their relationship to different dimensions of the social system.) The second refers to the manner of recruiting these elites. If they reproduce themselves, then society is managed by one or several ruling castes; if they are drawn only from the rich and propertied, then the society has a ruling class. The third factor refers to the manner of rewarding these elites for adequate performance. In some cases elites get more of the desirable things of life, in others less. As regards the Catholic priesthood, for example, a harmonious family life is denied, and celibacy is enjoined. In Plato's ideal state, the guardians were to forego earthly pleasures and comforts and cultivate ascetic tastes.

In addition, the social function of strategic elites must be distinguished from the individual purposes of their members. The drama of individual competition, of success or failure to get to the top, depends ultimately on the fact that there is a top to be gotten to. The sociological factors contributing to the emergence of different types of social pinnacles will be examined in the next chapter.

Notes

1. Joseph Schumpeter, *Imperialism and Social Classes* (1955), p. 111.
2. Alexis de Tocqueville, *Democracy in America,* Vol. I, The Henry Reeve Text as revised by Francis Bowen. Now further corrected and edited with a historical essay, editorial notes, and bibliographies by Phillips Bradley (1956), p. 438.
3. H. H. Gerth and C. Wright Mills (ed.), *From Max Weber: Essays in Sociology* (1946), p. 369.
4. H. J. Habakkuk, "England," in A. Goodwin (ed.), *The European Nobility in the Eighteenth Century* (1953), pp. 1-21.
5. Pitirim A. Sorokin, *Society, Culture, and Personality* (1947), pp. 260-1.
6. *Ibid.,* pp. 289, 292-3. Thus it is not generally true, as Claude Levi-Strauss would have it, that ". . . in human societies the actual forms of social order are practically always of the transitive and noncyclical type: if A is above B and B above C, then A is above C; and C cannot

be above A." See Claude Levi-Strauss, "Social Structure," in *Anthropology Today* (1953), p. 547. In societies with ruling classes and even more so with strategic elites, this statement does not hold true. It is possible and probable that an individual may hold high rank in one sphere and low rank in another.

7. Robert A. LaVine, "The Role of the Family in Authority Systems: A Cross-Cultural Application of Stimulus-Generalization," *Behavioral Science*, 5 (October 1960), pp. 290-5. Of the 518 societies studied by LaVine, 245 had and 273 had not developed a State. Of the 245 societies in which a State had developed, 170 also had social classes; of the 273 societies in which a State had not developed, only 32 had social classes.
8. Fustel de Coulanges, *The Ancient City* (1956), p. 325.
9. *Ibid.*, p. 325.
10. H. D. F. Kitto, *The Greeks* (1960), p. 161. For other discussions, see Fustel de Coulanges, *The Ancient City, op. cit.;* T. R. Glover, *The Ancient World* (1957), Chap. vi.
11. Henri Frankfort, *The Birth of Civilization in the Near East* (1956), p. 66.
12. *Ibid.*, p. 77.
13. *Ibid.*, p. 79.
14. *Ibid.*, p. 79.
15. *Ibid.*, p. 107.
16. Emile Durkheim, *The Division of Labor in Society* (1947), p. 182.
17. *Ibid.*
18. Pontus E. Fahlbeck, *Die Klassen und die Gesellschaft* (1923), Chap. ii, pp. 22 ff. Cf. several similar views noted in Charles H. Page, *Class and American Sociology: From Sumner to Ward* (1940).
19. Aristotle, *Politics* (1941), Book IV, pp. 1210-11. Italics supplied.
20. As Sorokin has observed, the hierarchical element is only one defining element of social class, else "any organized group is a social class." Pitirim A. Sorokin, *Society, Culture, and Personality, op. cit.*, Chap. iv. Dennis Wrong, in a perceptive article dealing with some of these problems, suggests the term "ladder hierarchies" to describe stratified bodies such as churches or armies, that may draw all of their recruits from the lower classes and yet be rigidly stratified. See, Dennis H. Wrong, "The Functional Theory of Stratification," *American Sociological Review*, XXIV (December 1959), No. 6, 773.
21. Paul Kirchoff, "The Principles of Clanship in Human Society," in Morton H. Fried (ed.), *Readings in Anthropology*, II (1959), pp. 259-71.
22. *Ibid.*, p. 266.
23. *Ibid.*
24. Karl Marx and Friedrich Engels, *The German Ideology* (1947), p. 39.
25. See Wilbert Moore, *Industrial Relations and the Social Order* (1947), Chap. iv.
26. See, for example, Karl Marx and Friedrich Engels, *The German Ideology, op. cit.*, p. 203.
27. Raymond Aron refers to three but in a somewhat different context. See Raymond Aron, "Social Structure and the Ruling Class," *The British Journal of Sociology*, I (1950), 1-16.
28. Karl Marx and Friedrich Engels, *The German Ideology, op. cit.*, p. 77.
29. This diagnosis was not uncommon in Marx's day, but his solution has

novel aspects. For in proposing to do away with the division of labor so as to regain the earlier social unity, the poverty of feudalism may be recaptured as well. For this reason, Marx insisted on the fullest development of the productive forces: only in a world without want would economic exploitation cease. Neither Marx nor Engels, however, provide more than a vague sketch of how prosperity can be maintained, in the absence of an organized division of labor.

The division of labor was singled out by many eighteenth- and nineteenth-century writers as a vital social force, but their reactions to it varied. Simmel, for example, favored the increase, rather than the abolition, of alienation between the worker and his work so as to leave the personality free for other, more important, matters:

"It could be imagined that, in the course of civilization, work on behalf of production becomes more and more a technique, more and more losing its consequences for the personality and its intimate concerns. While originally the two were fused, division of labor and production for the market . . . have later permitted the personality increasingly to withdraw from work and to become based upon itself. No matter how unconditional the expected obedience may be, at this later stage it at least no longer penetrates into the layers that are decisive for life feeling and personality value." Georg Simmel in Kurt Wolff (ed.), *The Sociology of Georg Simmel* (1950), p. 284.

Emile Durkheim, on the other hand, distinguished between a forced and a spontaneous division of labor, the latter compatible with men's natural talents and desires. He would have liked to see the forced division abolished but the spontaneous one develop further. Marx, however, considered the division of labor as largely forced—at least under capitalism—a view shared by de Tocqueville who wrote that "it advances the art and recedes the artisan," and who saw in this the foundation for a new and potentially even harsher aristocracy in the world than had ever existed before. See, Alexis de Tocqueville, *Democracy in America,* Vol. II (1956), 169.

30. See, for example, Karl Marx and Friedrich Engels, *Selected Correspondence, 1846-1895,* trans. Dana Torr (1942), esp. the following letters: Marx to Wedemeyer, 5 March 1852; Engels to Marx, 13 April 1866; Engels to Bebel, 18-28 March 1875; Engels to Conrad Schmidt, 27 October 1890.
31. Although Engels, for example, clearly specifies that "the law of the division of labor lies at the basis of the division into classes," he nevertheless considers exploitation of one class by another to be inevitable. "It does not prevent the ruling class" he goes on to say, "once having the upper hand . . . from turning its social leadership into an intensified exploitation of the masses." Friedrich Engels, *Socialism: Utopian and Scientific,* in Karl Marx and Friedrich Engels, *Selected Works,* Vol. II (1958), p. 151. Karl Mannheim also defines the ruling class as those whose "ownership and control of the industrial machine allows them to dominate the population," even though elsewhere he accepts the fact that ruling classes exist by virtue of their social leadership function and need not be exploitative. See Karl Mannheim, *Freedom, Power and Democratic Planning* (1950), p. 79.
32. C. Wright Mills rejects the term "ruling class" in favor of "power elite"

because he considers the former a badly loaded phrase which does not "allow enough autonomy to the political order and its agents, and it says nothing about the military as such." He also points out that "class is an economic term," "rule" a political one. See C. Wright Mills, *The Power Elite, op. cit.,* p. 277. Mills is right enough in the distinction he draws, but he does not always follow his own advice. Often the term "power elite" seems to be the same catch-all phrase that ruling class has been.

33. A. Bauer, *Les Classes Sociales* (1902), pp. 149 ff.
34. Nicolai Bukharin, *Historical Materialism* (1925), p. 303. Italics supplied.
35. *Ibid.,* p. 304. Italics supplied.
36. Leon Trotsky, *History of the Russian Revolution,* Vol. I (1960), p. 206. At one point, for example, he accords the ruling class a principal and essential role in social organization: ". . . when the sun of the old society is finally declining in the West . . . the privileged classes are now changed from the *organizers of national life* into a parasitic growth; having lost their guiding function, they lost the consciousness of their mission and all confidence in their power." *Ibid.,* p. 97. Italics supplied.
37. Joseph Schumpeter, *Imperialism and Social Classes, op. cit.,* p. 93. Cf. also Michels' remarks that the bourgeoisie of the seventeenth century was in the same state of intellectual inferiority regarding the monarchy and consequently lacked authority. Robert Michels, *Political Parties* (1959), p. 85.
38. Sylvia Thrupp, *The Merchant Class of Medieval London* (1948), Chap. v.
39. Ralf Dahrendorf, *Class and Class Conflict in Industrial Society* (1959), pp. 197-8.
40. *Ibid.,* p. 195.
41. *Ibid.,* pp. 301-3.
42. Franz Neumann, *Behemoth* (1943), p. 75.
43. Actually, a number of writers have been dissatisfied with the Marxist definition of ruling class and have tried to correct it. Wittfogel speaks of the "ruling elite" in "hydraulic societies" as representing the most powerful men of the state apparatus. Again the objection might be raised that since Wittfogel is evidently referring to the pre-eminence of the political elite, he could have dispensed with the term "ruling class" altogether. See, Karl A. Wittfogel, *Oriental Despotism* (1957), Chap. viii.
44. Nicolai Bukharin, *Historical Materialism, op. cit.,* pp. 305, 307.
45. G. D. H. Cole, "Elites in British Society," in *Studies in Class Structure* (1955), pp. 103-4.
46. Talcott Parsons and Neil Smelser, *Economy and Society* (1956), p. 290. The same essential point is made by Parsons in his excellent critical review of C. Wright Mills, *The Power Elite,* in "Power in American Society," in Talcott Parsons, *Structure and Process in Modern Societies* (1960), pp. 199-226.
47. As regards the recruitment of modern industrial managers, three separate studies have shown roughly the same thing: the majority of the managers of the biggest corporations come from upper middle and upper class families, and had fathers in business careers. See Suzanne Keller, *The Social Origins and Career Lines of Three Generations of American*

Business Leaders (1953); Mabel M. Newcomer, *The Big Business Executive: The Factors That Made Him* (1955); and W. L. Warner and James C. Abegglen, *Occupational Mobility in American Business and Industry* (1955). For a study of business ideologies that raises and answers some of these questions, see Francis X. Sutton *et al.*, *The American Business Creed* (1957), esp. Chap. xiv.

3. STRATEGIC ELITES: CONCOMITANT SOCIAL FORCES

▲

To explain why strategic elites have proliferated in the modern world, we must turn to the social processes that have shaped that world.[1] Elites proliferate because of four main social processes: (1) the growth of population; (2) the growth of occupational specialization; (3) the growth of formal organization, or bureaucracy; and (4) the growth of moral diversity. With the continuing operation of these four processes, elites become more numerous, more varied, and more autonomous.

In small, relatively undifferentiated societies with a primitive technology, social leadership ranges from a council of elders convening during communal crises to a more organized and permanent chieftainship. The early chiefs were primarily priests and magicians, and only secondarily political leaders. As the community expanded, the apparatus of leadership grew more complicated, so that during the Middle Ages in the West, for example, a coopted priestly caste existed side by side with a hereditary monarchy, a nobility of warriors largely but not exclusively hereditary, and a stratum of free citizens engaged in trade and crafts whose gradually accumulating wealth soon led them to demand more social power.

The industrial revolution permitted the rise of a new strategic elite and with it a new principle of recruitment. Henceforth, the possession of property—whether or not associated with inherited status—was to permit access to positions of leadership, thereby expanding the reservoir of potential candidates. In America, in part a colony for refugees from a quasi-caste society, property became decisive for access into the higher circles. This was due to the continued technological and geographical expansion of the United States as much as to a distrust of hereditary privilege.

Thus, a major trend has been neither a decrease in the importance of birth as the major criterion of selection and succession. This development has taken place whenever societies have expanded rapidly and have needed skilled personnel quickly. Individual merit has always been valued in human society, but institutional arrangements for its discovery and cultivation have varied. Conceivably these arrangements may become more firmly established in advanced industrial societies.

However recruitment patterns change in these societies, the organization of strategic elites is altered. They are more numerous now and more varied principles affect their composition and interaction than was ever true in the past. Strategic elites have emerged from ruling classes and castes, but they should not be identified with them. Strategic elites are new historical phenomena; the social and cultural circumstances that have led to their emergence are considered in this chapter.

Growth of population

Today, the world's population numbers more than 2.5 billion people and increases by some 34 million annually, nearly 4,000 per hour, more than one every second. The United States in 1800 had 5 million inhabitants; in 1962 it has nearly 200 million.[2] This growth in size can be paralleled in country after country. Its cause: the industrial revolution. The ancient civilizations that fashioned much of the moral order of the modern world were created by relatively small communities, and men feared the possibility of extinction due to underpopulation—hence the well-known biblical injunction to "be fruitful and multiply." Their population ideals so reflected these circumstances that the stipulated utopian communities seem infinitesimal by current standards. Plato and Aristotle designed their ideal societies on the scale of the Greek polis only three of which—Syracuse, Acragas, and Athens—numbered more than 20,000 citizens.[3] The ideal city-state was no larger than a medium-sized town of today, and its very size made possible its distinctive character—open-air democracy, intense communal participation, and a high degree of public spirit. With a growth in population, communities became more heterogeneous, organized, and complex.

The complexity that accompanies an increase in size necessitates more formal organization, more elaborate mechanisms of communication, greater specialization of work, and indirect rather than direct methods of management and supervision.[4] As Simmel has summarized the process:

> The large group creates organs which channel and mediate the interaction of its members and thus operate as the vehicles of a societal unity which no longer results from the direct relations among its elements. Offices and representations, laws and symbols of group life, organizations and general social concepts are organs of this sort. . . . Typically, all of them develop fully and purely only in large groups.[5]

One of the consequences of this growth in size was, as Spencer was among the first to state, an increase in the dissimilarity between the various parts of the expanding society. The importance of centralized social leadership increases. Those who man these positions of leadership in industrial societies are the strategic elites.

Growth of the division of labor

One of the differences between a local community and a more inclusive society lies in the scope and specialization of work. In a smaller and occupationally less differentiated community, all members must contribute toward its and their own survival. It tends to resemble a collection of like elements. In a society, members of an organized collectivity share unequal responsibilities—some assuming responsibility for the collectivity directly, some indirectly, and some not at all. A society may be described as a collection of unlike elements. Communities, though they can more readily act in concert, usually forego the advantages that elaborate differentiation provides; thus they are relatively poorer, but more unified morally. Cohesion and moral unity are more often a problem in complex societies; poverty and lack of development, in simpler communities.

One of the chief elements of social cohesion in simpler societies is work. Malinowski vividly shows how the routine of work in the Trobriand Islands cemented ties of friendship and kinship throughout the whole range of island villages.[6] But as the division of labor proceeds, this type of moral unity is seriously undermined. The members of the community are no longer able to judge each other's conduct in work, and therefore in life. What does the carpenter know of the world of the tradesman, or the peasant of the city artisan? The differentiation which accompanies the division of labor must be offset by parallel developments that unify the community once more, but on a more complex level. Centralized group organs emerge to perform some of the tasks that the membership once did for themselves. Among these tasks are, first, upholding moral unity and cohesion in the face of the daily division of work, habits, and outlook; and, second, co-ordinating these varied activities so as to avoid or settle intergroup discord and strife. Gradually, the internal group divisions grow so extensive that the community is no longer one in any but a moral sense. Centrifugal tendencies therefore must be balanced by centripetal ones, and in place of an actual uniformity there emerges an emotional, moral, and symbolic uniformity.

The division of labor has been viewed as the major force behind the advance of civilization by a number of thinkers—Adam Smith, Saint-Simon, Herbert Spencer, and Emile Durkheim. Durkheim observes that the development of the division of labor rests on the growth of material and moral density and on a concentration, rather than a dispersion, of individuals in a given territory.[7] Such a concentration must be followed by a multiplication of social relationships within the community. A growth in size that leads merely to a proliferation of like elements is not enough. There must also be an increase in the interconnections among them.

The preservation of social solidarity in a society increasingly differentiated morally, mentally, and occupationally, is a constant theme in Durkheim's writings. His notion that organic solidarity would come about spontaneously was not even to Durkheim himself entirely satisfactory. In dismissing Comte's suggestion that a new independent organ must be created whose function would be the coordination and reconcentration of men, ideas, and social goals, dispersed by the expanded division of labor, Durkheim reveals that he was at least considering some such possibility. He rejected this view, however, on the ground that such an organ could not regulate in detail the particular activities in all social spheres. His solution was to claim that organic solidarity comes about spontaneously.[8]

Durkheim, noting the growth of specialization in the occupational world at large, suggested that this specialization and subdivision would affect the highest centers of society, bringing about a functional differentiation of these centers. "The division of labor," he observed, "does not present individuals to one another, but social functions." [9] Durkheim's observations apply to changes in strategic elites: their greater numbers, greater diversity, greater complexity, and their more complicated interrelationships. One need only compare a technologically primitive society such as the Fiji Islands, with its "chief of all trades," and our own society, with a veritable plethora of chiefs. Note the number of activities of which the Fijian chief is in charge:

> The chief . . . organizes the activities in his district, directing work in the gardens, house building, and in fishing. . . . No decision of importance may be reached in the district without his approval. Funeral services, for example, may not begin until he has given the word. . . . The chief is also the arbiter of disputes within the district. . . . He holds the power of life and death over his subjects.[10]

Judge, executive, religious leader, social arbiter, ceremonial head—all are separate roles in modern societies, but they are fused into a single role in Fiji society. The social functions which this chief has to fulfill are identical with the social functions entrusted to the strategic elites of today: to organize productive work, to propitiate and communicate with supernatural powers, judge and punish offenders of the laws, coordinate communal activities, defend the community from enemy attack, discover new resources and solutions to life's problems, and encourage artistic expression. In the more primitive society, the personality of the chief is specialized; in the more advanced societies, the functions themselves have become specialized. This leads to an interesting paradox—that the simpler societies may develop more complex leaders than advance societies, leaders, that is, with more complex personalities and talents.

Increasingly, those who supervise differentiated functions in modern societies are specialists in full-time jobs. Today no stratum of hereditary aristocrats could carry on all the complicated affairs of the Establishment by simply attending informally to demands as they arise, or by discussing affairs of state, economy, the arts, and morality at the dinner table where church leader, financier, and prime minister consult one another as members of one family.[11] Specialization thus affects the strategic elites no less than the general population and makes of that common centripetal core group a divided and separate series of specialists. The consequences of this are the greater autonomy and independence of these elites, their smaller degree of cohesion, and the decreasing likelihood that any single elite can long exert absolute, arbitrary power. "When parts are little differentiated," Spencer remarked, "they can readily perform one another's functions; but where much differentiated they can perform one another's functions very imperfectly, or not at all."

No single strategic elite can today know all there is to be known, and none can perform all the functions involved in social leadership. The Renaissance man is no longer a viable ideal but a heroic myth. Specialized knowledge, training, and experience are the standards by which men in high places are judged. Nobility of blood was displaced by nobility of wealth, and the latter now appears to be making way for a nobility of expert skill and interests. A man may bestow his land, wealth, and social connections upon his son, but he cannot bestow his corporation position, artistic preeminence, or elected office. What has long been true of the Catholic hierarchy—its emphasis on the calling—is now becoming true of most, if not all, strategic elites.

Growth of formal organization and its social implications

Along with the growth in size and the division of labor in society, there has also been a growth of formal organization and of institutional differentiation. Society has come more and more to resemble that system of differentiated yet interdependent parts that theorists of the eighteenth and nineteenth century referred to as the social organism.

The growth of size and complexity make spontaneity inadvisable. There is need for planning, for formalized communication, and for coordination of diverse activities in separated institutional spheres. Reliance on particularly striking, devoted, and brilliant leaders is not enough—they may emerge too late or not at all. Positions of leadership must be established in advance of acute need, and individuals must be preselected to fill them.

In modern complex societies, a dichotomy exists between individual desires and communal needs, between the minority of dissenters and the majority of conformists, between the minority leadership presumably acting for the good of the whole and the majority of members subordinating themselves to this aim. As the core group becomes increasingly organized, it achieves that glimpse of immortality that Simmel attributed to the triad. To fix the start of this process is hardly possible nor necessary. The evolution began when collectivities first began to organize formally. Once the organized system, called society, ceases to be synonymous with the sum total of its membership, the paradox arises that while the society may be preserved, large portions of its members are destroyed; or conversely, the members may live and perhaps even live well, but the system decays.

The strategic elites, whose function is to act on behalf of the various aspects of the social system, likewise become dissociated from the membership that selects them. The cleavage between the system and its membership leads to consequences that have long been attributed to the evils in human nature, the corruptive effects of power, or the insatiable desire for domination and exploitation within man; yet they may be essentially a consequence of the difference between men acting *for* the system and men acting *within* and *under* it. As a result, the actions and indecisions of these elites, their ignorance and knowledge, their prejudices and vanities, become life-and-death matters.

The democratic ethos notwithstanding, men must become accustomed to bigger, more extensive, and more specialized elites in their midst as long as industrial societies keep growing and become more specialized, and as the technical need for formal organization increases. What is true of large-scale formal organizations is in this respect also true of the larger society:

> The organ charged with the responsibility of co-ordinating the work of all departments and of directing it in the service of the purposes of the organization as a whole is obviously the most responsible and powerful part of the whole structure. In commercial enterprise, it is usually called its "management" or "top management," but whatever its name, it is distinguished by the fact that it represents the unity of the whole organization in its diversity and is, therefore, the central repository of its authority.[13]

It is this development that Michels depicted, not without exaggeration, as the cause of the inevitable triumph of oligarchies in human affairs. "The sovereign masses," he wrote, "are incapable of undertaking the most necessary resolutions. The impotence of direct democracy is a direct outcome of the influence of numbers." [14] Large numbers, he continues, are unable to convene, and if they could, they could not synchronize activities. As a result, all responsibilities, powers of action, and decisions must be delegated to a selected group of representatives. Consequently:

> Organization implies the tendency to oligarchy. In every organization, whether it be a political party, a professional union, or any other association of the kind, the aristocratic tendency manifests itself very clearly. . . . As a result of organization, every party or professional union becomes divided into a minority of directors and a majority of directed.[15]

It is not always clear to what Michels attributes the evils of organization, for his hypothesis is not free from serious ambiguities. Organization itself does not make for oligarchy; the emergence of a professional leadership does, he claims, because "a strong organization needs equally strong leadership." [16] Yet the nature of the mass itself, not the leadership, is often responsible for oligarchical trends in even the most radical of parties. Full-time workers who occupy themselves with organizational details and who become skilled in persuasion, oratory, literary expression, and behind-the-scenes politics are transformed from the original servants of the members into their masters. Finally, he argues, democracy itself leads to oligarchy because democracy means large numbers, which in turn implies organization and delegation. Thus Michels alternately blames organization, specialization, human nature, and democracy for the rise of oligarchy.

Michels does not explain why a professional leadership, even granting its technical superiority to the mass, must become despotic. He merely implies that these leaders will tend to work for their own interests instead of for the good of all because they constitute but "a fraction of society." Whether this is true or inevitable, remains to be established. If leaders are bound principally by their functional roles in the organization and share few bonds of social origins, family obligations, political commitment, or religious faith—a possibility that C. Wright Mills, for example, viewed as highly unlikely—then, even though they are but a fraction of the membership, they may still work for the good of the aggregate whose welfare is in their hands. Nor is organization as such necessarily evil. Historically, the absence of organization in groups of large size often has been associated with the very worst abuses, arbitrariness, and tyrannies—as in the Greek tyrannies and Oriental despotism. Indeed, one answer to increasing organization may be not less but more organization of a certain type. In the Printers' Union in America, for example, the organization and persistence for many years of two groups of skilled, professional leaders prevented the abuses that Michels most feared, in that each kept watch on the other;[17] the British shadow governments illustrate a similar situation on a larger scale. It should also be pointed out that Michels assumes the mass of members necessarily remains indifferent and disinterested in the affairs of the organization and in the activities of the leaders they have chosen. As Bukharin has remarked, this rests on an "eternal category in Michels' presentation, namely the 'incompetence of the masses.'"[18] This incompetence, however, is neither a necessary nor a permanent attribute.

Max Weber contributed what remains *the* influential analysis of the role of formal organization in the modern world. Specialization, limited spheres of competence, hierarchies of offices, specified responsibilities, rights, rules, and rewards, are all elements of the rise of bureaucratization in the world. Along with Weber most writers exempt administrators and heads of bureaucratic organizations from the rules and regulations of the organizations they supervise. "Only the supreme chief of the organization occupies his position of authority by virtue of appropriation, of election, or having been designated for the succession. . . . Thus at the top of bureaucratic organizations, there is necessarily an element which is at least not purely bureaucratic." [19] The members of the strategic elites constitute administrators for the society at large and they, too, must be partially viewed as being exempt from the constraints imposed on ordinary members of society.

Consequently, members of strategic elites must be studied both as the heads of large-scale organizations bound by formal rules, and as unpredictable, spontaneous, and potentially creative or destructive leaders who may transcend these rules. In representing the total membership of organized or unorganized majorities in the social system, strategic elites are complementary to that membership. A compensatory not a direct reciprocity exists between strategic elites and the relevant mass—appearing unified where the mass is diversified; appearing small where the mass is large; appearing specialized where the mass is generalized. Strategic elites must perceive the whole of social life, be articulate where the mass is mute, and stand for the ultimate purposes of communal life, emphasizing the public rather than private interest.

Growth of moral diversity

Nostalgia for the small, intimate, familiar community has increased in proportion to its decline. Many would judge our modern world by its failure to live up to standards set by these communities, for in reliving the past men often transform it to suit their own desires. Many of the moral ideals of today, the standards of right and wrong, sacred and profane, were developed in these simpler communities and continue to be taught alongside the mores better adapted to an urban way of life.

But the communities of the soil that men cherished and defended with their blood bear little similarity to the far-flung societies of today. A world in which the construction of a single ship, the *Queen Elizabeth,* requires the labor of more than a quarter of a million people (Rome at its height as the center of the world had but one million people), and which serves 10,000 meals on a single day of its five-day transatlantic crossing, has little in common with the world in which our moral codes were first created. Traditions die hard and reluctantly, however, and many of the mores, though not the manners, of earlier nomadic and peasant communities are with us still. These mores survive in a society in which almost all else has changed. Modern industrial society is a world of *variety*. More people than ever before in larger communities must cope with a mechanized world in which even machines can think. The innumerable and growing number of occupations defy systematic and inclusive classification; over 40,000 occupational titles are used currently in the United States. In addition, there are regional, religious, racial, national, and personal differentiations. People belong to a multiplicity of groups and associations, separated from the majority of men by the work they do, by the things they know, by what they take for granted, by the people they habitually meet, and by the maps of the world that they carry inside their heads.

When Durkheim cited greater interdependence and reciprocal fulfillment as among the advantages of an expanded division of labor, he hardly anticipated the extensive division that currently exists. Today, when no one can know more than a fraction of these occupations and the ways of life they entail, men are more and more confined to occupational societies within their society. It is difficult, if not impossible, for all to be morally committed to the same goals, not only because of specialized occupational moralities, but also because the gap between the core values of a society and the personal values of individual members is growing wider. Individuals, though they still belong to the same society, no longer share all of its burdens and therefore cannot, except in the most abstract sense, live up to all of its ultimate moral claims. Today, only the strategic elites can do so. At the very time that a general morality has become crucial, in part because it is in danger of being lost, most individuals can do little more than pay lip service to the norms of the societies in which they live. Units have become so big and complicated that individuals feel powerless to alter or affect the shape of things to come. Societies, said Max Weber, are collectivities rationally organized for the achievement of consciously designated ends; communities function smoothly because its members *feel* that they belong together. In this sense, strategic elites resemble communities—they must feel committed to large collective purposes within a common cultural framework. Most people, in their everyday working lives, tend to refer to "they," the anonymous eyes and ears of the world or the men in control of things as sources of authority. The strategic elites, who are the originators rather than the instruments of social action, must be able, at least some of the time, to say "we."

Rise of functional elites

"The state," Aristotle wrote, "is a union of families and villages in a perfect and self-sufficing life." [20] Now, though families may still be included in this union, there are entire regions, huge cities, and even continents in the place of villages. The rise of strategic elites both reflects and reinforces the decline of local centers where much of history was once made. The shift of power and influence from the local to the national and now to the international scene has occurred in politics, business, religion, and the arts.

The victims of this shift are many. Chief among them are those centers that once captured the imagination—cities like Charleston and Boston in America—that live on rather than up to their reputations. The social landscapes of most industrial societies are dotted with similar places, of which even a young country like America has its share. New centers of power and influence have sounded the decline of old ones; a fatalistic view of the world has combined with the conviction that individuals no longer control their own destinies because the world has become too big, too impersonal, too unfamiliar.

The strategic elites themselves are caught in the struggle between local loyalties and national commitments, between regional attachments and national perspectives. The counterpart to this struggle may be found in many different types of societies throughout history, societies unable, institutionally, to keep up with demographic and geographic expansion and therefore unable to profit from it. The case of Mesopotamia is not atypical:

> The Sumerians had a phrase, "the black-headed people," to designate themselves as an ethnic unit; and the gods of Enlil and Anu, among others, were worshipped throughout the land. But this feeling never found expression in a political form; it remained without effect, it

seems, on the country's history. The particularism of the cities was never overcome.[21]

In time, Mesopotamia was to be invaded by neighbors, often in collusion with one of her own cities, until the final, successful attack by Cyrus, the Persian, in 539 B.C. This recalls the experience of Greece in the fifth century B.C. and that of Rome in the fifth century A.D. In each case the failure to control and curb the desires for local autonomy accelerated the decline of these civilizations. The inability to transcend sectional interests has plagued primitive societies as well, many of whom must manage to solve these problems without benefit of inclusive political organization. Various alternative measures—strict village exogamy, or membership in age-sets that override local village loyalties on specific occasions, or membership in far-flung trading associations—might be considered functional equivalents of political organizations such as the state.[22]

Advanced industrial societies, it appears, are currently on the way toward ever larger, functional divisions. This trend was anticipated by Saint-Simon, among others, who envisaged an international order based not on national but occupational coordination. Durkheim continued this line of thought. He favored the displacement of segmental, territorial solidarity by a comprehensive, functional solidarity based on occupational interdependence, residence becoming less and occupation more important. "A day will come," he prophesied, "when our social and political organization will have a base exclusively, or almost exclusively, occupational." [23] Increasingly it does appear as if local trading, academic, artistic, financial, and fashion centers are yielding ground, and territorial solidarities are making way for other kinds.*

Elites as minorities

Whatever the variations in opinion regarding the origin, organization, and current significance of strategic elites, there is essential agreement about their size. Generally, elites are assumed to be small in number in relation to the total population.[24] In fact, some of the distrust of elites by the populace stems from their being con-

* This may also be seen in fields such as entertainment, which used to be local and part of an area but is now national and part of an era.

spicuous minorities. Simmel cites an interesting instance of an attempt to make such a minority less conspicuous. In Venice, he tells us, "all noblemen had to wear a simple black costume: no striking dress was to call this small number of men in power to the attention of the people." [25] As to the actual size of these leading minorities, evidence is sparse. Few estimates, however, would have them exceed 3 per cent of any given population. Machiavelli, referring to the cities of his own day, thought that no more than forty to fifty men attained real power in any city.[26] Barnard calculates that 100,000 individuals occupy major executive positions in the United States; presumably he refers to executives in big business. In a population close to 200 million, 100,000 individuals amounts to one executive per 2,000 persons, or one tenth of 1 per cent of the total.[27]

Elites are also, though not always explicitly, minorities in other respects: (a) the positions they occupy—these being the topmost or central ones; (b) the attributes on the basis of which they were selected—possessing or appearing to possess some sort of excellence, be it wisdom, courage, intelligence, breeding, or some forms of expert knowledge and skill; (c) their social responsibilities—having a greater share of these than the rest of the population; and (d) their rewards—getting proportionately more of the good things of life.

Most writers are content merely to state, as a general conviction, that elites must be numerically small. But they do not further explore the matter. Three notable exceptions are Simmel, Michels, and Mosca whose writings contain explicit as well as inferential material which warrants examination.

Simmel traced the development of what he called central group organs to the growing size of the group, but also suggested that the maintenance of these organs depends in turn on their remaining small. This was especially necessary for aristocratic groups:

> If it is to be effective as a whole, the aristocratic group must be "surveyable" by every single member of it. Each element must still be personally acquainted with every other. . . . The tendency toward extreme numerical limitation, characteristic of historical aristocracies from Sparta to Venice, is not only due to the egoistic disinclination to share a ruling position but also to the instinct that the vital conditions of an aristocracy can be maintained only if the number of its

> members is small, relatively and absolutely. . . . It is very characteristic that . . . when Plato speaks of the Ruling Few, he also directly designates them, as the Not-Many.[28]

Simmel also suggests that both the absolute as well as the relative size of prominent members of a group should be taken into account. One individual, he points out, can less readily control a village of 100, than 100,000 men can control a society of ten million, though the proportions in each case are identical. But he did not further explain or develop this idea.[29] A recent study by Anderson and Warkov is germane to this problem. The authors sought to ascertain the relationship between the growth of an organization and the growth of its administrative component. They found that the larger the organization (in this case, hospitals), the smaller the proportion of personnel in administration. They therefore proposed three elements as intervening variables between an increase in the size of an organization and the size of its administration: the number of persons performing identical tasks; the number of different places at which work is carried on; and the number of tasks performed.[30]

Mosca attributes the necessity for minority leadership to the characteristics of organization. This minority, "to which the majority willingly or unwillingly defer," can organize itself and therefore obey "a single impulse," whereas the majority must ever remain unorganized and thus impotent.

> A hundred men acting uniformly in concert, with a common understanding, will triumph over a thousand men who are not in accord and can therefore be dealt with one by one. Meanwhile, it will be easier for the former to act in concert and have mutual understanding simply because they are a hundred and not a thousand.[31]

But aside from his insistence that the majority cannot, in principle, discover means of organization, Mosca does not say how the minority is able to do so beyond asserting that its small size will be helpful. In large part, Mosca was reacting against the sincere but naïve view that universal suffrage would eliminate the age-old problems of dominating minorities, dominated majorities, and despotism. But, one wonders, would 100 organized men be superior to 1,000 organized men? Is it not the absence of organization, rather than size, that accounts for the superiority of the small as against the large group? In any case, Mosca postulates an inverse relationship between the size of a population and the size of its ruling minority.

Michels agreed substantially with Mosca, considering an organized minority of professional leaders both indispensable and inevitable in mass societies. The mass is unable to act directly on its own behalf and must therefore delegate responsibility to professional representatives. The only hope for the mass of men is to win the right to choose its masters.[32]

Three different reasons have been suggested as to why elites must remain minorities: the structural features of hierarchical organizations; the search for desirable attributes which by definition are scarce; and the necessity for rapid communication which limits the size of the communicating parties, in this case, of the elites. These views illustrate the lack of agreement, as well as evidence, concerning the relation between size and effective minority leadership. It is generally agreed that elites must be minorities, but two contrasting qualifications have been maintained. It has been argued that elites are inversely proportional to the growth of the general population, and, conversely, that elites are directly proportional to such growth.

If strategic elites are viewed as analogous to administrators and executives in large-scale organizations in relation to the larger society, their relative size will depend on the degree of diversification or social and occupational homogeneity of that society. Where diversification is relatively slight, as in technologically primitive societies, these elites will be small and relatively uniform and unified. Where diversification is extensive and elaborate, as in technologically complex societies, the strategic elites will be diversified and relatively more numerous.

The fact that elites must be minorities has been evaluated in different ways. Aristotle favored the supremacy of the multitude rather than the few best because he felt the former's collective judgment to be superior in the long run:

> For each individual among the many has a share of virtue and prudence, and when they meet together, they become in a manner one man, who has many feet, and hands, and sense. . . . Hence the

> many are better judges than a single man of music and poetry; for some understand one part, and some another, and among them they understand the whole . . . if people are not utterly degraded, although individually they may be worse judges than those who have special knowledge—as a body they are as good or better.[33]

At the same time, Aristotle deplored the difficulties that arise as the size of the city increases. "Since cities have increased in size, no other form of government appears to be any longer even easy to establish." [34]

James Madison favored representative government as a way of controlling the "mischief of faction" and considered that the advantages of representation increase with the growth in size of the republic:

> In the first place, it is to be remarked that however small the republic may be, the representative must be raised to a certain number, in order to guard against the cabals of a few; and that, however large it may be, they must be limited to a certain number, in order to guard against a confusion of a multitude. Hence, the number of representatives in the two cases not being proportionally greater in the small republic, it follows that, if the proportion of fit characters be not less in the large than in the small republic, the former will represent a greater option, and consequently a greater possibility of a fit choice.[35]

Madison argues that since more people will participate in the election of the representatives in the large republic, better men are likely to be chosen. The representatives of the larger republic will have fewer local prejudices and broader tastes because they must please a larger and more varied group.

Michels had less confidence in the majority. In contrast to the writers just cited, he drew rather gloomy conclusions from his analysis of mass political parties. Inevitably, he warned, delegation of responsibility to selected leaders will lead to self-perpetuating elites and to despotism. "It is easier to dominate a large crowd," he observes, "than a small audience." Contrast this with Simmel's observation that other things being equal, "the larger the group, the smaller is the range of ideas and interests, sentiments and other characteristics in which its members coincide and form a 'mass.' Therefore, insofar as the domination of the members extends to their common features, the individual member bears it the more easily, the larger his group. Thus in *this* respect, the essential nature of one-man rule is shown very clearly: the more there are of those over whom one rules, the slighter is that proportion of every individual which he dominates." [36] Simmel maintained that although a tyranny is more oppressive in small groups (citing parents and their children as one example), it may be easier to dominate a large group. He who dominates a small group, Simmel concluded, can do so only because the members wish it, and their bondage, though voluntary, is the more complete and severe; he who dominates a large group has a wider but shallower reach. Thus Michels' hypothesis should be reformulated to include Simmel's telling insight: it is easier to dominate a large crowd than a small audience, but on fewer matters.

Thus strategic elites—administrators as well as leaders—will, on both grounds, be small in number relative to the total population. But it does not necessarily follow that they will be despotic minorities, since despotism depends on more than size. The possibility of despotism, however, is ever present.

In sum, at least four social forces have contributed to the emergence of strategic elites in their present form: a growth in size, division of labor, formal organization, and moral diversity. Advanced industrial societies are marked by occupational differentiation within functional sectors and by functional specialization among them. More and more, the political, economic, scientific, religious, educational, cultural, and recreational sectors are organizationally, occupationally, and morally autonomous. At the same time, overriding goals of these functionally specialized elites are as they have always been, the preservation of the ideals and practices of the societies at whose apex they stand.

Wherever they have emerged, whether in simple or in complex forms, the strategic elites had, and continue to have, roughly similar responsibilities. They symbolize the moral unity of a community becoming subdivided by emphasizing common purposes and interests. They attempt to coordinate and harmonize the diversified activities, combat factionalism, and resolve group conflicts. And they try to protect the community from external danger.

Increasingly, no single social stratum is likely to monopolize access to elite positions. The widely accepted model of society resembling a single pyramid is giving way to one with a number of parallel pyramids, each capped by an elite. The class system of industrial societies foreshadowed this trend in its stress on two principles: the status principle, depending on style of life and on qualitative distinction; and the achievement principle, depending on individual accomplishments in an impersonal market. Strategic elites stress both distinctions, for they are composed of men of proven ability as well as of men who represent a given set of moral ideals and a style of life adapted to their functional roles. The President of the United States, the president of a giant corporation, the top atomic scientist, and the leading writer of an era have little in common beyond their general cultural backgrounds and their achievement of prominence. How they arrived at their pre-eminent positions, what they must do to remain there, and how they affect the lives and fortunes of other men through the exercise of their functional responsibilities, differ for each.

The existence of an all-powerful economic ruling class is no longer valid. The economic sector is of course powerful and well-organized, and its leaders keenly interested in maintaining its influence and their power. But economic power is not the sole form of power even in a society obsessed by the idols of the market place. The political, the military, and the cultural functions have not generally nor even typically been carried out by leading entrepreneurs and their sons. In advanced industrial societies, wealth and property are never *all* that is needed to be accorded social honor.

The current business elite, for example, is better organized than ever before and at the same time less powerful than in the early stages of its rise to prominence. Moreover, a deep split is apparent between those entrepreneurs who have made the big time and those in the modest role of the small businessman. The first comprises the economic elite, an elite still in the making, which mirrors the contradictions of a rapidly expanding industrial society in that high birth and property most assuredly do not hurt the aspiring candidate although motivation, native ability, and training are equally or perhaps more important. Wealth may well continue to be an entrance ticket to the higher echelons, to the best schools, and to the self-confidence that accompanies these entries. Yet it is also true that the biggest corporations are most advanced in recruitment on the basis of merit irrespective of social background.[37]

Repeated reference has been made to the interdependence and functional differentiation among strategic elites as well as to their growing significance in occupationally, organizationally, and technologically complex societies. Their principal functional responsibilities will be examined in the next chapter.

Notes

1. Following Emile Durkheim, the causes of a phenomenon may be divided into two types: (1) the antecedent cause—in this case, strategic elites must be studied as outgrowths of the ruling castes, aristocracies, and ruling classes that historically preceded them, as was done in the previous chapter; (2) the concomitant cause—those forces that continue to operate and exert their influence. In this case, strategic elites must be studied in relation to the social forces that foster social expansion. See, Emile Durkheim, *Rules of Sociological Method* (1950), pp. 95 ff.
2. Julian Huxley, "World Population," *Scientific American,* LXCIV, No. 3, 64-7. Mankind appeared on the surface of the earth between 500,000 and one million years ago. At the birth of Christ, the world's population was approximately 350 million. In two thousand years, the population has grown from 350 million to 2,700 million. See, P. K. Whelpton, "A Generation of Demographic Change," in Roy G. Francis (ed.), *The Population Ahead* (1958).
3. H. D. F. Kitto, *The Greeks* (1960), pp. 72-3. The total population was of course much larger since the citizens constituted only a portion of the entire adult males of the community. At the outbreak of the Peloponnesian War the population of Attica numbered about 350,000—one half Athenian (men, women, and children), one tenth resident aliens, and the rest slaves. Sparta was much smaller in population though much larger in size—its 3,200 square miles, considered enormous by the Greeks, could be traversed on foot in two days. *Ibid.,* p. 65.
4. The elaboration of potential relationships with an expansion of group size is truly astounding. In a small group of seven members, the number of potential pair relationships is twenty-one. For a small household of ten members, the total number of potential relationships, including pair relationships, relations between a member and combinations of members, and relations among subgroups, reaches the fantastic total of 29,268. Theodore Caplow, "Organizational Size, *Administrative Science Quarterly* (March, 1957), pp. 484-505.

5. Georg Simmel, in Kurt Wolff (ed.), *The Sociology of Georg Simmel* (1950), p. 96.
6. Bronislaw Malinowski, *Crime and Custom in Savage Society* (1951), *passim.*
7. Emile Durkheim, *The Division of Labor in Society* (1947), Book II.
8. "The division of labor varies in direct ratio with the volume and density of societies, and, if it progresses in a continuous manner in the course of social development, it is because societies become regularly denser and generally more voluminous." *Ibid.*, pp. 262, 361.
9. *Ibid.*, p. 407.
10. Clellan S. Ford, "The Role of the Fijian Chief," *American Sociological Review*, III (August, 1938), esp. 542-50.
11. An excellent illustration of conflicts engendered by the growth of occupational specialties as distinct from family loyalties among the elite of a town is provided in Ibsen's *Enemy of the People*. The leading scientist who discovers that the town's water supply is polluted is virtually destroyed by his own brother, the Mayor, who fears that this discovery will, if publicized, ruin the town's tourist trade on which its survival depends. In the end, the scientist is silenced. "By the vote of everyone here except the tipsy man, this meeting of citizens declares Dr. Thomas Stockman to be an enemy of the people. Three cheers for our ancient and honourable citizen community! Three cheers for our able and energetic Mayor who has so loyally suppressed the promptings of family feeling!" The tension between family and community roles runs throughout the play. Henrik Ibsen, *Enemy of the People* (1942), pp. 151-2.
12. Herbert Spencer, *Principles of Sociology*, Vol. I (1896), Part II, Chaps. x-xii.
13. E. Strauss, *The Ruling Servants* (1961), pp. 34-5. "We are going to have to face the fact," writes one observer, "that there are going to be more and more industrial giants . . . bigger and bigger trade unions, and this means that as competition lessens, the importance that the decisions taken should be the right ones increases. It will not wreck the national economy if a small firm makes the wrong decision, but if I.O.I. does, it may." Laurence Thompson, *The Challenge of Change* (1956), p. 52.
14. Robert Michels, *Political Parties* (1959), p. 25.
15. *Ibid.*, p. 32.
16. *Ibid.*, p. 36.
17. S. M. Lipset *et al., Union Democracy* (1956), Chap. xi, pp. 219-37.
18. Nicolai Bukharin, *Historical Materialism* (1925), p. 310.
19. Max Weber, trans. in A. M. Henderson and Talcott Parsons, *The Theory of Social and Economic Organization* (1947) p. 335.
20. Aristotle, *Politics* (1941), p. 1189.
21. Henri Frankfort, *The Birth of Civilization in the Near East* (1956), p. 88.
22. J. G. Peristiany, "Law," in *The Institutions of Primitive Society* (1956), p. 45.
23. Emile Durkheim, *The Division of Labor in Society* (1947), p. 190. The distinction between local and national, and segmental and comprehensive power corresponds to Mannheim's classification of power into "com-

munal" and "functional" types. Karl Mannheim, *Freedom, Power and Democratic Planning* (1950), pp. 48-76.

24. An exception to the general view that elites are small minorities is provided by Dahrendorf, who maintains that this is no longer the case in advanced industrial societies, although he is of two minds about it. He notes that "the assumption that in any association the number of those subjected to authority is larger than the number of those in possession of authority does seem capable of generalization." But he is "hardly surprised to find that in many modern industrial enterprises almost one-third of all employees exercise superordinate functions. Delegation of authority in industry, in the state, and in other associations makes possible in industrial societies dominating groups which are no longer small minorities, but which in size hardly fall short of subjected groups." Here Dahrendorf seems to confuse responsibility *within* an organization with responsibility *for* it. Ralf Dahrendorf, *Class and Conflict in Industrial Society* (1959), p. 195.
25. Georg Simmel, *op. cit.*, p. 365.
26. Quoted in Mosca, *op. cit.*, p. 239.
27. Chester I. Barnard, *The Functions of the Executive* (1950), p. 289.
28. Georg Simmel, *op. cit.*, pp. 97, 105-7, 171-2.
29. *Ibid.*, p. 90.
30. Their findings thus challenge those of an earlier study by Terrien and Mills who found a direct relationship between an increase in the size of an organization and the size of its administration. However, closer examination dissolves the contradiction. The findings of Anderson and Warkov belong in the context of the first intervening variable (the number of persons performing identical tasks has grown); the findings of Terrien and Mills belong to the second (the number of different places at which work is carried on has increased). Frederick W. Terrien and Donald L. Mills, "The Effect of Changing Size Upon the Internal Structure of Organizations," *American Sociological Review,* XX (February 1955), 11-14. See also, Theodore E. Anderson and Semour Warkov, "Organizational Size and Functional Complexity," *American Sociological Review,* XXVI (February 1961), 23-8. Anderson and Warkov found that 12 per cent of the personnel in both large and small hospitals belonged to the administration of these hospitals. In postulating an inverse relationship between size of an organization and size of the administration, however, it would first be necessary to ascertain whether both the large and the small hospitals with identical proportions in the administrations were equally efficient and adequate. In the absence of any evaluation of their functioning, it is impossible to know whether the large hospitals operated as well as the small ones. It may still be true, ideally, that the larger the size the larger *should be* the administrative component, which is not to say that it will be.
31. Gaetano Mosca, *The Ruling Class* (1939), p. 53.
32. Robert Michels, *Political Parties, op. cit., passim.*
33. Aristotle, *op cit.* (1941), Book III, Chap. xi.
34. *Ibid.,* Chap. xvi.
35. James Madison, *The Federalist,* No. 10, in Richard D. Heffner, *A Documentary History of the United States* (1952), pp. 38-44.
36. Georg Simmel, *op. cit.*, p. 203.
37. Of the American business elite in 1950, for example, two thirds had

worked twenty years or longer to obtain the top positions in their firms, even though three fifths of this same group had been born to business families. See, Suzanne Keller, "The Social Origins and Career Lines of Three Generations of American Business Leaders," Unpublished Ph.D. dissertation, Columbia University (1953), p. 98.

4. THE SOCIAL FUNCTIONS OF STRATEGIC ELITES

▲

Strategic elites proliferate in advanced industrial societies because of antecedent historical conditions, currently operative social forces, and the functional requirements of large-scale social systems. The first two of these matters have been discussed in the two preceding chapters. We now turn to the question of the functional requirements of modern industrial societies.

The notion that elites subserve social functions is a fairly general one, found in one form or another in most writings on the subject. But few writers go beyond generalizations to trace the specific interconnections between elites and their social functions. Often these generalizations conceal such tautologies as the proposition that elites rule the community, or that elites are groups superior in status and power. Frequently, one or two types of elites are taken as the models for all types, a procedure that hinders the development of a comprehensive theoretical model. Without such a model, it is hardly possible to integrate and organize the varied relevant historical, anecdotal, and empirical findings.

The work of Talcott Parsons provides such a model. Parsons builds upon the work of a number of other thinkers who, though differing from him and one another in their methods and conclusions, also sought to discover the factors making for social stability and social change. Adam Smith, representing classical economic doctrines, thought of society as a self-regulating system propelled by myriads of independent, individual decisions registered in an impersonal market. A few decades later, Saint-Simon was no longer able to adhere to so mechanical a model, but he too sought to discover the factors affecting the social equilibrium. He saw this equilibrium as being actively promoted by a directing center consisting of the economic producers and technical and scientific experts—the key representatives of the emerging industrial society. Since wealth and technical knowledge were the mainsprings of that society, the decisions of economic and scientific experts were considered to be crucial for its fate.

Marx learned from both of these men. From Smith he derived the notion of society as a system of interdependent parts operating independently and almost outside of the individual consciousness. From Saint-Simon he acquired the conception of a directing agent—although he transformed it into the capitalist ruling class. Marx saw society as run by force, and since in his day this force was manifested most conspicuously in the economic realm, those in control of economic activity presumably controlled society.

Whatever their differences, Smith, Saint-Simon, and Marx similarly concentrated on one or very few factors as basic to the social order. Pareto further pursued these ideas. He tried to show, first, that although society was dependent on a common fund of values ("residues"), it also consisted of a dynamic set of competing and conflicting social forces. The equilibrium thereby established was at best precarious. Like Marx, Pareto retained the idea of a single group—in his case, the political rather than the economic elite—seeking to dominate society. Again like Marx, he saw the dynamic element in social life as a struggle between a powerful minority and the exploited. But this struggle was not between the powerful and the powerless, as Marx viewed it, but between the powerful and their rivals. Pareto argued that this conflict would continue as long as men exist; as long as there were minorities who rule there would be minorities who seek to rule.

In contrast to Marx, Saint-Simon, and Pareto, and despite the fact that he was preoccupied with problems of social control, Durkheim developed neither a single nor multistranded theory of power. He saw society as guided rather by moral norms which were either shared by all, as in primitive and simple societies or, distributed differentially, as in complex and advanced societies, especially among the major occupational groups.

In this century, one of the most ambitious and systematic attempts to delineate the nature of the social system is that of Parsons himself. In *The Social System* (1952) Parsons tends, in the manner of the classical economists and Durkheim, to present the social system as a machine without a driver. His more recent work, however, shows greater interest in questions of power and leadership.[1] Nevertheless, from an over-all perspective, Parsons continues to emphasize self-regulating social processes and mechanisms.

Each of the aforementioned thinkers presents a different, if one-sided, explanation of how the social system works. The classical economists stressed self-interest; Saint-Simon, the actions of economic producers and technical experts; Marx, economic exploitation of one class by another; Pareto, political dominance guided by the residues underlying the dynamic social equilibrium; Durkheim, reciprocal awareness of interdependence or moral consensus. Parsons, like Durkheim, is drawn to moral consensus as the basis of the social order and social continuity. The internalization of social norms in childhood and their maintenance in adult life (by means of a set of mechanisms referred to as pattern maintenance and tension management) play a crucial theoretical role in Parsons' scheme.

The suggestion that self-interest, moral consensus, socialization, or force plays a determinant role in social continuity is valuable only if it is not presented as an either-or choice, as has often been the case. Even if one agrees that these are important elements in social life, their actual significance and the concrete mechanisms through which they operate have not been systematically examined or empirically tested. Among these mechanisms, we propose, are the strategic elites.

If the analysis of the social system generally has been overly abstract, the analysis of elites has suffered from the opposite fault—too much descriptive detail and too little systematic theoretical interpretation. Several vivid portraits exist of such special elite groups as the robber barons, royal dynasties, and leading artists, but there is no comprehensive account of their respective social functions, though it is generally assumed that elites do have such functions and are thereby linked to the more enduring aspects of the social system.[2] Our task, therefore, is to indicate the principal interrelations of the most comprehensive of these analytical models of the social system to the empirical descriptions of various elites.

A functional model of the social system

Since the publication of *The Social System,* Parsons has increasingly refined his formal analysis of the dimensions of the social order and the components of social action. Some aspects of his theoretical scheme are particularly relevant for the formal analysis of elites.

The most general proposition in Parsons' theory is that societies are composed of differentiated yet interdependent units whose efforts and purposes are at least in some measure coordinated. Society is held together, on the one hand, by common values and institutional mechanisms, and on the other, by specialized activities and interests some of which, manifestly or latently, support these values. A society is a *system* of interdependent parts requiring a unified general orientation and direction so that the different parts do not work at cross-purposes. Moral order is the most general source of this unity, the realm of fundamental values, which defines and articulates the boundaries and limits of the society. These boundaries may vary, but today, Parsons would agree, national sovereignty constitutes one such cardinal reference point.

Every society, then, includes as essential elements both a set of common values and a set of differentiated but interrelated institutions and patterns of action. As we have seen, this differentiation increases with a growth in size and occupational specialization. Specialization occurs not at random but with reference to specific functional problems which in all social systems, if they are to remain systems, must be solved.

Parsons names four such functional problems, constituting fundamental exigencies of social systems: *goal attainment, adaptation, integration,* and *pattern maintenance and tension management.*[3] If societies are to achieve such collective goals as the maintenance of public welfare, freedom, progress, and sovereignty, institutional machinery must be developed for their implementation. Along each of Parsons' functional exigencies, more or less distinctive organized institutions and practices develop which in time come to constitute a special subsystem of society with specialized objectives and responsibilities. The goal attainment subsystem serves "to maximize the capacity of the society to attain its collective goals," by deciding when, where, and how available resources are to be utilized. The adaptive subsystem produces generalized facilities or means to attain these goals. The integrative subsystem maintains order and coherence among different parts of the system so that social solidarity is promoted and internal conflict minimized; its primary task is to link differentiated perspectives to the common moral framework. The pattern maintenance and tension management subsystem maximizes the motivational commitments and emotional well-being of individuals so that they may adequately perform and participate in social life. In short, the goal attainment subsystem defines and pursues common social objectives, the adaptive subsystem devises and utilizes the necessary means and facilities, the integrative subsystem promotes social morality, and the pattern maintenance and tension management subsystem safeguards individual and group morale.

According to Parsons, each of these four functional subsystems corresponds to a specialized institutional sector of society. The goal attainment subsystem is primarily concentrated in the polity, the adaptive subsystem in the economy. Each of these, although bound to the over-all moral framework of society, is partly autonomous; and because the same individuals perform different roles in the polity and the economy, some conflict between the two is unavoidable. Yet they share a common perspective in that their activities orient them to the *external* situation facing the society.

The integrative and pattern maintenance subsystems are primarily oriented to the *internal* situation—to states of mind, moral awareness and obligations, crises of conscience, and emotional tensions and strains. Thus one task of the integrative subsystem is to adjust conflicts arising among various subsystems and their competing claims, as, for example, when the polity favors tight money and high interest rates to prevent inflation and the economy favors low interest rates to promote investments. Parsons, in a recent essay, suggests that the legal profession, political parties, and interest groups should be classed with this subsystem.[4]

The pattern maintenance subsystem is principally concerned

with the morale of the units in the system—individuals and groups fulfilling the role obligations on which day-to-day operations of the system depends. Here the family and the school are crucial. They train individuals, with their various biological and emotional characteristics, for the duties they will assume in the economy, the polity, and other social spheres.

Preparing collective resources for successful encounters with the environment is the responsibility of the goal attainment and adaptive subsystems. These have predominant influence in societies committed to technical progress, military conquest, or industrialization. The two subsystems oriented to such internal matters as morality and morale are predominant in societies oriented to a speculative, contemplative, and expressive way of life. The distinction is really a question of emphasis, for all four functional problems are matters of concern in any society. A society is heading for trouble if its leaders are preoccupied *only* with its power position or its Gross National Product, neglecting such problems as friction between institutions, competition between covetous groups and individuals, and personal unhappiness and anxiety among its members. Yet, merely to keep a society harmonious or in high spirits is likewise self-defeating, since essential work would not get accomplished.

In constructing his model of the social system by means of analytical rather than historical building blocks, Parsons has avoided the pitfalls of various determinist explanations of the social order in which certain social factors are overemphasized because they loom large in the mind of the observer. He has attempted first to work out a model on the analytical plane. On this score he has succeeded: his model of the social system has closure, comprehensiveness, and is sufficiently abstract to permit generalization.

Difficulties arise when Parsons seeks to test his theoretical constructs empirically. The social institutions he has selected for this test are only imperfectly suited to their presumed functional responsibilities. The polity is concerned with more than goal attainment, the economy with more than adaptation, the family with more than pattern maintenance and tension management. Each of these institutions is an establishment with a long and complicated history of its own, and each serves several social functions. No precise correspondence exists between analytical system functions of major institutions and their concrete, and, in part, historically determined patterns of action.

This fact is particularly important in periods of rapid social change, when new needs, means, and values develop swiftly. Older, tradition-bound institutions are challenged and displaced by new institutions better able to meet changing situations. The family, once involved with all of the major functional problems of society, today plays a limited though still a significant role in society; its social form has changed from what MacIver calls a community to an association.[5] Today, the family's chief contribution to the functioning of the social system is reproduction and early socialization of children. But even this nuclear function is shared with other agencies, including peer groups and schools. For adults, the modern family is apt to be a repository of intimacy and strong personal sentiments, yet many adults turn to nonrelatives for attention. The psychological importance of the family as a refuge from the hurts of the world may well have increased, but its contribution to the solution of large-scale societal problems has declined. Functions the family once performed largely on its own are today shared with schools (socialization and education), courts (moral teachings and punishment for transgressions of the law), business corporations (production of the means of sustenance), and governmental agencies (welfare, protection, defense).* Parsons assigns to the family the function of "pattern maintenance and tension management"; but even this function is restricted to young children and thus hardly provides the most comprehensive empirical test of Parsons' model.

A second problem which arises in applying Parsons' analytical categories to current institutions stems from the fact that institutions themselves are abstractions. Institutions never act or deliberate or have crises of conscience or hostile impulses. The assignment to them of functional responsibilities therefore leads to reification of the social order.The normative order becomes confounded

* Because of its long and illustrious past and its control over important social machinery—most children are born, learn their first words, and acquire their first age and sex identities within families—the family's actual power over individuals is much more extensive than its functional power in the social system. The family has relinquished its hold on the social structure but not on the individuals whom it helps mold for participation in that structure.

with the factual order. Unwittingly, the implication that the state or the economy or the family ought to do such and such leads to the assertion that they do such and such.[6]

Societies regulate themselves and institutions act only in a metaphorical sense. Even in small and relatively homogeneous societies *men* must assume responsibility for the varied activities and operations of the social system. Why is this necessary? Why, if the functional model of society is accurate, cannot men simply follow its functional imperatives? The answer lies in the characteristics of social norms which, though they are guides to action, must not be confused with the actions themselves. If men were able to act as the rules dictate, they would be living in an "ideal" (or impossibly routinized) society, one in which the rational or logical structure corresponded perfectly with the social structure. In the absence of such a correspondence, some individuals must assume responsibility for translating functional prescriptions into workable rules. The individuals who do this for the social system are, in our view, the strategic elites.[7]

Study of the social origins and roles of these elites will help to avoid both of the problems depicted above. By shifting the level of analysis from norms and institutions to elites, the problem of reification disappears. These elites can never act solely in accordance with the functional requirements of their status. The moral and personal imperfections of men, the temptations of their surroundings, and also the characteristics of the social structure in which men participate prevent them from doing so. It is a sociological truism, applicable to leaders no less than to ordinary men, that individuals assume not one but many social roles. Those who act on behalf of the polity or the economy must balance their roles as leaders of these sectors against other roles as citizens and consumers. They may be oriented consciously and conscientiously to the fulfillment of their functional responsibilities, but they will rarely be oriented solely to them. By focusing, as we intend to do, on certain elites as the locus of functional responsibilities, we bring the model closer to empirical reality. The growth in size and complexity of industrial societies, accompanied by the increasing significance of large-scale organizations, centralized administration, and specialized social leadership, has brought these elites to the fore. Their emergence and proliferation, in fact, testify to the incapacity of older institutional arrangements to cope with the pace of social change.

Strategic elites thus provide an important missing link between society as blueprint and society as reality. The following pages attempt to show that these elites, as they are gradually taking shape in expanding industrial societies, may be roughly aligned with Parsons' major functional problems. This alignment leads to a typology and is in part a heuristic device which, we argue, aids effective analysis. The analysis itself—of the number and specific functions of diverse elite groups—requires rigorous empirical investigation, of which this study is at least a beginning.

Emergent types of elites

The elites associated with social leadership are becoming more numerous and specialized in complex societies—a trend confined not only to elites. Since the organization of the social system and the organization of strategic elites are to some extent interdependent, the proliferation and specialization of these elites may be linked to the structural-functional differentiation of the social system noted by Parsons.[8] The proposed classification is therefore only one possible way of ordering elites according to their major functional roles in society.

The pursuit of national goals or goal attainment is, according to Parsons, concentrated in the political sector of society. In the United States the elite that today appears to represent the public interest rather than more narrow segmental objectives consists of a relatively small group of national officials—the President of the United States, his Cabinet appointees, Senators, and Representatives —who are responsible for safeguarding the national interest and welfare. A dramatic example of the growing powers of this elite to speak for the whole nation was provided by the clash between the U. S. Steel Corporation and the President over a proposed price increase by the steel companies in the spring of 1962. The swiftness of the President's countermoves and the capitulation of the steel executives demonstrated that, for the moment at least, "the United States is bigger than United States Steel,"[9] and that what is good for U. S. Steel is not always good for the country. This marks an important shift in the internal balance of power from a time when the economic elite, in pursuing its own interests, appeared to represent the general interest. Today's economic objectives, important as they are, are only one among several desirable objectives, and the economic elite must compete with other elites for the allocation of national energies and resources. Economic achievements, once the main measure of social progress, must now be balanced against military strength, international prestige, mass education, and scientific breakthroughs. Accordingly, national anxieties and national pride in accomplishment focus on political rather than on economic elites. One of the first actions of Colonel John H. Glenn, Jr. upon his historic orbiting of the globe was to meet with the President and address a joint session of Congress, thereby symbolically linking his achievement to them and through them to the nation as a whole.

The achievement of economic growth, political stability, or scientific advance depends on the discovery and effective utilization of available means and facilities. Parsons refers to the application of these means as adaptation and assigns this function to the economic sector of society. No doubt the modern economies—and the economic elites—do contribute essential services to the realization of these goals, but they are not alone in so doing. At least three additional elites, we propose, are currently also concerned with adaptation: the military elite, consisting of the highest ranking officers, whose principal tasks involve the protection and defense of the society; the diplomatic elite, the ambassadors and ministers who supervise the external public relations of society; and the scientific elite, inventors of new techniques and controls over nature and men. The purpose of the adaptive subsystem, it should be kept in mind, is to discover and utilize generalized means to given ends; the production of wealth is only one of these means. Security, international good will, and new ideas and inventions are others.

Success in national undertaking depends as much on public understanding and support as on sound planning and organization. If men are to make personal sacrifices and to subordinate private interests to the attainment of common objectives, they must be morally aware of and committed to these larger purposes. Internal conflicts, grievances, and doubts must be resolved and clarified. Yet success in resolving such problems often implies social change, and social change, in turn, menaces traditional standards and universal beliefs. Leaders are looked to for moral guidance and reassurance. Such guidance and reassurance in the modern world is provided by the integrative elites—eminent clergymen, philosophers, educators, and "first families"—who endeavor to clarify and coordinate conduct and beliefs in the light of moral and ethical traditions. The expanded role of the military in national life, the social responsibilities of the giant corporations, and the growth of big government—all are a part of the new problems in a rapidly changing society which men face today.

Finally there are the elites—leading artists and writers, popular entertainers, film stars, and outstanding athletes—whose activities relate to less tangible but no less fundamental human needs. They are less well organized than many other elites, but they fulfill an important function for the social system—that of promoting social solidarity and morale (pattern maintenance and tension management in Parsons' terms). By their acts and in their persons, these elites stand for novelty, variety, and play; they provide legitimate fantasy outlets for unrealizable wishes and hopes, for grievances and torments, and for the anxieties and disappointments that life often brings. Their power lies in their ability to hold up to men a mirror of their dreams, of what they might have or still may become, thereby helping to meet their inexpressible or unacknowledged needs and secret desires. Leading actors, artists, composers, film stars, and even playboys on the grand scale, provide vicarious identities for their audiences and publics. Their work on the stage, the canvas, or the printed page portrays the dramas and tensions of real life, their imaginary solutions taking the place of those often unattainable in reality. Societies have always developed such mechanisms which simultaneously provide insight into the human situation and afford release from the pressure of collective forces on individual destinies.

External and internal elites

Parsons, it may be recalled, further classifies the four subsystems into two main types: those concentrating on external and those concentrating on internal system problems. The first, involving goal attainment and adaptation, deals with problems posed by intractable nature, other societies, or an unknown future. The second, involving moral integration and social solidarity, deals with moods, manners, and states of mind. This dichotomy is also useful in describing strategic elites, with the political, economic, military, scientific, and diplomatic elites on one side of the ledger, and the moral, aesthetic, religious, status, and intellectual elites on the other. Despite the increasing structural-functional autonomy of all strategic elites, there does seem to be a greater formal and substantive similarity between elites concerned with external problems and those concerned with internal problems.

During long periods of recorded history, internal problems such as morality and human solidarity received inordinate stress. Mankind did little to extricate itself from its enslavement to hunger, disease, and premature death. Since the industrial revolution, however, external problems have been emphasized, to the neglect of morality and morale. Demoralization, isolation, and estrangement are the bane of modern man. The official or public neglect of these problems is indirectly reflected in the intense private preoccupation with them. The tragedy of human existence, the irony of failure, the search by individuals for a meaningful life—none of these can be assuaged by economic, political, or diplomatic triumphs. In the long run, of course, preoccupation with neither external or internal problems is sound. In the first case, the society may prosper while entire strata are morally abused and personally desperate. In the second, individuals may be adjusted to their misery but do little to eliminate it.

Before considering some important differences between these two classes of elites it is important to note that neither exhaust the activities of the sectors they command. They are essentially the axes of these sectors, ultimately responsible for the successes and failures associated with them. But each sector includes an enormous variety of individuals and groups. Every instance of advice, encouragement, or sympathy, no matter when or where it is expressed, contributes to morale (pattern maintenance). Every ingenious or spontaneous solution to a crisis contributes to adaptation. Every discussion involving moral choices, proper conduct, injustice, and human cruelty contributes to integration. And every instance of pleasure and happiness—fleeting as it may be—contributes to goal attainment. The strategic elites are distinguished by the fact that their roles put them in charge of and make them responsible for long-range decisions and moral choices. Their range is thus broader and more inclusive than that of other participants. They are strategic precisely because they are the foci for the realization of collective aims. Their actions, words, gestures, impressions, and prejudices carry more weight than those of other men because they personify the aims, aspirations, and attitudes of multitudes. They come to stand for their sectors and all of their manifold ramifications. They are social models symbolizing the prizes of social life.

Modes of organization

Elites oriented to internal and those oriented to external problems differ in their modes of organization; not all are organized to the same extent. The American business elite consists of individuals holding leading positions in the largest corporations; the artistic elite, of persons enjoying a certain reputation among specific sectors of the public. The size of the business elite, in contrast to that of the artistic elite, is more or less predetermined by the number of positions available and is thus bound to an institutional framework. This has not always been the case, however. In ancient Egypt where sculptors and architects were technical experts, the artistic elite was more formally organized, resembling modern business elites. In ancient Rome the business elite exhibited many of the characteristics—spontaneity, individualism, and diffuseness—that we associate with the artistic elites of today.

One reason for this difference stems from the means used by elites to achieve their ends. Highly organized strategic elites depend for their success on the coordinated efforts of a variety of individuals and groups. The executives of Standard Oil could not carry out their functions without the cooperation of thousands of workers, specialized by skill and rank. Writers, painters, intellectuals, or actors, however, need only to organize themselves and apportion their time and efforts to produce books, plays, paintings, and performances. They need others to appreciate the results of their efforts—and to support them—but not to collaborate in realizing them.

In view of the tendency toward greater formal organization in many spheres, today's diffuse elites may be more organized tomorrow. This will depend in part on the supply of potential candidates available and on the demand for their products. In ancient Egypt, the demand for sculptors, architects, and painters during certain periods exceeded the supply and they were subject to compulsory recruitment. Similarly, science was once the province of the lone individual working for his own satisfaction. Today the great demand for scientific talent leads to formalized recruitment procedures.

The degree of formal organization of strategic elites, however, must not be confused with their specialization, another matter altogether. Strategic elites are formally organized when their spheres of activity have been systematically coordinated and structured, that is, bureaucratized. But regardless of the degree of bureaucratization, they are specialized in the sense that their activities do not, in principle, overlap. Strategic elites are more specialized today than ever before and more of them are also bureaucratically organized, but not all specialized elites are bureaucratized. Specialization is related to the division of labor; bureaucratization is related to the size, scope, and purpose of an undertaking. If an increase in the division of labor in society is accompanied by an increase in the available labor supply, bureaucratization then seems inevitable. In this connection it is interesting to note that of the two eminent social theorists, Durkheim and Weber, one chose the division of labor, the other, bureaucratization, as the leading social trend in advanced industrial societies.

The greater formal organization of the elites oriented to external problems suggests, as a further hypothesis, that these elites will in general be more despotic than the diffuse and less organized internal elites. This stems from their aforementioned dependence on the wills, motivations, and cooperation of many others, and it may explain why politicians or priests*—historically the elites of goal

* An elite that has belonged variously to the internal and the external strategic elites is that of the priesthood. When priests were *the* elite of goal attainment, they were both highly organized and despotic—whether one looks to ancient Mesopotamia or to eleventh-century Italy. But when, as now, they are chiefly associated with moral integration, they are neither as highly organized nor as despotic. The thousands of churches and the many faiths coexisting side by side was as unthinkable in the Middle Ages as diverse political systems coexisting in the same state would be today. Elites, in short, can and do shift their functional roles from one aspect of the system to another. The artistic elites were not always a part of the strategic elites,

attainment—have often been despotic. This hypothesis may also explain why those who organize the process of industrialization—the upper bourgeoisie of the nineteenth century, the Soviet leaders, or the emergent elites of Africa and Asia—frequently resort to despotic practices. Their despotism may stem from the fact that while their success is dependent on the efforts of many others in addition to themselves, the responsibility for failure rests solely on their shoulders.[10]

Instrumental and expressive aspects of elite roles

Strategic elites also differ in their public images and styles, which may be traced back, in part, to their classification along the external-internal axis. The elites primarily involved with goal attainment and adaptation tend to be judged on the basis of efficiency standards—how effectively and swiftly they get things done. The elites identified with moral integration and social solidarity tend to be judged according to their symbolic roles—what kind of impression they make on the public. All elites, of course, must try to satisfy both instrumental and symbolic demands. Generals may look the part splendidly, but are dismissed if they lose many battles; as, too, with corporation executives—their gray flannel suits and jutting jaws count for nothing if their firms consistently show little profit.[11] Artists, moral leaders, and members of high society, win half their battle by merely making the right impression. A mediocre actor often obtains a "heavy" role simply because he "looks like" a villain, just as appearing to be morally impeccable is often sufficient for those who would exert moral influence.

All strategic elites should thus create appropriate corporate images but such images are not equally crucial for all.

Strategic elites are both agents and symbols, and their public actions involve both instrumental and expressive features. In industrial societies, the elites primarily concerned with adaptive and goal attainment problems tend to be judged by what they *accom-*

---

certainly not when they were artisans for hire, as in some of the ancient civilizations. And it is not impossible that one day they may contribute to the formulation of national goals and policies in the light of aesthetic standards—and thus become involved with goal attainment. "Esthetics," wrote Maxim Gorky, "will be the ethics of the future."

plish, while those primarily concerned with integration and social solidarity tend to be judged by what they *represent.* The first type of elite is constrained to produce such tangible results as stability, victory, or a higher standard of living; the role requirements of the second type are directed toward intangibles—moods and states of mind, pleasure, the fear of death, and the will to live.[12] The differences in their functional responsibilities as well as their classification along the instrumental-expressive axis account in large part for different patterns of recruitment—a matter to be developed in a later chapter.*

Two main patterns of organization of social leadership may be historically identified: reliance on a single agent to assume responsibility for all four social system functions; and reliance on several agents, each of which specializes in one or more system functions. An example of the first is the chief in a small and comparatively homogeneous society who is at once high priest, king, leading warrior, and healer or saviour. When the society grows and specialization develops, the role of the chief is likely to be replaced by several specialized roles. The priest-healer, a role combining integration and pattern maintenance, is familiar in history rivaled only by the role of the king-warrior, a fusion of goal attainment and adaptation. With further growth in size, social leadership devolves upon an entire stratum such as a hereditary aristocracy, whose structural simplicity belies its functional complexity. As politicians and legislators, its members are identified with goal attainment; as landowners, soldiers, and scholars, with adaptation; and as noblemen and conspicuous consumers, with integration and pattern maintenance.

Each method has its advantages. The first clearly gains in unity what it may lose in efficiency, for a single agent is apt to be more unified in his acts than a group and far more unified than a number of groups cooperating with one another. But human limitations

* One problem requiring further attention and research is the extent to which each subsystem of society is in turn a complete social system unto itself. The economic elite, for example, performs the adaptive function for the society at large, but within the economy, this elite is identified with goal definition and goal attainment. Members of this elite, in short, wear two hats simultaneously, a possible source of confusion for them as well as for the public. In their larger social system roles, they are but one among several elites, whereas as leaders of the economic sector they are supreme within that sector.

being what they are, it is unusual, if not impossible, for a single agent to be equal to the demands of all four functional spheres.

The second method gains in efficiency what it loses in potential unity and cohesion. If a different group is assigned to a different functional sphere, each may become highly expert in its sphere, but the danger of rivalries, antagonisms, and misunderstandings among competing groups multiplies. One need only note the wars between monarchs and nobility, between popes and emperors, and the more recent conflict between scientists and priests. Rivalries among elites for supremacy may thus be expected to increase in highly differentiated societies with their differentiated elites. These elites, moreover, are both "individually necessary and jointly sufficient for survival." [13] They will become increasingly divergent in their patterns of recruitment, manner of reward, and public style. Signs of this development are evident not only in the United States but also, as we shall see in the next chapter, in Germany, Great Britain, and in the developing countries of Africa and Asia.

Notes

1. Talcott Parsons, *The Social System* (1952), esp. Chap. v; "A Sociological Approach to the Theory of Organizations," in Talcott Parsons, *Structure and Process in Modern Societies* (1960), pp. 16-58. Parsons generally continues to discuss social systems in terms of impersonal social mechanisms, such as socialization, institutional insulation, and role segmentation. Increasingly, however, he is coming to stress power, leadership, and ruling groups—although here he largely confines himself to the political sector. "The most general features of the institutionalization of power or political function in social systems," he writes, "is differential responsibility or leadership." See "Authority, Legitimation, and Political Action," in Talcott Parsons, *Structure and Process in Modern Societies, op. cit.,* p. 183. The economy, however, continues to be discussed very much as a mechanical system with its regulatory devices and processes such as "contract," input-output, and facilities and rewards. See, Talcott Parsons and Neil J. Smelser, *Economy and Society* (1956), *passim.*

2. One of the best attempts, by Sorokin, to systematize the study of elites foundered because Sorokin failed to link his various elite groups to the ongoing processes of the social system and thus left their influence sociologically unaccounted for. Sorokin, like Pareto before him, defined the elite as those individuals occupying high rank in "influential social groups—the state, church, class, language, and . . . other groups surveyed, including the professional groups. . . ." Sorokin, however, defines these elites as influential without locating the sociological sources of their influence. Why, for example, did he single out the state and the church but not the sphere of recreation? Pitirim A. Sorokin, *Society, Culture and Personality* (1947), p. 234.
3. The most explicit discussion of functional problems of social systems occurs in the following: Talcott Parsons, Robert F. Bales, and Edward A. Shils, *Working Papers in the Theory of Action* (1953), Chap. v, esp. pp. 172-90, 254-69; Talcott Parsons and Neil J. Smelser, *Economy and Society* (1956), Chap. ii, esp. pp. 46-85; Talcott Parsons, *Structure and Process in Modern Societies* (1960), esp. the following essays: "A Sociological Approach to the Theory of Organizations," esp. pp. 44-7; "Some Principal Characteristics of Industrial Societies," pp. 132-68; and "Authority, Legitimation, and Political Action," pp. 170-99. See also Talcott Parsons, "An Approach to Psychological Theory in Terms of the Theory of Action," in Sigmund Koch (ed.), *Psychology: A Study of a Science,* III (1959), 612-711.
4. Talcott Parsons, "A Sociological Approach to the Theory of Organizations," *Structure and Process in Modern Societies, op. cit.,* p. 46.
5. "There was a time," MacIver writes, "when the family seemed to comprehend the whole of life, but if so, it was not the family as we know it, but rather a family community which on the ostensible basis of kinship included a whole group of social interests." Robert M. MacIver, *The Modern State* (1926), p. 7. See also MacIver's more comprehensive discussion of the family in Robert M. MacIver, *Society* (1937), Chap. xi, pp. 196-236.
6. This is germane to Gouldner's observation: "In Parsons' terms organizations are social systems which are primarily oriented to the attainment of a specific goal. But an organization as such cannot be said to be oriented toward a goal, except in a merely metaphorical sense, unless it is assumed that its parts possess a much lower degree of functional autonomy than can in fact be observed. The statement that an organization is oriented toward certain goals often means no more than that these are the goals of its top administrators, or that they represent its social function, which is another matter altogether." Alvin W. Gouldner, "Organizational Analysis," in Robert K. Merton, Leonard Broom, and Leonard S. Cottrell, Jr. (eds.), *Sociology Today* (1959), p. 420.
7. For an application of Parsons' categories to a special type of human community, see Amitai Etzioni, "Functional Differentiation of Elites in the Kibbutz," *American Journal of Sociology* (March 1959), pp. 476-87.
8. An important question about any society, according to Parsons, is the extent of its structural differentiation or fusion "with respect to the four functional problems." "Our own society," he goes on to say, "is remarkable for the degree to which functional subsystems are structurally differentiated from each other." Talcott Parsons, "An Approach to

Psychological Theory in Terms of the Theory of Action," in Sigmund Koch (ed.), *Psychology: A Study of a Science, op. cit.*, pp. 612-711.

9. James Reston, "Kennedy Can Beat 'Em but Can He Convince 'Em?," *The New York Times,* April 15, 1962.
10. Drucker's observations are pertinent here: "We speak of 'organization' —the formal structure of the enterprise. But what we mean is the organization of managers and of their functions; neither brick and mortar nor rank-and-file workers have any place in the organization structure. We speak of 'leadership' and of the 'spirit' of a company. But leadership is given by managers and effective primarily within management; and the spirit is made by the spirit within the management group. We talk of 'objectives' for the company, and of its performance. But the objectives are goals for management people; the performance is management performance. And if an enterprise fails to perform, we rightly hire not different workers but a new president." Peter F. Drucker, "The Tasks of Management," in W. Lloyd Warner and Norman H. Martin (eds.), *Industrial Man* (1959), p. 196.
11. The distinction between instrumental and expressive aspects of elite roles is reminiscent of Max Weber's discussion of the differences between patrimonial rule with institutionalized charisma, and feudalism with personal charisma. Loyalty to office, specialized training, and elaborate formal organization are characteristic of patrimonial rule, whereas spontaneity, individualism, and admiration for natural gifts are characteristic of the feudal code. See Reinhard Bendix, *Max Weber, An Intellectual Portrait* (1960), pp. 360-8.
12. Robert Bierstedt's distinction between leaders and authorities, and authorities and experts, is applicable here. The formally organized elites consist largely of "authorities" and of "experts," whereas informally organized cultural and intellectual elites consist of "leaders." Authorities command, experts impress, but leaders influence, convince, and persuade. The basis of authority is formal office-holding, that of expertise, special skills, and that of leadership, force of personality. See Robert Bierstedt, "The Problem of Authority," in Morroe Berger, Theodore Abel, and Charles H. Page (eds.), *Freedom and Control in Modern Society* (1954), pp. 67-82.
13. For a discussion of this point, see Carl Hempel, "The Logic of Functional Analysis," in Llewellyn Gross (ed.), *Symposium on Sociological Theory* (1959), pp. 293-4.

5. THE EMERGENCE OF STRATEGIC ELITES: SELECTED CASES

▲

The long standing interest in the role of elites in society has so far not been matched by systematic as well as comprehensive inquiries into their nature and purposes. Most existing portraits are rather one-sided in their focus on the social origins and careers of elite members. In part this reflects the frequent, and inhibiting, identification of elites with the Marxist conception of a ruling class and the questionable assumption that a man's social background fully accounts for his manner of exercising power; it reflects also the absence of a theoretical framework for a synthesis of isolated empirical generalizations. The attitudes and ideologies of elites, their social, political, and personal relations are surely as significant as the social backgrounds that helped shape them, but they are more difficult to investigate and to interpret.

The few existing studies, however, may be used to support some of the main points made so far. Several recent inquiries, for example, provide valuable documentation of the specialized patterns of recruitment, training, and careers of national elites in the United States.[1] Others analyze the role of elites at the local community level in order to discover how monolithic or diversified their power structures are. Still others deal with the broad question of the characteristics of totalitarian rule and the growth of bureaucratic states, and, more recently, with the emerging elites in the developing nations of Africa and Asia. All of these provide some relevant material about elites, although they differ widely in definition of terms and concepts.

As the following brief overview suggests, the concept of an all-encompassing ruling class continues to exercise a firm hold on the thinking of various writers and leads to an underestimation, or a distortion, of the influence of specialized strategic elites in the modern world.

Elites in industrialized societies

THE UNITED STATES

The growing number of empirical studies of selected national elites has recently been supplemented by two attempts at a broader synthesis of the facts regarding their social make-up, their scope, and their methods of exercising leadership. The more comprehensive of the two, the late C. Wright Mills' *The Power Elite* (1956), represents a serious effort to interpret the emergence of diversified elites historically and sociologically.

In Mills' view, the members of three types of elites—business, political, and military—make most, if not all, the crucial decisions for the nation. He therefore concentrates on these elites, devoting considerable space to other elite groups such as the "very rich," the "celebrities," and "local society." But while Mills is keenly alert to a shift in the balance of political and economic power from the local to the national scene, he does not always clearly distinguish his three major types from the rest. Nor does he succeed in differentiating the concept of elites from that of social class. As Parsons has observed, Mills seems to identify the power elite (consisting of his three major types) with the upper class[2] which naturally leads him to overemphasize the importance of those social background factors which the two have in common and to minimize or ignore their differences.

Mills is engaged, throughout his book, in documenting two somewhat incompatible sets of facts: a strong, and in his view, indispensable link between the power elite and the upper class; and the absence of such a link, due to a growing functional specialization of the elites and hence their growing autonomy. At times, Mills considers the three elites as socially uniform and unified in purpose; at times, competitive and rivalrous.

Two main theoretical currents inform Mills' work. One stems from Marxist thought and appears in Mills' discussion of the three elites as essentially variants of the older type ruling class. The other derives from Max Weber's emphasis on the growing importance of public and private bureaucracies. The first leads Mills to stress the growing identity of interests and the greater interchange of personnel among the three elites; the second, their growing separation.

A definite inconsistency exists in *The Power Elite* between elaborate empirical documentation and sweeping generalizations without adequate supportive evidence. Nor is the empirical evidence itself always thoroughly examined. Indeed, Mills' own data do not firmly support his conclusions concerning the increasing social uniformity and ascending power of the leading elites in American society. The biographical information on which he relies reveals some striking dissimilarities in the backgrounds, education, and careers of the members.[3] He found considerable variation, for example, in regard to the occupational origins of the members of the three elites. Seventy per cent of the very rich and 57 per cent of the chief executives had fathers who were businessmen, but this was true of only 25 per cent of the political elite and of 21 per cent of the warlords. Similarly, as regards religious affiliation: three fourths of the very rich and two thirds of the political elite, but less than one half of the chief executives, adhered to the Episcopalian and Presbyterian faiths. As for the warlords, Mills simply states that they were "overwhelmingly Protestant." In effect, he provides considerable evidence supporting the thesis advanced in this book regarding the proliferation and diversification of the national strategic elites.

Floyd Hunter's *Top Leadership, U.S.A.* (1959) is far less sophisticated theoretically than Mills' book, but equally ambitious in its aim to delineate the top leadership group shaping national policy and to depict patterns of power in American society.[4] Using the reputational method, according to which selected informants nominate the individuals they consider to be most influential in local, state, and national affairs, Hunter compiled a list of several hundred top leaders across the nation. Using questionnaires, interviews, and informal polls, Hunter than attempted to ascertain the interconnections among these influential men and their individual as well as joint impact on the "development of public policy." [5]

One conceptual problem in Hunter's work concerns the categorization of national policy in rather gross, general terms, reflecting his pyramidal conception of power. Today, however, there is no single over-all public policy, but a series of distinct and separate policies reflecting distinct and separate political, economic, scientific, military and other objectives. Despite his unidimensional perspective, Hunter fails to find a single, comprehensive policy-making group in the nation. Without having anticipated the existence of a specialized national leadership, he is forced, at the end, to acknowledge its crucial importance:

> During my trips across country, I had reached a tentative conclusion that it would be difficult, if not impossible, to find any one issue or public policy in which a majority of the top leaders I had been interviewing would be interested. It was plain that interests of these men ran along business lines (their own), along regional lines . . . or in some cases interest lines crossed, as in free trade vs. tariffs. Speaking of the relatedness of national leaders, Clint Murchison of Texas said, "I think you are going to find that bankers know bankers, scholars know scholars, utility men know utility men, and politicians know everybody." I found this to be true, of course, but I also found more.[6]

Hunter's tendency to view national patterns of power and influence as reflections of patterns characterizing local communities leads him to underestimate the profound dissimilarities between the two. Citing one authority, he remarks that college professors, churchmen, and writers are not "making policy in this country today." [7] This is of course true—if one defines policy in political or economic terms. But if we locate the activities engaged in by college professors, or writers, in their functional contexts and relate these to the workings of the social system as a whole, then they do affect national policy. Education and the arts, as we mentioned earlier, do have strategic significance.

In a final effort to locate *the* group of top policy makers in the nation, Hunter selects a nucleus of one hundred powerful individuals who most consistently and frequently are considered to be nationally influential. These men, he insists, are not to be thought of as a clique running the country but as a "kind of reservoir of leadership on tap from which men are chosen to perform the important tasks of policy-making and/or to give status to any major policy proposal." [8] They are not formally organized or openly coercive but an informal group "representing many of the major influence groups." These leaders know each other personally, they know and are known by politicians, they belong to common clubs and associations. "They included the politicians, the men of wealth, and the military elite of whom Professor Mills speaks." [9] At the same time, however, they are unknown to many, perhaps even the majority, of local leaders working through traditional political or associational channels in their contacts outside the boundaries of their relatively isolated communities.

This again suggests that there is a cleavage between local and national channels of power, and that it is not advisable to study national patterns of power by means of the reputational method —better suited, it would seem, to local communities. National networks must be studied nationally. Hunter's findings that the most powerful men in America exercise both national and local influence may thus be an artifact of the method he used to compile his list of well-known leaders. His one hundred top leaders were, after all, nominated by local leaders residing in cities and towns across the nation. In order to nominate them, these individuals had to know them by name, which, in the absence of their own participation in national affairs, necessarily implied local contacts and activities among the top leadership. Many national leaders, however, have no such community links and are unknown to the community leaders trying to assess their influence.

Toward the end of his book, Hunter in effect acknowledges the fact that today the local community does not exercise national power. He then selects the agencies he does consider to exercise such power—"formal government and the economic corporation." [10] He thus has come around full circle: first seeking the locus of power in one hundred individuals with wide, informal social and interpersonal influence; and then, in two giant, impersonal, and highly organized national sectors. He fails to specify, however, which individuals in these large-scale organizations exercise the type of national influence he originally sought to discover.

The problem of describing and assessing leadership at the national level in the absence of an adequate and up-to-date model marks the work of both Mills and Hunter. Both tend to look for and thus to perceive a questionable unity and uniformity among men of power, and to force new empirical facts into an older theoretical frame. This is also true of most investigations—only a few of which will be discussed here—into leadership in cities and small towns.

E. Digby Baltzell's portrayal of the historical development of proper Philadelphians up to 1940 is one of the most interesting studies of recent years.[11] This is not a study of a strategic group, but an investigation of a social elite in a large city (as distinct from the small community). But while *Philadelphia Gentlemen* is an informative work and superior in scope to most elite studies, the previously mentioned analytical problems are apparent.

Baltzell's book is subtitled "Toward the Making of a National Upper Class." It, is however, a study of two segments of a metropolitan upper class—the Social Registerites and the *Who's Who* of Philadelphia. Comparing the socially most prominent and the wealthiest Philadelphians with the most successful Philadelphian professional men, Baltzell seeks an interconnection between the upper class (those in the Social Register) and the elite (those in *Who's Who*). In his view such a link is not only desirable but necessary because "leadership and the exercise and retention of power within a small and hereditary group of families is the ultimate end and justification for an upper class way of life." [12] This assumption may be valid, but Baltzell merely states it. In an economically stratified society there is always an upper class, to be sure, but whether or not this class is also active in other spheres and needs to justify its existence depends on historical circumstance—for example, the presence of rival groups or the energy of its members. Baltzell implies that an upper class is or ought to be a ruling class—by monopolizing political offices. Yet Philadelphia, in his own words, "provides an excellent example of a business aristocracy which has too often placed the desire for material comfort and security above the duties of political and intellectual leadership." [13] Baltzell takes these duties to be self-evident. But in a world in which one's occupation is apt to be a full-time job, business leaders rarely assume important duties in more than one sphere of public life. To influence political decision-making is one thing; to assume political leadership is something else. Nowhere in Western society has a business elite provided much intellectual leadership—not in ancient Rome, not in Renaissance Florence, not in eighteenth-century Britain, and not in twentieth-century America. Individual business leaders have encouraged such activities, but their role has generally been that of patron rather than creator.

Baltzell's use of the term *elite* is somewhat confusing, being so broad as to include all who have achieved distinction in some sphere—Senators, judges, professional boxers, movie queens, and artists. He does try, however, to develop a systematic scheme for elite analysis. An elite, he says, may be divided into three groups: those who occupy line or executive positions and who perform a goal integrating function by deciding upon the *ends* for which a given society will strive; those who provide the knowledge or *means* through which these ends are attained—technically equipped staff or professional people; and those who perform intellectual functions. An elite is composed, in short, of "organizers, technicians, and intellectuals." [14] This is a suggestive typology, reminiscent of Saint-Simon, but it is not fully developed. Why these elites rather than other types? Are all organizers, technicians, and intellectuals members of their respective elites or only some of them? If the latter, what is the principle of inclusion and exclusion? The problem is illustrated in Baltzell's application of this scheme to the Philadelphia scene of 1940 in which six elites and their functions are presented:

Elite	*Function*
1. Business elite	goal integrating function
2. Opinion and political elite	potential goal integrating function
3. Physicians and architects	technical function
4. Church and education	intellectual function
5. Artists and authors	unclassified function
6. Miscellaneous occupations	?

Not only do the elite categories seem to be somewhat vague—opinion and political elites are classified together; institutions (church) are classified with groups (physicians and architects); and one category has the puzzling heading, "miscellaneous occupations."

—but the corresponding "functions" themselves are not altogether convincing.

Part of the difficulty stems from Baltzell's effort to develop a general theory of elites from the study of a single city. Thus he presents the business elite as the elite of goal integration, whereas at the national level the business elite contributes to adaptation. Physicians and architects are important professionals, to be sure, but are not key decision makers for either the local community or the larger society. The military elite, increasingly influential at the national level, is nonexistent at the local level. Finally, artists and authors are classified as part of the elite, but Baltzell indicates no clear-cut function for them.

Baltzell's analysis presents a dilemma. His main effort seems to be devoted to demonstrating that the upper class, in failing to participate and succeed in political and cultural endeavors, is not living up to its historical role. But if his data are viewed from another perspective, it seems clear that Philadelphia is in a period of transition in which the traditional upper class has no choice but to share its leading position with other groups. This reflects, in a metropolitan setting, the changes toward specialization and expansion. Philadelphia appears to be shifting from upper class leadership to leadership by several functionally specialized elites. Baltzell's evidence suggests that the upper class is losing ground to achievement-oriented elites from a variety of ethnic and social strata. He finds that the younger members of the elite (the members listed in *Who's Who*) are less upper class than the older members; that politics and business have become functionally differentiated and the same group no longer participates in both sectors; that the family has lost ground to the school and the club as major socializing agents. This might have been predicted from a knowledge of certain major trends in advanced industrial societies. Philadelphia, as other cities as well as smaller communities, is caught in the pull of somewhat opposed social forces—a class hierarchy with an ascribed upper class at its head and a functional hierarchy capped by several emergent, specialized elites.

Similar trends may be at work in smaller communities, although at first glance the findings from the growing number of relevant studies reveal considerable inconsistency in patterns and practices. Such inconsistency may reflect the different assumptions underlying the research designs of different investigators. One such design, used by Floyd Hunter among others, relies on the aforementioned reputational method of ascertaining influential community leaders.[15] Several authoritative sources are asked for lists of leaders, whose names are then ranked by a panel of judges to arrive at a group of top leaders in the community. Another design utilizes a positional schema. The investigator outlines various relevant aspects of community power, locates the positions through which this power is expressed, and finally ascertains whether the individuals in the top positions in one sphere are the same as those occupying top positions in another. The two research designs have so far yielded quite disparate findings. Hunter and others have located a small, powerful group of economic leaders, often operating behind the scenes and away from the public eye, whose actions are decisive in shaping community policy.[16] Polsby and others have found not one but three elites—economic, political, and "society"—which are composed of different individuals and employ different patterns of recruitment.[17]

No consensus exists concerning the nature of local community leadership, but it is not clear whether this is due to differing strategies of research or differing theoretical assumptions.[18] Some investigators maintain, with supporting evidence, that business dominates the local scene; others claim, with evidence, that several elites share local power. Both conclusions may be empirically correct, the inconsistency reflecting only a genuine difference in the power structures of the communities studied.[19] If this is the case, variations in patterns of local power may reflect the fact that many key social decisions are no longer made primarily by the residents themselves. At the national level, inconsistent findings of this kind would have to be reconciled; at the local level they may indicate not inconsistency, but historical and social diversity.

Studies of community power structure, important and interesting in their own right, cannot replace systematic analysis of elites at the national level. Local communities as well as metropolitan areas are no longer autonomous enough to make key decisions without reference to the federal government, business corporations, and other national institutions.

The specialization and differentiation of strategic elites is not an American phenomenon but characterizes other modern societies as well. Nor is it a reflection of particular political arrangements, for it can be documented for societies with highly monolithic as well as with pluralistic political systems.

THE CASE OF NAZI GERMANY

The Germany of the 1930's and 40's faced problems of central social coordination similar to those of other advanced industrial societies. Franz Neumann, in his important study of Nazi Germany, stressed that the problem of determining the role of social classes, the relationship between rulers and ruled, and the cult of leadership "is perhaps the most difficult of all in an analysis of National Socialism." [20] Some of the difficulty may be attributed to Neumann's approach, for he was committed to a theory of *the* ruling class. Yet he writes:

> The essence of National Socialist social policy consists in the acceptance and strengthening of the prevailing class character of German society, *in the attempted consolidation of its ruling class,* . . . in the creation of a system of autocratic bureaucracies interfering in all human relations. *The process of atomization extends even to the ruling class in part.* It goes hand in hand with a process of differentiation within the mass party and within society that creates reliable elites in every sector.[21]

Both a ruling class and "reliable elites," he tells us, existed in Nazi Germany, the elites being ultimately controlled by the regime; but he does not indicate whether the regime consists of the ruling class or of a powerful elite. In his description of specific dimensions of the social system, Neumann challenges his own formulation of the existence of a ruling class. The ministerial bureaucracy, which grew extensively under National Socialism, he found to be a "closed caste," as eager to run a state efficiently as are businessmen bent upon business success. This bureaucracy was "the most important single agency in the formulation of policy, especially in the economic, financial, social, and agricultural fields." Its powers were wider than ever before, but they were not unlimited, "for it must compete with other bureaucracies of the party, the armed forces, and of industry." [22]

The party hierarchy itself, consisting especially of Hitler and his entourage, was not the all-powerful agency it was sometimes supposed. The relationship between party leaders and the ministerial elite was complex, but at the top each elite was relatively independent.[23] Finally, the "German army leadership, like the ministerial bureaucracy, is probably not National Socialist, strictly speaking. No one really knows anything about the exact relation between the party and the armed forces." [24] Later in the war, part of the army leadership turned out to be the most powerful German antagonists of Hitler and his staff.[25] The army, of course, did not rule Germany, but Neumann notes that it was "the sole body in present-day Germany that has known how to keep itself organizationally free from party interference." Its economic generals, in fact, encroached "on the party and the civil bureaucracies." [26] The army shared with the party and the industrial leaders the immediate short-range aims of preventing a German military defeat, but Neumann felt that such a consensus could not be maintained for long under peace-time conditions, since the army was out to preserve its own political and social status. Neumann concludes that "the ruling class in National Socialist Germany is far from homogeneous. There are as many interests as there are groups. Nothing holds them together but the reign of terror and their fear lest the collapse of the regime destroy them all." [27]

Neumann's study incorporates, implicitly, the rudiments of a theory of elites. He suggests that the Nazi system could conceivably develop a new type of ruling class resembling the supervisory board of the Continental Oil Corporation (a holding company for foreign oil holdings), consisting of party leaders, the army, the ministerial bureaucracy, and industry.[28] Neumann clearly recognized the signs of a new system of leadership and coordination. But he lacked a developed theory of strategic elites with which to catch his observations.

The case of Nazi Germany is particularly instructive for the problem under discussion, for it shows that strategic elites may develop within a totalitarian as well as within a democratic political framework. This development, a response to the growth in size, specialization, and large-scale organization, may be thwarted but not extinguished by a political dictatorship.

A more recent study of the role played by elites in the formulation of German foreign policy sheds considerable light on the social composition, patterns of recruitment, and political attitudes of some of the elites discussed by Neumann twenty years earlier.[29] Deploring the absence of systematic information about "income, social origin, and education" for the various elite groups in Germany, Karl Deutsch and Lewis J. Edinger have adduced a range of biographical facts unparalleled in similar investigations.[30] They note the "predominantly middle class" character of most of the elites studied, but one suspects that this may be an artifact of their inclusive definition[31] of middle class as consisting of such diverse occupational categories as "farmers, white collar employees, public officials, self-employed, in 'trade and commerce,' and 'free professions'." [32] Detailed examination of their data reveals a high degree of social differentiation among these elites with regard to geographic origins, military experience, age, religious affiliation, educational attainments, and careers. Especially noteworthy are "the difference in background between the current military and political elites," [33] the political indifference of the business elite, the striking social dissimilarities between Protestant and Roman Catholic church leaders, the youthfulness of the communications elite, and the relatively high accessibility of the political elite to men of working class background.[34] The trends noted by Neumann a generation ago appear to be quite characteristic among a number of strategic elites in present-day Germany.

THE SOVIET UNION

Many of the trends found in Western industrial societies also appear in the Soviet Union, although little precise information has been gathered from the perspective guiding the present inquiry. Writings on the Soviet elite have focused largely on the top party officials, the political elite. Most commentators, however, have included other elite groups in their descriptions. In addition to the traditional triumvirate—the leaders of the Communist party, the armed forces, and the secret police—the heads of various ministries and high-ranking intellectuals, artists, and writers are increasingly considered as potentially semi-autonomous forces cross-checking and competing with one another within the general framework of Soviet Communism. "Developments since Stalin's death," states a recent summary account, "suggest a trend toward greater independence of the various bureaucracies." [35] The possibility of such a trend was suggested by the composition of the Central Committee of the Party in 1952. Membership included party functionaries, government bureaucrats, high-ranking military men, scientists, and artists.

> While 46 members were full-time Party functionaries, there were also 37 government bureaucrats (excluding members of the Presidium who were ministers), 24 military men (not counting political commissars and military politicians like Voroshilov and Bulganin), and a sprinkling of scientists, artists, and the like. In other words, both symbolically and functionally, the Central Committee united, at virtually the top of the pyramid, the various groups that make up Soviet society.[36]

Officially, the Communist Party is the all-powerful judge of actions and decisions in almost all spheres of life in the U.S.S.R., but the viability of Soviet society requires specialized experts much as any advanced industrial society does. Industrial chieftains—administrative heads of "vast complexes of industry and agriculture, larger than the gigantic concerns of the West" [37]—are one such formidable group. A clash between these leaders and the heads of the Party has been said to underlie the Malenkov-Khrushchev struggle following the period of collective leadership after the death of Stalin.

But while the growing role of multi-interest groups is recognized and has been reported fairly extensively,[38] the trend persists of interpreting the Soviet system in traditional—and misleading—class terms. Edward Crankshaw, whose portrait of the Soviet Union in the post-Stalin era is otherwise first-rate, tends to confuse classes with elites. Crankshaw points out that virtually all factory directors, and most army officers, university professors, departmental managers in the ministries, collective farm managers, writers, and engineers—the elite as he calls them—are members of the Party. But he distinguishes between the political elite and these other groups in class terms: "The full-time Party functionaries . . . thus form the governing class; the rest form what is in effect the new Soviet bourgeoisie." [39] Such concepts were applicable to another and earlier type of social system, but not to a mid-twentieth century industrial society.

The recent Khrushchev reforms and programs clearly underline the rise and the appreciation of the expert in Soviet life. Kirichenko stressed this point at the Twenty-First Party Congress:

> Now life demands that there should be more specialists and experts in different branches of the economy among the leading Party, Soviet, business, and trade cadres.
>
> It is desirable, for example, that a rural district should be managed by individuals with agricultural training, or who are good and experienced practical men of affairs, experts in their jobs, and with organizing talents. Again, it is important that the secretary of the Party committee of a town largely concerned with machine building should himself be a specialist in that branch of industry or an experienced practical engineer who knows his job backwards. Again, it is necessary for a scientific establishment to be directed by a man in full command of the branch of science in question, and so on.[40]

These developments suggest that Party membership, still a badge of power, may gradually become more of a ceremonial certification of already powerful men who have risen to their eminent positions because of expert skills and experience.

It may be argued that efficiency and productivity in Soviet Russia today require functional differentiation and that therefore strategic elites, in the absence of a Stalin-like despotism, have proliferated. The Party can no longer control single-handedly the huge and complex U.S.S.R. any more than big business can run the United States. This is not to argue that business interests and ideology have ceased to be a powerful and dynamic force in America. In Soviet Russia, needless to say, the Communist Party plays a far greater role. In its name, both deeds and misdeeds continue to be justified, organized, and publicized. Centralized monolithic control, however, at least in the long run, is inconsistent with a social order in which specialization and expertise are in ever greater demand.

This demand, a conspicuous and inevitable feature of industrial societies, has also emerged in the newly developing nations. Between these nations and the Soviet Union of thirty or forty years ago, there are similarities. But with respect to the role and composition of strategic elites, as well as many other matters, there are also important differences which should be noted.

A note on elites in the developing countries

The leadership of the developing nations has received great attention in recent years. One reason for this is that periods of revolutionary transition are a time of severe conflict among competing elites. In this case traditional tribal leaders are seeking to maintain what progressive, Western-trained youth are trying to wrest from them. Throughout Asia, Africa, the West Indies, and the Middle East the social want-ad signs are asking, figuratively if not literally, for educated, skilled, and devoted men and women to help build the industrial foundations of their countries. Formal education is the single most important entrance requirement into the higher circles in Nigeria, Senegal, the West Indies, the Gold Coast, India, and many other countries.[41] In most of these countries, elites educated in Western terms often disagree violently with older, traditional elites about the process of industrialization, strong central government, the development of science, and universal education. Somewhat similar conflicts characterized the history of the Western world during its emergence from feudalism—but without the complication of colonialism. The West faced its own problems, however, for it was here that the industrial way of life first developed.

Today the mass of illiterate peasants—the majority of the populations of most of these developing societies—thus confronts fundamentally different moral and material orientations within the elites. And in the ensuing struggle, their society is taking shape. But whatever the divergent views and misunderstandings, once stabilization has been achieved, the members of these societies may never again participate in the dramatic spectacle of elites in sharp conflict about the nature and purposes of life, the meaning of the past, and the shape of things to come. Some such differences exist, of course, in industrial societies—for example, between economic and artistic elites—but both share certain fundamental conceptions and loyalties. These remain to be developed in the ex-colonial and industrializing countries. A vivid illustration of this situation is the present-day Middle East:

> For the stakes are nothing less than the meaning of Islam itself. Both modernizers and traditionalists wish to reorganize secular life within

> Islam. The question is: which Islam? . . . [the] conflicting appeals to Islamic doctrine could make sense only in two radically different real worlds of feeling and behavior. The Middle East may choose either world, but not both together.[42]

Do elites, in the sense in which we have discussed them, exist in these countries? Daniel Lerner suggests that there are elites but no followers. "The military regime," he quotes one Egyptian observer, "has really been seeking to create a class to represent." [43] Morroe Berger,[44] noting the predominant role played by the military elites in Egypt, the Sudan, Iraq, Turkey, and Pakistan in the designation of immediate national goals and the mobilization of available resources, attributes their pre-eminence not so much to their lust for power as to the timidity and impotence of native political and industrial elites.[45] It is questionable, however, in view of the specialized capabilities needed, whether the military will be able to fulfill this comprehensive role.

A closely linked problem concerns the recruitment of the emergent elites in these countries. The traditional two-class system, in Parsons' opinion, constitutes a significant obstacle to the industrial and scientific development of these countries.[46] Generally, the traditional upper classes have exercised the political and religious-cultural functions in these societies, relegating economic activities (as distinct from economic rewards) to the low-status peasant and working classes. This dissociation of the economic function from other functions of social leadership is likely to have profound consequences for the course of economic development. Berger likewise notes the problem posed by the need for specialized leaders in science and industry and the rejections of these activities by the current middle class as unworthy pursuits. Recruitment, consequently, is from the more deprived elements of the population whose outlook and interests are more radical than those of the traditional elites. An element of class conflict is thus injected into an already unstable and precarious situation. Parsons suggests that if the political elite in these countries is to be the chief agency for economic development and social change, then one essential problem to be solved is "where to find a subgroup of such a governmental class which will split off from the older tradition." [47]

Higher education is an indispensable attribute for those seeking access to the emergent elites in these societies, but it is not enough. Not all educated Asians and Africans either are or can be members of the strategic elites of their own countries. They must also use any other distinctive attribute they might possess, be it wealth, kinship,[48] or professional skills, to establish the specialized institutions and services that will help bring about the sort of world they presumably desire—a politically independent, technologically advanced, industrial society. The Asian, African, and Middle Eastern elites of the future will eventually have to face the fact that no single elite will be supreme, but that each will have to find its moral, symbolic, and functional place within a system of interdependent and specialized elites. Many of the studies to date have assumed a more or less wholesale displacement of the traditional elites by the modern. But this assumption rests on the dubious premise that the educated elite will be able to perform all of the strategic functions of the emerging industrial society—technological and economic, religious, political, moral, and cultural. A more realistic expectation is that, as in the West, different types of elites, varying in social as well as personal characteristics, will specialize in different functional problems.

Thus one important challenge facing the developing countries involves a choice among alternative values and the elites representing them. Another involves a shift from a diffuse ruling class to a series of specialized elites—some belonging to the traditional ruling elements, others to the modern, Western-educated stratum, and still others to the traditionally underprivileged masses. The social make-up of the elites that will eventually emerge may thus be even more diversified than in the West, and their moral cohesion, compatibility, and cooperation even more problematical.

Rank order among strategic elites

As the structure of social leadership becomes more complex, societies—whether fully or partially industrialized—face new problems of social cohesion and order among the strategic elites. In the remote past, social cohesion was furthered by the absolute preeminence of the religious-moral elites or by the fusion of moral with political or military functions. The specialization among elites, however, imposes a certain measure of equality among them—at least in the long run. The pre-eminence of an elite still occurs, but it is temporary, varying with time, place, and circumstance. This fact has led to various, and variously successful, attempts to discover the principles governing the hierarchy among elites.

Each of the scholars whose ideas were touched on earlier suggested a somewhat different principle. Marx assumed that those who control the means of production also control all major institutions. Pareto shared the widespread view that those with the readiest access to the state exercise paramount influence, because the state possesses ultimate resort to force. Mosca related the primacy of varying sections of the ruling class to the social forces prevailing during one or another epoch. In primitive societies, the social forces are chiefly war and religion, but as civilizations advance the number and kinds of social forces proliferate. Ruling classes rule because of their control over the main social forces—a tautological formulation, but one that points to the importance of social values in the predominance of different groups during different epochs.[49] Different opinions have been expressed, and a single elite has frequently been elevated to permanent stardom—be it the technological elite of Veblen, the managerial elite of Burnham, or the moral elite of Toynbee. Each of these elites, to be sure, has at times exercised absolute power but none has done so everywhere and always. The basis of their rank order thus needs to be explained.

The social position of elites (as well as their symbolic value) varies within and between societies, reflecting the absence of a universal hierarchy of values. The absolute predominance of an elite is possible only under fairly simple social conditions when a core elite enjoys a diffuse, over-all superiority by virtue not of its specific functional contribution to society but of its general attributes and characteristics. The imperatives of a given historical epoch—the relative importance of material scarcity, external threat, men's powers to understand and control their environment, and the severity of culturally induced tensions—determine which elite is supreme. In societies where material scarcity and little hope for amelioration prevail, religious and military elites tend to have first rank—the one to help or compel the members to adjust to the painful *status quo,* the other, to conquer new resources and supplies. In societies with the means to abolish material scarcity, economic and political elites tend to prevail. The crucial question is not adjustment but allocation. In the future, scientific and other culture-producing elites may become supreme. The goals of social systems may no longer be set by the need for sheer biological survival but by the possibilities for a richer, more interesting life.

Modern industrial societies are on the way to the third phase, not only as regards the variety of goals pursued by their elites but also in the specialized and partial contribution of each elite to the realization of these goals. The division of labor among strategic elites suggests that no single one can today claim an absolute, long-term superiority over the rest. The struggle for power may henceforth engage not only rival elites, as Pareto would have it, but also cooperating elites—in part autonomous, in part interdependent.

The functional differentiation among strategic elites does not, however, preclude the emergence of a relative hierarchy among them. It is generally agreed that modern industrial societies do not possess an "aristocracy of aristocracies," [50] but the temporary supremacy of one elite is the rule rather than the exception. This supremacy is quite delimited, as well as short-lived, because it is largely determined by which of the functional dimensions of the social system is ascendant at a particular time. The shifts in patterns of ascendancy are themselves a reflection of the fact that no single elite can today either designate or execute all types of collective undertakings.

The achievement of broad social goals in modern societies depends on a number of calculable and incalculable factors—including concerted action among the strategic elites. This involves a patterned sequence of actions, pushing first one, then another functional dimension—and the elites associated with them—into the foreground. Whether the national goals be those of democratic or totalitarian regimes, similar functional problems must be met in all. There is the need for effective exploitation of technical resources, including manpower and machinery (subsumed under the heading adaptation); the need for moral and ideological support by the public (integration); and the need for relaxation and emotional release. No one of these is absolutely more important than the others, although in different phases of the process different emphases prevail. Strategic elites move into ascendancy when their functions do likewise.[51] Since most societies pursue several goals simultaneously—the avoidance of war, the maintenance of international prestige, economic growth, space travel—several strategic elites may share the national spotlight at any given time.

Societies successful in the achievement of the goals they have set may either formulate new objectives or settle back and enjoy their achievements. Success may provide the impetus to social change, as there are ever new goals to be realized, new means to be devised, new conflicts and contradictions to be resolved, and new tensions to be released. Under these conditions, one would anticipate a corresponding rotation of elites. Or, the social system may become set in a customary mold unless or until some shock starts things moving again.

Even where the pursuit of success has been institutionalized, however, human error or the capriciousness of fate may prevent its attainment. Societies may become frozen at one or another "system phase" in their unsuccessful attempts to solve certain problems and the original objectives as well as the reasons for pursuing them may be forgotten or ignored. These are the periods in history when the future seems much like the past, when "there is nothing new under the sun." In such societies, the religious or moral elites tend to be supreme—reigning over the eternal mysteries of birth, death, and decay while proclaiming the futility and vanity of all things.*

The rank order of elites, therefore, is generally determined by the types of problems confronting a society, the priority accorded to these, and the functional and moral solutions proposed to solve them.

Societies, if they are to survive, require not only functional coordination but moral consensus, however loose and ill-defined. As

* Cyclical theories of history—as offered by Vico, Toynbee, and Sorokin—continue to enjoy a certain vogue, for, despite their mystifications, they contain a grain of truth based on the recurrence of similar types of leaders in societies otherwise exhibiting great material or moral contrasts. This leads to the tempting inference that similar individuals tend to recur in history. The similarities noted, however, reflect the roles these individuals are called upon to play at least as much as their psychological characteristics. That political despots may arise in many different places at different times has led some to postulate the existence of a political archetype in the collective psyche. But the recurrence of political despots may depend less on the individual characteristics of these men—there are probably always a sizeable number of potential despots available—than on the significance and relevance of their roles and functions at given periods.

they become more complex and the four functional sectors—goal attainment, adaptation, integration, and morale—become more differentiated, the problem of moral consensus becomes extremely complicated. Those entrusted with social leadership in various spheres must be able to act independently and yet strive to present a united moral front. Today, however, when each elite is specialized morally and functionally, each stands in some special relation to the core values of their societies and is to that extent relatively autonomous. The cohesion among these elites, therefore—their integration around common perspectives, their agreement on potential courses of action, and their moral autonomy—constitute important and complicated issues.

In the past, moral leadership, and the unity stemming therefrom, was often provided by a single group. Today no single elite is able to pre-empt such diffuse moral authority.[52] Each strategic elite represents a unique moral stand and this stand, as well as the capacity to fulfill the functional demands made upon it, determines the success of an elite in achieving and maintaining its superordinate position. Each elite may thus be expected to develop its own definition of what constitutes a "just and right cause," and each will also, on occasion, have to promote causes other than its own. Only in this way can there be even a semblance of moral unity in an age of moral diversity. The relationship between strategic elites and the moral order is the concern of Chapter 6.

Notes

1. This includes such studies—to be discussed more fully later—as C. Wright Mills, *The New Men of Power* (1948); Leo C. Rosten, *The Washington Correspondents* (1937); Morris Janowitz, *The Professional Soldier* (1960); Donald R. Matthews, *U.S. Senators and Their World* (1960); Robert Marsh, *The Mandarins* (1961); and several recent studies of business elites.
2. Talcott Parsons, "The Distribution of Power in American Society," in

Parsons, *Structure and Process in Modern Societies* (1960), pp. 199-225.
3. C. Wright Mills, *The Power Elite* (1956) Chaps. v-vii.
4. Floyd Hunter, *Top Leadership, U.S.A.* (1959), p. 66.
5. *Ibid.,* Chap. ii. This method is a variation of one used by Hunter in an earlier study of metropolitan leadership. See his *Community Power Structure* (1953).
6. *Ibid.,* p. 111.
7. *Ibid.,* p. 40.
8. *Ibid.,* p. 174.
9. *Ibid.,* p. 173.
10. *Ibid.,* p. 187.
11. E. Digby Baltzell, *Philadelphia Gentlemen* (1958).
12. *Ibid.,* p. 10.
13. *Ibid.,* p. 5.
14. *Ibid.,* p. 32.
15. Floyd Hunter, *Community Power Structure* (1953). For an able critique of the "reputational" method, see Raymond E. Wolfinger, "Reputation and Reality in the Study of Community Power," *American Sociological Review,* XXV (October 1960), pp. 636-44. For a recent study confirming the value of the reputational method for the location of influential community leaders, see William V. D'Antonio and Eugene C. Erickson, "The Reputational Critique as a Measure of Community Power," *American Sociological Review,* XXVII (June 1962), pp. 362-76.
16. This conclusion is consistent with the findings of the Lynds in the 1930's, regarding the emergence of the wealthy X family as the policy makers of Middletown. See R. S. and H. M. Lynd, *Middletown in Transition* (1937), Chap. v. The Lynds, incidentally, remark in passing that another equally wealthy family, the Y family, did not participate in community affairs, preferring to withdraw unto itself. This frequently noted finding has not, to my knowledge, been followed up, although it suggests that factors other than economic power determine the extent to which an economic elite will participate in, not to say dominate, community affairs.
17. Nelson W. Polsby, "Three Problems in the Analysis of Community Power," *American Sociological Review,* XXIV (December 1959), pp. 796-803. Polsby does not, I feel, sufficiently take into account the ethnic factor in New Haven (the community he analyzed), which may be subject to similar social upheavals as, for example, Boston during recent decades—where the social elite is Old Yankee; the economic elite a mixture of Old Yankee, New Italian, and New Irish; and the political elite New Italian and New Irish. The differences in ethnic recruitment patterns among these three elites may reveal less a functional separation in community leadership than an ethnic cleavage which may disappear as the various ethnic groups are "Americanized" further. See also, Wolfinger, *op. cit.,* for some support of this view.
18. Robert A. Dahl presents a telling critique of current elite studies, but his argument is weakened by an overemphasis on methodological matters before theoretical issues have been clarified. His definition of "ruling elite"—"a controlling group less than a majority in size that is not a pure artifact of democratic rules . . . a minority of individuals whose preferences regularly prevail in cases of differences in preference on key political issues"—is itself rather narrow. If there were no dissensus

under the conditions specified by Dahl, would this mean that the minority of individuals "whose preferences regularly prevail" is not to be considered an elite? See Robert A. Dahl, "A Critique of the Ruling Elite Model," *American Political Science Review,* LII (June 1958), 463-70. For an able and broader critique of studies of community power, see Peter H. Rossi, "Community Decision Making," *Administrative Science Quarterly* (March 1957), pp. 415-43. See also William V. D'Antonio, Howard J. Ehrlich, and Eugene C. Erickson, "Further Notes on the Study of Community Power," *American Sociological Review,* XXVII, No. 6 (December 1962), 848-54; Nelson W. Polsby, "Community Power: Some Reflections on the Recent Literature," in *ibid.,* 838-41; and Raymond E. Wolfinger, "A Plea for a Decent Burial," in *ibid.,* 841-8.

19. For two contending views of the differences between local and national elites, see Peter F. Drucker, "The Employee Society," *American Journal of Sociology,* LVIII (January 1953), pp. 358-63; and James B. McKee, "Status and Power in the Industrial Community: A Comment on Drucker's Thesis," *American Journal of Sociology,* LVIII (January 1953), pp. 364-70. Drucker maintains that management is the "new ruling group" in industrial society. McKee answers that "no one group can now be called a ruling group in industrial society." See also Robert O. Schulze, "The Role of Economic Dominants in Community Power Structure," *American Sociological Review* (February 1958), pp. 3-9.
20. Franz Neumann, *Behemoth* (1943), p. 297.
21. *Ibid.,* p. 298. Italics supplied.
22. *Ibid.,* p. 304.
23. *Ibid.,* p. 311.
24. *Ibid.,* pp. 311-12.
25. See, for example, Walter Goerlitz, *The German General Staff* (1953).
26. Neumann, *op cit.,* p. 312.
27. *Ibid.,* p. 323. This seems also to have held during certain epochs in Soviet history. Crankshaw, describing the situation following Stalin's death, characterized the mood of the surviving leaders as follows: "Their only hope was to stand together and pray that they would not hang together." See Edward Crankshaw, *Khrushchev's Russia* (1959), p. 37.
28. Neumann, *op. cit.,* p. 323.
29. Karl Deutsch and Lewis J. Edinger, *Germany Rejoins the Powers* (1959).
30. *Ibid.,* p. 61.
31. *Ibid.,* p. 125.
32. *Ibid.,* p. 139.
33. *Ibid.,* p. 86.
34. *Ibid.,* esp. the tables, pp. 135-41.
35. Raymond A. Bauer, Alex Inkeles, and Clyde Kluckhohn, *"How the Soviet System Works* (1960), p. 186.
36. *Ibid.,* p. 187.
37. Crankshaw, *op. cit.,* pp. 39-40.
38. "A good case can be made," writes a reviewer of a study of the Politburo, "that the Politburo is only a small portion of the soviet elite and, perhaps, an inadequate sample of it." Ralph Gilbert Ross, "Elites and the Methodology of Politics," *Public Opinion Quarterly* (Spring 1952), pp. 27-32. Another observer has pointed out that one continuing prob-

lem and complaint in Russia was the inability of the political manager to control the personnel decisions of the ministry under his command. See, Peter F. Drucker, *The New Society* (1950), p. 223. Merle Fainsod, in his comprehensive treatise, implies that while the Soviet political elite is supreme, other elites, though formally subordinate to it, are functionally indispensable. "The Soviet system of power has been constructed around a functional rather than a hereditary elite. . . . The privileges of members of the elite inhere in the offices they occupy rather than in their persons. . . . The security of the members of the elite depends on their ability to fulfill the demands which the leadership makes on them." Merle Fainsod, *How Russia is Ruled* (1953), p. 481-2.

39. Crankshaw, *op. cit.,* p. 66.
40. *Ibid.,* p. 91.
41. See "African Elites," *International Social Science Bulletin,* VIII (1956), No. 3, for a series of articles. See also M. Fortes and E. E. Evans-Pritchard (eds.), *African Political Systems* (1940); Thomas Hodgkin, *Nationalism in Colonial Africa* (1957); James S. Coleman, *Background to Nationalism* (1958), esp. chaps. vi, xviii; W. R. Bascomb and M. J. Herskovits (eds.), *Continuity and Change in African Cultures* (1959); G. A. Almond and J. S. Coleman (eds.), *The Politics of the Developing Areas* (1960); Hugh H. and Mabel M. Smythe, *The New Nigerian Elite* (1960); Simon and Phoebe Ottenberg (eds.), *Cultures and Societies in Africa* (1960); Melville J. Herskovits, *The Human Factor in Changing Africa* (1962); Daniel Lerner, *The Passing of Traditional Society* (1958); Melvin M. Tumin and Arnold Feldman, *Social Class and Social Change in Puerto Rico* (1961); and *Social Change in Latin America Today* (1960).
42. Lerner, *op. cit.,* p. 406.
43. *Ibid.,* p. 410.
44. Morroe Berger, *The Arab World Today* (1962).
45. *Ibid.,* p. 386.
46. Parsons, *op. cit.,* pp. 98-131, esp. pp. 116 ff.
47. *Ibid.,* p. 125.
48. Of the 156 members of the Nigerian elite interviewed by the Smythes, one third came from the old elite families, 45 of them sons of the old tribal chieftains. See H. H. and M. M. Smythe, *The New Nigerian Elite, op. cit.,* p. 87.
49. Cf. this with de Tocqueville's notion of the predominant importance of different "social facts" in different eras. "Upon close inspection it will be seen that there is in every age some peculiar and preponderant fact with which all others are connected; this fact almost always gives birth to some pregnant idea or some ruling passion, which attracts to itself and bears away in its course all the feelings and opinions of the time." *Democracy in America,* I, 100.
50. The phrase is Sorokin's. See his *Society, Culture, and Personality* (1947), p. 302.
51. The link between rank order and social function has been applied to the hierarchy among the different social classes in a society by Schumpeter: [There is] "a connection between the social rank of a class and its function . . . the position of each class in the total national structure depends, on the one hand, on the significance that is attributed to that function, and, on the other hand, on the degree to which that

class successfully performs the functions. Changes in relative class position are always explained by changes along these two lines, and in no other way." Joseph A. Schumpeter, *Imperialism and Social Classes,* (1955), p. 137.

More recently, Parsons has shown a strong interest in the relationship between the existing class structure and the emergent elites. Noting the dissociation of kinship from the exercise of political and economic power, the growing differentiation among different functional sectors, and the increasing autonomy of the political system, he concludes that there is no "ruling class in American society, no absolute hierarchy of prestige, and no top elite." See his essay, "A Revised Analytical Approach to the Theory of Social Stratification," *op. cit.,* p. 124; and Parsons and Smelser, *Economy and Society* (1956), pp. 286 ff.

Unfortunately Parsons does not systematically link his analysis of the functional aspects of the social system with his discussion of social classes in American society. He therefore accounts for top elite status not in functional but in occupational terms. Thus he is able to conclude that "there is no clear break between elite groups . . . and a broad band of what is usually called the 'upper middle class'." This is true only if people are compared not on their functional roles but on their styles of life and external attributes. The two may well resemble each other financially but not symbolically or functionally.

For an excellent recent discussion of the relationship between rank and social class, see L. L. Warner, "The Study of Social Stratification," in Joseph B. Gittler (ed.), *Review of Sociology* (1957), pp. 221-58.

52. Max Weber's studies of the world religions rest upon the search for such single groups as the "decisive exponents of the unity of culture." His emphasis upon the cultural sources of moral unity grew out of his despair at the disunity prevalent in his own time. Those who succeed in developing a theodicy of good and ill fortune which finds wide social acceptance will also succeed in pre-empting moral authority in society. This was the achievement of the itinerant artisans who first avowed the Christian faith, the mendicant monks who propagated Buddhism, and the medieval merchants turned Puritan. In other words, the moral outlook of an age is shaped by status groups whose social perspectives constitute a timely interpretation of fundamental moral values. We propose that this task is today performed by several strategic elites. See Max Weber, *Ancient Judaism* (1951); *The Religion of China* (1951); *The Religion of India* (1958); *The Protestant Ethic and the Spirit of Capitalism* (1950); and "The Social Psychology of World Religions," in Gerth and Mills, *From Max Weber: Essays in Sociology* (1946), pp. 267-302.

6. STRATEGIC ELITES AND THE MORAL ORDER

▲

A group of people, whatever its size, must continuously create a set of ideals for itself, an overarching set of moral rules defining the long-range goals toward which it should strive and to which it must orient itself *as a collectivity*. Such ideals, at once universal and abstract, do not exhaust all the rules necessary for day-to-day living, but they do provide a yardstick for the most important ones. While solidifying the collectivity, these rules also help differentiate it from others and thus contribute to the plurality of rights and wrongs that men live by and at times die for.

Durkheim has provided the best sociological analysis of the nature of moral rules and of the changes they undergo, along with the social and technological changes that accompany the rise of civilization. These rules have many functions for the various groups and individuals that compose a society. Above all, they are indispensable for creating and maintaining order and cohesion.

In his famous work, *The Division of Labor in Society* (1893), Durkheim explores the relationship between the nature of moral rules and the social milieu in which they arise. He distinguishes between two major classes of such rules: one developed under relatively simple, primitive conditions; the other under the complex conditions of modern industrial life. The first, *mechanical solidarity,* rests on the identity of collective aims; the second, *organic solidarity,* on reciprocal interdependence. Each set of rules and the practices associated with it comprise the collective conscience:

> The totality of beliefs and sentiments common to average citizens of the same society forms a determinate system which has its own life; one may call it the collective or common conscience. No doubt, it has not a specific organ as a substratum; it is, by definition, diffuse in every reach of society. . . . It is an entirely different thing from particular consciences, although it can be realized only through them. It is the psychical type of society, a type which has its properties, its conditions of existence, its mode of development, just as individual types, although in a different way.[1]

Durkheim does not indicate, however, where and in which groups or institutions this collective conscience is to be found. One principal reason for this is his adherence to a model of society as a nonstratified system, one in which there is continual feed-back between all or most of the members as private and as social individuals. The collective conscience, in short, is seen to exist in the average citizens of the society and yet have a life of its own. He does not say specifically where the collective conscience is to be located and in what or in whom it resides, but he does find some indicators of it—chiefly in the nature of law which prevails under both simple and more complex social conditions. Acts which offend the collective conscience tend to be strongly punished in all societies, but the nature of the punishment is more severe in simpler societies where repressive law reigns. In complex societies, restitutive law is prevalent. Specialized organs and functionaries are precisely defined and powers to punish are correspondingly circumscribed. The simple society with mechanical solidarity, predominantly repressive law, and a diffuse collective conscience gives way to a complex society with organic solidarity, predominantly restitutive law, and a differentiated collective conscience. Under mechanical solidarity, the individual is bound "directly to the society without any intermediary." Under organic solidarity, "he depends upon society, because he depends upon the parts of which it is composed." [2] The two types of societies differ as to their degree of specialization, the nature of their solidarity, and the extent of possible and permitted individualism. A general pattern of development may be identified in which a community based on identity and repressiveness gives way to one based on diversity and reciprocity.

The collective conscience and strategic elites

Durkheim nowhere refers to elites as such. Nor, except in passing, does he deal with the phenomenon of power; but he frequently alludes to them, and, as we shall see, his argument benefits from an application of the concepts we have utilized. Under conditions of mechanical solidarity, where individuals are presumably at one with the moral order, a directing center comprising the moral symbols of the collectivity is necessary. But since there is relatively little occupational and social diversity, this center, too, is unified and uniform. This sort of society, in short, needs but a single moral elite—priests, chiefs, or warriors—to serve as a focus and center of organized social life.

As societies become more diversified, the nature of the collective conscience and the relations of individuals to it change. The "common conscience consists less and less of strongly determined sentiments. Thus it comes about that the average intensity and mean degree of determination of collective states are always diminishing. . . ." [3] Religion tends to embrace an ever smaller portion of social life; political, economic, and scientific functions free themselves from religious ones. The "average intensity of the common conscience" becomes less intense as individualism becomes more widespread.

Since Durkheim gives no explanation of how political, economic, and scientific functions "free themselves" from religion, it is difficult to understand this development. Presumably, the process took place somewhat along the following lines: as men's abilities to control their environment increased, their reliance on supernatural explanations decreased; religion could no longer safeguard, regulate, and represent the moral unity because that unity had ceased to exist. The collective conscience as well as the occupational world became subdivided. This process, it may be reasoned, carried an important structural change: the single moral elite of priests was joined by other strategic elites, each gaining control of a distinct aspect of collective life and, generally, of the collective conscience.

In the more complex society, strategic elites express not only the common moral sentiments of the collectivity but also its differentiated aspects, providing simultaneously an image of social unity and social diversity. Instead of one common center there are now several such centers; instead of a single moral elite there are now several such elites. This has far-reaching consequences for individuals, the society, and the strategic elites themselves.

According to Durkheim, individuals in complex societies are no longer bound directly to the collective conscience by their beliefs, rituals, and "like-mindedness." They are bound instead to the occupational milieus in which they participate. Their moral outlook is increasingly determined not by the sum total of social life but by the particular aspects of the occupationally divided world with which they are personally familiar. The division of labor has extended from the economic sphere to all spheres: "The political, administrative, and judicial functions are growing more and more specialized. It is the same with the aesthetic functions." [4] Each occupation is developing a special moral identity of its own. As these occupational worlds become more differentiated, their members come to see the world differently, speak different languages, and possess different conceptions of happiness. Often they seem totally separate and even disconnected, although ideally they retain a certain measure of interdependence as each occupation contributes a specialized and socially valued product.

The agents acting on behalf of the collectivity thus begin to play a more crucial role in society and have more complicated tasks. Among the latter are three highly important functions: (1) to order the relationships between subgroups so that collective aims can be achieved; (2) to embody the ideal norms by which every collectivity is defined and on which its survival depends; and (3) to symbolize the solidarity of the differentiated collectivity through rituals and assembly—since such rituals and assembly are no longer feasible for the total membership of society (although, in a new form, this has again become possible through the mass media). Today, more and more specialized collective agents, related to the collectivity as a whole, are needed to remind the mass of men of their common ideal ends and to order and regulate the interrelationships among the great variety of subgroups that now coexist.[5]

As the divisions of labor advances, it leads both to a greater individualism and to a new kind of social solidarity. Social cohesion is now both spontaneous and reciprocal. But how does the division of labor—which implies greater specialization and segregation of institutions, services, and aims—lead at the same time to a deeper social solidarity? In particular, how does social solidarity become manifest once it ceases to be an outgrowth of direct personal moral obligations and sentiments, becoming, instead, an indirect effect of functional interdependence and interrelationships among subgroups? Durkheim never clarified this problem. His doctrine of organic solidarity is thus more a declaration of faith than a description of fact. As Parsons has observed:

> The general drift of his argument is to the effect that the division of labor itself creates solidarity. What he gives as an account of the mechanisms of this process is extremely sketchy, but the reader gathers that it is in his mind primarily a matter of habituation. . . . But this is clearly from his own standpoint an unsatisfactory account of the matter. . . . For where, in the mechanism of habit, is the element of obligation to be found? . . . The only real element of obligation still seems to be that involved in mechanical solidarity. . . . Durkheim has conspicuously failed to account for the specific element of organic solidarity beyond the very general formula that it must lie in features of the social milieu.[6]

Durkheim could have escaped this difficulty had he followed his own sporadic insights into the necessity for and the existence of a "directing center." This center, viewed in the context of the present discussion, is composed of what we have called the strategic elites. These elites, as the heads of functional sectors of society, see to it that the members perform their obligations within these sectors, but they themselves are obligated to act for and on behalf of the sectors.

Durkheim works all around the concept of elites without ever systematically developing this idea. He notes, for example, that as society becomes more complex a universal change occurs in relationships between the group and its individual members. In contrast to simpler societies, the individual ceases to be joined to the collectivity directly but is joined instead to what Durkheim calls the "image of the group," by which he seems to mean its chiefs, priests, or warriors. This image is conveyed by the conspicuous minority of men in leading social positions who embody Durkheim's collective conscience.

Durkheim traces the evolution of social organization from two types of mechanical solidarity (not one, as often asserted) to organic solidarity. When the collectivity is small enough so that all can participate in its affairs, the link between it and individuals is direct and their solidarity is mechanical. As the collectivity expands in size and diversity, a central organ develops—usually of priests, but also of rulers or warriors—whose task is to supervise the observance of common moral rules. The relationship between this central organ and individuals is direct, but that between individuals and their society is now indirect. The central organ serves as an intermediary between an expanding membership and the core values of the social organization containing that membership. Social solidarity is still mechanical because the emphasis is on uniformity of behavior and beliefs. With further expansion, the directing center itself becomes subdivided and specialized, and the linkages more complex. Individuals are generally tied most closely to their specific occupational worlds and to their colleagues; and each occupation is a subdivision of one of the functional spheres headed by a "directing agent." Directing agents of one sphere interact not with individual members but with the directing agents of other spheres. The solidarity this engenders is, in Durkheim's view, organic.[7]

The transition from mechanical to organic solidarity, therefore, comprises a shift from individual submission to the group to submission to the symbols of the group. These symbols, embodied in one or several directing centers, constitute the central authority on which group life henceforth depends. The function of these centers is "to create respect for the beliefs, traditions, and collective practices: that is, to defend the common conscience against all enemies within and without." [8]

There is also a difference in the severity of social sanctions in societies with mechanical as opposed to organic solidarity. In simpler societies, Durkheim observes, rulers and leaders tend to be much more despotic than in complex societies, although in both they provide special services to their communities. Their power rests less on what they do than on what they represent—the authority of the oldest and most important moral rules. Their power is more supreme in primitive societies because there the collective conscience is more supreme. In societies with an advanced division of labor, where social solidarity is based on interdependence and reciprocity, the collective conscience tends to be less arbitrary and comprehensive, and more spontaneous and voluntary. The central organ now depends just as much on the members of society as they depend on it. The arbitrary despotism of an earlier day has been banished. But while unilateral relations have been replaced by mutuality, the power of the central organ has not diminished; only its basis and justification have changed.

> No doubt it still enjoys a special situation, and, if one chooses so to speak of it, a privileged position, but that is due to the nature of the role that it fills, and not to some cause foreign to its function, nor to some force communicated to it from without.[9]

Durkheim thus arrives at the proposition that the directing organ in advanced industrial societies derives whatever privileges it possesses from its functional role in the social system.

Durkheim's analysis helps us to formulate the proposition that the survival of the traditions and taboos of complex societies depends more on the beliefs and values of their specialized strategic elites than on those of their total membership. Today, individuals cannot live up to all or even to most of the moral rules in existence. The moral demands typically made on them are those of day-to-day living—involving their homes and families, jobs, and perhaps clubs and associations. Moral obligation to ultimate ends, however, is the duty of strategic elites. It is they who are chiefly identified with them. Today the collective conscience may be considered to be the conscience of the men in strategic elite positions. This is not to say that average citizens are amoral or immoral, but rather that group membership is more fully integrated with specialized occupational milieus. Strategic elites, as heads of institutions and organizations serving collective functions, thus bear the general moral obligation that was formerly expected of all the members of society. The only solidarity that continues to affect all members is segmental or territorial, the latter being particularly significant during wartime, when to defend one's country is apt to be the highest aim.*

The preservation of the social order rests in part on the preservation of the moral order. All members of simple communities are expected to know and live up to the rules and norms of that order; in complex societies, some strata are considered more responsible and therefore morally superior to others. Today, the locus of ultimate moral responsibility rests, we suggest, with the strategic elites. Their fate depends not only on how effectively they perform their tasks—getting missiles launched, producing goods, desegregating schools, avoiding war—but also on their moral rectitude. Their public stance thus frequently tends to be rather stilted and formal—they are conscious of representing the moral force of society.[10] If a bank teller embezzles funds, it is enough to raise an eyebrow, but if a bank manager does so there is considerable moral indignation.

Since the strategic elites of today embody the central and ultimate ends of society, people tend to react to them as individuals formerly reacted to sacred symbols in the past—totems, priests, sacred rites, divine kings. But because of increasing secularism they are less sanctified. What one knows is always less hallowed than what one fears. The simple societies of which Durkheim writes were suffused by fear.[11] As fears decrease, so does the sanctity of leaders, although it may never be entirely effaced. Durkheim believed that those on whom men see themselves to depend will always be endowed with superhuman qualities.

> Also in the present day just as much as in the past, we see society constantly creating sacred things out of ordinary ones. If it happens

* It would be advisable for those studying crime, anomie, and moral conformity to take this change into account. Instead of expecting people to be concerned and even aware of the ultimate moral rules, one must expect them to be involved primarily with those occupational and social norms with which they are personally familiar. It is increasingly difficult to be aware of all the moral rules or to have any conception of the interrelatedness of such rules unless one occupies a position that permits one to survey the social organization. There are, therefore, two types of moral rules: those affecting the collectivity as such, and these are more familiar to and more relevant for the members of the strategic elites; and those affecting the lives of people in their day-to-day pursuits—sexual, occupational, and familial.

> to fall in love with a man and if he thinks it has found in him the principal aspirations that move it, as well as the means of satisfying them, this man will be raised above the others and, as it were, deified. . . . Opinion will invest him with a majesty exactly analogous to that protecting the gods. This is what has happened to so many sovereigns in whom their age had faith: if they were not made gods, they were at least regarded as direct representatives of the deity. . . . The simple deference inspired by men invested with high social functions is not different in nature from religious respect. It is expressed by the same movements: a man keeps at a distance from a high personage; he approaches him only with precautions. . . . The sentiment felt on these occasions is so closely related to the religious sentiment that many people have confounded the two. In order to explain the consideration accorded to princes, nobles and political chiefs, a sacred character has been attributed to them. . . . However, it is evident that this situation is due solely to the importance attributed to him by public opinion.[12]

Part of this sanctity stems from the fact that strategic elites must deal with life-and-death issues and are themselves confronting the mysterious, the powerful, and the unknown.

Durkheim's observation that functional "diversity induces a moral diversity that nothing can prevent" [13] has been elaborated and applied to the rise of strategic elites. As the collective conscience has become subdivided, it has been entrusted to specialized elites who must be not only technically proficient but also morally responsible for their particular functional spheres. The behavior of these elites serves as a reminder of the ultimate ends that bind a people pursuing their more confined, day-to-day activities. In this way, the strategic elites of complex societies are a link between past and future, a bridge to the moral survival of all. If any persons today receive the homage, reverence, fascinated interest, and anxious ambivalence reserved for sacred entities, it is the strategic elites who embody an ideal image of society, and in whom man worships and hates himself.[14]

Increasingly, the strategic elites of modern societies are entrusted with the preservation of the moral as well as the material order. But since these elites have themselves become functionally and institutionally differentiated, they have two moral roles to play. One concerns the defense of the moral order on an absolute level—here they represent a united front toward their society or the world itself. But since they are also differentiated, they must develop and defend moral principles more specifically related to their respective functions. Thus, at times, they must make a public show of their moral accord, at times, of their moral differences.

Moral differences among strategic elites

Moral principles or norms, like many other cultural phenomena, illustrate the law of duality in regard to cause and effect. Moral principles are, among other things, actions supported by an "ought," as when people first derive profit from exchange and then work out a scheme whereby such a profit is considered morally desirable. In this case, the moral principle follows from the action. People are expected to pursue profit even if this conflicts with their other interests and desires. In this sense, moral principle is the cause of action. New moral beliefs are ever being added to and dropped from the cultural storehouse as life changes, and this in turn changes ways and patterns of life. This holds for both the more abstract cultural level and the relatively concrete institutional level. Strategic elites function primarily at the institutional level.

Since strategic elites have different functions, facilities, and personnel, they emphasize and influence different aspects of the moral system. The members of each elite share and emphasize a distinctive set of values which represents a special sector of the collective life. They are identified with these values and norms not only by the public but in their own eyes as well. These elites also are subject to *general* legal and moral norms—they are expected to be law-abiding citizens, virtuous, and honorable. But each elite has its own special definitions and criteria of these virtues. The private sexual morals of business leaders are not as relevant for their public roles as, say, those of moral or religious leaders. Business leaders would be morally condemned however, if they displayed the authoritarianism expected of military leaders. Just so, the morality of politics is not that of business. Pretensions to superiority by birth would be out of place among Nobel Prize winners where superiority is attained by achievement.

Except in a highly general and abstract sense, then, each elite is judged by differing moral standards, although each is judged by some standards. This exacerbates the moral diversity, if not confusion, that characterizes advanced industrial societies, which according to our view stems not only from the conflict of standards between the traditional past and the dynamic present, and between the pressures of expediency and of morality, but also from the functional and hence moral semi-autonomy of the strategic elites.

The moral diversity prevailing in highly differentiated societies is bound to affect deep-rooted moral attitudes and preferences. For one thing, an absolute morality within a single society would involve a great narrowing of horizons and impoverishment of spirit. The collective conscience, once unified in its homogeneity, is today unified only in its diversity. The members of society, if they are to benefit from this variety, must be prepared to accept several, sometimes contradictory, moral postures. This view has certain similarities to the discussion led by Karl Mannheim, of the moral relativism stemming from increased cross-cultural contact. Today, however, it is no longer primarily a cross-cultural but an indigenous problem, as people are confronted by seemingly incompatible norms and models. Social insulation of institutions and general ignorance about a wide variety of principles and practices help limit the degree of moral confusion in the social order. More and more people are closely familiar with only segments of their society—chiefly those of work and private life; they leave the rest to those "in the know." Since they are not deeply involved in other spheres, they are apt to be more tolerant of the unfamiliar and the unusual.

Consequently "those in the know," the members of strategic elites, have greater moral responsibilities (which they need not always be aware of or live up to) than most persons. If disunity and disagreements are to be kept under control, the members of one elite must keep a sharp watch on others, lest one of them tries to impose its particular values and goals. There is today then the possibility both for greater complexity of moral life and greater chaos. To keep the scale between complexity and chaos tilted in favor of complexity, members of the different elites must have access to each other, communicate with each other, and learn to appreciate each other's moral frames of reference. The upright, fastidious financier may find distasteful the more light-hearted, disorganized, spontaneous existence of the artist, but he must try to understand this life style so contradictory to his own and find some way of integrating it with his own conception of the world. Without this kind of understanding and partial integration, societies may be faced by extreme conflict among the elites themselves, unmitigated by any sense of unity or ultimate purpose.[15]

The moral problems brought to the fore as differentiation among strategic elites increases are similar to those of earlier epochs. These problems were intensified with the decline of the preeminence of religious leadership in society. With the rise of differentiated political institutions, secular leadership began to encroach upon areas previously reserved for religious leaders; the conflict between these two elites marks much of the history of ancient Egypt, and, more recently, the history of the West through the Middle Ages.

With the rise of science, conflict among elites increased. The trial and condemnation of Galileo by the Inquisition, involving the clash between Copernican theory and biblical scripture, is a famous instance of this conflict. This seventeenth-century trial was a forerunner of many later contests between science and religion concerning questions of the origin and meaning of life and the universe.

In the twentieth century, this conflict, once viewed as more or less settled, is flaring up again—now between science and the polity. Giorgio de Santillana draws a suggestive parallel between the recent Oppenheimer case and the Galileo trial of three centuries ago:

> The usefulness of both scientists to society was clearly recognized. Both of them had delivered the goods: Galileo the prestige of his telescopic discoveries, Oppenheimer the atom bomb. The trouble came when the scientists went on to exert their influence, however tentatively and respectfully, on matters of high policy. Galileo's book was a discreet but transparent attempt at getting the Church to change its mind on a fundamental scientific issue. Oppenheimer, too, expressed definite views about the over-all strategy for which his individual contributions formed an important part.[16]

In both epochs, as long as science did not interfere with cherished moral beliefs supervised by already established elites—in one case religious, in the other political—it was free to pursue its activities. But when their discoveries reached the point of having revolutionary implications, some scientists understandably felt compelled to take a larger view of their work, their social roles, and their times.

Like other aspiring candidates from less privileged groups, newly risen elites face the opposition typically confronted by *arrivistes* in many times and places. Why, today, as at times in the past, do not the older established elites simply absorb the new discoveries of scientists or other specialists without admitting their progenitors into their own ranks, thereby benefitting from these discoveries without relinquishing their prerogatives? The answer lies, I think, in the kind and extent of specialization that has divided the strategic elites morally and functionally. For as the realm of the knowable has become so specialized and detailed as to defy mastery, the realm of the unknown has also become specialized. The area of the unknown, the province of religious leaders, was once as vast as the area of the known was small. Gradually, however, as the latter expanded, the area of the unknown became delineated. We are now faced not only with cosmic uncertainties, but political, economic, military, moral and scientific ones as well—each confronted by specialists. It is highly unlikely today for the president of a large corporation to seek the advice of a religious leader about economic matters; nor does the nuclear physicist characteristically turn to the political leader for help.

The older established elites themselves find their powers limited precisely by their ignorance of new fields. The church in the seventeenth century was in a position similar to that of the government in the twentieth—it lacked technical knowledge of the scientists it was judging.[17] It was only a matter of time before the leaders of the church capitulated to the leaders of the newer sciences—at least to the extent of no longer judging the objective merits of their work. Similarly in the twentieth century, political leaders face strong pressure to make room for leading scientists and other specialists on whose knowledge military planning, economic expansion, and a host of other matters now depends and without whom effective public policy can no longer be made.[18] More and more, leading scientists not only receive rewards accruing to those who are entrusted with positions of key importance to society, but they share the moral responsibilities and problems reserved for those in high places.*

Cohesion among strategic elites

In modern industrial societies, each strategic elite represents both the common moral framework and a particular functional sphere. This poses some difficult problems. Ideally, the members of each elite must not only seek to align themselves with other elites but also to retain their special identity; they must be knowledgeable of the duties and goals of all without over-valuing those of a particular elite. This is a large order. Leading literary men often are poorly informed about the sciences and politics; politicians are frequently ignorant of the arts; and scientists are apt to be naïve in politics. Yet since the members of all strategic elites, to be effective, must keep sight of their common goals, they should have some knowledge of the concerns of each, a task becoming more difficult as specialization increases.

This is one reason why modern societies periodically proclaim their common goals in a public and official manner. Primitive societies do so through collective rituals, industrial societies through formal announcements of annual programs and intentions. The sheer declaration of common goals seems to renew and strengthen the collective identity,[19] by suggesting the existence of a fundamental moral consensus.

Not all observers agree that such a consensus actually exists. They stress the aimlessness, chaos, and fragmentation of modern life and the threat this condition poses to collective survival. As suggested earlier, however, this view rests on untenable premises, among them the notion that all or most people must be committed to the *same* norms and values if a society is to cohere. But such is not the case in modern industrial society, for this kind of unified moral accord is no longer socially essential nor, in fact, pos-

* This, incidentally, points to an important difference between the developing and the industrialized countries. In the former, the general assumption is that only governmental elites will be responsible for over-all policy. Scientists, educators, and technicians are needed and trained as rapidly as possible, but there is as yet little appreciation of the fact that eventually the political elite will have to yield to the leaders in other strategic spheres. Their current superordinate role is at best temporary.

sible. What is required for effective social life is moral accord among the strategic elites: they must have some loyalties and goals in common. As societies become more differentiated a considerable degree of cohesion and consensus is needed at the top.

That such consensus is difficult to achieve goes without saying. That it has always been so in large complex societies is less widely known. Part of this difficulty is the product of the historical dialectic itself—every proposed collective large-scale effort encounters opposition not only from its opponents but from the people engaged in realizing it. Commitment and doubt often go hand in hand within the same individuals as well as within the same societies.[20] The point need not be labored that doubt and conflicts are necessary: societies advance both as a result of achievements and as a result of disagreements and struggles over the ways to attain them. This is where power struggles play a major and indispensable role.* Loyalty to common goals does not preclude conflict over how they are to be realized.

Nevertheless, the absence of moral consensus is often held accountable for severe problems besetting modern nations. De Tocqueville, who considered the leading manufacturers and their legal aides to be the new aristocracy of industrial society, found this group distinctively different from preceding aristocracies in that there were now men of wealth but no class of wealth: "these rich individuals have no feelings, or purposes, no tradition or hopes, in common." [21] Max Weber analyzed the development of modern Germany along similar lines, focusing on the moral conflict between the old landowners and the new capitalists; this conflict, ultimately won by the capitalists, nevertheless marked the victors with an authoritarian stamp sharply contrasting with the ideal of civil equality.[22] Discussing post-World War II France, Raymond Aron noted that "a society can only survive and prosper if there is true collaboration" and a "unity of opinion and action on essential points" among the various groups in the elite. He described the contemporary lack of such unity: "In France the com-

* This is true of both advanced industrialized societies and developing ones. In most of the latter there is probably a consensus that poverty must be conquered, ignorance eliminated, and autonomy secured. But thereafter agreement ceases as rival groups and potential elites struggle for the triumph of their conceptions of how to attain these ends. Ultimately all major power struggles involve opposing visions of the future.

munists and the non-communists are not in agreement on the direction of our diplomatic policy and so on the mission which the community is called upon to play." [23] In the past, ties of kinship and social class prompted moral consensus among elites; today as these have come to play a lesser role, new sources for a unity of outlook need to be developed.[24]

Moral compatibility is important for the development of social cohesion among strategic elites, but it is not alone decisive for such cohesion. The latter also is promoted by facilities for exchange and communication and by personal compatibility among the members of different elites. These three factors are of course interrelated—if there is a basic moral accord, mechanisms for sustained and intimate communication will be found which in turn will lead to more personal contacts. But with the greatly expanded size and complexity of society, opportunities for personal exchange and contact among members of the elites have lessened.

These opportunities were far more readily available when the scale of things was smaller, when institutions "were at the level of men's eyes," and when distance and time were men's collaborators, not their adversaries. Social and geographical distance increasingly separate elites from the public and often from each other. Small and relatively self-contained worlds are emerging in which policies and programs are often developed in semi-isolation. But leaders in the different spheres of social life would benefit from an exchange of views if only to discover the reasons for their disagreements or the possibilities for potential agreement. This agreement need not be in the form of explicit rules and regulations. On the contrary, to be truly effective it must develop organically and below the threshold of full consciousness. The most substantial and creative consensus is that which exists covertly.[25]

The specialization of function and recruitment practices among different elites raises the possibility of a different personality type predominating in each, some more, some less, compatible with one another. The role of personality factors among members of strategic elites deserves a study in itself, particularly the degree to which personal characteristics impede or aid the members to realize their social objectives and to live up to the demands of their social roles. The successful man, like other men, is a blend of the occasion, the role, and the personality, but once success has been attained his personality may prove in certain circumstances to be crucial. The megalomania of Hitler, the paranoia of Stalin, the trepidation of Chamberlain, the courage of Churchill—all became historically significant, if not decisive. Some individuals are unable to share power or are compelled to win out at all costs, this as much as moral dissonance or social distance can prevent or inhibit the collaboration of groups whose very existence depends on collaboration.

Robert Michels is one of the few writers who has given serious attention to the role of personality factors among elites, and although his material is largely anecdotal, his observations are suggestive.[26] He found, for example, that the leaders of radical parties are often consumed by personal hatred for one another, and that this leads to frequent and bitter clashes among them, to the detriment of themselves and the parties they represent. Mutual jealousy, envy, competitiveness, greed, vanity play a significant part in the creation of oligarchy. Resulting rivalries, according to Michels, have two components: an objective component involving principles, tactics, and goals; and a subjective one, involving jealousy and envy. Frequently, he observed, differences over principle lead to personal hostilities, but just as frequently the latter assume the guise of clashes over principle.[27]

Personal animosities, prejudices, and ignorance, inevitable as they may be, affect both the elites themselves and the publics they serve and represent. Strategic elites are composed of leaders whose various publics are generally the same individuals—the general public. The latter's members, of course, play different roles and therefore are associated with different specific publics, each of which may be of primary interest to a specific elite. The public of the political elite is made up of citizens and voters; that of the economic elite, of workers and consumers; the military elite perceives a public of soldiers and civilians; the religious elite, of souls and sinners. Each strategic elite has a specialized perception of the general public, formed by its own interests and the nature of the specific public with which it is associated. This perception becomes more specialized as elites become more differentiated. In the past when elites were more homogenous, their perceptions of the general public were likewise more homogeneous.

This specialization, however, has its limits. If social order is to be maintained, it becomes necessary at some point for the members of each elite to know a considerable amount about the activities, intentions, and aspirations of the others. The political elite is supported by taxes, but the availability of taxes requires that people be employed and is therefore largely dependent on the actions of the economic elite. The position of the economic elite depends upon the performance of the workers in their employ. The latters' efficiency rests in part on the separation of work and play, the responsibility of the recreational elite. Each strategic elite in short must round out its particular perceptions and preconceptions concerning the general public (or mass) by becoming aware of those of other elites.

To the various social ills that have periodically afflicted the social order a new one has been added: the problem of social cohesion among strategic elites no longer united by ties of blood, social status, and wealth, but by functional interdependence. How to preserve and maintain their unity without stifling their diversity is a serious, and as yet unsolved, problem.

Notes

1. Emile Durkheim, *The Division of Labor in Society* (1947), pp. 79-80.
2. *Ibid.*, p. 129.
3. *Ibid.*, p. 167.
4. *Ibid.*, p. 40.
5. The common conscience has, in this way, become specialized. Even simpler societies, Durkheim notes, were not uniform and homogeneous: "To simplify the exposition, we hold that the individual appears only in one society. In fact, we take part in several groups and there are in us several collective consciences." *Ibid.*, p. 105*n*.
6. Talcott Parsons, *The Structure of Social Action* (1949) p. 321. "Durkheim," Parsons concludes, "has conspicuously failed to account for the specific element of organic solidarity beyond the very general formula that it must lie in features of the social milieu." *Ibid.*, p. 323.
7. According to Durkheim, this type of social solidarity is the first step toward individualism and a break with tradition. "Rather than dating

the effacement of the individual from the institution of a despotic authority, we must, on the contrary, see in this institution the first step toward individualism. Chiefs are in fact the first personalities who emerge from the social mass. . . . In dominating society, they are no longer forced to follow all of its movements. Of course, it is from the group that they derive their powers, but once power is organized, it becomes autonomous and makes them capable of personal activity. A source of initiative is thus opened which has not existed before then. There is, hereafter, someone who can produce new things and even, in certain measure, deny collective usages. Equilibrium has been broken." Durkheim, *op. cit.,* p. 195. Note that equilibrium and stability are not identical.

8. *Ibid.,* p. 84. Some actions, Durkheim notes, are severely punished even though they do not incur strong public disapproval or even great public interest, such as the injury done to "a governmental organ." "The smallest injury to the police power calls forth a penalty, while even repeated violations of contracts, or constant lack of correctness in economic relations only asks for amends for the loss. . . . Why is this privilege accorded to what is sometimes called the social brain?" *Ibid.,* p. 84.
9. *Ibid.,* pp. 181-2.
10. Eisenstadt has observed in the case of Israel: ". . . mobility and aspiration to elite status are closely connected not only with a fuller social participation but also, and perhaps mainly, with a more active and independent one, the main characteristics of which are the feeling of *closer* relations to the main social values, the emphasis on the symbolic importance of one's own performance of various roles connected with these values." S. N. Eisenstadt, "The Place of Elites and Primary Groups in the Absorption of New Immigrants in Israel," *American Journal of Sociology,* LVIIX, No. 3 (November 1951), 222-31.
11. "We do not believe," an Eskimo told his questioner. "We only fear." Quoted by Paul Radin in *Primitive Religion* (1957), p. 52.
12. Emile Durkheim, *The Elementary Forms of the Religious Life* (1954), p. 213.
13. Emile Durkheim, *The Division of Labor in Society, op. cit.,* p. 361.
14. Mosca was among those who realized that what is important for the preservation of society is not so much the morality of the people as the morality of the "ruling class." See Mosca, *The Ruling Class* (1939), pp. 50 ff.

    The suggestion that the strategic elites are necessarily more generally obligated to observe broad social norms, particularly those relevant for their functional sphere, receives support from yet another quarter. Durkheim found that army officers had higher suicide rates than enlisted men, and he persuasively related this to the over-integration of the officers with military norms. A recent study of suicide suggests the same pattern to be at work in other occupational milieus. See, Elwin H. Powell, "Occupation, Status, and Suicide: Toward a Redefinition of Anomie," *American Sociological Review* XXIII, No. 2 (April 1958), 131-40.
15. This appears to be true in most groups—there must be some coalition between the leaders of groups, no matter how uneasy or precarious, else the group may not accomplish its aims; so too in the smaller nuclear

family unit, the husband and wife must present a differentiated but emotionally unified common front to the child else he may be irrevocably divided in his struggle to align with one of the parents against the other. See, for example, the remarks of Robert F. Bales "The Equilibrium Problem in Small Groups," in T. Parsons *et al., Working Papers in the Theory of Action* (1953), p. 149.

16. Giorgio de Santillana, "Galileo and J. Robert Oppenheimer" in *The Reporter* (December 26, 1957), pp. 1-18.
17. Santillana writes: "It is permissible to speculate about what would have happened if Oppenheimer, together with Fermi, Bethe, and two or three other authorities in theoretical physics, had stated in 1942, as Heisenberg did in Germany, that the atom bomb was not feasible. No one could really have known except them. . . . Heisenberg was certainly a patriotic German and a very great physicist, yet, after extensive exploratory work with his colleagues, he gave up—and not even Hitler could say anything." *Ibid.*, p. 10.
18. Drucker's comments are pertinent here: ". . . management can only be one leading group among several; in its own self-interest it can never be and must never be *the* leading group. It has partial rather than comprehensive social responsibility—hence partial rather than comprehensive social authority. Should management claim to be *the* leading group—or even to be the most powerful of leading groups—it will be either rebuffed and, in the process, be shorn of most of the authority it can claim legitimately, or it will help into power a dictatorship that will deprive management as well as all other groups in a free society of their authority and standing." Peter F. Drucker, "The Tasks of Management," in W. L. Warner and H. Martin (eds.), *Industrial Man* (1959), p. 193.
19. Such a declaration, including a list of American national goals, is contained in a recently published report of the President's Commission on National Goals, *New York Times,* November 28, 1960, pp. 20-3. The report divided the major national goals into two kinds, domestic and foreign. On the domestic front, the chief emphasis is on the fullest development of the individual, on equality of opportunity irrespective of sex, race, religion, or ethnicity, perfecting the democratic process; and the advancement of education, science, technology, and the arts. It also calls for a "growing economy" which is at the same time a "democratic economy," for an improvement in general living conditions, and for the promotion of social security and welfare. The document is a superb illustration of the moral dilemma faced by those currently trying to articulate national goals, in trying to reconcile different, if not opposed, principles: individualism on the one hand, and Federal Aid and some minimum type of planning on the other.

    The goals mentioned as worth-while in this report compare favorably with those proposed by Clark Kerr *et al., Industrialism and Industrial Man* (1960), pp. 42-3.
20. The alternation between periods of harmony and of conflict has been considered a timeless and universal historical phenomenon by some writers. Bazard, following Saint-Simon, divided history into "organic" and "critical" epochs, the latter characterized by social disorganization and anomie. "Today scientists amass facts but there is no coordination among them; in industry competition and individual interests are para-

mount; and even the poets no longer express any but anti-social sentiments. The poet is no longer the divine singer placed at the head of society to serve as an interpreter to men. . . ." The "today" he referred to occurred in 1830. Quoted in Emile Durkheim, *Socialism and Saint-Simon* (1958), p. 214.

21. De Tocqueville, *Democracy in America,* II, 170.
22. Max Weber, "Capitalism and Rural Society in Germany," in H. H. Gerth and C. W. Mills (eds.), *Essays From Max Weber* (1946), p. 371. Weber predicted that some of these problems would arise in the United States as soon as land became scarce, population dense, and occupations highly differentiated.
23. Raymond Aron, "Social Structure and the Ruling Class," *The British Journal of Sociology,* Vol. I (1950), No. 2, 1-16.
24. Trotsky describes the aristocracies of nineteenth-century Europe as having a "supernational" character, "bound together as they were by ties of birth, inheritance, scorn for all those beneath them, and last but not least, cosmopolitan adultery in ancient castles, at fashionable watering places, and in the courts of Europe." Leon Trotsky, *The History of the Russian Revolution,* I (1950), 66.

    Some, notably C. Wright Mills, claim such a transcendent identity for the members of the various national elites in America today. But as already indicated, Mills overstates the case even with respect to the evidence he himself puts forth. Moreover, by concentrating on the "power elite" and ignoring other members of the strategic elites such as artists and religious leaders, the social diversity increasingly characterizing the strategic elites is obscured.
25. Such consensus is more difficult to achieve today than in the past. "If Socrates Had Lived in Scarsdale," reads the title of an indictment of modern urban life, "he'd probably never have known Aristophanes or Xenophon or Plato because that crowd of writers and intellectuals all lived in Greenwich village and he wouldn't have known Pericles and Aspasia and that government bunch because they all lived in Washington." John Crosby, *New York Herald Tribune,* November 18, 1960.
26. See also Harold D. Lasswell, *The Psychopathology of Politics* (1930).
27. Robert Michels, *Political Parties* (1959), pp. 196 ff.

    A clash over principles and the personal animosities and rivalries this reflects or engenders may be one price to be paid for the social and functional differentiation among strategic elites today. Another may be the feeling of personal insecurity and anxiety arising from the absence of strong solidarity, the lack of an acceptable and convincing ideology for elites. Such insecurity may stifle originality and individuality among the members of the various elites no less than among the general public. Originality of behavior and outlook is often closely associated with homogeneity of values and background. Group solidarity makes for a degree of personal autonomy and individuality not otherwise possible. Members of established aristocracies have been distinguished by their close adherence to a group code and style of life as well as by their disregard or transcendence of this code. It remains to be seen how and whether the members of the various strategic elites will solve this problem of group allegiance and personal distinction.

7. THE SYMBOLIC ROLE OF STRATEGIC ELITES

▲

Society in general—not only Boston—may be defined as a state of mind that exists because and to the extent that men acknowledge it. Collective survival hangs on the thread of collective belief, and institutions are only as strong as the imaginations of their supporters. Social indifference or disbelief, more than active opposition, may undermine collective survival. One widely used antidote to this threat is for the guardians of the social order to clothe that order, its institutions and human representatives, in mystique and mystery. Collective rituals emphasize this precarious balance between life and death, birth and decay, by dramatizing miraculous achievements and triumphs over forces of destruction.

Love, power, and death—three main bonds of social solidarity—are used by groups to maintain the interest, attention, and support of their memberships. As long as men remain fascinated, the individual, the group, or the society wielding that fascination is able to assert itself. Every great leader thus relies on secrecy, every great teacher on leaving some things unexplained. And the best myths are those whose riddles remain unsolved. Elites, as guardians of collective life, similarly develop an aura of mystery and mystique, rooted in social distance, difference, and hierarchy.

Success in life demands the enactment of social roles that depend not only on deeds but on appropriate manners, gestures, and styles, that is, on symbols and promises. Merit is appreciated but so is "the appearance of merit," [1] and this last depends on symbolic skill and on the power to evoke appropriate public response. If this is true in general, it is particularly true for the strategic elites whose members must convey an image of superiority and merit for the sake of their public identities and for the creation of communal solidarity. "The rulers themselves," writes one authority, "benefited the country by their existence. They personified it, and their state of health and fortune affected its welfare; the ritual prohibitions to which they were all subject were intended, by preserving their own persons, to protect the country as a whole." [2] These rulers, or their modern counterparts, the strategic elites, are not only actors but social objects as well.

If the members of these elites are to be generally understood and followed, they must succeed in developing a public image which facilitates the symbolic exchange between themselves and their publics. Such an image is fostered by similarities in dress, manner, and modes of speech as well as by less tangible qualities reflecting upbringing, education, and career experiences. If their actions are to be comprehensible to a wide audience, they must be similarly interpreted by those to whom they appeal and their behavior must be fairly consistent with the image with which they are associated. The members of particular strategic elites thus will generally appear to be similar sorts of men. (Here, as elsewhere in social life, stereotyping is inevitable.) As a partial consequence, the social type recruited in each strategic elite tends to become patterned, for if symbols are to be socially effective they must be both general and familiar.

Strategic elites are both collective agents and collective symbols. In their role as agents, the instrumental aspect comes to the fore—how and how well they perform their leadership roles. In their symbolic roles, the expressive elements predominate—the sort of public impression they make. The warrior of old, in addition to being skilled in strategy and tactics, had also to look the part. A business tycoon of today must not only manage his firm but suggest through his appearance and bearing some of the characteristics to which success in business is conventionally attributed. Strategic elites are also social objects in at least three respects: as authority figures and decision-makers; as bearers of moral authority; and as men of renown, success, and distinction inspiring envy and emulation.[3]

Three kinds of collective symbols

Many writers have referred to the symbolic functions of elites. Maurice Halbwachs speaks of "the whole society" as being "concentrated in the emperor" or "certain individuals," arousing in others "faith in the Church, family feeling in the domestic group, political conviction in the parties." [4] Halbwachs thinks of this process, however, not in sociological but in social-psychological terms: particular individuals are seen to have special capacities or gifts for conveying the central tendencies of groups. We suggest that all strategic elites can convey this sense of the normative, irrespective of any individual gifts for so doing.

For analytical purposes, the social role of strategic elites as collective symbols may be divided into three parts—the cognitive, the moral, and the expressive. The cognitive refers to elites as technical experts and authorities who know what to do, and how to achieve given goals. Since the members of society cannot acquire first-hand familiarity with all the ways of the world, strategic elites as collective symbols are expected to provide such information by representing authoritative "know-how." Strategic elites also have *moral* roles—representing standards of right and wrong, these being no longer familiar to or shared by all the members of the collectivity. Finally, strategic elites have expressive roles as objects of love and hate, admiration and envy, emulation and resentment. The social solidarity upon which the ultimate fate of a society depends requires shared emotional attachments as well as shared goals and terminal values. Strategic elites become the collective symbols around which these attachments crystallize. They are expected to know, to judge, and to please. Their behavior is appraised in terms of its cognitive, moral, and expressive impact.[5]

The symbolic importance of elites is often referred to but generally this is taken to mean their role as moral arbiters or as representatives of traditions. The symbolic import of their cognitive and expressive behavior is largely ignored.[6] Yet, when strategic elites are as differentiated as they are today, this three-fold distinction becomes increasingly important since the different elites, in considerable measure, become specialized in these symbolic dimensions. In earlier types of social leadership groups, such as aristocracies or ruling classes, all three symbolic roles were fused to a greater degree.[7]

The symbolic cognitive role of strategic elites provides an authoritative frame of reference for the members of society and thus helps them interpret deeds and events affecting them. Individuals generally inform themselves about the details clearly affecting their own self-interest, but usually they do not have the time, opportunity, or inclination to investigate other aspects of social life. It is by observing the various strategic elites that members of society become more knowledgeable and informed about the several worlds around them.[8]

In their symbolic moral role, strategic elites reinforce social solidarity and moral behavior. Their public appearance generally stresses this moral aspect—perhaps to remind men of their common identity and destiny. And this moral identity has to be learned not once but many times.

> . . . as time goes by [writes Halbwachs] beliefs tend to grow feebler and opinion hazier, since they spread among a fairly passive human group not naturally disposed to make the necessary effort to grasp them. So there has to be a section of the group which is constantly reinforcing them, where they become clearer and more effective; and within this section certain individuals who concentrate these beliefs and opinions within themselves, and who hold them so strongly that they radiate out amongst the whole group. . . . It is always the role of a few to stand most clearly for common tendencies and to fortify these by their example at least.[9]

In short, organized societies require specially endowed and designated individuals to keep alive and strengthen the moral faith.

The expressive symbolism of strategic elites refers to the provision of intrinsic gratification to men, to the emotional responses they provoke and arouse. This is one of the most fascinating yet least understood problems concerning strategic elites. What is clear is that different societies encourage and create quite different expressive behavior. Compare the restraint and reticence of the British public servant with the informal, "democratic" approach of American business and political leaders. Societies also sometimes greatly change their modes of expressive responses from one generation to the next. In this sense, strategic elites like other collective creations provide clues to more fundamental collective dispositions and preferences. Which physical traits are highly valued or what manner of speech is most appreciated provides insight into widely shared aesthetic preferences and standards, standards which often become established with great rapidity. (Barely a few weeks after President Kennedy's assumption of office, the new First Lady became a national symbol of beauty and style.)

Strategic elites may also be considered as collective projections, serving as models and mirrors of the ambitions, hopes, and strivings of masses of men. Since models must exhibit virtues, apparent if not real, if they are to inspire emulation, strategic elites tend to represent the ideal aspects of their positions and activities. Members of the society have a great deal at stake in this emotional and symbolic investment, and miscalculations and errors, though "all too human," are not readily excused. The men at the top are expected to be more than human. Great expectations can easily turn into great grievances. People are dependent on strategic elites not only for those matters in which elites are commonly expected to excel but with respect to deep, and often unacknowledged, wishes and aspirations. Identifying with elites when things go well, they may turn swiftly against them when things go poorly, for what is at stake are the self-images of men and their longings for strength, courage, success, and acclaim. These collective projections thus include components expressive of the deeper need-dispositions of personalities, particularly those, according to Parsons, that are imperfectly integrated:

> Insecurity in the psychological sense is one of the persistent and ubiquitous aspects of the malintegration of social systems . . . in most social systems there are incompletely gratified needs to feel that "everything will be all right." It is very natural indeed that these needs should be projected on persons who occupy expressive leadership roles. There is, then, very generally an exaggerated trust or expectation that the leader will "take care of everything" in such cases.[10]

This dependence on elites can lead to exploitation and self-denial. It is not uncommon for people to suffer privations while their elites live in comfort and luxury. This situation occurs, in part at least, when the deprived identify with and *vicariously* partake in the advantages of the privileged. De Tocqueville, discussing political subordination, remarked:

> In some nations, the monarch is regarded as a personification of the country; and the fervor of patriotism being converted into the fervor of loyalty, they take a sympathetic pride in his conquests, and glory in his power. There was a time under the ancient monarchy when the French felt a sort of satisfaction in the sense of their dependence upon the arbitrary will of their king; and they were wont to say with pride: "We live under the most powerful king in the world." [11]

Identifying with the powerful, men rejoice over their triumphs and despair over their defeats even when they themselves stand neither to gain nor to lose—materially—therefrom.

Instrumental and symbolic functions

In addition to instrumental and moral differentiation among strategic elites, there is an important symbolic differentiation. Without the latter the boundaries among otherwise differentiated elites could hardly be maintained. Each elite, even when concerned primarily with highly instrumental activities, has a strong component of expressive symbolism.

This symbolism, serving as a short cut to communication between elites and the public (or the several publics) and among the elites themselves, is mediated by certain visible traits or signs on the basis of which a public identity is created and transmitted. In the past, this identity was fostered by differences in official attire. Sartorial distinctions still characterize the members of some elites—military officers, diplomats, religious leaders. But generally this distinction is no more, probably due to the availability of mass media such as newspapers and television, one of whose chief tasks is to establish the identity of public figures for their readers and viewers.

One of the few studies of the symbolic devices used by elites is William B. Brown's *The People's Choice*. It examines the image of presidential candidates in American election campaigns with some highly suggestive results. Using campaign biographies, the author traces this image from Washington to Kennedy. The candidate himself, his birthplace, parents, siblings, wife and children, professional colleagues, and friends—all are presented in a set of stereotypes combining wish-fulfillment with history. Concerning the candidate's ancestry, for example, there is considerable ambivalence about whether to stress the virtues of his hereditary stock or his achievement, but wherever possible ancestry is supplied and is usually traced back to pre-Revolutionary times. The campaign biographies of most candidates lay claim to "sturdy, tyranny hating Old World ancestors who battled in the cause of religious or political liberty." [12] Fathers tend to be civic models for their sons, mothers the epitome of Christian virtues. The ideal setting is that of rural America of the eighteenth century, though there have been some changes with time. The mother is now more intellectual, the father a companion to his son. But these innovations are grafted onto the older images. The candidate's campaign biography usually blends three traditionally reputable occupations by having the candidate participate in each in turn—farmer, lawyer, and businessman. Brown concludes that campaign biographies are not only propaganda but also a clue to the symbol of "the ideal citizen of the Republic."

> As he sits before the hearth in his own unpretentious house awaiting the verdict of the people, one sees a plain, simple man of modest means, surrounded by a dutiful, loving wife and adoring children, a man of practical good sense and boundless energy, a man of deep but unostentatious piety, of impeccable moral character, and of sturdy republican virtues—an enduring symbol of the ideals and aspirations of the Republic.[13]

Whether the candidates' lives do in fact conform to this image is not as important as whether they will be perceived as such and what happens when they do not conform. Collective symbolism has a good deal of leeway built into it, the image being so varied and many-sided that even if a candidate lacks one or two desirable traits he usually has high marks on others. His acts will tend to be interpreted not only in light of his official role and the demands currently made upon him, but also in terms of his symbolic relation to the traditional image, as the recipient of unfulfilled desires and needs of a collectivity that has fashioned its leaders in its own image.

Although the relative importance of these symbolic elements among elites requires further study, it is clear that they play a prominent role in two types of strategic elites generally neglected in sociological investigations—the recreational and the artistic. For these elites, the symbolic or expressive function is more significant socially than their moral or instrumental one. The recreational elite—the "celebrities" as C. Wright Mills calls them—are an interesting case in point. These stars of screen, television, and Café Society have a more important social role (which may not even be clearly perceived by them) than is usually attributed to them. They represent the self-indulgence, glamour, and exciting and romantic personal life desired in some degree by the members of their publics. The latter, with the help of private and public gossip, are apt to be familiar with minute and intimate details of the lives of their idols. The social position of the recreational elite in modern industrial societies is unique. In feudal society, this elite was closely associated with the political leaders and thus its social base was fairly secure. Today, as a differentiated elite relatively unattached to any center of power, it is subject to the vicissitudes of fashion and taste. The "idols of consumption," representing a kind of collective pleasure principle, are created as well as destroyed by sudden shifts of interest and attention. What arouses one generation leaves another one cold. Neither the reasons for these changes nor their social significance have been adequately analyzed, but systematic investigation might well provide clues to collective fantasies about pleasure, license, and luxury. The members of the recreational elite feel the precariousness of their positions, and sometimes go to great length to secure it against public fickleness. Many idols, in short, transform themselves into their public images, and some of them, we know, are individually ruined in the process.

The artistic elite, similarly without anchorage in a power group, represents quite different expressive traits, principally those associated with individual creativity, idiosyncrasy, and nonconformity to traditional values. As the recreational elite must largely conform to their public's conceptions of an exciting life, so the artistic elite is expected to conform to the popular image of creative nonconformity. Leading actors, critics, and writers have therefore been both dangerous and essential to the communities in which they lived—dangerous because originality implies nonconformity and nonconformity in most societies tends to be punished. When this nonconformity is practiced by members of a strategic elite, the problem is magnified. Conversely if social life and thought are to be renewed and fresh, these "dangerous" individuals are essential. Artistic, as well as the recreational, elites have thereby been simultaneously exalted and punished. In the social drama they are half heroes and half villains. Their gifts are envied and admired, but their morals are not above suspicion, and their originality or individuality often condemns them to unpopularity and public disapprobation.

Formally organized strategic elites, in which cognitive or moral aspects predominate, are likely to have the most clear-cut and restrictive public style with but little personal or individual variation. Members of elites that are more diffuse, relatively unorganized, and in which expressive traits are accentuated tend to be much freer to project their own individual personalities onto their public roles. In the first case, the institutional office and the person are less distinguishable, in the second, they are quite distinct. An elite may change its expressive character with time. The American business elite of the last century seems to have been much less uniform in visible external attributes than it is today when the image of the professional manager predominates.

Each strategic elite becomes a sort of anthropomorphic entity, an amalgam of social function, social ideal, and social need. They are mirrors of society into which the many project their desires for fortune or fame and in which the few flash back appropriate images. The public may be large and diversified as in expanding open class systems or small as in stable closed class systems, the needs may be intense or weak, and the elite images may be more or less adequate.

Symbolic reciprocity between strategic elites and their publics

The analysis of strategic elites requires not only an examination of their functional roles, their symbolic images, and their expressive and instrumental activities; it should also include consideration of their particular publics. Study of elites themselves as collective projections provides important clues about the publics they serve and represent.

Many observers, de Tocqueville and Simmel among them, have recognized that an often unacknowledged reciprocity exists between elites and other members of society. The latter look to the elites, usually not directly, but through a series of intermediary groups, as the embodiments of society's ideal values and as individuals crowned with success. In an open class system, elites symbolize the possibility of attaining the prizes of social life; in closed class systems, they demonstrate their "innate" superiority in alone having access to them.

This reciprocity between strategic elites and the rest of society may take unexpected forms as when unskilled workers vote for an ultraconservative candidate, or when soldiers gladly forfeit their lives in a war for their king, or when people wait for hours to catch a glimpse of the royal family. The nature of the bond and the bondage is then difficult to fathom. Elites wishing to retain their emotional and aesthetic appeal ought not, in short, to neglect their symbolic roles.

When elites do not effectively perform their instrumental functions—individually and collectively—they are displaced. The same holds true, though here we are on highly speculative ground, if they fail to fulfill their symbolic function by losing touch with the public's expectations or by breaking the bond between themselves and their followers.

Something of this kind befell the Boston Brahmins. Their financial influence and economic position are still substantial, but they play a minor role in the public life of Massachusetts today (the Saltonstalls and Lodges being notable exceptions). Their snobbish exclusion of the Irish and Italian immigrants, their aloofness and indifference to people with alien customs and tastes, deprived them of their role as dominant status models of the community. With fewer people to imitate them and look to them as dominant social arbiters and exemplars of distinction, their demise was inevitable. The rejected Irish and Italians, producing their own models and social codes, pushed the Yankee blue-bloods aside. Today, the "Proper Bostonians," still economically powerful as a class, are social anachronisms, isolated from the pulse of the community.

Similarly, Mosca notes the harmony between serfs and their lords in the Middle Ages when both lived side by side on the same estate, often taking their meals together, and freely exchanging ideas and opinions. This harmony dissolved in hostility once these lords assumed definite "social airs." It was not the material advantages of the lords that incurred bitterness in their serfs, for they were wealthier, better dressed, and in command of the situation in either case. What was considered inexcusable was the lords' attempt to set themselves apart by adopting the manners of the Court and imitating its style of life. The privileges of the lords had been accepted by the serfs on the ground of the formers' greater responsibilities, but the serfs were not willing to grant them superior personal dignity and self-respect. When the lords broke the implicit reciprocity by patterning themselves after a new model, the serfs grew openly resentful. Elites, in effect, must be not only responsible but responsive to the members of society.[14]

Reciprocity between elites and their publics does not imply, of course, an identity of aims and actions. Members of elites often come up from the ranks, represent their publics, and are bound to them, but they differ from their publics: strategic elites are socially superior, they act and decide for all, and they often risk the lives of others. Their failures and successes are thus more visible, their failings more reprehensible, and their virtues more splendid.

Reciprocity between elites and other members of society may be obscured by institutionalization and routinization. Once institutions have been firmly established, specific individuals assume leadership roles, but they may or may not be ideally suited for them. And while their personal characteristics are of public interest they usually do not affect the institution itself substantially. Nevertheless the reciprocal tie, the symbolic link, continues to exist. This tie can be simulated and manufactured in a large, differentiated society more readily than in a small, intimate community. As societies expand, there is a tendency to accept *obiter dicta* if they come from what the public considers the right source. This is so, partially, because of ignorance about the details of various aspects of organized social life, and, partially, because, as Chester I. Barnard has described it, the "zone of indifference" seems to become larger.[15] Indifference accompanies ignorance.

Strategic elites, as collective symbols, are largely the products of the societies in which they function. The individuals "who seem the most active of all," writes Halbwachs, "the only truly active members of the group have been shaped by it in its own image . . . and all their originality and prestige derive from the fact that they concentrate within themselves a larger part than most of the collective representations, and can hold them for a longer time." [16] Durkheim insists that the authority of the socially powerful must be sought not in their character but in the nature of the societies which they rule and influence. "As for the personal superiority of the chief," he writes, "it plays only a secondary role in this process. It explains why the collective force is concentrated in his hands rather than in some others, but does not explain its intensity." [17]

Men become emotionally involved with their elites whose members they consider to be both like and superior to themselves.[18] This complex bond has been observed in many types of leader-led or superior-inferior relationships. De Tocqueville points out that the mutual regard binding masters and servants is based on the fact that each fills a position he can neither relinquish nor lose. On the one side are obscurity, poverty, and obedience for life, and on the other fame, wealth, and command for life. The two are distinct and inextricably tied.[19] Simmel probably meant this when he wrote that in "innumerable cases, the master is the slave of his slaves." All leaders are also led, for they depend on their followers as much as these depend on them. The absence of this reciprocity accounts for the particularly oppressive tyranny exercised by a group over its individual members.[20] Slaves or servants, in turn, often imagine themselves in their masters' place and so mitigate the facts of subordination by fantasies of superiority. As Michels has noted, the chosen of the people appear to be the creatures of the people, and this is agreeable to "the *amour propre* of every citizen who says to himself: 'Without me he would not be what he is; I have elected him; he belongs to me.' " [21]

The symbolic relationship between elites and followers may be observed more clearly in small groups involving direct leader-follower interaction. Findings from such studies are suggestive in this connection, though they cannot replace macroscopic analysis. Fritz Redl, for example, following a line of thought initiated by Freud, who saw the "leader" as one around whom group processes crystallize, utilized children's groups to demonstrate that such crystallizations can take some ten different forms, and that not all of these result in leader-follower relationships. According to Redl, there are many ways of reacting to the central person—the group may view him as an object of identification based either on love or fear, or as an object of loving or aggressive drives, or as an object of ego support, and so on.[22] Redl limits his observations to small informal children's groups and is careful not to apply his findings to larger social aggregates, but his approach may be useful in the study of the social psychology of strategic elites.

Thus different spheres may "create" and reward different personality types among the strategic elites, for each elite tends to be associated with a distinctive type of collective projection. The President of the United States probably is often loved as a kind of ego ideal, whereas a major corporation president does not need to be "lovable" but powerful, efficient, and effective. Some generals evoke more fear than affection among their followers; great writers or artists sustain fantasies of individual autonomy, license, and freedom among their admirers. The larger the number of strategic elites, the greater the variety of collective projections and identifications. Moral demands may be satisfied by identification with priests and philosophers; aggressive dispositions by army leaders or agitators; unconventional desires by recreational celebrities; possibly, criminal dispositions by powerful gangsters. Study along these lines might reveal a good deal about the motives that play a part in inducing particular individuals to assay this or that elite status. The corporation executive who does not expect to be loved may be more adequate in his role than one who does.

It would be interesting to pursue these speculations more systematically in a context in which both the collective expectations and individual motivations among the incumbents of strategic elites are relatively accessible—especially in smaller communities where the interplay between collective projections and elite characteristics is more direct and visible. The individual's personality probably plays a more important role in small than in large groups. As groups expand, relationships become less personal, and leadership becomes not so much an attribute of personality as a quality of a role within a specified social context.[23] Leaders in small groups must be able to perform many functions similar in certain respects to those we have assigned to strategic elites, such as symbolizing the ideals of the members, assessing the opinions of members on issues relevant to the group, and maintaining group traditions.[24] In Charles Horton Cooley's words, a leader must "be a great deal of a man." He must be emotionally and intellectually superior to as well as in tune with the rest. He must transcend the limits of the group and yet adapt himself to the feelings and needs of the members. If he succeeds, his fame and power may even transcend himself. A "function of the great and famous man is to be a symbol, and the real question in other minds is not so much, Who are you?, as, what can I believe that you are? What can you help me feel and be? How far can I use you as a symbol in the development of my instinctive tendency?" [25]

The reciprocity between leaders and led, between elites and their publics, works both ways. It affects the perceptions and evaluations of the leaders as well as those of the led. In their assumption of elite roles, leaders often project their own expectations and desires onto the public, exacting a degree of voluntary submissiveness quite inconsistent with other aspects of social reality. In their desire to be able to "count" on their various publics, they tend to appraise them as less knowledgeable and more loyal than is in fact the case.[26] This is a subject largely unexplored by social scientists. Little is known about the projections made by publics onto their elites, but even less is known about the projections of elites onto their publics.

Symbols and sentiments

Public reactions to elites are marked by ambivalence despite the fact that people identify with and admire them. There is what Michels called the "political gratitude" of the public, the gratitude felt by the crowd for those who speak and write on their behalf. If the members of the public are not grateful, argued Michels, it is a sign that they are torn by competing loyalties.[27] Yet, as Simmel realized, the ruler is in some measure

> almost always an adversary. Man has an intimate dual relation to the principle of subordination. On the one hand he wants to be dominated. The majority of men not only *cannot* exist without leadership; they also *feel* that they cannot; they *seek* the higher power which relieves them of responsibility; they seek a restrictive, regulatory rigor which protects them not only against the outside world but also against themselves. But no less do they need opposition to the leading power, which only through this opposition, through move and countermove, as it were, attains the right place in the life pattern of those who obey it.[28]

Strategic elites are ambivalent symbols because they represent both an ideal difficult to attain and real groups with visible privileges. The balance between admiration and envy is an uneasy one, as people covet or renounce the prizes of life, resenting or identifying with those who have obtained them. Yet, the need to approve and admire often prevails over the need to reject and condemn. For strategic elites are also visible symbols of social continuity, representing a society's hard won and precarious solutions to the pressing problems of life. This, together with vicarious identification, makes for, though it does not guarantee, the triumph of admiration over envy.

People seek a part of themselves in the social mirrors displayed by their elites, and they hope to encounter a flattering, gratifying reflection. This may help to account for the persistence of inefficient, ineffective, and abusive elites. Once an elite type has become firmly entrenched, public attachment and identification tend to preclude a sober, dispassionate appraisal. People come to judge their elites as they would judge themselves in their place: they make allowances and excuses and draw the veil of illusion over their eyes. Throughout history, elites have lingered on long after their actual reign has ended, living in the memories of men they never knew. As with King Arthur, so with many great men immortalized in legend:

> Yet it is not the King Arthur of history—whether he wore a toga and fought in Roman crest and breastplate or was merely a savage Celtic

> chieftain who triumphed over heathen invaders little more savage than himself—with whom we are concerned today. It is the King Arthur of legend, who was created by poets hundreds of years after his death from fragmentary memories handed by word of mouth.[29]

It is as collective symbols that strategic elites survive long after their deeds and misdeeds have ceased to matter. By knowing them we come to know some of the secrets of history, some of the buried longings of peoples.

Notes

1. Hugh Dalziel Duncan, *Communication and Social Order* (1962), p. 209. Duncan's discussion of the symbols of social hierarchy is highly suggestive. See esp. pp. 179-245.
2. Lucy Mair, *Primitive Government* (1962), p. 180.
3. This distinction runs through much of the classic and contemporary writings in sociology. See, e.g., W. I. Thomas and Florian Znaniecki, *The Polish Peasant in Europe and America,* 5 vols. (1918-1920); Charles Horton Cooley, *Human Nature and the Social Order,* rev. ed., (1922); Robert M. MacIver and Charles H. Page, *Society: An Introductory Analysis* (1949); and most recently, Talcott Parsons, "An Approach to Psychological Theory in Terms of the Theory of Action," in Sigmund Koch (ed.), *Psychology: The Study of a Science,* III (1959), pp. 612-711.
4. Maurice Halbwachs, *The Psychology of Social Classes* (1958), p. 17.
5. For the background of this three-fold distinction, see Talcott Parsons, *The Social System* (1951), pp. 142 ff. See also, S. M. Lipset, "Political Sociology," in R. K. Merton *et al.* (eds.), *Sociology Today* (1959), pp. 81-115. Lipset differentiates between the "effectiveness" and the "legitimacy" of a political system but omits its appeal.
6. This is true, for example, of all the papers on the newly emerging African elites in: "African Elites," *International Social Science Bulletin,* VIII (1956).
7. Thus, for example, De Tocqueville remarks: "In aristocratic societies the class that gives the tone to opinion and has the guidance of affairs, being permanently and hereditarily placed above the multitude, naturally conceives a lofty idea of itself and of man. It loves to invent for him noble pleasures, to carve out splendid objects for his ambition. Aristoc-

racies often commit very tyrannical and inhuman actions but they rarely entertain groveling thoughts . . . the effect is to raise greatly the general pitch of society." Alexis de Tocqueville, *Democracy in America,* II, 45. See also Max Weber, "National Character and the Junkers," in Gerth and Mills (eds.), *Essays* (1946), pp. 386-95. Weber deplores the lack of just such an aristocracy in Germany and the impossibility of using the social form of German gentility "to mold and unify the nation in its gesture as a *Herrenvolk.* . . ."

8. This authoritative function of strategic elites resembles an earlier function of religion, one it has to this day in more primitive societies. "Another important function of religion may be the provision of authority for belief and action. Unity of action in ritual assembly and on other occasions is not merely suggested by the religious patterns. It is enjoined. A particular type of order in the social universe is not merely offered as a solution to the problems of divergent aims. It is presented as the only true solution, and the only one which is morally acceptable. . . . The authority function of religion removes the dilemma of choice from many social situations which would otherwise be embarrassing. For this it substitutes the notion of rightness. . . . One of the methods of reinforcing adherence to the authority is to endow its modern representatives with more than ordinary human powers." Raymond Firth, "Religion and Social Reality," in William A. Lessa and Evon Z. Vogt (eds.), *Reader in Comparative Religion* (1958), pp. 124-33.
9. Maurice Halbwachs, *op. cit.,* p. 17.
10. Talcott Parsons, *The Social System* (1951), p. 403. Note that Parsons confines the projection of collective needs of this type to those in expressive leadership roles. In our view, such projections are typical for all leadership roles among the strategic elites. See also *ibid.,* pp. 399 ff., where Parsons discusses the instrumental and the expressive aspects of leadership roles.
11. Alexis de Tocqueville, *Democracy in America,* I, 251. Cf. also Durkheim's observation that societies acquire self-awareness through their governments. Suppress the Roman patriciate, he says in effect, and the city of antiquity is no more. Without loyalty to the monarch or to the feudal lord, the societies do not exist, and "could not maintain themselves." Emile Durkheim, *Socialism and Saint-Simon* (1958), p. 148.
12. William Burlie Brown, *The People's Choice, The Presidential Image in the Campaign Biography* (1960), pp. 144-5.
13. *Ibid.*
14. Gaetano Mosca, *The Ruling Class* (1939), Chap. iv. See also Durkheim's remarks regarding the absence of conflict between capital and labor during the Middle Ages when the two were "almost on an equal footing." Emile Durkheim, *The Division of Labor in Society* (1947), p. 353.
15. Chester I. Barnard, *The Functions of the Executive* (1950), pp. 168 ff. "Zone of indifference" is the expression used by Barnard to describe the limits within which orders are accepted without conscious questioning as to their acceptability by those who must follow these orders.
16. Maurice Halbwachs, *op. cit.,* p. 19.
17. Emile Durkheim, *op. cit.,* p. 196.
18. Halbwachs has expressed this as follows: ". . . mankind's thought needs to embody itself in human beings of its own kind, but which it

imagines far above itself in intelligence and instincts, to embody these very tendencies in them as though they were both their trustees and their source." *Op. cit.,* p. 17. Trotsky, in his description of the reasons for Miliukov's failings as the leader of the Russian Kadet Party after the Revolution, explicitly uses a mirror-image: "The everyday bourgeois did not like Miliukov because Miliukov too prosaically and soberly, without adornment, expressed the political essence of the Russian bourgeoisie. Beholding himself in the Miliukov mirror, the bourgeois saw that he was gray, self-interested, and cowardly and, as so often happens, he took offense at the mirror." Leon Trotsky, *The History of the Russian Revolution,* I (1960), p. 189.

19. The social-psychological processes involved here are highly interesting. The identification between master and servant makes the master look at his servant as an inferior part of himself, whereas the servant over-identifies with the master, assuming his personality and his privileges in fantasy because he considers him a superior part of himself. De Tocqueville, in fact, suggests that one profound distinction between the "American Democracy" and other forms of government is that the reciprocal tie between superiors and inferiors has been broken. There is no bond between rich and poor, they being connected neither by habit nor duty. The "manufacturing aristocracy" is accordingly more likely to make use of the working population than to govern it and guide it. Alexis de Tocqueville, *Democracy in America,* II, 190. See also the well-known discussion of the master-slave relationship by Georg Friedrich Hegel, in J. N. Findlay, *Hegel: A Reexamination* (1962), Chap. iv.
20. Simmel, with his usual keen insight into group processes, is led to remark that the lower the social standing of a group, the less likely it will allow one of its own members to rule it, whereas the higher its social standing, the more likely that one of its members (or peers) is permitted to assume this role. Where everyone has a low image of himself and of his peers, none will be found suitable to pass judgment on the rest, but where everyone has a high opinion of himself and his equals, all can pass such judgment. Kurt Wolff (ed.), *The Sociology of Georg Simmel* (1950), p. 219.
21. Robert Michels, *op. cit.,* p. 220. See also pp. 62 ff. Cf. the remark by Odin: "It is Molière, and no other, who wrote the great plays which so to say *all of France dictated to him.*" A. Odin, *Genese des Grands Hommes* (1895), p. 134. Italics supplied.
22. Fritz Redl, "Group Emotion and Leadership," in A. Paul Hare, E. F. Borgatta, and R. F. Bales (eds.), *Small Groups* (1955), pp. 71-86.
23. Some relevant points are made by Cecil A. Gibb, "The Principles and Traits of Leadership," *ibid.,* pp. 87-95. Leadership, notes Gibbs, "is not usually an enduring role unless an organization is built up which enables an individual to retain the role after he ceases to be qualified for it. In this case leadership becomes domination or mere headship" (p. 89).

The unconscious bond between leaders and followers is all too often interpreted as a one-sided dependency of followers on the leader. In particular, the leader's paternal qualities are accentuated, frequently to the exclusion of other types of qualities. This may be true as regards kings or powerful chiefs but not of all types of leaders. Not all leaders are "father figures," although some may be, and perhaps all were at some point in the past when patriarchal institutions were stronger. Similarly with the members of various elites. Some symbolize authority; others, license; and still others, human generosity. For a sensitive discussion that nevertheless stresses the paternalistic element, see Sebastian de Grazia, *The Political Community* (1948), p. 114.

24. Kamla Chowdhry and Theodore M. Newcomb, "The Relative Abilities of Leaders and Non-Leaders to Estimate Opinions of Their Own Groups," in Hare *et al., Small Groups, op. cit.,* pp. 235-45. See also Ferenc Merei, "Group Leadership and Institutionalization," in E. E. Maccoby, T. M. Newcomb, and E. G. Hartley (eds.), *Readings in Social Psychology* (1958), p. 525. A good summary of the characteristics needed by leaders to perform their leadership roles is contained in George C. Homans, *The Human Group* (1950), Chap. xvi. For a discussion of a number of small group studies, see Michael Olmsted, *The Small Group* (1959).
25. Charles Horton Cooley, *Human Nature and the Social Order* (1902), Chaps. viii, ix. See also Richard T. Morris and Melvin Seeman, "The Problem of Leadership: An Interdisciplinary Approach," *American Journal of Sociology,* LVI (September 1950), 149-56.

    Not all the members of strategic elites are leaders, but some of them are and perhaps more of them should be. Those who are not leaders may be experts in particular fields of endeavor. Others may be wielders of legitimate power, that is, authorities. Some men may be all three. All members of strategic elites must be at least one. For a good analysis of these three forms of social superiority, see Robert Bierstedt, "The Problem of Authority," in Morroe Berger, Theodore Abel, and Charles H. Page (eds.), *Freedom and Control in Modern Society* (1954), pp. 67-82.
26. In a study of American military life during the Second World War, it was found that officers tended to overestimate the favorable and underestimate the unfavorable reactions of enlisted men toward Army life and toward themselves. Samuel Stauffer *et al., The American Soldier,* I, 396 ff. See also Robert Michels, *Political Parties,* p. 68, where he discusses the "megalomania" of leaders as a result of the adulation surrounding them.
27. Robert Michels, *op. cit.,* p. 60.
28. Kurt Wolff (ed.), *The Sociology of Georg Simmel, op. cit.,* p. 193.
29. Arthur Bryant, "Camelot's King: Man and Myth," *New York Times Magazine,* December 11, 1960.

8. RECRUITMENT, RESPONSIBILITIES, AND REWARDS

▲

Two sets of conditions bring the perennial problem of the recruitment of strategic elites to the forefront of collective attention: when societies undergo rapid changes and need new men with new skills on short notice; and when the incumbents of elite positions fall short in the performance of their tasks. The second situation often is related to the first. New needs exacerbate leadership inadequacies of long standing, and thus press for organizational changes in recruitment and selection.

Prevalent patterns of recruitment to the leading positions in politics, in science, in recreation, and in industry reflect the strains between two irreconcilable tendencies in social life—the need for order and the need for change. If the social leadership becomes so conservative as to be immune to new ideas and social developments, the pressure of unfulfilled needs mounts until that leadership declines, resigns, or is violently displaced. If it is so receptive to the new as to neglect established traditions, social continuity is endangered. Whatever balance is achieved between these two tendencies is usually short-lived.

As the preceding chapters indicated, modern industrial societies are characterized by a growing autonomy among the four functional spheres—goal attainment, adaptation, integration, and morale—and by a growing moral, instrumental, and symbolic differentiation among the strategic elites. As a result of a growth in size, specialization, and formal organization, strategic elites have grown in number and in variety. Because of the premium placed on skill and experience, strategic elites are increasingly becoming nonhereditary, functionally specific, and non-permanent. The chief legitimate principle of selection today is proven merit of a particular, delimited sort. Whether this merely reflects the current technological transition from the machine age to the atomic age, it is too soon to tell. In the foreseeable future, however, this pattern is likely to prevail.

In the following pages we shall review four main aspects of elite recruitment and selection: What attributes are considered desirable? Where are the candidates possessing these attributes to be found? What mechanisms are available to obtain the desirable candidates? How can desirable candidates be attracted? The answers to these questions will provide clues to patterns of social mobility in a society during given periods, to how open or closed the "top" is considered to be, how accessible or inaccessible are the channels to the top, and for whom, and what people in general expect regarding their own chances to climb the heights and how satisfied they are with their progress toward this goal.

Historically, two main principles of recruitment to strategic elite positions have contended with each other or have shared an uneasy truce. One principle is based upon the presumed superiority of biological and social inheritance. The other stresses achievement and demonstrated merit in one or a series of tasks, such as skill in war, appropriating possessions, or passing examinations. These two principles are integrated, in varying ways, into the basic value systems of societies, permeating their institutions and their notions about human perfectability, the possibilities for a better life, and the desirability of change. Analytically it is therefore possible to distinguish between sets of values that morally approve or condemn individual competition for the prizes of social life. These moral preferences do not appear to occur at random; they often reflect objective opportunities and limitations. Where the social strata are conceived of as fairly fluid (usually because they are still in process of formation), social mobility, especially upward mobility, seems right and proper. Where they are fairly fixed, such mobility seems undesirable. The moral attitude toward social mobility may be independent of its actual occurrence, however, for as is well known, a limited sort of mobility exists even under caste systems.[1] It is rather the desire for and the reaction to such mobility that may be expected to vary as moral emphases vary. In the more rigid system the parvenu tends to hide his humble origins; in the more fluid one he may boast of them. Since moral perspectives do not always correspond to actual conditions, the inadequate feed-back between social ideals and social realities permits the existence of social mobility without moral sanction, or its absence despite such sanctions.

The democratic ethos notwithstanding, competition, achievement, and mobility are desirable or undesirable not on rational but on moral grounds. "A philanthropist," writes Mosca, "would certainly be tempted to inquire whether mankind is happier—or less unhappy—during periods of social stability or crystallization when everyone is almost fated to remain in the social station to which he was born, or during directly opposite periods of renovation and revolution, which permit all to aspire to the most exalted positions and some to attain them." [2] Both the inquiry and the answer, he adds, would be difficult.

The accessibility of strategic elites depends on certain features of the social organization—the size, the extent and amount of the division of labor, the relative rate of technological and economic growth—as well as its system of values. And all of these act and react on each other, a change in any one of them having repercussions on the rest. When a society is in process of expansion, because of internal differentiation or external conquests or contacts, upward mobility is necessary lest this expansion be thwarted. Such societies stress the desirability of upward mobility and its imputed advantages for the individuals. But once a plateau has been reached—usually at some point of diminishing returns—the opposite tendency emerges.

Some social mobility exists in all societies; what varies is its extent, its amount, and its moral definition. Likewise, all societies contain tendencies toward social crystallization. The two are not mutually exclusive but competing principles. Just as aristocratic societies despite their emphasis on station and birth permit the rise of "inferior" men, by ennobling them, marrying them, or in other ways buying them, so achievement-oriented societies exhibit the aristocratic tendencies they officially condemn.

Desirable attributes

Mosca and others have defined elites according to their possession of some attribute, real or apparent, by virtue of which their decisions and actions carry weight. These attributes vary from society to society and from generation to generation, but they may be classified into three main types: *ascribed, achieved,* and *functional.* Ascribed attributes refer to characteristics which differentiate individuals but which they are powerless to produce in themselves, such as sex, color, and age. Achieved attributes—honor, wealth, or popularity—may be attained by individuals through their own efforts. Some persons are more successful in this than others, but, apart from the "injustice" in nature's distribution of gifts, individuals do have some control over their fate. Functional attributes refer to characteristics associated with particular contributions to an ongoing social process—leadership, creativity, problem-solving, efficiency, or combinations of these. These attributes characterize not the individuals as a whole but the particular roles they assume.[3] The individual who is elected President or pope is assigned the qualities that a President or a pope presumably should have irrespective of the qualities he actually possesses.

These three types of attributes may coincide empirically even though they must be kept distinct analytically. The American business elite is at once a functional elite—in that it supervises the production of economic goods and services, an elite of achievement —in that its members did not inherit their positions, and an elite of ascription—in that its members are typically male, white, and middle aged. In this case, as in more and more cases in modern industrial societies, a new balance is emerging between ascription, achievement, and performance, reflecting changed and changing ideas of what constitutes merit. Increasingly one asks not, "Who is this person?" but "What has he done?"

Which criteria are emphasized for the different elite positions depends upon specific functional, moral, and technical needs and the talents available to satisfy them. The American business elite today is generally recruited from among those with the necessary technical qualifications, but its members are also selected according to the "moral fitness" of the candidates and their perceived capacity to uphold rather than undermine the moral climate in large-scale industrial organizations. The medieval Catholic Church was primarily interested in the moral qualities of available candidates but also appreciated their competence in handling men and ideas and their missionary zeal. Individuals sometimes consider themselves members of an elite merely because they possess one of the three types of elite attributes—maleness, say, or higher education, or wealth. But it is never a single attribute that distinguishes strategic elites; it is rather a combination of the three.[4]

All societies expect their elites to be committed to the general social and moral framework as well as to the specific norms of the institutional sphere in which they operate. Without such moral commitments, societies are endangered at their most vulnerable point: the relativity of all values—a relativity which only a firm faith can counteract. Consider Mannheim's observations regarding the Soviet Union. He saw that although the Soviet Union had managed to eliminate social class as a recruitment factor to its ruling core (it was the only industrial society, he claimed, to have done so), it had not solved the problem of moral continuity at the top levels. In the absence of hereditary succession, the political loyalty test is used to obtain such continuity, but in the process, new problems of inequality and exploitation emerged.[5]

An important fact concerning criteria of recruitment to strategic elites is whether they are finite or infinite. Land is clearly a finite criterion for there is only so much of it, and if recruitment to elites is confined to those possessing land, all those without it are excluded in advance. When someone acquires land, moreover, someone else loses it. The same situation holds for the sale and purchase of offices and commissions.

Criteria such as the possession of money, skills, and certain kinds of education are clearly not of the same order, because there is no preordained upper limit to them. One's possession of money or a skill does not prevent another from also having it. Consequently, those who are excluded from potential access to top positions are not as likely to blame the social system and will not as readily turn their resentments against it; they are more apt to blame successful individuals rather than the rules of success. In the

United States, where the absence of strong class feeling against the existing economic order among the relatively deprived has puzzled both foreign and native observers, resentment generally turns against individual capitalists not capitalism. This is partly due to a general belief in equality of opportunity. But this viewpoint is also strengthened by the absence of an unambiguous measure of actual opportunity, and the belief that one man's success need not deprive another, at least no specific other.

Both ancient and modern societies, despite significant differences in their social make-up, have demanded some proof of the excellence of their strategic elites. But while most moderns agree that "governors should excel their subjects," they no longer define excellence as comprehensively as did Aristotle, the author of this view. Today it is not general virtue that is sought but a particular virtue, not general wisdom but a special kind of wisdom. Virtue, loyalty, and ability are still considered to be desirable traits of leaders, but there is disagreement as to where these are to be found. In part this reflects the fact that the ancient and modern societies differ in the distribution of these qualities, in part, that ideologies as to who possesses such qualities have changed. In pre-industrial societies, the virtues of leadership were attributed to certain strata linked by kinship ties; in industrial societies the link between blood and ability has been severed, and these virtues are no longer believed to be concentrated in any single group.

The search for candidates

For hereditary elites the problem of locating candidates is relatively simple—they produce them. For nonhereditary elites the problem is more complex and historical solutions of it have varied. When strategic elites are functionally fused, a single social stratum can usually be counted on to supply the necessary personnel, through birth or through some other means. But when strategic elites are functionally differentiated, as in industrial societies, any one group is rarely an adequate source of supply for all elites—though some group affiliations are preferable, hence more advantageous, than others, resulting in the informal exclusion of certain groups. With more positions open than there are candidates to fill them, social restrictions are apt to be minimal; where there are fewer positions than candidates, restrictions are apt to be relatively severe.

In pre-industrial societies with sharply drawn social boundaries, access to elite positions was limited to special groups not because birth and wealth were considered to be the ultimate tests of merit but because the well-born or wealthy were expected to possess the desired attributes of leadership to a greater extent than other groups.[6] In a class-stratified social system, certain personal and social qualities tend to go hand in hand, and for certain types of elites, this fact is significant. Barnard observes that in big-business organizations, status compatibility within and outside the organization must be maintained for effective functioning of the organization:

> Where in a general society a low status is assigned based, e.g., on race, nationality, sex, age, education, ownership of property, or family, it is difficult in general to acquire high status in formal organizations in that society; and where there is high social status it tends to facilitate high organization status, though less so in democratic than in aristocratic societies.[7]

Barnard is saying in effect that big-business executives typically are selected from those groups enjoying a generally high status in the society—white, native born, college educated, upper middle class males—which, as we shall see in the next chapter, is exactly the case in the United States. This particular set of attributes, however, is not directly associated with the scientific and artistic elites. Thus Barnard's observation of elites does not hold for all. In fact, elite recruitment from a limited circle of men united by ties of ancestry and wealth is not typical of industrial societies. Just as no single criterion is adequate for the placement of persons into strategic elite positions, so no single group can supply all potential candidates for these elites. This calls for an extension of the base from which elites are selected and of the groups from which they are drawn.

The membership of strategic elites today, as compared with earlier times, is more representative of the society. But elites continue to comprise select minorities, and are not necessarily elites recruited from more liberal than within a narrower segment of the social order. As Mosca has shown, democratic recruitment is compatible with autocracy, and aristocratic recruitment with liberalism. The Roman Catholic Church makes its decisions autocratically without consulting the broad membership, yet recruits new members from the rank and file. In Great Britain, liberalism and the recruitment of strategic elites from restricted social circles go hand in hand. The ancient city-states extended suffrage to all male citizens, but office holding was confined to select groups of families. Suffrage is universal in modern industrial societies, but access to some strategic elites is often informally restricted to the higher social classes.

Selecting desirable candidates

Once relevant criteria are determined and the group boundaries delineated, the problem remains of how to select the actual from the potential candidates for elite membership. At least seven different selective mechanisms have been used historically: (1) *Biological reproduction*—as incorporated in hereditary monarchical systems, which may or may not be combined with male dominance and primogeniture. (2) *Co-optation*—whereby an elite chooses its successors, as in the case of governing boards of many corporations.[8] (3) *Election*—selection by a large heterogeneous population united by formal legal ties from among alternative candidates, as in modern democracies; as well as selection by an already highly elevated group of one of its members for high office, as in the choice of a king by the nobility or the election of a pope by the College of Cardinals. (4) *Selection by rote*—whereby individuals are chosen according to a fixed numerical principle. If the group is small enough, every member may hold office in turn, as in some university departments with rotating chairmanships. In other organizations, every tenth or hundredth person may be chosen. Selection by rote implies a certain equivalence among members of a group—either with respect to the presumably equal distribution of capacities necessary for given offices or the assumed irrelevance of special talents for such offices. Thus Simmel calls the reforms of Cleisthenes, who instituted a Council of 500 members composed of fifty men from each of the ten *phyles,* "one of the greatest historical innovations." "The rational idea of constituting a representative body out of the total group, on a wholly numerical basis, transcends the stage of development characterized by the 'century' . . . for the first time in history the purely numerical division is used for establishing governmental units as symbols of the population." [9] (5) *Purchase of elite positions*—a prominent procedure used in France and China during some periods; exists where diploma qualifications for office prevail. (6) *Forcible appropriation*—as when men usurp political power, wealth, or symbols of prestige or excellence. (7) *Training and formal preparation for elite positions*—a mechanism found in both earlier and present-day societies. The Chinese literati or Mandarins were chosen from among the successful candidates in the open examinations for the Chin-Shih degree, with the winners of the highest degree obtaining the highest offices; the examination system was essentially a selection and not an appointment device for there was always a number of successful candidates who did not assume offices.[10] Such selection, however, is not identical with specialized training for elite positions. The latter is illustrated (in utopian terms) by the guardians of Plato's *Republic* who were to be trained from birth for their later elite duties. The Incas provided a similar formal and specialized education for the members of the nobility and the monarchy. Contemporary societies do not generally train individuals for specific elite roles from birth but rather select them—although in some cases such selection proceeds early enough so as to qualify under both patterns.[11] Selection on the basis of examination is becoming an important method of choosing potential leaders for certain leadership positions in industrial societies. It is also gaining ground in some of the developing countries where education is viewed as the chief vehicle of progress. In parts of Africa, many adults want their children to enter "intellectual professions" rather than business—so highly valued, at least until recently, by many parents in Western societies.[12]

These seven mechanisms of selection may be grouped into three general procedures: hereditary succession, appointment from the top, and election from below. What may be inherited varies. In aristocracies it is a general social status; in caste systems, a specific occupation along with a general moral status; and in class systems, property and access to educational opportunities. Concerning appointment, men may be chosen for special skills or for evidence of certain moral commitments. Election may be either formal as in the case of the political elite in the Western democracies or informal as in the arts and entertainment sphere where the audience registers its sentiment by accepting or rejecting a particular artist or performer.

More than two thousand years ago Aristotle summarized the fundamental principles of elite recruitment and selection. It is both a tribute to his genius and an indication that some things have remained about the same over a wide span of history that these principles still have considerable validity.

> I will now inquire into appointments to offices. The varieties depend on three terms, and the combinations of these give all possible modes: first, who appoints? secondly, from whom? and thirdly, how? Each of these admits of three variations: (A) All the citizens, or (B) only some, appoint. Either (1) the magistrates are chosen out of all or (2) out of some who are distinguished either by a property qualification, or by birth, or by merit, or for some special reason, as at Megara only those were eligible who had returned from exile and fought together against the democracy. They may be appointed either (a) by vote or (b) by lot.[13]

We would add only two points to Aristotle's original three. In addition to asking who shall choose the members of each strategic elite, from among whom, and how, we would also ask on the basis of what attributes are they chosen and for how long.

With respect to each of these several points there is no comprehensive procedure that would include all of the strategic elites of industrial societies. Some elites stress ancestry, others educational attainments, still others long experience and training. Some elites are elected, others appointed, and others born to their positions. No single attribute is generally advantageous, and no single selection mechanism applies to all. The members of some elites have relatively short tenure while that of others is lifelong. Occupational and educational achievements of distinction are still concentrated in the higher classes, but that does not alter the more important fact that the link between social class and access to strategic elites has become in many societies indirect and informal. Ascribed attributes have in general decreased in importance while achieved and functional attributes have increased.

These changes surely are generally perceived in modern societies, for people are usually alert to their opportunities even when, as often happens, they fail to make use of them. These changes have stirred new hopes in the hearts of many of those who were once categorically excluded from getting to the very top. These observations suggest the following note of caution.

The decline of heredity and the rise of individual achievement as principles of recruitment have increased opportunities to gain access to strategic elite positions. But the absolute number of individuals that can belong to any of these elites is still very limited. Strategic elites continue to be small, select minorities; the majority of men continue to be excluded from direct participation at the highest echelons in every sphere. Many are called and few are chosen, and large numbers of individuals continue to strive for the top in vain. The "democratization of expectations" may therefore lead to a more intense preoccupation with success in industrial societies precisely because fewer arbitrary social barriers now separate the strategic elites from the mass of men. But although direct access to the strategic elites is denied to the many, indirect access has become ever more possible and necessary. The mandate of rulers, thinkers, and warriors no longer comes from heaven or sacred lineage but from the people in their roles as citizens, consumers, and audiences. People are still persuaded, duped, charmed, misled, and abused—but they cannot be ignored. The long-range planning that goes into an American presidential campaign is preoccupied not merely with winning over the political bosses but the people whom these bosses supposedly control—people who have the vast power to endorse or reject. The accessibility of strategic elites, necessarily confined to the few, is thus counterbalanced by their accountability, increasingly extended to the many.[14]

Attracting desirable candidates

The creation of a sound plan to obtain suitable candidates for strategic elite positions is only a first step. It is one thing to know what one wants and another to get it. Here we face the problem of incentives, of the ways in which subjective desires and capacities are linked with objective necessities.

All societies offer rewards to men assuming leadership positions. Some rewards are tangible material benefits such as money, land, cattle, or slaves, while others are intangible such as social honor and influence. The specific rewards used to interest potential recruits to elite positions depends on the social definition of scarce and desirable values, and their distribution.

Study of such rewards provides important clues about the nature of opportunities existing in a particular society. The same rewards do not everywhere play the same role. In African tribal society, a man with a thousand head of cattle is obviously wealthier than a man possessing only ten, but this wealth does not add substantially to his comforts. The wealthy man cannot consume his cattle; he can use them only to attract and support dependents and thereby to acquire power over other people. Here wealth is not an intrinsic reward but a "facility." [15] In industrial societies, wealth can be used to obtain possessions rather than to give them away.[16]

In addition to tangible rewards, societies also rely on other appeals, such as prestige and influence. All strategic elites enjoy the attention, if not always the approval, of the public. This attention and the accompanying prestige may be their own reward, or the only reward still available to groups whose functional importance has declined. The lofty social status of British peerage, for example, is not matched by affluence. "A large proportion of today's peers," writes Anthony Sampson, "both new and old, have difficulty in making ends meet. It is no consolation for an Earl to be able to go in to dinner before a Baron if he can never actually afford a dinner party." [17]

The nature of the rewards used to attract candidates to different elite positions largely determines what types of candidates will present themselves. Our knowledge of these processes is inadequate, but it seems reasonable to suppose that individuals who seek power will not pursue a movie career, that those seeking great wealth will not become clergymen, that persons valuing independence and initiative will not enter the Civil Service. Max Weber in his classic essay on the social distribution of power divided types of rewards into economic or class power, status or social power, and political or party power.[18] To these three types of rewards may be added a fourth that has come into prominence with the rise of large-scale administrative organization—positional or functional power and the status of "expert" attributed to individuals having such power.

Weber's essay, in fact, is not directly concerned with the function of rewards for society but with their effects upon the psychology of individuals within society. He suggests how, but not why, rewards and the resulting privileges may be obtained and maintained. He does not make explicit the relationship between rewards and services or obligations. Without this, the role of individual desires in the distribution of rewards may be unduly exaggerated. Nor does he mention other types of rewards such as fame, reputation, popularity, or glory—although in constituting sources of power, these too appeal to men.

Rewards play a two-fold role in the recruitment of elites: they motivate individuals to assume the responsibilities of elite positions; and they maintain the values of hierarchical social positions. If there is a profound imbalance between responsibilities and rewards, the structure of the social hierarchy may be impaired. If a worker were to receive greater rewards—material, moral, or personal—than a manager, the status of the manager would be undermined. Rewards thus maintain the value of hierarchical positions as well as the level of motivation to fill them. They are inducements to individuals as well as indicators of positional rank. Some rewards must always be differentially distributed in relation to strategic importance of positions. But the reward need not be material. In many societies hierarchies of prestige are not accompanied by differences in material benefits. Gluckman, in describing a whole series of primitive tribal societies, remarks that none of these societies have any luxuries. Chiefs cannot "build palaces, have luxurious feasts, wear jewels or costly robes." The wealthy man can show his economic superiority only by giving his wealth away. "From North America, Oceania, and Africa, in tribes which have chiefs, aristocrats and slaves, reports all speak of the essential equality of living standards between all these groups." [19] Elites (chiefs) and social classes or castes (aristocrats and slaves) exist, but there are no material differences between them.

Rewards also have a symbolic function for the social order. If strategic elites are rich, honored, and admired, other members of society by virtue of their psychological identification with them also feel rich, honored, and admired. To oversimplify the point, the social superiority of their elites boosts the egos of the mass of men. (This may be why disaffection from elites results in resentment of their most obvious privileges more than of their moral abuses.) Moreover, to the extent that official ideology stresses the attainment of scarce values by those who most deserve them, the visible proof that some do attain them buttresses social ideals. It also serves as evidence that the elites have a right to their lofty positions because they possess these scarce values. Thus multiple aims are furthered by the distribution of distinctive privileges to strategic elites.

Finally, because societies interact with one another, the collective impression made by their strategic elites influences the opinions others have of them. Consequently, the unequal distribution of rewards has internal and external functions as well as psychological, social, and symbolic significance. Clearly, it is impossible to dispense with differential rewards to strategic elites in modern industrial societies.

Responsibilities and rewards

Leaders of a society or of an organization are apt to stress their responsibilities, the "burdens of office," and the costs of their obligations, while members are apt to stress the leaders' visible rewards and benefits. Yet the unequal distribution of responsibilities is as widespread a feature of human societies as is the unequal distribution of rewards—which suggests a possible connection between these two phenomena. In the past, elites often enjoyed what many viewed as excessive privileges, but these privileges were to some extent "deserved," sociologically speaking. Unfortunately there is no clear-cut line between "deserved" and "excessive" privilege—hence the persistent possibility, if not the likelihood, of the exploitation of men by despots, tyrants, sybaritic leisure classes, and self-seeking overlords. Men are capable of extraordinary excesses as well as of incredible endurance and submission to what they consider their fate.[20]

Demands for excessive privileges and unusual prerogatives do not seem to follow automatically or naturally from the sheer fact of assuming leading positions in society. They seem rather to be related to the significance and elaborateness of the functions assumed: the wider and broader these are, the more exalted the position of leaders and the more resigned or acquiescent the members. Hocart observed that the original priest-king was probably not "a person of great majesty; prosaic, at times grotesque, his humdrum function was to ensure a regular supply of food and a satisfactory birthrate by the best means inference could suggest, whether dignified or undignified." He ascribes the rise in kingly pomp and circumstance to the expansion of kingly functions, of the boundaries of the kingdom, and of the ambition which "impels every man to magnify himself in the eyes of his fellows." [21] The counterpart to this is the dependency of the subjects on their king in hope of relief from "psychic, physical, economic, ethical, religious, and political distress," [22] which may lead to the subjects' eventual abdication of self and their exploitation and abuse by those they have put into power.

In turn, however, kings and other social leaders are expected to solve the most pressing problems of collective life. Theirs are large assignments and the price for failure may be death. Their privileges and benefits are exceptional, but so are their responsibilities, and the demands on their time, energies, and personal resources.[23] This is increasingly true of modern leaders who must "earn" their positions—in business and politics no less than in the arts and sciences.[24] Responsibilities and rewards thus form parts of a whole and may be discussed jointly. And each is linked to recruitment, for rewards are the spur to the expenditure of effort that the duties of strategic positions demand.

Patterns of recruitment

All established methods of elite recruitment aim to discover the "best" available talents, although definitions of the "best" vary as greatly as do cultural assumptions as to where to find it. No method of recruitment of elite personnel is *intrinsically* superior or inferior, but it should be functionally consistent with the social and cultural system. Different patterns of recruitment attract different types of talents, and the particular talents highly valued in a society help to determine the particular methods of recruitment used in that society. Where a knowledge of sacred texts is greatly admired, the selection of leaders will stress some type of intensive formal training.

Where moral qualities and attitudes of "fair play" are stressed, potential leaders will tend to be bred for their tasks in a more informal manner.

The two main principles governing access to strategic elite positions are inheritance and achievement. Much has been written about the advantages of each, but a good deal of this literature reflects the personal preferences of the observers. Yet each principle, as embodied in a method of selection of leaders, has both advantages and disadvantages for the social system and for individuals striving to attain elite positions within that system.

INHERITANCE

Even in an age which stresses the universal rights of man, equality of opportunity, and individual achievement, the advantages of the hereditary transmission of functionally important positions cannot be entirely ignored. Where traditions are precarious, heredity provides a succession of persons loyal to these traditions. People born and bred to their positions acquire the requisite habits, skills, and outlook at an early age, thereby developing an emotional attachment to both the prestige and the responsibilities of their high status.

Max Weber, even while praising the advantages of "universalistic" criteria of evaluation, favored hereditary dynasties not only because he saw them as the preservers of legal government—and ultimately of the freedom of the citizens—but also because he saw them as the guardians of the ideals of the past, creating and defending high moral and intellectual standards. Such standards cannot be developed overnight and they cannot be sustained by the mentality of the *parvenu.*[25] "As a carrier of political tradition, training, and balance in a polity," he wrote, "there is no doubt that a stratum of landlords cannot be replaced."[26] De Tocqueville noted that an aristocracy "conceives a lofty idea of itself and of man. It loves to invent for him noble pleasures, to carve out splendid objects for his ambition. Aristocracies often commit very tyrannical and inhuman actions but they rarely entertain groveling thoughts . . . the effect is to raise greatly the general pitch of society."[27]

Michels specified another advantage of aristocracy and hereditary monarchy—the beneficial effects of permanence of social position for the management of the general affairs of society. Like the landed proprietor, the hereditary prince, "having an eye to the interests of his children and his successors," almost always "abstains from a policy which would hopelessly impair the vital energies of his country." [28] This feeling for the soil and the past provides a measure of continuity and stability even while it makes for an inevitable conservatism and resistance to change. A proprietary attitude toward the land and its fate characterizes the born aristocrat and is a source of his pride and prejudices. Thus, Tolstoy answered his imaginary "liberal" critics, in what was to have been a chapter in *War and Peace,* by reaffirming his aristocratic loyalties in these terms:

> I have written thus far only about Princes, Counts, Ministers, Senators, and their children, and I fear that henceforth there will be no other characters in my history. Perhaps this is not good and will not please the public—but for all my desire to have as many readers as possible I cannot gratify such a taste, for a number of reasons: . . . because the lives of merchants, coachmen, seminarists, convicts, and peasants appear to me to be single faceted and boring . . . because I can in no way comprehend what a policeman, standing in his sentry-box, is thinking and feeling . . . finally (and this, I know, is the very best reason) *because I belong to the very highest class, to society, and I love it.*
>
> . . . I dare to say that I am an aristocrat, by birth and by habit and by situation. I am an aristocrat because for me, to remember my forebears . . . is not only not shameful but is especially joyful. I am an aristocrat because I have been brought up from childhood in love and respect for the highest classes, and in love for refinement . . . I am an aristocrat because . . . neither I nor my father nor my grandfather have known want, nor the struggle between conscience and want. . . . All this is perhaps very stupid, criminal, insolent, but there it is. And I warn the reader in advance what sort of man I am and what he may expect from me. There is still time to close the book and expose me as an idiot and a reactionary.[29]

Among the advantages of hereditary transmission of elite status are early exposure to the desired standards of belief and conduct among those destined to assume it, the development of a deep emotional identification between power holders and their successors, and the institutionalization of relatively clear-cut methods of admission and exclusion. However, as members of aristocracies must subordinate their personal wishes to collective practices and codes of long standing, the grip of the past on the present is often excessive. Conflicts over the patrimony are all too frequent; younger children resent the "unfair" superiority of their eldest brothers, and quarrels and recriminations poison the family atmosphere: aristocratic families though socially privileged are not necessarily happy families. Frequently the rebellious younger members chafe as much against the restrictions and taboos of their established status as do their nonaristocratic peers against the lack of it.

One of the major disadvantages of inheritance as a principle of recruitment is the capriciousness of human genes and uncertainty regarding the transmission of specific capacities. The divergence between high status and individual ability has plagued aristocracies in many societies. In addition, there is the problem of the unreliability of human motivation. Those to the manor born are not always eager to preserve their birthright. As with aristocrats of wealth so with other hereditary elites: "Great fortunes are made by those who have not only the capacity but the desire to make them, and the desire is more likely to be strong when ability feels itself restricted and confined by poverty. . . . a large inheritance obviously facilitates the acquisition of more wealth, but at the same time reduces the incentive to acquire it." [30] When men are placed by birth into elite positions without regard to their inclinations and talents, the result is often lowered morale or lowered efficiency or both. Hereditary elites are thus prone to boredom, incompetence, and stagnation. Most aristocracies have been unable to solve this problem satisfactorily, short of abandoning the hereditary principle itself.

SELECTION BY MERIT

Election, appointment, or self-selection of elite leaders has the advantage of enlarging the reservoir of potential candidates. "It has correctly been emphasized," writes Simmel, "that the system of big industry gives the exceptionally gifted man more opportunity to excel than did anything prior to this system." [31] By avoiding a major weakness of hereditary recruitment—the oppressive weight of dead traditions on the living—selection on the basis of merit encourages and rewards the spirit of enterprise and is better suited to a world in flux. In Mannheim's words:

> People who make their way in life by self-help are frequently men of new ideas and values, men of initiative and mental alertness, whereas conservative groups, which for generations have mainly upheld and preserved what others have achieved, are less likely to produce men willing to take risks and receptive to new ideas . . . the self-made man making his way from "rags to riches" often develops a keenness most desirable in a society bound to change. If these mental traits are discouraged or neutralized by over-assimilation, society loses resources for change and adaptation.[32]

Selection on the basis of achievement is likely to occur when members of strategic elites must possess specialized training as well as recent knowledge. Societies in which the principle of dynamic differentiation and growth has been developed cannot rely on family transmission of skills and attitudes because the teachings of the fathers are out of date by the time their children are grown. Moreover, as societies expand and grow more complex, so do their strategic elites; they reach a stage where the supply of candidates would be inadequate were it confined to particular classes or groups.

Selection on the basis of achievement also has its problems. Initially, the chief difficulty is that of recognizing merit among aspiring candidates, and later, of maintaining cohesion and morale among the successful ones. Simmel, though agreeing that "the special talent now has a much greater chance of rising to a higher position," was convinced that an aristocracy of merit "cannot be realized empirically. One reason is that, thus far, no procedure has been found by which 'the best' could with certainty be recognized and given their positions. Neither the *a priori* method of breeding a ruling caste, nor the *a posteriori* method of natural selection in the free struggle for the favored position, nor the (as it were) intermediate method of electing persons, from below or from above, has proved adequate."[33]

But the chief drawback is the absence of a cohesive set of beliefs and standards which men, especially members of strategic elites, must share, at least in some degree. The advantages of recruiting proven "experts" may be lost if they are bound to their narrow specialties and lack broader perspectives. As George Bernard Shaw quipped: "To make a democracy work you need an aristocracy; to make an aristocracy work you need a democracy," particularly, one might add, in large, diversified, and centralized societies.

The spirit of cooperation among the various strategic elites depends largely upon a common social heritage, a heritage which must be rooted in some subsection of society if it is to be more than a vague set of abstract principles. Until recently it was generally rooted in the interests and outlook of a single social class. In closed class systems, where strategic elites develop a corporate consciousness based on their common origins, their very unity—not necessarily of specific but of general aims—may make them oppressive and arbitrary. In open class systems, where strategic elite positions are accessible to a wider range of groups, and particularly in highly differentiated industrial societies, such a corporate consciousness seems to be lacking. This may be all to the good if it results in a series of sharp ideological exchanges and conflicts leading to a new and more viable synthesis, but it may also lead to disruptive rivalries and struggles. How to attain a workable balance between these two tendencies—social rigidity and social fragmentation—is one of the problems of our time.

The recruitment of strategic elites from a single social class is, of course, no guarantee of their cohesion and sense of direction, particularly if the class system is in the process of a general decline and decay. Moreover, subgroup loyalties need not be class loyalties. There are many possible ties among men other than their social and economic standing. Members of strategic elites, drawn from a wide variety of environments, may nevertheless develop strong *esprit de corps* and a sense of common social mission. Friendships, common ideals, shared schooling, and the sheer experience of success are likely to produce deep attachments. Artists have usually constituted a fraternity that holds together, especially in the face of danger to its self-esteem, and yet artists for many centuries have come from a wide variety of backgrounds. Generations of creative men have demonstrated that professional identities forged on the way to the top may be as binding as class identities.

Social inheritance and achievement of strategic elite positions are likely to prevail in different eras. Typically, inheritance characterizes traditional societies in which strategic elites are few in number, homogeneous, and in which elite capacities and skills are readily acquired through effective socialization early in life. Recruitment on the basis of achievement characterizes expanding societies in which complexity and diversity are the rule and in which elite capacities and talents require lengthy and specialized training and the inculcation of powerful motivation.

Hereditary elites have the advantages of earlier and more effective socialization of their members, greater social cohesion, and more intense *esprit de corps*—formed as much by early training as by social snobbery and exclusiveness. And though their sense of family and class honor is associated typically with a social conservatism which lessens their adaptability to change, this also makes for stability. Society may gain in unity of direction what it loses in flexibility.

The problems of nonhereditary elites (whether elected or coopted) are exactly the reverse. Recruited from a wider range of social groups, they have more diversified interests and talents and are thus more responsive to challenge and change. This is especially true where tenure in elite positions is relatively brief. But these qualities may work against the development of cooperation and collaboration.[34] More serious is the danger, in societies that stress democracy, equality, and the accountability of leaders to their publics, of elites failing to develop a sense of their elite identity—under the mistaken notion that to do so would be undemocratic. An implicit assumption of elites as undemocratic or exploitative can stifle the development of coherent programs and perspectives. This in turn makes it difficult for the public to debate the merits or demerits of particular objectives. The vacuum will as likely as not be filled not with creative and timely proposals but with traditional and "safe" beliefs. Excessive individualism and competitiveness no less than excessive conservatism may prove socially destructive in the long run. So may the ideological void left when men seek to deny or dare not accept the facts of their elite status. In modern industrial societies the trend is away from recruitment based on inheritance toward recruitment based on achievement. Particular problems of these societies therefore lie in the moral and ideological sphere.

"Aristocracies," De Tocqueville remarked, "seek not to better the society but to preserve it"—which may account in large part for their eventual decay. Today, societies can be preserved only by effective accommodation to rapid social and technological change. In the atomic and space age, societies must keep in step or perish, and their strategic elites must either help them move into the future or perish with them.

In the following chapter, patterns of recruitment to strategic elites in the United States—with some illustrative material drawn from other modern societies—will be examined and compared. The discussion in the preceding chapters suggests that we shall find no uniform over-all pattern because each strategic elite has its own moral, functional, and symbolic characteristics. Nevertheless, we can predict some common elements among these strategic elites, for they are part of the same society and share certain values. Since wealth and higher education are still quite strongly class-linked, we can also expect to find social and cultural similarities among elites in which higher education and specialized, prolonged training are indispensable. Finally, we anticipate no uniform pattern of elite recruitment because contemporary industrial society has no uniform social core group.

Notes

1. See, for example, the brief, lucid discussion by Taya Zinkin, *Caste Today* (1962). For a lucid, comprehensive discussion of this, see Pitirim Sorokin, *Social Mobility* (1927), Chap. vii.
2. Mosca, *The Ruling Class* (1939), p. 68.
3. This resembles the concept of "locus" proposed by Emile Benoit-Smullyan in his important theoretical paper, "Status, Status Types, and Status Interrelations," *American Sociological Review,* IX (April 1944), 151-61. Regrettably, the author did not elaborate the distinction and integrate it with his conception of "status" and "situs."

4. Aristotle, *Politics,* p. 1212. Aristotle lists three criteria for recruitment in oligarchies and democracies: number, wealth, and virtue; oligarchy existing when the rich, who are also noble, and the few govern; democracy, when the free, who are also poor, and the majority govern. And since there are several different forms of democracy and oligarchy, there are also several different combinations of attributes. Further, he distinguishes between the personal and social qualifications of candidates for the highest offices. The criteria of wealth, numbers, and virtue are social criteria in the sense of setting limits as to who should be considered. But those who actually hold office must also exhibit certain personal qualities, chief among which are loyalty to the established constitution, great administrative capacity, and virtue and justice of the kind proper to each form of government. This list is not too different from one proposed for a very different sort of world at a much later date. Chester I. Barnard selects the following qualities of leaders: vitality and endurance, decisiveness, persuasiveness, responsibility, and intellectual capacity. Barnard, *Organization and Management* (1948), pp. 80-110.
5. Karl Mannheim, *Freedom, Power, and Democratic Planning,* "The Ruling Class in Capitalist and Communist Society" (1959), pp. 77-107.
6. Aristotle, *op. cit.,* Book III, Chap. xii, p. 1193. Aristotle understood the distinction clearly even though he recommended recruitment on the basis of individual excellence as well as birth and wealth. "When a number of flute players are equal in their Arts," he observes, "there is no reason why those of them who are better born should have better flutes given to them; for they will not play any better on the flute, and the superior instrument should be reserved for him who is the better artist. For if there were a superior flute player who was far inferior in birth and beauty, although either of these may be a greater good than the art of flute playing, and may excel flute playing in greater ratio than he excels the others in his art, still he ought to have the best flutes given to him, unless the advantage of wealth and birth contribute to excellence in flute playing, which they do not. Moreover, upon this principle any good may be compared with any other."
7. Chester I. Barnard, *op. cit.,* p. 210.
8. For an excellent discussion of this point, see Philip Selznick, *TVA and the Grassroots* (1949).
9. Simmel, in Kurt Wolff (ed.), *The Sociology of Georg Simmel* (1950), pp. 106-7.
10. Robert M. Marsh, *The Mandarins* (1961), p. 83.
11. Barnard, *op. cit.,* p. 106. As Barnard has stated, the current efforts are directed toward selecting the best of those available: ". . . the most perfect selection would not suffice to give adequate leadership if the supply of the 'raw material' were of inferior quality." In a recent article a similar distinction is drawn between what the author calls "sponsored and contest" mobility. "Under contest mobility the object is to train as many as possible in the skills necessary for elite status so as to give everyone a chance to maintain competition at the highest pitch. Under sponsored mobility, the objective is to indoctrinate elite culture in only those presumably who will enter the elite, lest there grow a dangerous number of 'angry young men' who have elite skills without elite station." Ralph H. Turner, "Sponsored and Contest Mobility," *American*

Sociological Review, XXV (December 1960), No. 6, 855-67. The author refers to "the elite" of Great Britain as exemplifying the norm of sponsored mobility, thus by-passing the problem of a diversity of elites, and of the mobility norms they exemplify.

12. P. Mercier, "Evolution of Senegalese Elites," *International Social Science Bulletin,* VIII (1956), 441-52. See also Daniel Lerner, *The Passing of Traditional Society* (1958), p. 238, who notes that throughout the Middle East higher education is so prestigeful that Egypt, for example, is already oversupplied with secondary school graduates with nothing to do. The same holds true for Iran. *Ibid.,* p. 363.
13. He adds, that for different offices, the officers may be differently chosen. Aristotle, *op. cit.,* p. 1230.
14. For a recent discussion of "accessibility and accountability," see William Kornhauser, *Politics in Mass Society* (1959), esp. pp. 51-60. This distinction parallels Mosca's between aristocratic and democratic recruitment patterns, on the one hand, and between autocratic and liberal patterns of decision-making on the other.
15. For this distinction see Talcott Parsons, "A Revised Analytical Approach to the Theory of Social Stratification," in R. Bendix and S. M. Lipset (eds.), *Class, Status and Power* (1953), p. 103.
16. Opinions as to the merits of material rewards for public service have varied. Plato and Aristotle disapproved of them. Plato turned his "guardians" into virtual ascetics, and Aristotle presupposed wealth among candidates for public office precisely in order to avoid their later being tempted by the possibilities of material gain. He suggested, instead, that "every state should be so administered and so regulated by law that its magistrates cannot possibly make money . . . for the people do not take great offense in being kept out of the government —indeed, they are rather pleased than otherwise at having leisure for their private business—but what irritates them is to think that their rulers are stealing the public money; then they are doubly annoyed; for they lose both honour and profit." Aristotle, *Politics,* Book V, Chap. viii, p. 1248.

    A similar view prevailed in the early trade union movement in Europe. Michels describes the manual workers as "exacting masters" who were not willing to pay their party leaders adequately. They wanted employees to serve for the love of the cause and not with an eye to material gain. This, however, apparently lessened the motivation to serve at all. Michels, *Political Parties* (1959), pp. 123 ff.
17. Anthony Sampson, "What's in a Title," *New York Times Magazine,* January 15, 1961.
18. Max Weber, "Class, Status, and Party," in Gerth and Mills (eds.), *From Max Weber* (1946), pp. 180-95.
19. Max Gluckman, "The Origins of Social Organization," in Morton H. Fried (ed.), *Readings in Anthropology,* II (1959), 246-58.

    Rewards as inducements and rewards as indicators of rank are not easy to distinguish and are often confused. This appears in part to contribute to the controversy over the functional causes of social stratification.
20. An interesting article in this connection is Helen Codere, "Power in Ruanda," *Anthropologica* N. S. Vol. IV (1962), No. 1, 45-85.
21. A. M. Hocart, *Kingship* (1927), p. 238.

22. Max Weber, "The Sociology of Charismatic Authority," *op. cit.,* p. 245. According to Weber these are the contributions of the charismatic leader.
23. Among the Shilluks of the White Nile, according to Sir James Frazer, the king was put to death if he grew ill or senile "lest with his diminishing vigour the cattle should sicken and fail to bear their increase, the crops should rot in the fields, and men, stricken with disease, should die in ever-increasing numbers." Sir James George Frazer, *The New Golden Bough,* edited and with notes and foreword by R. H. Gaster, p. 225. For other examples, see Hocart, *op. cit.,* Chap ii.

    The burdens of high office are related, at least implicitly, to the privileges attached to such offices. "Servitude," Henri Frankfort has observed, "loses much of its sting if authority rests with those to whom faith has attributed the power of safeguarding the existence of society. . . . A certain amount of arbitrariness, even of despotism, is taken for granted in the great; it is their privilege, but only if it is counterbalanced by a sense of responsibility for the land and for those who will till it." Henri Frankfort, *The Birth of Civilization in the Near East* (1957), p. 107. See also Fustel de Coulanges, *The Ancient City* (1956), p. 326, and Sebastian de Grazia, *The Political Community* (1948), pp. 75-6.
24. Michels describes how the heavy burden of mental and physical labor has resulted in a large proportion of socialist agitators succumbing to mental disorders. Michels, *op. cit.,* p. 57. And Matthews remarks that the price of political power is high: "few Americans could live under the job's tensions, moral dilemmas, intrigue, and insecurity." Matthews, *U.S. Senators and Their World* (1960), p. 90. The same holds true for Supreme Court Justices. See Anthony Lewis, "The Justices' Supreme Job," *New York Times Magazine,* June 11, 1961.

    The moral and technical demands made on party workers in the Soviet Union provide a further illustration: "The party man must exhort, explain, and defend. When volunteers are called, he must rush to volunteer—to work on Sunday or to move to Siberia. He must not get drunk. He must *not* be seen in Church. And no matter how exemplary his behavior, when things go wrong and hundreds are at fault, he gets the blame. Because they appreciate the difficulties of life in the party, non-party Russians judge members as they would everyone else, without special envy or resentment. They know that Communists live well for their station in life, but they know also that the Communist is always at work. He is known to sacrifice much of his individuality for the vague satisfactions of organizational triumph." Max Frankel, "The 8,708,000 Elite of Russia," *New York Times Magazine,* May 29, 1960, p. 49. Italics supplied.
25. Max Weber, "Capitalism and Rural Society in Germany," *op. cit.,* p. 370.
26. Max Weber, "National Character and the Junkers," *ibid.,* p. 386.
27. De Tocqueville, *Democracy in America,* II, 45.
28. Michels, *op. cit.,* p. 102.
29. Quoted in Kathryn Feuer, "The Book That Became 'War and Peace'," *The Reporter* (May 14, 1959).
30. Josiah Wedgwood, *The Economics of Inheritance* (1929).
31. Georg Simmel, *op. cit.,* p. 294.
32. Karl Mannheim, *op. cit.,* p. 105.

33. Georg Simmel, *op. cit.*, pp. 294-6.
34. Peter Bachrach suggests that one way to correct the imbalance between centralized elites and a fragmented mass is to reduce the power differential, not by trying to promote elite consensus, but by increasing and stimulating popular discussion, awareness, and consensus. See "Elite Consensus and Democracy," *The Journal of Politics*, XXIV (August 1962), No. 3, 439-53.

9. SOCIAL BACKGROUNDS AND CAREERS OF SELECTED ELITES IN THE UNITED STATES

▲

The problem of the recruitment of elites centers on the selection of the right men for the right jobs. Two principal methods of selection, as we saw in Chapter 8, are biological and social reproduction. Biological reproduction implies that those currently in elite positions are expected to transmit these positions to their offspring. Social reproduction implies that individuals are expected to attain elite status by means of self-selection, competitive examination, election, or co-optation. Where the demand for candidates is relatively stable, a social class or group may monopolize access to elite positions by producing its heirs. Where demand is expanding, this monopoly will be broken—at least for the period of the expansion. The accessibility of elites increases under three sets of conditions: (1) if, under stable social conditions, a social class loses its monopoly of access as a result of inadequate reproduction, as was the case with many aristocracies; (2) if, as a result of demographic and social expansion, the number of openings increases so that biological replenishment must be supplemented by other forms; and (3) if, as in the arts or the sciences, the skills demanded are such that personal preference or unusual talents play a decisive role.

Currently all three conditions, especially the latter two, may be observed. Strategic elites should therefore be more widely accessible to a variety of groups and strata than they have been in the recent past, for what constitutes need at the top constitutes opportunity below. Examination of the patterns of recruitment to these elites should show whether there has indeed been a change in the sources and in a nature of the successful candidates.

Social characteristics of the members of various elites have long been of interest, but systematic investigations of elite recruitment are rare.[1] The best of these studies to date concern the American business elite at different periods in recent history.[2] Despite differences in the concepts, samples, and methods used, most of these studies agree that the American business elite is also a social and economic elite, but that it is becoming more accessible to lower-class aspirants. These conclusions challenge predictions concerning the inevitable decrease of elite circulation and the consequent consolidation of a ruling class.[3]

The question arises, however, whether the business elite is representative of all elites in a society. If one assumes the coexistence of a number of functionally differentiated, partly autonomous groups of elite decision-makers—each a king in its particular province—a focus on the business elite cannot provide insight into the general accessibility of the higher circles. Studies of recruitment must therefore extend to other strategic elites in American society, to see whether the postulated changes toward expansion, proliferation, and specialization are characteristic of all or only some of them, and whether there is now more or less social heterogeneity than formerly.

A second question concerns the trends in recruitment patterns within each elite. To the extent that these elites are part of a common pattern, they will be similarly affected by the main trends of the times. But to the extent that they are unique, the demand for new blood and new skills should reflect their specific needs. The leaders of business, of the military, of diplomacy, of politics, and of sciences will be more responsive to technological changes than religious or artistic leaders. And since the former were previously less accessible to the lower classes, they should now exhibit the more striking and suggestive changes in patterns of recruitment and selection.

We will thus attempt a comparative assessment of the social origins, educational attainments, and careers of the various strategic elites in American society at mid-century. Our main interest will be in tracing the majority patterns and, where possible, suggesting long-range trends. Unfortunately, conceptual and methodological problems, including inadequacies of the samples used in various studies, permit us to do no more than sketch in existing patterns and propose some possibilities for more systematic research in the future. Before turning to the available information, some methodological considerations are in order.

Problems of definition and boundaries

Most studies of elite groups do not readily lend themselves to the sort of comparison we have in mind—namely, an assessment of the same set of selective characteristics of all or of most strategic elites in a single society at a specific epoch. Such a comparison calls not only for a range of information currently unavailable, but also requires an acceptable conceptual framework, similar logical and operational definitions of terms, and comparable categories of information. In the absence of these, collection and interpretation of reported findings are difficult. Consider the simple datum that in the United States in 1950, 15 per cent of the business elite came from wage-earner backgrounds but only 3 per cent of the diplomatic elite did. Do these two sets of figures mean that the business elite is five times more accessible to aspirants from lower status backgrounds than the diplomatic elite? Or that aspirants from such backgrounds are more attracted to a business than to a diplomatic career? Or that other factors such as schooling and early work experience account for the disproportion? Or that bias at the top is responsible? We cannot answer these questions because we do not know enough about the distribution of aspiration among the various economic levels. The little we do know cannot as yet be clearly linked to such important factors as the structure of careers and the role of education in channeling aspirations. Existing patterns of recruitment presumably reflect social values as well as individual aspirations and opportunities—the problem is to discover the relative contribution of each and their varied combinations for the different elites.[4]

Some of these difficulties might be surmounted if we had comparable information permitting us to take stock of those social characteristics that the various elites have in common and those which are divergent. The unique constellation of traits for the different elites cannot be properly assessed if the similarities among them are neglected or ignored. One aim of this book has been to show that these elites are functionally interrelated, that the variety of existing elites is not just a matter of chance or the haphazard working out of a random social process. Sharing and dividing the task of social, moral, and cultural leadership, they may be expected to reveal both common and divergent social characteristics.

The use of a conceptual scheme facilitates the search for essential information because it provides reasons and justifications for seeking particular facts and a basis for interpretation.[5] It also provides some standards as to how much information is needed for comparative purposes and to fill in existing gaps in our knowledge. Even if the conceptual scheme proposed here—of a series of functionally interdependent, partly autonomous, strategic elites with special moral, instrumental, and symbolic characteristics—is highly tentative, it does help us avoid certain common errors. In attempting to appraise the current accessibility of different social strata to the top of American society, we are not content to cite just one or two elites in evidence, but endeavor to discover patterns of access to a number of different elites from each of the four broad functional categories.

A key problem, as yet unresolved, concerns the definitions of elites employed in different studies and demarcation of their boundaries. "The genius of great affairs," remarked Bagehot, "abhors nicety of division." [6] So it is with elites. To date, most studies concentrate on a portion of the elites in question. Studies of the political elite center on senators, Cabinet members, Chief Executives, and state governors; the business elite, on leading officials of selected corporations; the scientific elite, on leading scientists; the diplomatic elite, on selected ambassadors and ministers.[7] None of these studies is exhaustive either of the entire elite or even the portion selected for special attention. The problem of definition thus remains a serious one. Further, in order to differentiate strategic elites from leading professional men such as envoys, politicians, military officers, and artists, one needs criteria for separating the very top echelons from the rest and observing how these are linked to the performance of the strategic social functions discussed earlier. Perhaps the very top should include only ambassadors sent to major world powers, Senators in key committees, four-star generals, Chief Executives and Cabinet members, the heads of the key government bureaus, and the most acclaimed luminaries of the arts. But still the problem of definition remains: for what is considered "key" and "most important" varies with the criterion employed, such as the scope of responsibility, originality, staying power, individual excellence, or social influence. One problem for research is to see how, where, and whether the elites selected on the basis of these varied criteria overlap. For some elites—those occupying formal positions in large-scale organizations in business, politics, diplomacy, and the military—boundaries are relatively clear-cut and depend on the number of organizational levels included. For elites of scientists, artists, writers, educators, and entertainers, the problem is more complicated. Here, various criteria of top status, each with some claim to validity, may be employed.

There is also the matter of comparing items of information that are not strictly comparable since no agreed upon inventory of items has as yet been established. We know something of the geographic origins of some leading American scientists, but little about their ethnic origins. We know that two-fifths of the American business elite in 1952 had attended one of the Big Three colleges (Harvard, Yale or Princeton), but we lack such information about higher civil servants, leading intellectuals, and members of high society. And since comparative information for other societies at the same historical epoch is also sparse, it is difficult to assess the historical as distinct from the functional aspect of recruitment.[8]

Once an agreed upon inventory of items exists and an elite census is underway (itself a formidable, if not a prohibitive undertaking), the categories utilized will have to be more carefully defined. The habit of comparing proportions of elite members coming from "business" as distinct from "professional" families has only a rough usefulness at best, since these categories are clearly too inclusive of a wide range of socioeconomic possibilities.

Finally, there is the problem of the nature of inferences made from empirical data. This—the fit between concepts and data—is the Achilles heel of scientific advance. Take, for example, the relationship between scientific eminence and religious affiliation, a subject that has been extensively studied.[9] Both in Europe and in the United States Roman Catholics are under-represented among scientists generally, as well as among prominent or remarkable scientists. This may reflect an affinity between religious values and particular forms of social success as Merton, following Weber, has argued.[10] But it may also reflect historical tradition and the greater conventionalism of Roman Catholics—social prejudice at the top, or self-imposed restrictions below. In fact, due to the intertwining of religious with ethnic and economic status, this finding may reveal less about the influence of religion than about the socioeconomic and ethnic milieu in which this religion is practiced. We have as yet no basis for deciding which of these plays the decisive role. Religious affiliation may be related to social ascendancy in different ways, and the analyst must elucidate, not assume, the various possible relationships before deciding on their meaning.

This leads us to consider the broader utility of information on the social recruitment of elites. Aside from human interest in and curiosity about great, prominent, or famous men, such information reveals something about two distinct sets of issues. One relates to the society in which elites participate, the other, to the character of the elite members themselves.

Careful studies of social recruitment and ascent help to assess the degree of flexibility of the social structure at the highest peaks, and this is of interest to ambitious men at all social levels and will color their expectations about success. The characteristics, skills, and knowledge typically required for different elite positions is utilized both by the young appraising their chances and by those advising them. It is an interesting psychological fact that men generally must strive higher and reach farther than their capacities permit if they are to achieve unusual things—unusual, that is, in relation to their milieus and talents. It also seems true that individuals, in their pursuit of excellence or conspicuous success, need models to emulate. Elites constitute such models for the society at large.[11]

Studies of elite recruitment—as Daniel Bell has pointed out [12]—also help explain certain changes and shifts in style (as in painting or drama), or in types of decisions, or in the ways power is exercised. These may reflect shifts in recruitment patterns, that is, in the sorts of men who get to the top.* Here as elsewhere, the data

* One of the most intriguing problems concerns the link between patterns of recruitment and patterns of motivation among those who succeed in

to be sought will be governed by the questions raised. If one wishes to ascertain the link between elite status and social class affiliation, one must ask one set of questions and collect one set of facts. If one seeks to ascertain why individuals pursue different kinds of success, the concepts and methods will have to be appropriate to that intention.

Turning now to *our* main question—the relationship between changes in the needed numbers and skills of elite personnel and changes in recruitment patterns—we find that this question cannot be properly answered at this time. For some elites there is no such information at all, namely, the leading artists, writers, and composers, and prominent clergy of the different religious faiths. For others—screen stars,[13] journalists,[14] and leading scientists[15]—the information is not up-to-date. Nor are the studies whose findings will be referred to equally successful in avoiding the conceptual and methodological difficulties we have outlined. Still, they do enable us to make tentative inferences into the patterns of recruitment to various coexisting elites in contemporary American society. More firmly established conclusions will have to await the results of future research.

Social origins of strategic elites

We shall now review selected aspects of the social origins and careers of different elites, summarizing only the most consistent major findings. For the sake of clarity and simplicity of presentation, the laborious details of methods and results are presented in a separate appendix at the end of the book.

The most commonly used indicators of social origins are social class, as revealed by fathers' occupation and sons' educational attainments, and social status, as indicated by religious affiliation,

---

attaining elite status. One needs to know not only the characteristics of successful candidates but also those of the aspiring candidates at different levels. As yet we do not have this information, but it might constitute a good next step for those engaged in elite studies. One can obviously infer little from the social data if such data pertain to but a fraction of successful individuals and omit the larger numbers who have tried to succeed but failed. Once such information is available, it will be possible to relate the findings both to social and to motivational factors. This is where the sociologist and the psychologist need to join forces.

lineage, and ethnicity. These are by no means the only desirable indicators (information on family income, father's education, educational and occupational attainments of grandparents and siblings would also be most useful), but they are the only ones for which we have comparative evidence.

Before examining the social origins of current elite groups, it would be helpful to indicate what we might expect to find. Given the existence of an upper class in nineteenth-century America, united by ties of family, wealth, property, and high social status, we should expect to find social class continuing to play a significant role in the recruitment of many elites. A class-stratified society is, after all, one in which opportunities for education, for acquiring wealth and property, and for developing special talents and ambitions are class-linked by definition. Once established, such patterns and the styles of life and thought they give rise to are difficult to change, if only because families, the chief units of social classes, see to it that they persist. Social class is therefore apt to be influential in the recruitment of elites in which ascribed characteristics play a highly significant role. Where achievement is emphasized, it should be less significant. Thus for elite recruitment as a whole, social class will be a variable rather than a constant element.

In line with the noted technological, demographical, and bureaucratic expansion of American society in the last fifty years, we should expect all elites to be more open to outsiders than they were in the past. The rapidity of these changes has resulted not only in increased demands for more of the same talents, but also for more unusual and new talents. The need for specialists has transcended the boundaries of social class.

SOCIAL CLASS: ACHIEVED ATTRIBUTES

Turning now to the data, it appears that social class factors continue to play a significant role in the recruitment of the political, business, military, and higher civil service elites as well as the judicial, scientific, religious, opinion, and entertainment elites.[16] Even the incomplete and uneven data on social class backgrounds leaves little doubt that the various elite members, typically drawn from the middle classes of society, are the offspring of business or professional men who could afford to encourage their sons to obtain at least a college education. Yet a minority of each elite comes from upper as well as lower class backgrounds. No social class is entirely excluded, nor (except for high society) does a single class monopolize access to any of these positions.

The lowest social stratum of manual workers, however, is only minimally represented among most elites, although those of religion, sports, entertainment, and education may be more accessible. The prevalent middle-class pattern lends support to those social critics who perceive an increasing rigidity in the social hierarchy and who focus on the lack of extensive upward mobility for those born in the lowest social class.[17] Yet, since wealth and property were, during the past century, characteristic of those admitted into the higher business, political, military, and diplomatic circles (see for example the studies of the business elite of 1870),[18] their continued importance should not come as a shock. The important question is whether a change may be noted away from the traditional pattern to one more attuned to modern times, where value is placed on skill, talent, and motivation.

As is shown by the data in Appendix III (pp. 307-8), there has been such a change. And this change is all the more marked for those elites that were previously least accessible to lower-class representation. In view of the tenacity of privilege, these proportions are still very small, but they do reflect expanding rather than contracting opportunities for lower-class aspirants—paralleling the expansion of opportunities at lower levels of the social structure.

Whether a similar trend exists in the elites of stage, screen, sports, and the arts, cannot be answered at this time as there is no precise information available. For these elites, however, such facts are less relevant, although interesting, because they have apparently always been more accessible to lower-class individuals, and because particular individual talents and motivations play a far greater role here than in the more formally organized elites of business, politics, diplomacy, and defense. In fact one might postulate a somewhat opposite trend for these elites, whose social prestige has increased of late—namely, a possible increase in college-educated middle- and upper-class recruits, paralleling the increase in the prestige and financial rewards of elite status in the arts, films, and education.

The main findings regarding the social class origins of various elites may be summarized as follows: (1) the majority of elites are predominantly middle class and college educated; (2) a minority are lower class and lack a college education; (3) sparse data on trends suggest that the proportion of lower-class recruits to these elites may be increasing. It should be stressed, however, that while the majority of these elites originate in middle-class business and professional families, their backgrounds show considerable social and economic diversity, and include a number of different income and occupational levels, and a great variety of occupational types —teachers, business owners, business executives, independent and salaried professionals, but also clerks, salesmen, and office workers.

The importance of social class in recruitment varies. Thus the proportion of wage earners' sons has been small in all elites, but is greater for some than for others: only five out of one hundred military officers rose from the ranks of wage-earner families, but fifteen of every hundred business leaders did. College education is virtually indispensable for some strategic elite positions, but the proportion of college graduates varies from 60 per cent among the current business elite to 90 per cent among the current Senators, and presumably it would be 100 per cent for the top scientists. There is a preferred, even typical pattern, but not a uniform one. Before we consider the meaning of these findings, it is necessary to turn to the second aspect of social origins—ancestry, religion, nativity, and ethnicity. These constitute assets or liabilities in their own right, irrespective of their link with social class. In most elite positions in a pluralist society with a definite hierarchy of preferred ascribed attributes, men are preferred to women, whites to Negroes, Protestants to Jews, and native-born, old family stock to immigrant or second-generation stock. The data are too sparse to do more than suggest patterns, but it is clear that an inquiry into the distribution of ascribed attributes yields somewhat different results from the previous discussion of achieved attributes among members of strategic elites.

SOCIAL STATUS: ASCRIBED ATTRIBUTES

The members of most strategic elites are white, male, native-born, of British or Northwest European descent, and of the Protestant (especially Presbyterian and Episcopalian) faiths. (See Appendix IV, pp. 308-9.) In fact, the elites appear to be more homogeneous as regards these ascribed attributes of race, religion, ancestry, and sex than with respect to achieved attributes such as wealth or education. This is less true for the recreational and artistic elites, who are generally believed (though not definitely known) to be more accessible to women, Negroes, and immigrants.[19]

As with social class, however, there are signs of a change. The highest proportion of individuals possessing less favored social characteristics occurs in the latest generation of the elites in business, defense, and diplomacy. (See Appendix V, pp. 309-12.) No study has found an increase in exclusive characteristics of elite members in the latest generation. Some elites, however, are less accessible to minority group candidates than others. In the military and diplomatic elites, for example, nativity, ethnicity, and religion are more salient than for the "idols of consumption" in entertainment and sports.

According to the information gathered in Appendix IV, the social characteristics of elite members also affect patterns of ascent. The individuals who attained elite status even though they lacked preferred ascribed attributes possessed or acquired wealth. Of the twenty-nine business leaders in 1950 of South Irish or Southeast European descent, three tenths were self-made men—a proportion ten times greater than that for the business leaders of British descent. Jewish business leaders had quite different patterns of mobility from those of the Roman Catholic or Protestant faiths. Three fourths of them came from business families (compared to 57 per cent among the Protestants, and only 38 per cent among the Roman Catholics). The Jewish business leaders also included the smallest proportion of lower-class men. Only 16 per cent of them came from farmer and wage-earner backgrounds, as compared to 25 per cent of the Protestant and 62 per cent of the Roman Catholic business leaders. Finally, the Jewish business leaders had less formal education than the others (almost one fifth were not high-school graduates; only one out of three were college graduates). Comparable figures for Protestants show two out of three to have been college graduates; among Roman Catholics, however, only one out of three. Jewish business leaders apparently achieved elite status in business by rising from middle and upper-class families also engaged in business, whereas Roman Catholic business leaders rose to business prominence from lower class status via the expanding business bureaucracies.

Donald R. Matthews notes distinctive patterns of success for Republican and Democratic Senators. The Democrats had higher social class positions (as indicated by father's occupation) "but were also more often immigrants, Catholics, Jews, and members of relatively lower prestige Protestant denominations." They also had more formal education than their Republican counterparts, but at the lesser known schools.[20]

Keller compared the career paths of three separate groups of diplomatic envoys—Protestants from lower-class homes, Jews, and Roman Catholics—and though the numbers are small, the findings are sufficiently interesting to warrant a more elaborate study with larger samples. Those lacking economic status (the lower-class Protestants) were largely of old family, British stock who started at the bottom of the social class hierarchy and worked their way to the top via politics. The majority had had no college education but "read" law and later ran successfully for political office. They were high on status attributes but low on class attainments. The Roman Catholic diplomats, half of whom originated in lower-class homes of railroad workers, farmers, and manual laborers, succeeded primarily as bureaucrats via a slow upward climb in corporate, military, or foreign service hierarchies. Jews succeeded via family position and prestigeful education. (See Appendix IV, pp. 308-9.)

A question now arises: How much do these patterns reflect self-selection, and how much the preferences of electorates or of members of selecting boards? Most likely, these two elements interact as traditional selection patterns in the various fields limit both the chances and the expectations of success among different types of candidates. To establish this interaction precisely, one would need to know the distribution of aspiring as well as successful candidates. Such information as is currently available suggests that the poor may need the "proper" ascribed attributes for successful entry into the elites whereas minority group members may need the right achieved attributes. Those who possess neither stand the least chance of such success. But what about those who possess both?

If elites are narrowly defined, social class and social status play a crucial role—particularly in politics, business, the military, the judiciary, and diplomacy. Thus, Matthews noted that a key group of patrician Senators—although comprising only 7 per cent of all postwar Senators—were concentrated in the most prestigeful Senate committees, were disproportionately represented among Senate leaders, and were also "heavily over-represented among the chairmen of committees." These Senators, descendants of America's old families of wealth and lineage, also have the greatest staying power in the Senate. (See Appendix VII, pp. 317-19.) Among the business elite of 1950, Keller also was able to identify such an elite of elites—the upper and upper middle class, Protestant, Anglo-Saxon business leaders concentrated in the older, established business fields.[21] A similarly exclusive group could be located among the top envoys to the most important European posts in the present century.[22] Thus where the boundaries of elites are sharply drawn, the pull of social class and social status is still extremely powerful, though no longer all-powerful.

Are the pinnacles of American society more or less accessible now than in the past? The answer depends, as we have just seen, on how broadly or narrowly these pinnacles are defined, and which specific elites are involved. If elites are formed on the basis of the relatively free play of diverse social and psychological forces, success is largely a function of individual motivation and objective requirements. However, inasmuch as existing societies have a tradition of class-patterned opportunities and aspirations, the men at the top continue to reflect not only variations in individual talents, but also, and perhaps more strongly, the distribution of social facilities. The hold of the past, however, is not uniformly characteristic of all elites. What is more, the trend is toward expanding opportunities for lower class and lower status aspirants.

Education and careers

As indicated at the beginning of this chapter, patterns of recruitment change not only in response to demands for greater numbers of elite candidates, but also because of changing objective requirements. Increasing specialization prompts an increase in the demand for highly trained specialists. This has long been true of leading artists, writers, athletes, and intellectuals whose members have generally not been able to rely solely on family connections for success or on prestigeful class affiliations and college diplomas. Increasingly, this pattern will also come to prevail among elites where such connections did once play a decisive role in recruitment. Selected aspects of this trend are summarized below.

1. *Formal education:* The importance of higher education, observed in the society at large, may also be observed for various elite groups. A college education, plus advanced post-college training, are characteristic of elites that may differ substantially in other respects. Such training, indispensable for most members of the economic, military, diplomatic, and scientific elites who must master complex and new skills, is becoming increasingly essential for political leaders, journalists, and even creative artists. Since the world has become more complicated and less comprehensible to the technically unsophisticated, those who guide opinion or express the main currents of feeling and thought must be informed about that world if their work is to reflect the most significant trends of the times.[23]

2. *Specialized apprenticeship:* Early commitment, prolonged specialized training, and intensive preoccupation with work, long characteristic of careers in the creative arts, are now evident for the elites in other fields. Members of the military, diplomatic, business, political, and scientific elites increasingly choose their life's work early, devote themselves to a thorough course of formal and informal training, and work many years for the top prizes. The professional politician was predominant among postwar Senators, the corporate manager among the business leaders of 1950, and the specialists with extensive in-service training among the leading generals and admirals. The highest proportion of foreign service career officers (though still a minority) occurred in the latest decade studied (See Appendix VIII, pp. 319-24.) And scientists, clergymen, and educators have all felt the impact of specialization, although how this has affected the careers of the top leadership in these fields is not yet known. (See Appendix VI, pp. 312-17.)

This professionalization is reflected in the extensive post-college training of the members of the various elites. For example, one-sixth of the business elite, two-fifths of the diplomatic, one-half of the political, and all of the judicial have been trained as lawyers.

As formal rules and procedures increase, those familiar with the handling of rules and regulations assume prominent roles. (See Appendix IX, pp. 325-6.)

3. *Specialized career paths:* Within each elite, the specialist is on the rise. And patterns of ascent and selection are accordingly numerous and varied. They range from periodic elections following grueling campaigns for some members of the political elite, to the co-optation of presumably qualified individuals who have climbed to the last station before the peak in the big corporations, to the overnight stardom in the world of entertainment, to the fame that awaits the novelist who has written the great American fable. The individual who aspires to success in big business should be prepared to devote twenty years or more to corporation life. The would-be diplomat who dreams of negotiating on vital matters of peace and war will have to achieve distinction in business or one of the professions, or commit himself to the foreign service for perhaps twenty-five years, before that dream becomes reality. Everywhere careers are lengthened, with success coming only after years of hard work in a specialized field. (Appendix VI, pp. 312-17.) Summarizing the evidence for the 1950 business elite, Keller remarks on the pervasive and noticeable impact of lengthened career spans, of more intensive and earlier devotion to a single industry and, increasingly, to a single company, and of the older ages of men on achieving top success in the world of big business. Clearly, regardless of social class backgrounds, the latest generation of business leaders has been marked by the altered, bureaucratic patterns of business success.[24] The American trend is paralleled in other industrial societies. According to a recent comprehensive study of the managerial elites of twelve countries:

> . . . advanced industrial development—whether in capitalist, socialist, or communist economies—demands a professionally oriented managerial elite. Access to managerial positions increasingly must be based on competence. And competence becomes ever more dependent upon specialized professional training and experience. As a consequence, the managerial class in the more advanced industrial societies inevitably tends to become an elite of competence, which means that education and training, rather than family ties or political connections, must inevitably become the principal avenue of access to its ranks.[25]

These findings challenge C. Wright Mills' contention that the interchangeability of the power elite has increased in recent years.[26] Indeed, the available evidence suggests that it is becoming more and more difficult to move from one elite sphere to another. Peter Drucker's comments seem to be closer to reality:

> . . . the skills, the competence, the experience of management cannot, as such, be transferred and applied to the organization and running of other institutions. In particular, a man's success in management carries by itself no promise—let alone a guarantee—of his being successful in government. A career in management is, by itself, not a preparation for major political office—or for leadership in the Armed Forces, the Church, or a university. The skills, competence, and the experience that are common and therefore transferable are analytical and administrative—extremely important, but secondary to the attainment of the primary objectives of the various non-business institutions.[27]

4. *Work and leisure:* Hard work and prolonged effort are the lot of most members of strategic elites in modern complex societies. Fulfilling the obligations currently attached to elite status is at the very least a full-time occupation. No worker today is more tied to his machine than the business executive to his desk, the scientist to his laboratory, or the artist to his studio. As a result, throughout the industrial world, leisure as such is no longer a mark of distinction.

5. *Insecurity of tenure:* Although individuals are increasingly achieving elite status, this status, once won, has grown less rather than more secure. Retirement, dismissal, defeat, or rejection inevitably face members of strategic elites. In a world that demands flexible accommodation to rapidly changing problems of national and international scope, tenure at the top is apt to be brief and uncertain. The political leader may fail to be re-elected or reappointed, the general may be stripped of his command, the star may lose his public following, the business leader may have to resign. These men constantly run the risk of losing the places they did so much to win. Most of them are confronted with the prospect of fixed retirement that pays little heed to their actual physical and mental powers. For the hereditary elites of old, entrances were signalled mainly by birth, exits mainly by death. There was no fixed

route to the top because most of the members were already at the top. If the rules of the game were observed, one's status was secure. This pattern of the past survives only in the Social Register of the present day—a strategically unimportant reminder of a bygone era.*

6. *Age at success:* Lengthened career spans mean that the members of elites are generally older upon achieving success than was true in the past. Previously cited studies suggest that whereas top rank is achieved fairly frequently among entertainers at a relatively young age, about 60 per cent of the business, political, diplomatic, and military leaders are over fifty years old at the peak of their careers. The greater the degree of formal organization of an elite, the older its incumbents.

7. *Rewards:* Another general trend is that of rewarding elites according to their services rather than their station in life. The feudal principle of recompense and responsibility on the basis of ancestry and social position has almost disappeared. Today payment for services is usually in the form of salaries rather than in the form of land or other types of fixed property. Some of these rewards (if they are sufficient) can be passed on to progeny, but *not* the positions on which they depend. The likelihood of the emergence of fixed status groups is thus diminishing.

Rewards, like careers, have also become specialized. Financial recompense ranges from the relatively modest earnings of diplomatic, military, and political elites, to the immense salaries of the members of the business elite and screen idols.[28] Moreover, different elites are associated with different types of rewards. The business elite has inordinate wealth but little public prominence; the diplomatic elite, little wealth but considerable public prestige. The political elite has power as well as prominence, and the artistic, scientific, and intellectual elites may achieve personal fame. Members of high society retain local prestige, and religious leaders pos-

* Aside from birth and marriage, the only way to gain entry into the Social Register is to be recommended by someone already listed, whereupon an advisory board decides whether the candidate warrants consideration. If it decides in his favor, the original sponsor receives a form letter asking for four or five additional letters of recommendation from other members. If all goes well, the applicant then gets a blank requesting the information for his listing.

sess moral power in local communities. No single strategic elite monopolizes all or even most of the rewards currently available.*

Internal and external elites

In reviewing these patterns of backgrounds and careers, it is evident that the elites previously described as being concerned primarily with external problems are somewhat more distinctive than those entrusted with internal problems.

In an age that emphasizes the conquest of space and the utilization of new sources of energy, those elites concerned with providing the technological and organizational means for the achievement of these goals will play a particularly strategic social role. This is surely the case in the United States today where headlines are devoted in considerable measure to the leaders of politics, science, business, defense, and diplomacy. It is these elites, moreover, that are increasingly formally organized, recruited, and apprenticed. And it is here that professionalization and specialization are most pronounced. It is here, too, that the Anglo-Saxon model predominates.

Elites concerned with internal system problems of morality and morale exhibit a greater social heterogeneity. This is partly due to the absence of formal organization and formalized procedures for recruitment. The primary responsibility of these elites—moral and religious leaders, first families, leading educators and opinion leaders—is to clarify and coordinate belief and conduct, to interpret an ever-changing reality in the light of certain collective ideals, and to formulate or reassert ideologies related to life in their times. Recreation and sport elites are also characterized by apparent diversity of background and career. The absence of tight formal organization attracts individualists of all stripes and puts a high premium on socially sanctioned egoism.[29]

The political, military, business, and scientific elites, on whom the actual push into the atomic era largely depends, reveal the greatest social uniformity in origins and careers. Their middle class

* This may have significant repercussions on the distribution of incentives for different elite candidates since individuals vary in the rewards they desire.

beginnings, religious affiliations, ancestry, and professionalization of careers, all tend to converge toward a common pattern. There thus appears to be a strain toward social homogeneity among strategic elites whose social functions—in this case, the formulation and achievement of broad, long-range goals—are similar.

Paradoxically the elites of opinion, morality, and morale—once the most rigid arbiters of men's conduct and beliefs—are today relatively diversified. When societies were loosely organized and regionally and linguistically divided, these elites, in particular the religious and moral thinkers, were unified and monolithic. Today, as the rest of society becomes ever more formally organized and centralized, it is they who mirror the need for differentiation and flexibility. Each of these elites, in its own way, passes judgment on current problems by bringing a minority view to bear on the general culture of their age. Their separate efforts thus help relieve the pressure exerted by the despotic majority on those who do not readily fit in with the mainstream. "High society" is often deplored as a social anachronism, but its existence perpetuates the survival of a world view different from that presented in the mass media, in the mass factories, and in the giant cities. In its insistence on its version of traditional (even if outmoded) standards, it shows that its members are not content to follow any and everyone. Similarly, the religious vision of a divine order and divine justice may not be compatible with the skeptic's view of the world, but its existence is one more guarantee against the leveling of tastes and standards in that world. The more numerous these elites, therefore, the greater the protection against ideological and moral absolutism.

Some implications

Increasingly, the topography of the American social structure appears to consist of a number of peaks, each scalable by highly specialized methods adapted to the social and organizational terrain. The decline of the hereditary transmission of elite status is manifested in all leadership groups except that of high society. Privileged groups still predominate in some elites, but privilege is not a prerequisite for success, and although wealth and high social status are very advantageous in some elites, they no longer determine access to the top echelons in business, politics, and culture.

Recruitment of elite members, however, is not as yet a random process. The link between material means and education persists, and the appeal of various types of success is unequally distributed in the different strata of society. Yet, even the elites least open to lower class and lower status aspirants are becoming more accessible. At the highest pinnacles, the boy of privilege, no less than the "poor boy who made good," must achieve and maintain his elite position by hard work, competitive merit, and intensive application of effort throughout most of his adult life. This trend weakens and may eventually break the age-old link between elite status and upper-class status.

The family system—the major link between social classes and the generations—will likely play a diminished role in elite recruitment in the future. In the past, the family was the chief school for both kings and carpenters, and thereby contributed to the continuity of the social order, even as it inhibited the adaptability of this order. The family could only teach what it knew, and much of what it knew were the class codes and ideals by which it lived. It was not necessarily the best nor the most efficient school, and in allowing little leeway to the young it was even tyrannical, but for centuries it was almost the only school.

Today, social and technological changes have deprived the family of the capacity to prepare the future generations for the lives they are to lead. This function is gradually being transferred to other agencies, still in process of formation, whose knowledge and resources are more up to date. Parents are separated from their children not merely by the natural course of the biological life cycle, but also by the accelerating tempo of the sociological life cycle. Once, a goal of most children was to know as much as their parents; today, having only this knowledge would condemn children to ignorance about large and important areas of life. Understandably, more and more parents know less than their children, and this affects not only the psychology of family relations, but the structure of the institution as a whole.

Historically, the influence of the family in class-stratified societies stemmed not only from its power in socializing the young, but also from its powers to reward them later in life with status, property, education, or access to important positions in society. Now, elite positions, though bringing high rewards to their possessors, some of which may be passed on to their children, are usually neither secure nor transferable. Upper and upper middle-class individuals, along with their less fortunate peers, must win such positions through their own efforts. No matter how much this principle may be violated in practice, it is more genuinely observed today than it was one hundred years ago. And once the link between social position and the family system has been broken, the perpetuation of inequality along fixed generational lines may be abolished.

Current patterns of recruitment can hardly be expected to mirror all of these changes equally. These must be perceived rather as part of a shifting balance of social forces—including tradition, self-selection, objective requirements, and public (which includes elite) expectations—each acting on and reacting to the others. The recruitment of elites in American society today reflects the pull of social class, the push of individual merit, and the invisible hand of tradition.[30]

Of course, the suggested trend in elite recruitment in advanced industrial societies may be no more permanent than parallel trends during other expanding epochs in history. Writing of the eighteenth-century Prussian civil service and the heterogeneous origins of its elite members, Rosenberg could be referring to our own day:

> It was indeed an unusual melange of individuals who managed to enter the evolving elite of "public law bureaucrats." . . . Drawn from many walks of life, these social stragglers, when thrown together into the hierarchy of commissioned Hohenzollern servants, suddenly faced each other as professional associates in a joint enterprise. Collectively they formed a distinct functional status group. As individuals, however, they differed sharply among themselves in class origins, education, and occupational background, personal ability and achievement, the amount and sources of income, and, consequently, also in their tastes, attitudes, loyalties, and modes of living.[31]

But he also notes that the most noteworthy component of this service class consisted of "indigenous nobles." Reminiscent of our own day is the fact that even "titled aristocrats were now impelled, before they were entrusted with definite duties, to give the impression of competence."[32] Soon, however, the merit system became linked to a new form of spoils system. Although the permanent hereditary rights to particular offices had been broken at least in principle, family hold on positions and on special branches of the service prevailed, along with other forms of nepotism. In practice, the new emphasis on professionalization and competence became overshadowed by the old stress on family obligations. However, the ideas and ideals had been transformed, and this left its mark on the new system. In time, the Prussian aristocracy was effectively displaced by professional middle-class bureaucrats.

The likelihood of a relapse to some form of hereditary privilege in the modern industrial world is tempered by one important new difference between that time and ours: the nature of the skills and knowledge demanded. Today, these skills can only be acquired individually, and the knowledge on which they are based is ever-changing. With the spread of science, men and their leaders are beginning to learn that knowledge is proximate rather than final, that the discoveries of today may be anachronisms tomorrow. With the institutionalization of this kind of social change, entrenched classes or groups will be less able to monopolize elite positions in the future.

The prevalence of achievement and performance standards and the rise of new patterns of socialization also signifies the decline of the amateur and the rise of the expert—not merely as an adjunct of, or an auxilliary to, those in power, but as a wielder of power.[33] And since experts are made, not born, the circulation of elites increases, along with the variety of individual and of social types recruited into each elite. This consequence of changing social and moral conditions decisively alters the principles of social cohesion and of social balance, not only in the society at large, as Mannheim anticipated, but also, and perhaps especially, at the top.[34]

The almost legendary cohesiveness of British upper-class sons raised and educated by gentry families and public schools has never been characteristic of a society like the United States whose class system is of recent vintage and whose aristocratic traditions were slight from the start. However, the American equivalent—a more or less unified wealthy upper middle class tied by ancestry, property, race, religion, and national descent—has provided a sense of cohesion that should not be underestimated in a mobile, rapidly expanding society. This type of cohesion is difficult to sustain, not to say create, under modern conditions. As Mannheim has vividly shown,[35] with the decline of the medieval church in western

Europe, the idea of one absolute truth was replaced by that of relative truth, varying with the social vantage point of the observer. This phenomenon, which can lead to a sense of anomie described by Durkheim,[36] is now affecting the very heights of the social structure. Elites, in participating in a common enterprise, need a common set of binding moral principles, but, being specialized, they also need an ethic of separateness. This ethic is no longer created *for* them in the homes and schools of their childhood, but *by* them in the corporations and laboratories, the party hierarchy and studios, of the modern industrial world.

Common values among otherwise disparate elites—no longer joined by race or caste pride, nor by ethnic, economic, or religious exclusiveness—may perhaps be furthered by their experience in a society whose culture stresses achievement of that great and rare unifier, *success*. Most members of most elites approve of ambition, self-discipline, and hard work because this is their common lot. And the awareness that theirs is an uncommon destiny contributes to their appraisals of men and events, and enters, though does not determine, their decisions and conduct. The sheer fact of elite membership entails certain similar experiences: the necessity to supervise subordinates, the responsibilities of power and influence, the temptation to self-indulgence, the enjoyment of similar privileges. But this community of experience does not lead to a community of interests. The latter demands a self-assurance which helps elites accept their existence, instead of, as seems the case in the United States, denying or camouflaging it.[37] It also calls for a set of articulated beliefs and ideals justifying the social superiority required by elites to perform their functions. Today, when individual achievement is supposed to determine such superiority, the possession of ascribed attributes such as race, sex, or descent, while pertinent, is no longer morally relevant.[38] New factors must take the place of these earlier promoters of elite identity.

Elites must be capable of developing self-images that stress their communality and their uniqueness. They must consolidate their identities, images, and aims around ideologies that justify and at the same time illumine their specialized, autonomous roles in a joint destiny.[39] Only in this way will they be able to "transmit and safeguard the best elements of tradition," and "develop dynamic ideas" to promote their own claims—which increasingly transcend national boundaries—as well as those of their nation and of humanity.[40] The "end of ideology" may well be the beginning of ideology, for "the end is where we start from." [41]

Notes

1. The nineteenth-century studies of elite recruitment concentrated on men of genius, "great men," and "leaders" or "creative artists." Social backgrounds, to the extent that they were studied at all, were generally used to document the greater contribution made by the higher classes of society, serving thereby to bolster genetic explanations of genius and creativity. See, for example, Francis Galton, *Hereditary Genius* (1871); Havelock Ellis, *A Study of British Genius* (1904). The methodological inadequacies of these studies—as for example their definitions of creativity, and the shortcomings of samples drawn without regard to national boundaries—were soon apparent. And around the turn of the century, studies appeared concentrating on great, successful, or famous men in specific fields. See, for example, J. M. Cattell, "American Men of Science," *Science* XXIV (1906), 732-44; Gustavus Myers, *History of the Great American Fortunes* (1907).
2. These include, among others: Frances W. Gregory and Irene D. Neu, "The American Industrial Elite in the 1870's," in William Miller (ed.), *Men in Business* (1952), pp. 193-212. In the same book, see also William Miller, "The Business Elite in Business Bureaucracies," pp. 286-307. F. W. Taussig and C. S. Joslyn, *American Business Leaders* (1932); C. Wright Mills, "The American Business Elite: A Collective Portrait," *The Tasks of Economic History* (Supplementary Issue to the Journal of Economic History), V (December 1945), 20-44; W. L. Warner and James C. Abegglen, *Occupational Mobility in American Business and Industry,* 1928-1952, 2 vols., and *Big Business Leaders in America* (1955); Mabel M. Newcomer, *The Big Business Executive* (1955); Reinhard Bendix and Frank W. Howton, "Social Mobility and the American Business Elite," *The British Journal of Sociology* IX (March 1958) No. 1, 1-14. For additional references to American studies, see S. M. Lipset and Reinhard Bendix, *Social Mobility in Industrial Society* (1962), Chap. iv.
3. C. Wright Mills, for example, in *The Power Elite* (1956), continually struggles to reconcile two opposed perspectives regarding the power elite in American society, namely that it is unified and becoming more monolithic and that it is diversified and becoming less so. See esp. Chaps. i, ii, and xii, and *passim.*
4. An effort at such a comparative analysis—of political elites throughout

the world—is contained in the surveys of the Hoover Institute. See H. D. Lasswell *et al., The Comparative Study of Elites* (1952).

5. Lasswell recently put forth some proposals relevant in this connection. See, H. D. Lasswell, "Agenda for the Study of Political Elites," in Dwaine Marvick (ed.), *Political Decision-Makers* (1961), pp. 264-89.
6. Walter Bagehot, *The English Constitution* (1901), p. 3. See also Charles S. Peirce, "The Century's Great Men in Science," in Ray Ginger (ed.), *American Social Thought* (1961), pp. 45-63.
7. For a discussion of these studies, see Appendix II.
8. A notable exception is the recent comprehensive analysis of the managerial business elites in twelve countries. See Frederick Harbison and Charles A. Myers, *Management in the Industrial World, An International Analysis* (1959).
9. For a summary of such studies see, Robert K. Merton, "Puritanism, Pietism, and Science," in Merton, *Social Theory and Social Structure* (1957), rev. and enlarged ed., pp. 574-606, esp. the bibliographical postscript, pp. 595-606.
10. *Ibid.*
11. In societies valuing achievement, a knowledge of the stereotypes about existing elites may be an important clue to the distribution of ambitions and aspirations in different social groups. In the absence of precise information, a marginal pattern may loom as the typical one, and some individuals may exclude themselves from certain careers because of mistaken notions concerning the role played by race, religion, or diplomas therein. It is commonly thought, and perhaps rightly, that screen stars are more likely to be drawn from lower social strata than are other elites. However, a cursory examination of small samples of such stars suggests that this pattern may not be typical, and that it may differ for male and for female stars. If this should be confirmed by further investigations, it would lead us to take a closer look at the reasons for this prevalent misconception.

    Even though elites represent only a small fraction of the total population, their visibility and symbolic impact are enormous, and there is reason to suppose that their collective characteristics affect popular expectations about opportunities for "getting ahead." In providing a notion of what the upper limits of mobility are, elites are perceived as models to be imitated or as models beyond one's horizons. For a somewhat contrary view, see S. M. Lipset and Reinhard Bendix, *Social Mobility in Industrial Society* (1962), p. 278.
12. Daniel Bell, *The End of Ideology* (1961), p. 70.
13. Leo Rosten, *Hollywood* (1941).
14. Leo Rosten, *The Washington Correspondents* (1937).
15. With the exception of Anne Roe's book, *The Making of a Scientist,* there are virtually no recent studies of the scientific elite (as distinct from scientists generally who have been more widely studied). Cattell's study is half a century old, and Visher's omits many aspects of social background that one would include today. See S. S. Visher, "Environmental Backgrounds of Leading American Scientists," *American Sociological Review* XIII (February 1948), No. 1, 65-72. For a summary of such studies, see Bernard Barber, *Science and the Social Order* (1952), pp. 134-8.

16. See Appendix I.
17. For example, Paul Goodman, *Growing Up Absurd* (1962), Chap. iii. Gabriel Kolko, *Wealth and Power in America* (1962), esp. Chap. vii.
18. The studies by William Miller and his associates leave no doubt of that. See William Miller (ed.), *Men in Business, op. cit.,* esp. F. W. Gregory and I. D. Neu, "The American Industrial Elite in the 1870's" and William Miller, "The Business Elite in Business Bureaucracies"; also Suzanne Keller, *The Social Origins and Career Lines of Three Generations of American Business Leaders,* Unpublished Ph.D. dissertation (1953).
19. A study of 100 women listed in *Who's Who in America* for 1926-1927 showed that one-third had attained eminence as authors, one-fifth as artists. Persis M. Cope, "The Women of Who's Who: A Statistical Study," *Social Forces* VII (December 1928) No. 2, 212-23.
20. Donald R. Matthews (1960), *U.S. Senators and Their World,* p. 46.
21. Suzanne Keller, *The Social Origins and Career Lines of Three Generations of American Business Leaders, op. cit.,* Chap. vi.
22. Suzanne Keller, *Twentieth Century Ambassadors,* Unpublished manuscript.
23. The percentage of college graduates among the various elite groups studied was as follows: Hollywood stars of the 1930's—18 per cent; Washington Correspondents—52 per cent; Business elite of 1950 (Keller's figures)—61 per cent; Higher Civil Servants (Bendix figures) —80 per cent; Diplomats (Keller's figures)—81 per cent; Military—Air Force, 73 per cent; Army, 85 per cent; and Navy, 98 per cent; Senators —91 per cent.

    The relationship between higher education and general upward mobility has recently been questioned by Anderson who showed that in Great Britain, the United States, and Sweden, a good deal of upward as well as of downward mobility occurs independently of schooling. He suggests that education has more influence on upward mobility in the United States than in the European countries studied. C. Arnold Anderson, "A Skeptical Note on the Relation of Vertical Mobility to Education," *American Journal of Sociology* LXVI (May 1961), No. 6, 560-70. Apparently higher education is very closely related to recruitment into the strategic elites.
24. Suzanne Keller, *The Social Origins and Career Lines of Three Generations of American Business Leaders, op. cit.,* p. 173.
25. Frederick Harbison and Charles A. Myers, *op. cit.,* p. 79.
26. In fact it would seem to be less and less possible for a corporation executive to step into a general's shoes, or for a general to assume a leading position in politics, and for them to make a good job of it. Such interchange can occur more or less successfully only if these men are to be used as figureheads (as when a retired general becomes chairman of a board in industry); this also provides a real or illusory image of unity of the several elites—a unity sorely threatened by the increasing differentiation and autonomy among them. See, C. Wright Mills, *The Power Elite, op. cit.,* p. 287 and Chap. xii.
27. Peter F. Drucker, "The Tasks of Management," W. L. Warner and N. Martin (eds.), *Industrial Man* (1959), p. 191.
28. Most Senators, according to Matthews, must maintain two residences,

entertain, and pay for trips on their salaries of $22,500 plus expenses. D. R. Matthews, *op. cit.*, p. 90.

The financial recompense of big business executives is exceptionally high. Of the 900 top executives studied by *Fortune* magazine, 80 per cent earned more than $50,000 annually, and this does not include shares of stock, pension and retirement plans, and expense accounts. "The Executive Life," *Fortune,* pp. 17, 19. Parsons refers to the "high financial remuneration" of business executives in contrast to government and professional men but feels that it is relatively smaller than the fortunes inherited by the entrepreneurs during the past century, although it is of course larger on an absolute level. Talcott Parsons, "The Distribution of Power in American Society," in *Structure and Process in Modern Societies* (1960), pp. 199-226. See also Gabriel Kolko, *Wealth and Power in America* (1962), Chap. iii.

No matter how high a man's salary he will manage to spend it. In 1948, Conrad Hilton spent $550,000 as follows:

Taxes	$352,000	Maintenance of 2 homes	$32,000
Charity	80,000	Boat expenses	6,500
Family & Friends	36,000	Clothing	4,000
Insurance & Premiums	11,000	Savings	21,000
Club dues & Entertainment	12,000		

From Osborn Elliott, *Men at the Top* (1959), p. 24.

According to Janowitz, only a handful of military men at the top earn over $20,000 a year. Morris Janowitz, *The Professional Soldier* (1960), p. 183.

In the United States foreign service, Career Ambassadors earn $20,000 annually, Career Ministers, $17,500.

In the 1940's, only 2 per cent of the clergymen with college degrees earned $7,500 or more, but we do not know if this applied to the elite of the clergy as well. The figure is cited in Ernest Havemann and Patricia S. West, *They Went to College* (1952), p. 33, Chart 7.

Only one-fifth of the leading journalists studied by Rosten in the 1930's were earning more than $7,500 at that time. Leo Rosten, *The Washington Correspondents* (1937), p. 248.

29. In the large organization, it has been suggested, individuality is sacrificed to the organization and the type recruited into its top echelons is therefore strikingly uniform. "In the large organization even the risks associated with the selection of leadership are reduced. Organization replaces individual authority; no individual is powerful enough to do much damage. Were it otherwise, the stock market would pay close attention to retirements, deaths, and replacements in the executive ranks of the large corporations. In fact, it ignores such details in tacit recognition that the organization is independent of any individual." John Kenneth Galbraith, *The Affluent Society* (1958), p. 102.
30. Sjoberg has argued that the class system at present is both rigid and fluid, and that both are necessary—rigidity for the sake of integration in a highly specialized industrial order, and fluidity for meeting the ever growing need for trained specialists. Gideon Sjoberg, "Contradictory

Functional Requirements and Social Systems," *Journal of Conflict Resolution* IV (1960), No. 2, 198-208.

31. Hans Rosenberg, *Bureaucracy, Aristocracy and Autocracy. The Prussian Experience 1660-1815* (1958), pp. 60-1.
32. *Ibid.*, p. 72.
33. The expert is a specialist in a particular field. Of course, as Janowitz and others have shown, such specialists need not be narrowly defined. *The Professional Soldier, op. cit.*, Chap. ii.

    Samuel Grafton, TV comment on the news, December 17, 1962, Channel 13, made the following observation: "One caught a glimpse of the President as what, I am convinced, history will some day call him —a kind of ARTIST OF DECISIONS. He has objectified the decision-making process. He looks at it with an amazing detachment, as a sculptor, perhaps, looks upon the carving process. He talked of how 'mistaken' decisions abroad started both World Wars, and of how a mistaken interpretation of our intentions by China started the Korean war. Time and again he used the word 'decision,' and in his use of it, it is not a word denoting *power*, but a word denoting skill. . . . Mr. Kennedy seemed tonight, more than ever, the cool, clear-headed, professional of decision-making. No wonder he bulks so large in a country in which the word 'executive' has come to have so many golden and glamorous meanings." Quoted by permission of the author in a personal communication to me January 5, 1963.
34. Note, however, that Mannheim emphasizes the negative impact of this phenomenon. "Indeed, the more elites there are in a society the more each individual elite tends to lose its function and influence as a leader, for they cancel each other out." Karl Mannheim, *Man and Society in an Age of Reconstruction* (1940), p. 86. This need not be the case however, for if one views these elites as linked to the tasks of the social system and proliferating in number and kinds as these do, then the elites do not cancel each other out but supplement each other.
35. Karl Mannheim, *Ideology and Utopia* (1949), p. 58.
36. Emile Durkheim, *The Division of Labor in Society* (1947), Book III, Chap. i.
37. Daniel Bell, *op. cit.*, p. 89.
38. But recruitment on the basis of individual merit rather than ascription will not alter the elite unless these individuals also are permitted to bring new ideas and new moral values along with them. If new men are inculcated with old principles, however, the net result will not be very different from what it was. Such a situation is vividly described by an observer of the recruits at Sandhurst, the British training ground for the military elite. He was shocked by what he calls the "feudal" attitude among the officers and the sense of caste pride coupled with a personal belief in the individual "right to command." "Where I had expected to find a professional officer corps, I found a caste rooted in its own conception of superior, God-given status." Simon Raven, "Perish by the Sword," in Hugh Thomas (ed.), *The Establishment* (1959), p. 79. Earlier, however, the author had indicated that the virtues which the new Army "wished its new entries to possess were of a long-established nature." *Ibid.*, p. 56. Since the ideals had not changed along with new methods of recruitment, these new men were soon turned into old type military officers. One wonders, however, whether and for how long

these ideals can survive the modern conditions of military life in peace and war.

39. Daniel Bell argues that as a result of the "new nature of decision making, its increased technicality," the older elites are being displaced. He mentions the "managerial executive class," the old style military leaders, and Southern traditionalists. "The Dispossessed—1962," *Columbia University Forum,* V (Fall 1962), No. 4, p. 12. I think this is partly true but somewhat exaggerated. It seems more likely that instead of being altogether displaced these elites are merely being asked to move over and make room for some newcomers. They may of course react to this as Bell describes, but then he is diagnosing not the facts of the situation but their fears about it.

40. Karl Mannheim, *Freedom, Power, and Democratic Planning* (1950), p. 106.

41. In the current period of transition between the old and the new, the formation of informal coteries and operational cliques in politics, and perhaps in other spheres, provides a partial sense of community and continuity of interest. These should increasingly be challenged and supplemented by counter-cliques and coteries, equally well-organized, if the outcome is to lead to more than the preservation of established vested interests.

    Richard H. Rovere, "The American Establishment," *Esquire* (May 1962), seems to be referring to just such a unifying clique whose attitudes seem regularly to prevail in important national affairs, although he caricatures them.

    Richard Rose, in "Anatomy of British Political Factions," *New Society* (11 October, 1962), pp. 29-31, refers to "operational parties" composed of a "group of individuals with representation in Parliament which seeks to further a broad range of policies through political action." These operational parties are "elitist, London-based, and concerned primarily with the small political world of Westminster. . . . The functional requirements of a major operational party seem to be: leadership, an ideology, technical expertise, *cadres,* and a communication network."

10. THE RISE AND FALL OF STRATEGIC ELITES

▲ The spirit and vitality of a society, its resiliency and the sense of well-being among its members, are greatly dependent upon the character of its strategic elites. The latter's high visibility, apart from their power to do well or ill, makes them a collective focus of expectations and a collective target for grievances. Whether a street-corner gang or a giant corporation or the state itself, the pervasive influence of the leaders on the general emotional and moral climate of the membership is apparent. What affects these leaders is apt to have widespread social impact. Their triumphs and disasters frequently are the triumphs and disasters of all.

One of the striking facts about these strategic elites, leading Pareto to remark that history is "a graveyard of aristocracies," is that they do not endure. And along with their rise and fall, the fortunes of the collectivities dependent on them likewise rise and fall. Their "fall," often prolonged over several generations, sentences whole generations to a loss of direction and frequently to moral confusion. No wonder that the death of kings has been a subject of drama and myth.

The survival of strategic elites is therefore no less important for the fortunes of men than is the survival of the individuals and social groups to whom they are attached, though our understanding of this aspect of social structure and change is limited. In addition, there has been a tendency to confuse two distinct dimensions of the problem. One refers to the processes whereby individuals or groups gain access to or lose their hold on elite positions. This, "the circulation of elites," as Pareto expressed it, depends on the biological and the socio-psychological replenishment of elite members. The second dimension of the problem involves not the individuals or groups comprising these elites but the functional significance of their activities. As the latter changes so does the significance of traditional elites. The landed gentry is superfluous in industrial societies not because its individual members are incompetent but because the functions performed by the gentry have either been superseded or are now performed by groups better adapted to modern industrial life. Similarly, the decline of capitalist dynasties and the rise of a new managerial elite parallel the change from family to corporate capitalism. Thus as social organization expands or contracts, social positions and the demand for the skills associated with them likewise grow more or less numerous. When elite positions and activities lose their social importance, it is not enough merely to effect a change of personnel. When elite individuals lose their effectiveness, however, their exchange and replacement are in order. There are then both individual and sociological explanations for the rise and fall of strategic elites, and being separate phenomena they deserve separate consideration.

Circulation of elite individuals

BIOLOGICAL FACTORS

Present-day notions about the causes of the rise and decline of elites recall those nineteenth-century thinkers who, in keeping with the Darwinian temper of their day, saw social uniformities largely as reflections of underlying biological laws. In the struggle with nature and with men, those who survived were viewed as the fittest. But what if the "fittest" failed to survive, as long historical experience attested? The answer, some writers thought, must lie in a flaw in their biological make-up, which was unapparent at first but which gradually claimed more and more victims until finally entire lineages were extinguished.

Inquiries into the historical decline of elites frequently led to the conclusion that celibacy and sterility were its chief manifestations.[1]

Many members of hereditary aristocracies, it could be shown, married late or not at all, had few children, especially male children, and were increasingly victimized by disease and high mortality rates in infancy and childhood. The most impressive and thorough demonstration of such a biological demise of an aristocracy is Fahlbeck's study of the causes of the gradual extinction of 3,000 noble lineages of Sweden.[2] The Swedish nobility was formally established as an estate in 1280 and officially abolished in 1860. During these six centuries, the majority of noble lineage died out, one third surviving but one generation, and few of them beyond the fourth. Fahlbeck found that celibacy and infertile marriages were presumably the most common causes of the extinction of the noble houses.[3] In a fascinating series of tables, he showed the increase of both from generation to generation. He also found the same forces to be at work to a lesser degree on the surviving lineages. Here, too, the proportion of noble heirs marrying, begetting male offspring, and surviving from generation to generation was small.

Fahlbeck sought the explanation of aristocratic demise in the realm of biology, namely, in the enfeeblement of noble stock with the passage of time. Similarly, Ammon and Lapouge accounted for the weakening of noble stock as due to their nervous and mental exhaustion and their sexual intermingling with lower classes. The lower classes, in their view, stand to gain from this in the long run, since the higher classes are fated to die out. Galton explained the sterility of peers by their marriages to heiresses, who, he announced, were naturally less prolific than other women. The observed sterility of the higher classes is not due to some fault in the males, he argued, but in the females.[4] Pareto speculated that the dying out of hereditary elites might lie in the fact that the richer classes, while having proportionately fewer children, could save all of them, including the feeble, whereas the poorer classes could save only the strong. But, as he pointed out himself, this obviously does not explain the decline of co-opted—that is appointed—elites.

These writers and others took great pains to adduce biological reasons for the extinction of aristocracies of birth as well as of merit, but none did so convincingly. In fact, a comparison between aristocracies and other groups,[5] which few thought of making, suggested similar patterns to be at work in all. Thus Ammon noted a decrease in the number of children by generation even among factory workers, and indicated his growing dissatisfaction with traditional biological explanations.[6]

These thinkers also resorted to psychological explanations, typically singling out the greater nervous strains and stresses to which leading thinkers, artists, and statesmen were exposed, the burdens of command in art as in war, and the drawbacks of the sedentary life.[7] But this would hardly explain the decline in fertility among later generations of factory workers or merchants.

One wonders how much the findings on celibacy and sterility reflected the changing social fortunes of particular hereditary lineages and groups at whatever social level. Most of the nineteenth-century studies, for example, unwittingly utilized data from groups that were either rising or falling in the social scale, reflecting the shift from feudalism to industrialism. But, as has been suggested, both upwardly and downwardly mobile families tend to have fewer children than stationary families. A recent study of individuals listed in the Social Register and in *Who's Who* showed their marriage and fertility rates to be higher than those of individuals listed in *Who's Who* alone.[8] Baltzell suggests that upward social mobility may well be the intervening variable between social class and fertility. Those who wish to move up in the world often tend to curtail family size in order to facilitate the process, whereas those who reside at the top need make no such concessions to economic and social ambition. Similarly, Fahlbeck found that for married members of the Swedish aristocracy the average number of children was 4.3, leading him to conclude that infertility did not cause the decline of the lineages whose members did marry.[9]

It is not unreasonable, therefore, to suggest that the findings regarding the biological decimation of noble families and of men of genius may reflect their shifting social and historical fortunes. Even Fahlbeck's monumental study does not avoid this possibility, for the Swedish nobility was at the height of its influence by the middle of the seventeenth century and declined until its formal abolition in 1860. His careful recording of christenings and burials, however, was not evaluated against this background. A group in historical and social decline tends to grow defensive, to hoard its diminishing capital, and to contract its commitments and obligations. At best, the future is uncertain, as the world for which one was raised is being usurped by upstarts alien to one's sense of values. In such an atmosphere, one's pride of self and caste is wounded if not extinguished. One may seek to live out one's life, but not to create life anew. Similarly, great artists, writers, and thinkers have rarely had a secure existence—depending on the favor of some patron or on the meager support of a few connoisseurs. Few artists die rich. This general condition of insecurity combined with the demanding nature of an artistic career go far to account for their observed pattern of sterility and celibacy.

The failure to marry and beget offspring may thus reflect psychological and social factors as much as biological ones.[10] It may be true, as Fahlbeck concluded, that "the angel of death hovers over lineages as it does over individuals," but these lineages need not all die of natural causes. Psychological and sociological factors play as important a role in the decline of given elites as do biological ones.

PSYCHOLOGICAL FACTORS

Whatever the specific genetic aptitudes of hereditary elites, they also exhibit special peculiarities due not to their biology but to their "upbringing which has brought out certain intellectual and moral tendencies in them." As serious as their failure to reproduce themselves is their inability to transmit intellectual superiority—an aptitude "with which heredity has least to do. The children of men of highest mentality often have very mediocre talents." [11] The continuing survival of hereditary elites is thus precarious from the start, because social continuity depends on the transmission of cultural values and habits of mind and character as much as on biological reproduction. Hereditary elites incapable of living up to their traditional responsibilities are as surely doomed as if they were merely disinclined to assume them. Nonhereditary elites, though they recruit rather than raise potential successors, face a similar problem. And both are vulnerable at exactly the same point: the link between the generations, the point at which the past is entrusted to those eternal "nouveaux arrivistes," the new generation.

The lack of capacity among potential heirs is only one source of instability. Equally uncertain is the heirs' desire to follow in the footsteps of their fathers. It is in the nature of youth to rebel, but it may nevertheless make a difference whether the rebellion is temporary or permanent, and whether it leads them to reject all or only a part of their birthright.

There have always been children who have preferred to make their own way in the world, because of an interest in some special field of endeavor or because the occupations decreed for them by family tradition have been distasteful. And whether they go their own way or are held in check by the firm hand of their elders, the results are sociologically, though not psychologically, similar—given elite positions are either unfilled or, worse, filled inadequately.[12]

If reluctant heirs fail to find alternative employment without loss of status, they may return to the family fold. But no aristocracy can rely on this circumstance, and all have devised means to curb such rebelliousness by curtailing their heirs' powers or by subduing their spirits. In so doing they have often won temporary reprieves, but have failed to halt the tide of decline. Profligacy, mismanagement, indifference, or passive conformity on the part of the heirs have proved too formidable. Thus, the English aristocracy devised the "strict settlement" as a means to preserve its estates from generation to generation, only to discover that while this did indeed curtail the power of the heir to do harm, it also curtailed the power of the father to discipline him. The chosen eldest son, at his marriage, signed a deed of settlement guaranteeing the descent of the estate intact for the coming generation by greatly limiting his power to sell or mortgage the estate. But in protecting corporate interests against the errors and abuses of individual members, this regulation also prevented the father from using the threat of disinheritance as a means of disciplining the heir apparent. The father could neither withhold a portion of the estate from him nor distribute it among the rest of his children. Profligacy, immorality, and irresponsibility—hard to prevent and even harder to control—were thus a continual menace. For, as has been observed: "Wealth and leisure are likely to produce great diversity of character and taste . . . but unless the members of such a class are restrained by religious feeling or strong moral conventions, their lowest common denominator is apt to be dissoluteness of manners. Gout was the occupational disease of the English aristocracy, and mistresses a frequent by-product of their arranged marriages." [13]

Every landed gentry has worried about how not to exhaust the lands and estates on whom its economic fortunes, and those of the ever present idlers, dowagers, and numerous unproductive relatives, depend. Sound management, however, seems to have been quite rare. In England, most gentry families went from relative affluence to absolute impecuniousness in no little time.

> The first generation might inherit money as well as land from the founding father, and sometimes, too, economical habits. In succeeding generations the family was apt to acquire the characteristic habits of the class to which it had risen; it exhausted the reserves, accumulated debts, and became increasingly vulnerable to changes in the economic climate. This was a tendency only, which might be checked or reversed by a variety of circumstances; vast estates and wide connections gave the great families a certain immunity, but the tendency is clearly visible in the rise and decline of families among the smaller gentry.[14]

This pattern is familiar in societies as separate in time and space as China, Sweden, England, ancient Egypt, and the city states of ancient Greece.

Problems of economic mismanagement and incompetence, grave as they were, could be mitigated by employing the services of an astute overseer. But the problems of indifference, boredom, and a deadly, because passive, conformity were less amenable. Men at the top, whatever their advantages in comfort and luxury, suffer certain disadvantages peculiar to their station, among which the burdens of ancestry, material security, and social pre-eminence rank high.

The injunction to honor the past and its traditions, familiar to all aristocrats, can stifle creative impulse in the best of men, and result in that civilized hesitancy before life that marks many of the scions of great old families.[15] The more glorious the past by comparison with the present, the more firmly the dead claim the living, making them unfit for life in the here and now. To look upon the present with old eyes and the spirit of another time and place dooms men to a hand-me-down existence of borrowed ideals and achievements.[16]

In describing the upbringing of the gentry youth in old China, Fei shows how deeply spontaneity and individuality had to be suppressed for the sake of family and caste solidarity. They were taught to be content with their place, to rejoice in security, and to accept the past as the measure of all things. Not unnaturally, this produced in them a sense of the futility of all effort, and created resigned, conservative, cowardly, and obedient men.[17]

In a world of want, luxury can become a curse. The awareness that one need not, like most other men, struggle for the means of livelihood saps one's initiative. What can be the spur for children born to high social position, except the negative one of fear of losing that position? And fear makes some men timid and cautious, others, reckless and defiant—both extremist reactions. Those spared such fears seem to be faced with equally unpleasant alternatives—a profound indifference to the world and its cares, or a compulsive preoccupation with pleasure. Thus aristocracies, in a move toward self-protection, tend to make virtues of austerity, self-denial, and noblesse oblige, hoping to counteract the natural seductions of their environment. But this itself often breeds boredom—if the pleasures of life are denied and the challenges eliminated, what remains? [18]

If boredom is the typical affliction of those born to old wealth, profligacy afflicts those born to new. The offspring of men who have achieved their elite status rarely have the same drives as their fathers had. Having been raised in affluence, they are often better prepared to enjoy it than to increase it. This may coincide with the covert desires of their fathers, whose capacity for enjoyment was exhausted in the struggle for status—in reaping what their fathers have sown, the sons may satisfy personal as well as parental impulse.

Both first-generation and birth elites thus have ample opportunity to become parasitic human beings. That many do not is remarkable. Their birthright is a security they did nothing to win, an affluence that only remoteness from the mass of men can make morally bearable, and a future that offers little challenge.[19] To reject that world means to be different, and to be different requires the kind of courage that their entire upbringing has been at pains to suppress.

The young aristocrats who rebel against their unearned advantages may thus be among the more spirited and creative individuals within the higher circles. Significantly, these rebels often enter the arts—an area permitting the greatest individuality, and yet having long and deep traditions, a past to live up to.[20]

The rebellion of the young reflects of course more than unresolved family dramas. The world to which the young are reacting is a different kind of world, and their refusal to follow in the footsteps of their elders may indicate not obstinacy but a sound instinct for the realities of life. The son of a British Lord, for example, pursuing a political career must renounce and refuse his title for the sake of his political future.[21] Social change will understandably involve the younger generation more than their elders.

Typically, the circulation of elite individuals involves upward or downward social mobility and is expressed in the rise or reversal of economic fortune, in the presence or absence of success, in the maintenance or loss of occupational position, and in a gain or loss of reputation. At the top levels, the immediate cause of such a rise and fall of individuals is aging and death. The deeper biological and psychological factors, as yet poorly understood, are celibacy, sterility, and indifference or incompetence.

Strategic elites must also be prepared to confront age and death, but as they are not hereditarily recruited they are immune to the scourge of celibacy and sterility. Nor are they apt to succumb to boredom, self-indulgence, anomie, or rebelliousness, since they are not forced into a prearranged life. These pressures are either reduced or entirely absent. Since in principle no one is summarily excluded from access to strategic elite positions, no one need assume such positions without desiring them. In advanced industrial societies where strategic elite positions are individually attained and lost, the circulation of elite individuals is objectively prevalent and morally preferred.

Circulation of elite positions

The rise and fall of individuals and groups into and out of strategic elite positions is eternal—here accelerated, there slowed down—increasing as recruitment on the basis of individual achievement increases. Similarly, elite *positions* themselves and the groups associated with them also undergo transformation. That is, there are social changes affecting not only the types recruited into elite positions but the very bases of these positions.

External and internal changes, such as the rise of new ideas and inventions or the emergence of new world powers, are generally followed by changes in the organization and recruitment of strategic elites. The religious elite is prominent in an age of faith, but subordinate in an age of science as its previous function is subdivided among a number of new elites, or both the elite and its particular function wane. Similarly, a stratum of landowners is superfluous in industrial societies, displaced by corporation executives, engineers, and scientists. In short, environment is always a factor in the rise and fall of elite positions. As Mosca observed, ruling classes decline when they cease to find scope for the capacities through which they rose to power and when what they have to offer loses its importance.[22] The changes ushering in these social reorganizations may have their sources in internal or in external developments, or in both. It is not always possible to tell which. Max Weber, for example, concludes that the decline of ancient civilization was due primarily to the drying up of the sources of slave labor. This he classifies as an "internal" cause—but this is debatable.[23]

These social forces are often imperceptible because they gather momentum only gradually and because the illusion of permanence is necessary both for men and the institutions they create. But whether internal or external forces are held responsible for shifts in the importance of particular elite positions, the elites themselves are always directly involved in their own decline—either by their failure or imperviousness to adapt to change. Nor is this failure solely a result of the short-sightedness to which men in high places are prone. They may correctly perceive and interpret the warning signals along the way but be powerless to turn the tide.[24]

Neither is some flaw of character or incapacity to master men and events necessarily the cause of their undoing. Both success and failure play a role: failure, because it necessarily leaves needs and expectations unfulfilled, and thus presses for new men to solve the perennial problems of life; success, because it brings about irreversible changes that call for a reorganization at the top. Success means growth, expansion, and a change in the number and kinds of interrelationships among men. Thus strategic elites, adequate at one stage of social development, may cease to be so at a later one. The previous organization then becomes a hindrance to the realization of new goals. Often the old elites struggle manfully with the avalanche of new problems until they exhaust their resources or make apparent the inadequacy of existing institutions, and, consequently, their own inadequacy. The ensuing struggle may be more or less violent, depending on the intensity with which the old guard defends its traditions and the new attacks them. Civil wars are generally considered the most terrible for they destroy in each participant a part of his common heritage and thus a part of himself. The final victory is never a total one. So it is with the civil wars of strategic elites: the dethroned elites hover like departed spirits over their triumphant successors.

However strategic elites are displaced, then, they always participate in their own death—either by their obstinate refusal to change or by their inability to keep in step with the tempo of the times. Indeed, Pareto claims that elites are never really overthrown from without but only from within, that they lose their right to live because they have lost their will to live. There is some truth to this claim. Elites, collectively, are prone to develop certain characteristic weaknesses as are their individual members. Of the various ills that may befall them, three are paramount: conservatism, routinization, and loss of faith.

CONSERVATISM

A certain amount of conservatism is desirable and necessary for the designated guardians of social tradition. As collective standard bearers they must uphold the traditions that link the past with the future. But as leaders they must be receptive and alert to new developments. Few individuals can do both jobs well simultaneously. Privilege and power may naturally make men conservative but when combined with a legitimate emphasis on the preservation of cherished traditions, the past no longer simply upholds and supports the present but governs it. Aristocracies, especially those of the blood, gradually become wedded to ancient rituals and set themselves apart from the common life of men. The ensuing estrangement between elites and the public is the surest portent of a mortal struggle to come.

Ultimately, it is social distance which accounts for the fatal conservatism of elites. Yet, some social distance is necessary and desirable if elites are to play adequately their roles as experts, models, and collective symbols. If they are to represent different aspects of the collectivity, particularly the moral dimension, they must be larger than life, yet draw their inspiration *from life*. Strategic elites must resemble the Arabian princes of fairy tales who disguised themselves at night and went among the people to listen to their talk. In the garb of beggars and common men, they learned the thoughts and feelings of the populace. Such nightly visits, in symbolic form, are necessary for elite groups, because without open channels of communication extending in all directions, the best of men become stultified and their best impulses become obsolete. Strategic elites cannot live apart and yet make decisions for a world.

Excessive social distance seems to have always accompanied the downfall of elites. It encourages preoccupation with the creeds and deeds of ancestors, an adherence to fixed canons of taste, of style, and of speech, and an inflated notion of innate self-worth—all of which provide an illusory sense of permanence. As the following observations illustrate, the same tendencies may occur in very different contexts:

> The early British conquerors behaved like all the early conquerors, parading round with their Indian women or elephants, and spent many years without returning home. A later generation brought out English wives, took frequent leave, and created an unbridgeable gulf between themselves and the entire Indian population. Their incomparable standards of justice and honest administration counted for little against the Pukka Sahib complex and the deliberate refusal of all social or human contacts. . . . With each generation, as the material triumphs of the British regime grew more manifest, so did its alien character, and it might be argued that the Indian Empire was lost on the playing-fields of Haileybury.[25]

Mosca makes the same point for an earlier era. In feudal times,

> the Baron knew his vassals personally. He thought and felt as they did. He had the same superstitions, the same habits, the same language. He was their master, harsh sometimes and arbitrary. For all of that, he was a man whom they understood perfectly, in whose conversation they could share, at whose table be it in a humble station, they often sat, and with whom they sometimes got drunk. . . . In the Middle Ages the first peasant revolts broke out not when feudalism was harshest but when the noble lords learned to associate with one another, when the courts of love—a conscious quest of good

manners—had begun to give them polish and to alienate them from the rustic ways of the lonely castle.[26]

And James Reston, a perceptive observer of high politics in America, comments:

> The greatest danger in this city is that civilized, intelligent men do forget in this heady atmosphere who they are and where they came from. More important, if not deflated once a month by a loving wife, they fall victim to the most deadly habit in Washington, which is that they begin to think they actually are what they represent. No doubt this is what Woodrow Wilson had in mind when he divided the men who come to Washington into two classes: those who grow and those who swell.[27]

Whence comes this social distance, this insuperable barrier between men and their elites? Some of it, as already indicated, is desirable; leaders must be set apart from the rest in some special way.[28] When elites were bred rather than recruited, the social distance between them and the public may simply have been a reflection of the general social structure. Today additional factors are operative. One of these factors is isolation and secrecy at the top, the latter of which is vital lest all action be paralyzed. But this secrecy also has another side that destroys confidence, openness, and the flow of ideas and sentiments. For secrecy means isolation, and for elites, isolation ultimately is a sentence of death.[29]

Structural reasons also account for the tendency of top men to get cut off from the general membership of society. For one thing, they cannot socialize with subordinates without destroying their mutual sense of place. Consequently the opportunity for an informal exchange of ideas is lost. Also, men in top positions usually depend on formal sources of information, which is likely to have passed through the hands of self-designated censors, reporting only that information *they* consider desirable. "This circumstance of social structure," writes Merton, "makes for an informational lag. Considerable numbers of people in the organization become alienated from the established norms long before this comes to the attention of the authorities whose job it is to uphold these norms. . . ." [30]

The "blindness of the upper class of the old regime and the way they encompassed their own downfall," which puzzled de Tocqueville, stemmed, in part, from the lack of free exchange of information and opinion between them and the larger public, and the social distance thereby fostered.[31] The aristocratic astigmatism of elites is directed not only toward other men and events but also toward themselves. All ruling groups tend to lack the capacity to see themselves objectively, perhaps because they do not move in an environment in which there is that "free public life" that leads to an exchange of views at all social levels. They meet with adulation and attention wherever they go, have few confidantes and many rivals, and come to believe that they are the centers of the universe. This happens in the most democratic environments, among strategic elites that are popularly elected as well as those born to their positions. Consider T. H. White's description of Lyndon Johnson as Majority Leader in the Senate:

> For Johnson, the United States Senate is more than the Senate: it is faith, calling, club, habit, relaxation, devotion, hobby, and love. For him the Senate, with its hallowed traditions, is the most glorious instrument of government known to man, and each facet of its life—its majestic decisions, its sordid little deals, its prickly personalities, its open clashes and backroom intrigue—fascinates him. Over twelve years the Senate has become almost a monomania with him, his private domain, and *he confuses the United States Senate with life itself.*[32]

Obviously this sociological blindness can attack all types of elites—hereditary and nonhereditary. Lukacs, the important Marxist theoretician and literary critic, indicts the bourgeoisie for this very failing. Admitting that the capitalistic system is more rationalist than all preceding social systems, he tries to show that it is irrational at precisely the point where all societies are irrational: in the ways in which the ruling class perceives and defends itself and its mission. For example, the least defensible aspect of entrepreneurial capitalism was the recurrence of economic crises bringing suffering to workers and marginal producers alike. And although the theoretical solution—economic planning—lay at hand and had in fact been developed by the bourgeois economists themselves, the bourgeoisie could not afford to make use of this solution. For to accept the scientific solution would have been tantamount to accepting its own dissolution, and of this the bourgeoisie was incapable. No class,

Lukacs argues, is capable of this. Thus the bourgeoisie is involved in a basic contradiction between its illusion that it is the master of the capitalist process and its awareness that it must become its ultimate victim. It must therefore develop an ideology to mask this contradiction, and in doing so becomes cynical, hypocritical, and cut off from social and historical reality.[33]

Even if one rejects this conception of the bourgeoisie, one can hardly quarrel with the contention that the bourgeoisie is unable to contemplate, not to say hasten, its own demise. In this, however, it is not unique. Lukacs' conclusion applies to all types of elites, including strategic elites. The latters' sole advantage lies in the fact that their greater differentiation requires them to be self-critical in only a limited sphere and thus to have a relatively wide scope for the critical scrutiny of other elites. The harm caused by their self-deception is thus more limited. The literary elite can write about the decline of, say, the economic elite with admirable detachment, but could not contemplate its own displacement (as distinct from the displacement of rival authors) with anything but incredulity. Conversely, the economic elite can contemplate without pain the death of the novel, hence of novelists, but view its own disappearance as inconceivable.

ROUTINIZATION OF ATTRIBUTES

If complacency, conservatism, and social estrangement from the world of reality are the typical afflictions to which hereditary aristocracies are prone, selection by rote and the resulting staleness in processes of recruitment are those of nonhereditary elites.[34] Max Weber observed that the chief problem of deterioration in family charisma is the "drift of aristocratic privilege toward social snobbery and the monopolization of advantages without commensurate performance," whereas the chief problem of deterioration in institutional charisma "is the drift of functionaries and education toward specialized performance at the expense of personal inspiration or substantive rationality." [35]

Once a given set of criteria is decided upon as relevant or desirable, selection becomes more efficient, even to some extent more impersonal, but precisely because of this it may become automatic and mechanical. Thus the enthusiastic young scientist of one generation becomes the model for the selection of future generations of scientists in external attributes of style, manner, and training but not in the one quality that gave him uniqueness and life—his enthusiasm and genius. Excessive standardization of selection procedures, particularly in giant organizations, is difficult, if not impossible, to avoid. Yet this is probably as damaging to the continued vitality of strategic elites as were snobbery and inhumanity to the old aristocracies. For in time, the social type recruited into each strategic elite will tend to become routinely patterned, in part because it is difficult to determine a man's true capacities in advance of his exercise of them and in part because the symbolic functions of elites demand a certain superficial resemblance among their members. Symbols must be both general and familiar if they are to be socially effective, and selection tends increasingly to favor individuals with the proper social and personal style.

This routinization of selection—as when candidates to particular positions must have attended certain schools or conform to a certain physical type—is greater and thus a greater danger among strategic elites attached to large-scale organizations. Here the "pathologies of status systems" are most evident. As Barnard has observed, whatever the advantages of status systems, such as the distribution of responsibilities according to capacities and interests, one of their main disadvantages is that they "unduly restrict the circulation of the elite." No matter how men are selected, errors will occur and inferior men will be found to occupy superior positions. As status tends to become primary and the individual comes to symbolize that status, he is increasingly judged not according to his actual but to his expected performance. Thus the symbolic importance of a particular status limits the objective evaluation of those occupying it. Even if officials are found to be incompetent they may be retained lest their removal prove injurious to the organization. Once status systems become ends in themselves instead of means to the fair distribution of abilities, responsibilities, and rewards, men are selected not on the basis of how effective they are but how effective they seem to be, that is, how well they satisfy the symbolic requirements of their roles.[36]

This routinization of selection eventually leads to a discrepancy between substance and spirit, and to the triumph of ritualism. Strategic elites cease to be models of inspiration and become caricatures of contempt because they have lost the faith of those on whom they ultimately depend. This in turn may lead them to lose faith in themselves.[37]

LOSS OF FAITH

Observers of both ancient and modern societies agree that the decay or decline of elites is accompanied by a decrease in self-confidence, a "failure of nerve," a loss of faith among them. This has led at times to the hasty conclusion that this loss of faith is a cause of their decline. But as we have seen the decline may be unavoidable in the face of internal or external change, and the loss of faith may reflect a sociological condition and represent the collective anticipation of death. Nonetheless, many writers stress the loss of self-confidence as if it were the primary cause of the greater decline. "We may regard it as an established historical law," writes Michels, "that races, legal systems, institutions, and social classes are inevitably doomed to destruction from the moment they or those who represent them have lost faith in their own future." During the French Revolution, as well as in ancient Rome and in Imperial Russia, the moral conquest of the old by the new preceded the actual triumph of the latter. The ruling classes retained their privileges and prerogatives long after they had lost their right to them within their own hearts.[38] Stalin told H. G. Wells, as reported by Sir David Kelly, former British Ambassador to Russia, that the "rich experience of history teaches that as yet not a single class has voluntarily given way to another class. There is no such precedent in the whole of world history." The Ambassador disagreed:

> But I can find no warrant in history for this statement—on the contrary, one of my most positive beliefs is that the replacement of one governing minority by another is always due either to foreign conquest or to loss of confidence by the governors in their own mission. . . . When I was a child three or four thousand British Civil Servants and sixty or seventy thousand British troops governed several million Indians. It is ridiculous to suppose that this handful ruled so many millions by force; they governed by the hypnotic effect of prestige, because they believed in their divine right to be there.[39]

Whence comes this loss of faith which has so often been observed to accompany the fall of empires and kingdoms? Marx, the rationalist, saw it as the natural reaction of certain sections of the ruling class to the inadequacies of the existing order, and hence to their own inadequacies, making them break away to join the "class that holds the future in its hands." [40] But this often-repeated assertion is hardly an explanation.[41] Aristocratic critics of democracy have suggested that democratically elected elites are unsure of themselves from the very start and therefore can have no fundamental faith in themselves.[42] But they have been unable to prove this assertion because they have usually interpreted "faith" to mean a particular faith or a specific set of principles and values dear to their own hearts.

In fact, the relationship between the decline of an elite and its loss of self-confidence has never been carefully analyzed, and our knowledge of this important process is very limited. The few existing hypotheses generally apply only to the political elites. Yet it would not be especially difficult to obtain information on the decline of given families as social arbiters or of stage and screen idols. Such information could seek to answer the following questions: How do the individuals affected save their wounded self-esteem? What kinds of defenses do they create? How many of them break with the old to join the new—because they are realists or because while ceasing to believe in themselves they have not despaired of life in general, or simply because they cannot bear to watch their own funerals? To study the process of dethronement and displacement in relatively selected and delimited groups may facilitate its study in larger groups.

The behavior of declining elites has widespread repercussions on the rest of society. If they insist on going down with the ship, these elites seal not only their own doom but also that of the entire crew; if they decide to forfeit their places, they give the rest of humanity a chance to live. These issues are relevant because strategic elites, too, must come to terms with the idea of their own eventual death. Within any given sphere, moreover, a continual shifting of social types occurs, a process almost as mysterious as it is persistent. Usually, however, it is more characteristic of elites that are informally organized and less tradition-bound. Consider the entertainment sphere. The comedians of ten years ago have had to make way for the satirists of today, the singing styles of yesterday seem dated now, and the idols of the parents are not the idols of their children. When, where, and how this process starts and gains momentum is still not well known. But a necessary first step in its study is to question the assumption of a one-sided causal connection between a loss of self-confidence among elites and their ensuing decline. It would appear that this is rather a two-way and probably a multi-dimensional process.

When elites fail to keep pace with a world in continual flux—because of traditionalism, social distance, and social self-deception—their mastery over men and events is bound to wane. Their first important errors of judgment result in a gradually intensified suspicion of their powers and decline of public confidence. Sensing that they are losing hold on the public, the response of elites may be a redoubling of effort, or panic, or the first seeds of self-doubt and moral uncertainty. Moral uncertainty spreads as rapidly throughout human communities as does information about a new source of honey among communities of bees—in both instances, no words need be exchanged. Thereafter the stage is set for future errors, uneasily anticipated by the public. The elites must face up to their own fears and doubts as well as to the subtle distrust, the growing anxiety, the mocking challenge, or the resignation gradually spreading through the community. Add to this the inevitability of error in a world in flux, and it is easy to see how the confidence of the public *and* the elites now desperately courting that public will continue to be badly shaken. Mosca reminds us that a "widespread skepticism will in time disintegrate the social order." Once this skepticism extends to the "political formula," or to the collective myth that justifies particular forms of rule, the end is near. "It is perhaps for this reason," he adds, "that all strong and long-lived societies have cherished their 'traditions' even when these have ceased to correspond to current reality and when the educated can no longer believe in them. Socrates was put to death because his rationalism attacked these very traditions." [43] We cannot conclude then that the loss of faith among the strategic elites of a society is the chief cause of their decline—though this process should be systematically studied. Their loss of faith may be rather a consequence of the decline of their cause. The rival hypothesis thus reads: strategic elites lose their faith in themselves when their relevant publics have lost faith in them.

GENERATIONAL DISCONTINUITY

The circulation of elite positions hinges not on the succession of individuals but on the succession of generations. Every year three million infants are born in the United States who will see the world differently from others partly because they were born at one particular historical moment. Not all of them will stress their generational ties above other ties, but some of them will, and at times, all of them will.

New movements succeed or fail to the extent that they capture the attention of the youth ever in search of a faith of their own. In times of rapid social change, the youth is always more abreast of current affairs than their elders because they experience these changes not as changes but as absolutes. And disagreement between the generations, if not conflict, is usually the result.

The sociological importance of the "generation" was stressed by certain French and German thinkers in the eighteenth and nineteenth centuries, among them, the historian Leopold von Ranke, the genealogist Ottokar Lorenz, the literary historian Kummer, the art historian Pinder, the sociologist Comte, and the philosopher Dilthey. All recognized that men born at the same historical moment possess a potential, though not always an actual, bond lending a certain conceptual and perceptual unity to their reactions. Initially this generational concept was thought to clarify the causes of social change and account for the rhythm of social life by linking it to the biological laws of birth, death, and aging. Unfortunately, this model was deceptively simple and inadequate. It turned out that in the types of societies with which these men were concerned social change was far more rapid than biological change. The problem thus became one of discovering the cutting points that separate or divide one generation from another. This problem is still unsolved, and the concept, though potentially powerful, has been largely neglected. Not even Karl Mannheim's stimulating discussion could bring it to life again.[44]

The generational continuities and discontinuities of strategic elites would be a fascinating and profitable subject of study. For the wishes and perspectives of the younger generation have always been of considerable importance in the succession of elites. Indeed, the loss of support of their own young may have hastened the decline of hereditary elites. For the young are usually the first to break away, if such occurs, going off on their own or joining new movements that better express their visions of the world and the future.

Now that strategic elites are becoming both differentiated and nonhereditary, it will be interesting to see whether and how the generations will assert themselves. In one way the likelihood of such self-assertion was greater under a system of hereditary elites because parents could only try to fashion their children in their own image, but they could not select their children according to how well they already fit this image. Where the elders choose their successors—as among co-opted elites—the possibility is high that they will choose those most closely resembling them and therefore the past. Where elites are formally or informally elected by the public at large—as in politics, the arts, and entertainment—new generations can more readily assert themselves.

The notion of generational discontinuity is implicit in Pirenne's famous thesis about the different stages of capitalism. Each period of capitalism, he argued, demands a different type of capitalist, which is not to be found among the descendants of the capitalists of the earlier epoch. This is so because the spirit of enterprise is neither genetically nor socially transmitted from generation to generation within families. How the innovative type of capitalist emerges, Pirenne left unspecified. In thus registering his disagreement with Marx, he concluded that there are as many classes of capitalists as there are different stages of economic history.[45] And he saw economic history as a succession of types of men temperamentally and morally adapted to the various economic stages. The enthusiasm and responsiveness to challenge of the aspiring entrepreneur gives way to the placidity and self-satisfaction of the businessman who has already succeeded. Now concerned primarily with preserving his gains and living in comfort, the incentive or the capacity for innovation is lost. Progress is thus linked to sucessive generations.[46]

Pareto also distinguished between established and aspiring elites in terms of the self-absorption of the one and the self-sacrifice of the other. He did not specifically invoke the concept of the generation, but he implied such a concept throughout his discussion of elite circulation. He begins by noting that not only hereditary elites but co-optive or appointed elites also decline in time and that the supposed biological "causes" adduced to explain the first can hardly apply to the second. The second phenomenon, he argues, requires an explanation in its own right.

Every governing elite, Pareto declares, can survive only by continual replenishment from the subordinate masses—preferably from the healthier rural elements. Thus the individual circulation of elite members is an indispensable condition of the continuity of elites. But even where this individual circulation is operative, elites may decline, mainly because of the general moral decline that sets in once they are in power. Recruitment is held partially responsible, for every criterion of selection in favoring some men and excluding others leads to the eventual selection of mediocre men—cautious and conservative men who will simply preserve what others have attained. Such individuals do little more than cynically manipulate the masses so as to preserve their own power long after any ideals have ceased to inspire them. A profound imbalance develops between the manipulative elites and the masses who look to them for guidance. This imbalance can be righted only if one group yields its place and makes room for a new elite with its ideals still intact and better adapted to the changing times. But since no elite gives up its social position voluntarily, a counter-elite must develop that will eventually grow strong enough to overthrow those in power and step into their places.

The old and the new elites stress different types of skills, aims, and personalities, each group developing a surplus of certain qualities and a deficiency in others. This imbalance alone creates pressures for change. The reigning elite develops individualistic, greedy, self-centered, corrupt types—the "foxes"—who are shrewd and clever at chicanery. The rival elite develops and attracts men of confidence, strength, idealism, and group-feeling—these Pareto called the "lions." It is the fate of all foxes to be overthrown by the lions, and it is the fate of all lions to become foxes.[47]

Pareto never explains why the governing elite must eventually grow cynical, except to imply that the debilitating effects of age and the corrosive effects of power are at fault. And though he would have liked to use his model of the governing elite as the model for all elites, it is clearly not applicable to all. The rise and fall of schools of painting, schools of thought, moral beliefs, or styles of beauty can hardly be attributed to cynicism among the elites involved. In addition, if there is a continued revitalization of elites through recruitment of new members from below, why does the moral decline and loss of faith occur at the top? Pareto, himself puzzled by the decline of co-opted elites, lamely suggested that this is due to their tendency to choose as successors men with mediocre qualities. Whether he meant by this persons similar or inferior to themselves is not clear.

Michels, in discussing different types of working class leaders, gives us one clue to the problem. He describes the men who join the socialist movement early as idealists who are out to win a cause, not to accumulate personal advantages. But once the cause has been won, the cynics, egoists, and cowards start to join the organization and may even become dominant. Thus the moral character of the elite changes not because the members of the original elite (the early leaders) necessarily grow conservative or cynical, but because their relative influence declines once success is attained. The original movement, initially small and dedicated to the cause, attracts opportunists of every stripe as it expands and these extend their immoral influence at the expense of the original leaders.[48]

Michels' discussion takes us a little step ahead, for he suggests that the later candidates for socialist leadership are morally inferior men. In reference to strategic elites, this means that the supply of candidates may stay constant, but that its character may change. Once institutions become established, they may attract those who prefer safety and security to challenge and change. Social rigidity and conservatism thus may result despite the circulation of elite individuals. It is not that co-opted elites tend in time to choose mediocre men—as Pareto supposed—but that the men who present themselves as candidates may be more mediocre at a later period. In and of itself, upward mobility into the strategic elites does not guarantee that these elites will avoid the pitfalls of rigidity and routinization to which they are prone. This method of recruitment is far preferable (it is probably indispensable) to other methods available in industrial societies, but in the last analysis, it is only as effective as the candidates it attracts. This illustrates once again the reciprocity and interpenetration of strategic elites with the collectivities they represent. The character of an elite depends on the ways in which it is recruited, on the moral, instrumental, and personal qualities of its members, and on the purposes and projects it entertains.[49]

In summary, several prominent factors are operative in the failure of elites to survive: their inability or reluctance to reproduce themselves when inheritance of elite position was the expected pattern; the degeneration of their creative powers due either to the inbreeding of incapacity or to the selection of unsuitable candidates; and certain social afflictions such as conservatism and excessive social distance from the mass of men and their problems.[50]

In this chapter we have tried to isolate the chief dangers confronting elites, some of which have been overcome, others of which are still with us. If the existence of leading minorities is inevitable, so is their rise and fall. For only through a change in the types of men at the top can new inventions, new experiences, and new ideas become part of the whole community. Thus the decline of elites may reflect not only the failure to meet the ever-present challenges faced by man and society, but also result from their successes. Whichever the cause, it will determine the response of the declining elite to its fate, to which in turn the public reacts. There are many ways of dying and as many reasons. Some elites have passed from history gracefully; others violently, seeking to pull everything down with them. Whether men will suffer much or little at the death of their elites depends in substantial measure on the latter's maturity and realism.

Strategic elites in modern industrial societies are protected against the biological disabilities that threatened hereditary elites, but they are not equally protected against the psychological and social disabilities of social distance, conservatism, and the routinization of attributes. As regards each of these, members of the elites and their publics must make a conscious effort to minimize their occurrences and ill effect. Today, the variety of existing strategic elites is itself insurance against a general stultification at the top: if one strategic elite should succumb, there are others to carry on their functions. In the past, the stultification of one part of the strategic elites affected all parts because of the greater homogeneity and fusion of functions. The current heterogeneity and diffusion thus have conspicuous advantages over and above those already enumerated.

The circulation of elite individuals is evidently greater under the current system than under earlier ones, with respect to absolute numbers and the variety of abilities and qualities being tapped. The circulation of elite positions is likewise likely to continue. One of the sources of this circulation is the fact that ultimate ends require interpreters to make them concrete and tangible. But many interpretations are always possible; and the very articulation of one interpretation creates counter-interpretations. Moreover, although strategic elite positions must be assumed by minorities, these minorities can always be challenged and displaced.

The members of each strategic elite must therefore learn or be taught to expect that they too will be displaced. Societies that do not grow tend to decay. Thus elites must aim for success and growth and be prepared to yield their places even if they are successful. In time, all elites, the successful and the unsuccessful, must surrender their powers and withdraw from the center of the social stage. They may continue to have a place in the memory of men, as did the Furies in the hearts of fifth-century Athenians, but they will not again decide and act for the multitude. Therein lies the renunciation eventually demanded of all strategic elites, and this renunciation remains the most important lesson they have yet to learn.

Notes

1. See among others, Vilfredo Pareto, *Systemes Socialistes,* Part I (1902); Pitirim A. Sorokin, *Social Mobility* (Chap. xv), "The Factors of Vertical Circulation," pp. 346-377 (1927); Otto Ammon, *Die Gesellschaftsordnung und Ihre Natuerlichen Grundlagen* (1895); Francis Galton, *Hereditary Genius, An Inquiry Into Its Laws and Consequences* (1871); Francis Galton and Edgar Schuster, *Noteworthy Families* (1906).
2. Pontus E. Fahlbeck, *Der Adel Schwedens* (*und Findlands*), "Eine Demographische Studie" (1903).
3. *Ibid.,* p. 98. Of the 1,452 extinct lineages with sufficient information

as to causes of death, 40 per cent of the last surviving male offspring did not marry; 24 per cent were married or widowed, with no children; 17 per cent were married or widowed, with daughters only; and 17 per cent were married or widowed, whose sons died in infancy.

4. Galton, *Hereditary Genius, op. cit.* When this "explanation" did not help him account for the equally striking rates of sterility among the judges of England, he held their late marriages to their mistresses responsible.
5. Francis Bacon, *Selected Writings* (1955), p. 20. Many groups of "great men," leading artists, writers, and men of genius, have similarly been shown to be relatively sterile, leading Francis Bacon to observe that the "noblest works have proceeded from childless men; men which have sought to express the images of their minds, where those of their bodies have failed. So the care of posterity is most in them that have no posterity."
6. Ammon, *op. cit.*, p. 147. His specific words are: "Die Frage scheint mir noch nicht genuegend studiert zu sein." In her study of the merchant class of thirteenth-century England, Thrupp found that this class was barely reproducing itself. Only two thirds of the sons of merchants followed in their fathers' footsteps. Without outside recruitment, the merchant class would have died out. See, Sylvia L. Thrupp, *The Merchant Class of Medieval London* (1948), esp. Chap. v.
7. Fahlbeck, *op. cit.*, p. 168. Fahlbeck is among the few writers who does not find nervous and mental illnesses to be greater in the higher classes. Nor does he find immorality to be greater among later generations of hereditary aristocrats, saying that they were not rich enough and too religious for that. Nonetheless he is puzzled by the biological decline of the aristocracy, and finally becomes somewhat mystical, asserting that man must pay for his superior knowledge and sensitivity not with his own life but with the life of his offspring.
8. E. Digby Baltzell, "Social Mobility and Fertility Within an Elite Group," *Milbank Memorial Fund Quarterly,* Vol. 31 (October 1953), No. 4, pp. 411-20. The two groups comprised 226 Philadelphians listed in both the Social Register and in *Who's Who,* and 544 Philadelphians listed only in *Who's Who.* Of course we would also have to know whether the members of the Social Register who are listed in *Who's Who* are representative of all the members of the Social Register. If not—and the exclusion of the isolates, the playboys, and eccentrics would suggest that they are not representative—the finding is more interesting as to what it reveals about the members of *Who's Who* than about the members of the Social Register.
9. See also, Corrado Gini, "Real and Apparent Exceptions to the Uniformity of a Lower Natural Increase of the Upper Classes," *Rural Sociology,* Vol. I (September 1936), No. 3. He also found that at times the average number of children is highest for the upper classes, though he thought this was offset by their lesser marriage rates and longer lifespan.
10. H. J. Habakkuk, "England," in A. Goodwin (ed.), *The European Nobility in the Eighteenth Century* (1953). Wars are another oft-mentioned "cause" of the extinction of hereditary elites. Habakkuk blames the War of the Roses for the decline of the medieval English nobility and its acceptance of new blood—"worthy" outsiders—into its ranks. Fahlbeck, however, did not find death in war to be a significant cause of the

extinction of the noble lineages he studied—only 59 out of 1,452 extinct lineages could be traced to war casualties.

11. Mosca, *The Ruling Class* (1939), Chap. 2. Mosca goes on to point out that this is why "hereditary aristocracies have never defended their rule on the basis of intellectual superiority alone, but rather on the basis of their superiorities in character and wealth."
12. See, Robert Michels, *Political Parties* (1959), p. 264. Michels presents a long list of what he calls the "types who defect from privilege to progress" (he is referring to middle and upper class individuals who join socialist movements), among whom are the young idealists, the satiated rich, the anxious rich, malcontents, neurotics, and ego maniacs who, feeling insufficiently appreciated by their own class, seek quick successes elsewhere.
13. Habakkuk, *op. cit.,* p. 20. Another device designed to assure motivation among the young was the use of sibling rivalry as a spur to competitive excellence, as in the Middle Eastern monarchies. While possibly improving the quality of the candidates, an unfortunate by-product of this struggle over the patrimony was a series of bloody fratricidal wars that poisoned family relations for generations.
14. *Ibid.,* p.8.
15. The Boston descendants of old families have been brilliantly described by Elizabeth Hardwick: "These unhappy men carry on their conscience the weight of unpublished novels, half-finished paintings, impossible historical projects, old-fashioned poems, unproduced plays. Their inevitable 'small income' is a sort of dynastic flaw like hemophilia. Much money seems often to impose obligations of energetic management; from great fortunes the living cells receive the hints of the possibilities of genuine power, enough to make some enormously rich Americans endure the humiliations and fatigues of political office. Only the most decadent and spoiled think of living in idleness on millions; but this notion does not occur to the man afflicted with ten thousand a year. He will commit himself with a dreamy courage to whatever traces of talent he may have and live to see himself punished by the New England conscience which demands accomplishments, duties performed, responsibilities noted, and energies sensibly used. The dying will accuses and the result is a queer kind of Boston incoherence. It is literally impossible much of the time to tell what some of the most attractive men in Boston are talking about. Half-uttered witticisms, grave and fascinating obfuscations, points incredibly qualified, hesitations infinitely refined—one staggers about, charmed and confused, by the twilight." Elizabeth Hardwick, "Boston," in *A View of My Own* (1962), pp. 145-59.
16. By using the past as a yardstick for the present, one is virtually asking to be left behind, and passed by, as was the American Henry Adams: "Something had been thinned down or defeated in him; and we must suppose that by his time New England had been turned into a forcing house. His attachment to democracy made him a dashing critic of Europe at first; but when detachment set in, he quickly caught the defect of the detached mind: *its tendency to stick to out of date evidence*. . . . Adams was a snob, a very intelligent and imaginative one, but still a snob." V. S. Pritchett, "The Man Who Snubbed Himself," *New Statesman,* March 14, 1959, p. 371. Italics supplied.
17. Hsiao-Tung Fei, "Peasantry and Gentry": An Interpretation of Chinese

Social Structure and Its Changes," in Reinhard Bendix and S. M. Lipset (eds.), *Class, Status, and Power* (1953), pp. 631-651.

18. Amy Kelly, *Eleanor of Aquitaine* (1957), p. 42. Boredom or *accidia* was one of the seven deadly sins in the Middle Ages—proof that it was not an uncommon tendency, especially, one would suppose, among the chatelaines, though it spared not even the queen. Of Eleanor of Aquitaine, her biographer wrote: "In the eight years since she had come up from the lively courts of the south, she had exhausted the Ile de France as a theater of interest. Paris offered no proper arena for women, for duchesses, for queens. She was bored with dialectic, bored with universals, with discourse upon the unfathomable nature of the Trinity, bored with bishops and with abbés and the ecclesiastical conclaves over which they presided, bored with dedications and with pious pilgrimages. She was not a little bored by her overlord, by his naïveté, his scruple over trifles, his slavery to ritual, his lingering immaturity."

19. See R. K. Merton, "Continuities in the Theory of Social Structure and Anomie," in *Social Theory and Social Structure* (1957), pp. 161-194, p. 191. It is clear that here is a source of anomie not usually included in discussions of this term, though Durkheim did originally use it to refer to those whose economic fortunes had changed for better or for worse, but not to those born to high positions. In a society in which individual achievement is strongly emphasized, particularly achievement of economic and material position, those born to high positions are morally handicapped. A society that stresses earning one's privileges places peculiar burdens on those not earning yet enjoying them. To pretend to work for the good things of life when one possesses them is hypocrisy. Yet not to work where everyone works is acutely guilt-provoking. But what to work for—in a society that stresses what one already has—is a bewildering and embarrassing predicament. Unless they find an activity that is rewarding and meaningful—whether in the arts or in philanthropy—such individuals are likely to be among the most miserable of beings. Certainly this source of anomie should be added to the two main types discussed by Merton, who distinguishes between the anomie produced by a discrepancy between the moral right to upward mobility in the face of objective barriers, and the anomie that results from the moral condemnation of mobility that has in fact occurred. The individuals thrown into the particular confusion designated as anomie are, in the first instance, those who fail to move up; in the second instance, those who succeed in doing so. I am now suggesting a third type, namely, individuals who are at the top without having done anything to get there. The findings on the higher suicide rates among some elements in the higher classes may reflect this type of anomie rather than, as Powell suggested, the altruistic self-effacement of those in the more responsible occupational positions. See, Elwin H. Powell, "Occupation, Status, and Suicide: Toward a Redefinition of Anomie," *American Sociological Review* XXIII (April 1958), No. 2, 131-139; see also, Austin L. Porterfield and Jack P. Gibbs, "Occupational Prestige and Social Mobility of Suicides in New Zealand," *American Journal of Sociology* LXVI (September 1960), No. 2, 147-152. Porterfield found that the upper-class suicides in New Zealand were downwardly mobile rather than stationary, but he gives no further details. No studies to date have examined the suicide rates of specific strategic elites. Offhand, one

would feel that the suicide rate among the pattern maintenance elites would be higher than among the integrative elites, but this is mere speculation.

20. E. Digby Baltzell, *Philadelphia Gentlemen* (1958), p. 47. Baltzell found that of the Social Registerites who had also achieved status as revealed by their inclusion in *Who's Who,* the younger generation was twice as likely to have gone into the arts and literature than the older. Unfortunately the age limits are too broad—younger, including men under sixty-five; older, including men sixty-five and over.
21. *New York Times,* July 29, 1961, p. 6. This has been dramatically headlined by the case of Anthony Wedgwood Benn who was both a member of the House of Commons, to which he had been duly elected, and a member of the House of Lords. Upon the death of his father, he assumed the title of the second Viscount Stansgate, thus having no right to sit in the House of Commons. He then attempted to rid himself of his peerage by claiming that he was not of noble blood. However, on July 28, 1961, the High Court of Justice ruled that there was no way of getting rid of an unwanted peerage, and Benn lost his right to sit in the House of Commons and therewith his political position. In a brief statement following the verdict, he expressed confidence that "discrimination against the nobilty would eventually end," adding by way of justification that "Catholics, Jews, free-thinkers, and women were all once excluded from Parliament."
22. Mosca, *op. cit.,* Chap. 2. If a social force such as religion declines in importance, says Mosca, then the section of the ruling class whose position was dependent on the control of religion will also decline. If the entire ruling class had been dependent on religion, then the entire ruling class would either have to change its character by adapting to the new or be overthrown. "Thus the growth of new social forces and the decline of old forces is in general correlated with the constant process of change and dislocation in the ruling class."
23. Max Weber, "Die Sozialen Gruende des Untergangs der Antiken Kultur," in *Gesammelte Aufsaetze zur Sozial und Wirtschaftsgeschichte* (1925), pp. 289-311. Though his essay concentrates on the slave supply as the chief determinant of the shift from an urban to a rural way of life, in actual fact one could—as Weber in effect does—argue that the death of the urban culture, which was after all the substance of ancient civilization, was equally significant. The "twilight sleep" to which he refers may just as well have been caused by the abdication of the urban patriciate.
24. A fine account of the decline of an aristocracy, as seen through the eyes of one of its most civilized, lucid, and sensitive members, is contained in Guiseppe Di Lampedusa, *The Leopard* (1960).
25. Sir David Kelly, *The Ruling Few* (1952), p. 7.
26. Mosca, *op. cit.,* p. 112.
27. James Reston, "To the Great Men's Ladies, God Help Them," *New York Times,* January 20, 1961.
28. S. A. Stauffer *et al., The American Soldier,* I (1949), p. 393. In this connection see Stauffer's remarks on the characteristic differences in the attitudes of officers and enlisted men to almost all aspects of Army life, with the officers holding more favorable ones.
29. Thus it is disturbing to learn that such secrecy is likely to stay with us

as regards advanced developments in nuclear physics. "The world being what it is today and is likely to be for a long time to come, secrecy and applied nuclear physics are words that must be joined together." Conant, *Modern Science and Modern Man* (1952), p. 31. Any top establishment is full of mysteries, some being in the nature of things, others in the nature of men. Thus, White, in discussing the sprawling network of power enclaves in American society at the local political level, writes: "Where true power lies in these hundreds of revolving, dissolving, nascent and fading political groups is known only by the local folklore, *below the threshold of public report* . . . The laws of libel, the decencies of political reportage, the conventions of friendship and custom, the obstacles of distance and parochialism, all effectively conceal the ever-changing topography of American politics." T. H. White, *The Making of the President* (1961), pp. 136-37. Italics supplied.

30. Robert K. Merton, *Continuities in the Theory of Reference Groups and Social Structure, op. cit.,* pp. 347-348. He adds: "Belated concessions to the now patently changed norms of the organization serve only to make apparent to all how much the previously existing authority has declined." This may be why—as de Tocqueville, de Coulanges, and Pareto, among others, have warned—"governments" that become "humanitarian" or that try to improve conditions after having been blind to the need for such improvement, are signing their own death warrants. For by their yielding at that point they are publicly proclaiming both their previous incompetence and their current apprehensiveness.
31. Mary McGrory, "The Optimist," *New York Post,* August 2, 1961, p. 3. Thus in an interview, Attorney General Robert F. Kennedy expressed his opinion that relatively few people—even within the inner though not the innermost circles—dare to speak up to the President. "The number of people who do is quite limited. The Attorney General is not only allowed but expected to talk back, and has observed with surprise the reluctance of people to speak freely before the chief executive." De Tocqueville, *The Old Regime and the French Revolution* (1955), p. 143. This is why de Tocqueville suggested that political freedom is "no less indispensable to the ruling classes to enable them to realize their perils than to the rank and file to enable them to safeguard their rights." As the French nobility did not participate in a "free public life," their views were the views of their fathers and "they could not move with the times."
32. Theodore H. White, *op. cit.,* p. 132. Italics supplied.
33. Georg Lukacs, *Geschichte und Klassensbewusstsein* (1923), pp. 57-93.
34. Max Weber, in Gerth and Mills (eds.), *Essays,* "The Sociology of Charismatic Authority," pp. 245-252; "The Meaning of Discipline," pp. 253-264; and "The Social Psychology of the World Religions," pp. 297-299. Routinization of attributes appears at first glance to be similar to Weber's conception of "routinization of charisma," as it may well be. Weber referred specifically, however, to the process of transition from charismatic leadership to bureaucratic or traditional domination. He was chiefly interested in the transformation of spontaneous social movements inspired by the unworldly, impassioned heroic leader into institutionalized establishments led by formally and rationally designated authorities. Just as Weber extended Rudolf Sohm's original concept of charisma from the sphere of religion to all social spheres, so the concept

of routinization of charisma can be extended to apply not only to the continuity of spontaneous social movements but to the continuity of any established social pattern.

35. Reinhard Bendix, *Max Weber, An Intellectual Portrait* (1960), p. 314.
36. See C. I. Barnard, "The Functions and Pathologies of Status Systems," *Organization and Management* (1948), pp. 207-244.
37. Chung-li Chang, *The Chinese Gentry* (1955), p. 115. This routinization will adapt itself to different systems of selection. Chang describes how a Chinese Emperor of 1727 had to combat the breakdown of the examination system by instituting the purchase system! "Recently"—these are the emperor's words—"I see that among those who rise through the examination system, not only are many careless and perfunctory, but many are also corrupt and lawbreaking. The practice of teacher-student examiners and successful examinees, and classmate relationships associated with favoritism and appeals to feelings, is seen everywhere and is unbreakable. If the official career should be left completely to those who rise through examinations, they would just firmly join together and work in their private interests against the public interest. This is of great harm to the public welfare and to the livelihood of the people. The purchase system should be appropriately expanded." Favoritism plays a role in the recruitment of all nonhereditary elites, directly and indirectly. Men naturally prefer those who resemble them, sharing their values, habits, and beliefs, and come to see them as superior to other candidates who may nevertheless be equally or better qualified.
38. Michels, *op. cit.*, p. 243. A society "which lacks a lively faith in its own right is already in its political death agony." *Ibid.*, p. 242. The German poet Heinrich Heine prophesied in 1843: ". . . for communism it is an incalculable advantage that the enemy against which the communists contend has, despite all his power, *no firm moral standing*. Modern society defends itself simply because it must do so, without any belief in its own rights, and even without any self-respect, just like that ancient society which crumbled to ruin at the coming of the carpenter's son."
39. Sir David Kelly, *The Ruling Few* (1952), p. 5-6.
40. Karl Marx and Friedrich Engels, *Manifesto of the Communist Party* (1848), p. 109.
41. The sentence—a portion of the ruling class breaks away and joins the class that holds the future in its hands—is one of the most cryptic phrases in Marx's writings, tantalizing enough to be systematically studied, though no one has as yet done so. It is astonishing that this sentence is continually reiterated as if it stated a truth instead of a provocative hypothesis. *Ibid.*
42. For a recent discussion of such views, see William Kornhauser, *The Politics of Mass Society* (1959), Chaps. i and ii, esp. p. 66.
43. Mosca, *op. cit.*, Chap. ii.
44. Karl Mannheim, "Das Problem der Generationen," *Koelner Vierteljahrshefte Fuer Soziologie,* VII (1928), 157-185. Mannheim leans to Heidegger's view that a generation is a group of people participating in a common historical and social fate. He then proposes some additional conceptual distinctions that need not be discussed here. Clearly, however, Mannheim has not solved the problem of the boundaries between generations. Rather, he has by-passed it. His formulation is useful only for ex post facto explanations rather than for predictions,

since one cannot know who has participated in the same historical fate until the fateful era is past.

45. Henri Pirenne, "The Stages in the Social History of Capitalism" (Address delivered at the International Congress of Historical Studies, London, 1913), pp. 494-496.
46. For a discussion of the general relationship between age groups and social structure, see S. N. Eisenstadt, *From Generation to Generation* (1956). Eisenstadt does not deal with the problem of the "generations" as it was first posed by the European thinkers; rather, he seems to be concerned with the relations between youths and their elders and with the ways in which youths become integrated with the world of their elders. He thus defines youth largely in terms of adolescence. But as already indicated, the generations cannot be defined solely in their relation to the physiological life-cycle. Some generations may be so defined, others not. Thus, sociologically, two groups may be only five years apart in age and yet belong to two different and even opposed generations, whereas other groups may be thirty years apart and belong to the same sociological generation.
47. Pareto agrees with Marx that the rise of the new elite depends in part on the disaffection of a portion of the old elite who in leaving the foxes and joining the lions contribute their superior wits to the latter's superior strength assuring eventual victory. Like Marx, he presents a ready-made conclusion without accounting for it. See also, Marie Kalabinska, *La Circulation des Elites en France* (1912), pp. 109-10.
48. Michels, *op. cit.*, pp. 212-213.
49. Max Weber, "The Protestant Sects and the Spirit of Capitalism," Gerth and Mills (eds.), *Essays,* p. 320. In this connection Max Weber's comments are pertinent: "According to all experience, there is no stronger means of breeding traits than through the necessity of holding one's own in the circle of one's associates."
50. Arnold J. Toynbee's *A Study of History,* Vols. I-VI (1934-1959), is chiefly concerned with the distintegration and to a lesser extent with the rise of civilizations. These volumes warrant careful study for their detailed descriptions and illustrations based on materials from societies all over the world and encompassing a time span of some six thousand years. Conceptually, however, these volumes do not advance our understanding because most of the concepts are used tautologically. Toynbee speaks of a "creative minority" successfully responding to challenge when a civilization (which he defines in global terms) is in the process of growth, and of a "dominant minority" still challenged and still responding but no longer successfully when the civilization is in process of decay. But he does not enable us to pick out the characteristics that would help us identify a creative as distinct from a dominant majority independently, that is, in advance of a knowledge of their historic roles. In the absence of independent criteria, however, it is impossible to judge the actions of these minorities except after the fact. See also M. F. Ashley-Montagu (ed.), *Toynbee and History* (1956), particularly the essays by Pieter Geyl, Hugh Trevor-Roper, and Pitirim A. Sorokin.

11. ELITES, EQUALITY, AND FREEDOM

▲ This book seeks to clarify the nature and goals of strategic elites in modern industrial societies. Every society has a core group representing its unity and potentiality for common action. This group assumes different forms depending upon such circumstances as size of population, availability of skills, the division of labor, and the modes of biological and cultural survival. In advanced industrial societies the core group consists of several elites, each possessing distinct social functions and organized in distinct ways. These elites are responsible for the material and moral well-being of diverse groups and of the national community as a whole. The make-up, capacities, and decisions of elites both reflect and influence the characteristics of the societies in which they emerge.

Recapitulation

We began by raising four major questions about these elites. We asked first about the number of elites and the social conditions surrounding their emergence. It was proposed that the number of elites varies, depending upon the extent of social differentiation and centralization. Currently, four types of elites, performing a number of basic social functions, may be identified. These constitute the *strategic elites,* and are to be distinguished from the ruling castes, aristocracies, and dominant classes of the past whom they resemble in general social purpose while differing in specific organization. As societies become more differentiated internally, the core group becomes more differentiated and specialized. Strategic elites thus "represent" both the unity and internal diversity of society.

Our second question concerned the more specific functions of these elites. Using the social system model developed by Talcott Parsons, four basic types of elites are currently identifiable: goal attainment elites—those organizing the attainment of general social purposes; adaptive elites—those developing the means to achieve these goals; integrative elites—those articulating general moral standards and beliefs; pattern maintenance elites—those reflecting the general morale of the members of society. These four types were shown to operate within the same over-all social framework but to perform specialized tasks.

Strategic elites were also differentiated according to whether they are primarily concerned with problems internal or external to the social system. Integrative and pattern maintenance elites were depicted as concentrating on internal problems involving moral conduct and individual aspirations; whereas goal attainment and adaptive elites were described as focusing upon such external problems as relations with the outside world and plans for the future. The latter elites tend to emphasize the instrumental aspects of their responsibilities and are highly organized; while integrative and pattern maintenance elites tend to stress the symbolic aspects and are more diffuse and individualistic in orientation. These four types of strategic elites do not represent an exhaustive classification, necessarily. In the United States, for example, at least ten such strategic elites may be identified currently, but a shift in population, scientific discoveries, new ideological currents, or other changes may result in the emergence of new strategic elites.

The functional and symbolic differentiation of strategic elites is paralleled by their moral differentiation with respect to the core values of the social system, each being linked more closely with some of these values than with others. In the past, the social core group was morally unified in large part because it was recruited mostly from a single social stratum on the basis of kinship or wealth, and its members had roughly the same social standing and shared a similar world view. Today strategic elites are not unified in the same sense. Pressing new problems have resulted. Thus, their differentiation should not grow so great as to threaten the potential unity of the collectivity, but it cannot be so slight as to ignore the actual diversity of a rapidly changing society. The compatibility and communication among these elites, therefore, are social problems of the first magnitude. No less a problem involves the interchanges between these elites and the larger public whom they simultaneously lead and serve and for whom they constitute ideal, if ambivalent, social models.

The third question concerned the recruitment, responsibilities, and rewards of these elites. The analysis of uneven and scanty empirical data about various types of elites supported our theoretical expectations. Each of the four main types of strategic elites is now recruited in a different manner and from somewhat different elements of the total population. Goal attainment elites are usually elected, adaptive elites are generally appointed, pattern maintenance elites are chosen by public favor, and integrative elites follow no set pattern. Each exhibits its own characteristics, incentives, responsibilities, and rewards. This variety of practice reflects the variety of the urban and industrial way of life.

The fourth question raised the problem of the survival of strategic elites and its impact on social continuity. Historical and empirical evidence suggests that it is the destiny of elites to decline whether they fail or succeed. Their death, however, may be necessary or premature. When elites are displaced by the forces they themselves have brought to life, their demise is necessary, a prelude to the new. But when they succumb to the diseases of sterility or apathy, their death is premature and avoidable. Today, when strategic elites are selected from a wide range of highly motivated individuals, one cause of their premature death has been brought under control. In one sense, of course, elites never die completely, for they live on in the memories of men and nations, and in this symbolic survival achieve a certain immortality.

SOME TRENDS

The social composition of strategic elites in highly industrialized societies reflects the following social developments: (1) *The conquest of poverty and the possibility of securing the minimum necessities of life.* Man no longer needs to exploit his fellow man for survival. Fear of hunger, the dreams of material luxury, the insatiable craving for material security, and the pursuit of possessions as ends in themselves—all are slowly giving way to new motifs reflecting the greater material security and equality among men. In turn, these changes may affect the behavior of the strategic elites whose distinctive status is becoming symbolized less by luxury and material splendor and more by special responsibilities and styles of work. (2) *The importance of specialized training and technical excellence in the selection of core groups*. The application of intelligence to the material, moral, social, and individual needs of mankind is beginning to transform the world, which was long governed by primitive hungers of the body and terrors of the mind. The revolution in the use and appreciation of human intelligence, one of the great revolutions of our time, is already reflected in the social composition of the strategic elites in the most advanced societies. (3) *The decline of the social class and kinship complex that has been a fundamental part of social structures since the beginnings of recorded history*. Neither of these institutions may entirely disappear, but their combined hold on the world is being broken. The family, still the chief institution for the reproduction and early socialization of children, can no longer guarantee material gains and social positions for its young, and has thus lost much of its social power. Moreover, the family, in being widely dispersed and organized into small individual units, has become a means to private self-expression rather than a training ground for public existence. Where it was once the springboard into society, it is now more of a refuge from it.

The rise of individual achievement as the chief principle of recruitment to strategic elite positions has already had repercussions on kinship and social class. A social hierarchy persists, but it is a hierarchy that is reconstituted with each generation. Whatever the injustices or regrettable features of this system, it does not have those based largely upon birth and hereditary privilege. Earlier class systems rewarded individuals on the basis of the accomplishments of their forebears: status was largely ascribed. In present-day societies, individual achievement receives more and more weight—in industry, politics, and cultural life. No scientist wins the Nobel Prize because of his father's scientific attainments or his social pedigree. (4) *The complexity of the core group encourages variety in styles, ambitions, personalities, and perspectives among its members.* The destiny of entire peoples no longer hangs on the fortunes of a single group or class. With a number of alternative models to choose from, human communities are not as readily overwhelmed by the disenchantment of the ruling few. Each strategic elite represents only a particular conception of life and a way to the future. None represents the one and only way.

SOME DANGERS AHEAD

Some of the new developments concerning elites are no more beneficial socially than the patterns they are displacing, but given the size, division of labor, and technological advances, they are unavoidable. Conspicuous advantages accrue to a social order led by a variety of elites rather than by a single uniform social class or group, but so do potential perils. One cause for concern is the rift between the leadership and the rank and file of organizations, which so preoccupied Michels. E. H. Carr speaks for many when he warns of this danger in connection with the emergence of specialized leaders in the different spheres of social life: "In the first place, the interest of the leaders are no longer fully identical with those of the rank and file, since they include the special interest of the leaders in maintaining their own leadership—an interest which is no doubt rationalized, but not always justly, as constituting the interest of the whole group. The leaders, instead of remaining mere delegates of their equals, tend in virtue of their functions to become a separate professional, and then a separate social, group forming the nucleus of a new ruling class . . ." [1] Unfortunately neither Carr nor Michels explains how occupational specialists are transformed into a cohesive and permanent social group with interests of their own to defend. The only way to form this sort of ruling class is to link privileges to the kinship system from generation to generation. But in the absence of this link—and we have shown its great decline in the society now in the making—no permanent ruling class can emerge. Specialized leaders will still have some common ground—in fact they must if their organizations and the society at large are not to consist of segregated enclaves of competing groups—but this common ground will not enable them to subvert the public interest as a matter of course. Exploitation may take other shapes in the future, but not that of distinctly privileged social castes perpetuating themselves and their kin. That era in human society is on the way out.

A second and graver danger lies in the informational gap between specialized leaders and the public, a gap that nullifies many of the rights available to the public on paper. Ignorance of the public often encourages leaders to resort to irrational methods of persuasion and communication. In an age of mass communications, the power of leaders to manipulate public opinion is extraordinary. "The spectacle of an efficient elite maintaining its authority and asserting its will over the mass by the rationally calculated use of irrational methods of persuasion is the most disturbing nightmare of mass democracy." [2] The best safeguard against this danger is for the public to become literate, informed, and thus potentially critical of decisions and proposals made by leaders.

Another problem, singled out by Max Weber and others, is the emergence of a new type of aristocracy—an aristocracy of diplomas—which will determine social status as property qualifications once did. But while educational certificates may supplant pedigree and property as marks of distinction and honor, they cannot produce permanent hereditary aristocracies. The crucial distinction between the world of yesterday and today (figuratively speaking, since most countries still live in worlds of yesterday) is that achievement not birth determines social standing, and educational qualifications, skills, experience, and training must be individually achieved. The most skilled individuals will be highly rewarded, of course, but the rewards will be merited and nontransmissible.[3] Moreover, one cannot compare realistically the technological experts in a highly dynamic industrial society with the ritual experts in a highly static one. The Chinese literati had to master ancient texts, whereas modern executives and statesmen must master the most recent developments in science and industry, foreign affairs, and even military technology. The Chinese could and did reserve the majority of government positions for the gentry, though in principle anyone with the appropriate training and ambition could compete in the metropolitan examinations leading to these positions; in fact, some poor peasant boys generally passed these examinations. What was then an unusual condition becomes endemic in advanced industrial societies—provided, and this is indispensable, that educational facilities are made generally available. If not, a minority of the well-to-do may monopolize educational opportunities at the cost of maintaining and expanding the society.

The postulate of advanced industrial societies being led by a new ruling class sharing a single set of attributes is thus contrary to currently ascertainable trends. Rather, such societies include a number of coexisting pyramids, each with its own internal hierarchy, folklore, rituals, and prizes. Strategic elites resemble the top cards of different suits in a deck of cards—the ace of spades must share his lofty place with the elites of the other three suits. One elite may be temporarily superior to others in terms of priority or attention but in this it resembles the trump cards that vary from hand to hand.

Certainly the problem of the concentration of power is a serious one, if only because of what Max Gluckman calls the "frailty in authority," [4] but it is no more serious now than it has always been. If people permit their leaders to think, feel, and decide for them, they may of course become passive pawns. Although today it is less necessary for people to yield their independence because they have more powers and greater rights than ever before, they must be aware of these powers and make use of them.

Some prospects: The changes ahead are no doubt many, but only two types are here singled out for comment. These touch upon some of oldest human desires, earliest dreams, and most persistent questions of mankind. They involve the problems of human equality, freedom, and the inevitability of despotism. All societies have had to grapple with these, and no society has as yet succeeded in solving them.

Equality

"Where there is no vision," quotes the Book of Proverbs, "the people perish." Men living in communities preserve such visions in the myths they create. One such myth is that of equality, ancient yet ever new because ever unrealized.

Equality may refer to individuals, groups, conditions of life, aspirations, opportunities, or rewards. In modern times it has referred primarily to opportunities for changing one's station and achieving one's worldly standing. Individuals differ in their abilities and desires, and it is felt that these differences should find their own level through the expenditure of individual effort, not through traditional assignment. Accordingly, men have protested less against the inequalities of capacities—regrettable as these might be—and more against the inequalities of social conditions. Inequalities of rewards are accepted if they are seen as reflecting differential responsibilities, but they too continue to arouse controversy. Men resent less the existence of a social and occupational hierarchy than the basis for inclusion or exclusion from it.[5] "If the institution of classes or castes sometimes gives rise to anxiety and pain instead of producing solidarity," Durkheim observed, "this is because the distribution of social functions on which it rests does not respond, or rather no longer responds, to the distribution of natural talents." [6]

In the transition from feudalism to industrialism, increased demand for skilled men naturally resulted in an expansion of opportunities. New sources of wealth and status made social mobility not only possible but necessary since expanding societies cannot rely on inheritance to fill all available positions. Social mobility has never been totally absent in any society, but it was for long periods disapproved of in principle. Not until the industrial revolution did social mobility become morally right in the eyes of most people. This was especially true in such societies as the United States that had no feudal or aristocratic past. From its beginnings, men believed in equality of opportunity for themselves and their children:

> They might be poor; they would not remain poor. They might be out of work; a job was waiting around the corner. They might be half-literate; their children would go to college . . . he [the American] never needed to assume as the Englishman did, that there was some allotted station in life that was his, and others that were, almost *a priori*, beyond his reach.[7]

Equality of opportunity is only partially captured by figures on upward social mobility, though the extent of this mobility was and continues to be both absolutely and relatively high.[8] The opportunity for social mobility is greater in industrial than in agricultural societies, but its extent is nevertheless limited by the existence of the social hierarchy. And that hierarchy is based, by definition, on inequalities. Lipset and Zetterberg write: "If a country is 90 per cent peasant, even with completely equal opportunity, most children of peasants must remain peasants. Even if every non-peasant position is filled by a peasant's son, only about eleven per cent of them could change their occupation. On the other hand, if a country undergoes rapid economic transformation and the proportion of non-manual positions increases to, say, one half of all positions, then 50 per cent of the children of manual workers would have to secure non-manual work in order to meet the criterion of equality." [9] We do not know if there was absolute equality of opportunity here—we only know that there was more of it.

Another mainstay of the belief in equality of opportunity was the early American's increasing similarity in styles of life, dress, and consumer expenditures. Foreign visitors often were unable to recognize the members of the different social classes from external criteria alone. "The European was fascinated by the general air of prosperity, the free-and-easy relations between persons on different social levels, the lack of social distinctions, class hostilities, class jealousies, class political issues." [10] This situation continues today, strongly abetted by mass production and mass spending.[11]

Moreover, American ideals differed from those of Europe in that moral equality was approved of in principle. Different types of work were differentially rewarded both materially and psychologically, but the fundamental distinction was between those who worked and those who did not. Idleness among the upper classes in older feudal societies indicated their "innate" superiority. Here, the idle and unemployed were held in contempt. The dignity of man was based on the positive evaluation of labor. Accordingly, members of strategic elites work exceptionally hard and are accorded high prestige not despite but because of their labors.

If we now ask how and whether strategic elites have affected the existence of social inequalities, we must conclude that they have both furthered and reduced them. They have furthered inequalities because as a result of the growth in number and variety of strategic elites, available top positions have also multiplied. Furthermore, as birth and ancestry decrease while individual talent and capacity increase as criteria of recruitment, more varied types of individuals are able to achieve these coveted positions. When strategic elites were drawn largely from privileged minorities connected by wealth and ancestry, entire strata of human beings were permanently exalted and permanently depressed. Not individuals but the social categories to which they belonged were admired or condemned.

Some individuals, no matter how excellent their moral and intellectual qualities, were automatically excluded from the highest ranks. Conversely, other individuals, no matter how base, were automatically included. Such a system institutionalized self-hatred among the inferior strata and self-love among the superior, each of these feelings often unrelated to the personal qualities of the individuals involved.[12] In addition to differences in economic and material well-being, and the gross excesses in self-indulgence and in exploitation of others which this system engendered, it also led to the indignity and humiliation of men. For the influence of masters on their subordinates extended farther than their authority. The master, as de Tocqueville observed, was obeyed for himself because obedience to the class of masters was extracted and internalized.[13]

Strategic elites can never assume such an all-embracing influence over the inner lives of men. Whatever subordination they demand of the citizens is limited in time, place, and circumstance, and is usually related not to the whole man but only to certain roles. Men may continue to pay homage to what they consider evidence of personal magnificence, but they are less likely to sanctify or to despise entire groups of human beings. Where power is limited, the worship of power is likewise limited.

Moreover, since the superiority of strategic elites will be confined to the specialized spheres with which they are identified, their superiority in one area does not preclude their subordination in others.[14] And where personal competence is prized and rewarded, incompetence is condemned and punished. Thus strategic elites have no permanent or absolute claim to their positions. This alone prevents them from establishing permanent personal empires.

Yet the very existence of strategic elites perpetuates a hierarchical social order and a hierarchical view of individuals. If this is accompanied by important differentials in material and moral well-being, it may well act as the spur to effort that many nineteenth-century thinkers[15] considered a conspicuous advantage of inequality. But it may also lead to that frenzied search for security and status that others have deplored. Since inequalities of reward are part and parcel of complex societies, equality is in principle unattainable, producing discontent among all strata of the population —even among those at the very top. A spirit of competition is engendered that knows little satisfaction because it is directed toward no fixed goal. The price of ideological egalitarianism is thus persistent discontent and spiritual disorder. Social order can reign only if men are content with their lot. "But what is needed for them to be content, is not that they have more or less but that they be convinced that they have no right to more or less." [16] Thus the acceptance of inequality is seen as a source of spiritual tranquillity, provided, Durkheim would add, that the existing inequalities reflect natural inequalities and do not do violence to men's material and moral needs.

The proliferation of strategic elites therefore goes hand in hand with the continuance, if not the expansion, of equality of opportunity, principally because the criteria of recruitment and selection emphasize individual achievement rather than group inheritance of social positions. Inequalities among men, however, continue as they always have—they are not eliminated by altering the patterns of recruitment and selection of strategic elites. Instead, they depend upon the actions of these elites in their various functional spheres and upon the interaction between strategic elites and the rest of the community to whom these elites are increasingly accessible and accountable. Yet, the sheer accessibility of strategic elites does not automatically lead to greater public well-being. This can be created only jointly—with the public demanding a better life and elites attempting to provide it. The public needs to be sensitive to its possibilities and desires, elites alert to their responsibilities and opportunities. The dialogue must be continuous and many-sided, consisting of arguments and controversies as well as declarations and reassurances. This calls for self-confidence on both sides. There is some reason to believe that this self-confidence is less firmly developed among strategic elites in societies imbued with the egalitarian spirit. Under egalitarian conditions, de Tocqueville stressed, public leaders cannot develop that loftiness of purpose and exalted notion of self that true leadership requires. Leaders in America struck him as servile, debasing themselves like courtiers by flattering the majority that had raised them to preeminence. He saw as inevitable that leaders of democracies (he was especially concerned with political and local leaders) would reflect the mediocrity, pettiness, and narrow-mindedness of their electors.[17] Similarly, Max Weber believed that only landed aristocracies could develop and safeguard genuine cultural values and superior ideas.[18] And Mannheim considered the lack of exclusiveness of elites in modern society as a sign of impending deterioration.

Part of this argument is well taken. If strategic elites are to lead, innovate, and inspire men to the attainment of social goals, they must accept their superiority—however temporary. Consequently, leaders of democracies must develop an ideology of superiority without its degeneration into moral arrogance or status snobbishness. This ideology, to be well founded, need not be rooted in untenable beliefs about racial or genetic superiority. Pride in excellence of achievement, commitment to large purposes, attachment to fine ideals—these have always inspired leaders, whatever their endeavor. And they must inspire today's elites if a deadlock between the traditionalism of collectivities and the timidity of leaders unaware of their rightful superiority is to be avoided. Ultimately, leaders in politics, the arts, science, and recreation must give the people a sense of direction. This they can hardly do if they ask directions from those looking to them for guidance. Elites and the mass of men must accept the principle of inequality in talents and responsibilities without succumbing to a servile dependency or indifference.

An uneducated and uncultivated majority can raise up inferior leaders, too closely modeled after its own image, but this need not always be the case. Much depends on what is done to elevate the tastes, skills, and habits of the majority. The rise of literacy, the spread of comforts, the increase in variety, and the reduction in drudgery may make it possible for the majority to fashion superior leaders as it once was for the aristocracy. One may deplore the decline of the landed aristocracy, made the more alluring by legend, but one cannot for all that restore it to life. What can be done is to expend collective energies in raising the tastes and ideals of the majority. For ultimately it is that most maligned of social creatures—the mass—that creates leaders, and its leaders will be only so good as the social soil from which they spring. For the leaders this means the development of self-confidence, independence of mind, courage, and human sympathy as well as professional excellence. For the mass it means the development of intellectual faculties and moral vision.

The reciprocity between strategic elites and the collectivity must engender mutual respect and sympathy. Yet it must not preclude the distance and reserve necessary for a proper appreciation of their respective differences in responsibilities and power.[19]

We agree with Tawney that the desirable equality is not that of "capacity or attainment, but of circumstances, and institutions, and manner of life." We deplore that inequality which "is not inequality of personal gifts, but of social and economic environment." We are "concerned not with a biological phenomenon but with a spiritual relation." [20] As Alfred Marshall argues, "the question is not whether all men will ultimately be equal—that they certainly will not—but whether progress may not go on steadily, if slowly, till, by occupation at least, every man is a gentleman. I hold that it may be and that it will." [21] Marshall was justified in his optimism, for in the past century social and a good measure of economic equality has been added to the civil and political equality won during the past three centuries. Men are equal in status and in rights before the law, in political life, and with respect to a basic minimum of economic welfare and security. Today poverty and unemployment, although shocking in an affluent society, are the lot not of the majority but of a minority of men.[22] Economic and occupational categories continue to be unequal but not the human stock assigned to them. Increasingly individuals have equality of opportunity to achieve unequal statuses. Whether or not they will make use of these opportunities in the absence of compelling advantages to be gained is still a moot question. Contentment with one's lot may ease the spirit and simultaneously destroy ambition. But while the argument has some plausibility, it cannot be answered at present since it rests on notions of ambition developed under conditions of relative discontent. Men may not stake all for the attainment of material possessions or political power, but they may be moved by the attainment of excellence, reputation, or a life well-lived.

It is here that the composition and selection of strategic elites portends the shape of things to come. For one of the striking features of elites, as societies become more complex technologically and occupationally, is their greater functional, symbolic, and moral variety. Variety has become the new value in the social order. It is reflected in the greater number of strategic elites, in recruitment and selection patterns, in individual talents and abilities desirable in the different memberships, and in the general stress on differing skills and ideas. Hence on the cultural level there are now a number of social models to choose from and various moral standards by which to judge men. The tyranny of an exclusive minority or a sweeping majority is receding. The spell of the dominant creed—whether in art, in science, or in politics—is breaking. Mankind is on the threshold of a new era—that of diversity—which is another term for an important form of freedom.

Freedom and despotism

Throughout history, mankind has been hungry for bread and liberty. And since the division between rich and poor went hand in hand with that between leaders and led, the battle against the tyranny of hunger and that against moral oppression were one and the same. Men hoped to defeat both in one stroke. Today, in advanced industrial societies, the battle against hunger has been won and the material gap between the haves and have-nots substantially reduced. But the distance between leaders and their publics persists. Some have reacted to this with the charge of hypocrisy, others have resigned themselves to exploitation and domination as part of the "nature of things."

At first glance these reactions are comprehensible. Strategic elites continue to be small minorities exerting enormous influence as decision-makers, as models to be imitated, and as privileged groups receiving more than their share of honor and comforts. And they have increased in number. Nevertheless a general pessimism seems unwarranted because the proliferation of strategic elites is a protection against rather than indication of the inevitability of exploitation and despotism.

TYPES OF DESPOTISM

Saint-Simon, Max Weber, Durkheim, and Mannheim, among others, have pointed out that the nature of power determines the perversion of power. Where power is all-inclusive and personal as in absolute monarchies, despotism will also be all-inclusive and personal. Where power is institutionalized and impersonal, despotism will be institutionalized and impersonal. The tyranny of the group, it is generally agreed, is harsher than that of the law because its authority, both moral and physical, is formally unlimited. The power of the judge, or expert, or bureaucrat may be resented because it is impersonal and objective, but it is a power that rests on an implicit reciprocity between the rules and those subject to these rules. The power of the patriarch, though often tempered by personal identification and admiration, rests on no such reciprocity: the fate of the individual is largely dependent on the whims of his master. The capriciousness and arbitrariness of power, hence of despotism, are therefore far greater under personal, comprehensive rule than under impersonal and specialized rule. And even if we assume that the so-called lust for power has not diminished, the context in which power may currently be expressed is no longer as favorable to power-hungry individuals as it once was. Strategic elites, representing specialized and separate centers, find their power to be specialized and limited. The only way to prevent abuses of power is to control the powerful, and the dispersion of strategic elites constitutes such a control. The heterogeneity of elites has also contributed to the decline of direct coercion and the rise of persuasion, a striking characteristic of industrial societies. As the pressures making for despotism have grown less intense, there is more hope of freedom under a system of numerous, specialized, and morally differentiated strategic elites than under systems of aristocracies and ruling classes. This change for the better can be understood by examining the three main sources of despotism: technological monopoly, psychological excesses, and social distance.

Technological monopoly: According to Michels, who largely based his discussion of oligarchy on the revolutionary socialist movement in nineteenth-century Europe, the sheer expansion of an organization increases the power and potential likelihood of despotism among the minority of technically qualified leaders. The latter's centralized position, plus their monopoly of information and skills in communication and persuasion, guarantees the leadership's superiority over the membership.

Strategic elites are also composed of technically qualified experts, but their greater functional specificity (an element slighted by Michels, who was dealing with only one social sphere) limits their powers. The proliferation and partial autonomy of strategic elites, their variations in composition and recruitment, and differing moral perspectives decrease the likelihood of an omnipotent oligarchy. In addition, these elites critically examine—and thereby check—each other's actions and decisions. Thus limited power leads to limited abuses.

Psychological excesses: The exercise of leadership often brings out the worst in men. Ideals and noble aims are forgotten as leaders, driven by vanity and egoism, become entrapped by the temptations of power. This holds especially for leaders who achieve their positions through their own efforts. Michels finds, for example, that ex-manual workers turned socialist leaders are particularly incorrigible in this regard—jealous of their newly won authority, capricious, and loath to accept contradiction or criticism.[23] Those born to high position tend to be estranged from the common run of men from the start and develop exalted notions of innate superiority as a matter of course. One could argue that the tyranny of the newcomers to power is but an exaggeration of the style of power exhibited by their predecessors—the only style with which they are familiar. Thus the French bourgeoisie, once it came into power, assumed the mode of life, many of the usages, and even the mentality of the feudal nobility—a phenomenon that has occurred in other times and places. The parvenu imitates the model he displaces. Just as revolutionary movements retain more of the past than they abolish, so revolutionists come to act like the masters they had promised to destroy.

There are additional reasons why men, once they have gotten a taste of power, are eager to retain it—among which is the reluctance to forego privileges and comforts, particularly where the discrepancy in material standards of life between leaders and led is high. Leaders are also disinclined to relinquish power if the subsequent loss of position implies a return to obscurity.[24]

Paradoxically, this lust for power can also stem from an intense and lofty idealism. "The bureaucracy which is most faithful and most efficient in the discharge of its duties is also the most dictatorial." [25] Men may become despotic and exacting for the sake of a creed, a movement, or an organization, demanding a degree of obedience for the sake of a cause that they would not demand for themselves. This may even meet with the secret wishes of the members: "one easily expects of the collectivity not only what one cannot achieve, but also what one does not care to achieve . . . the group interest . . . entitles, or even obliges, the individual to commit acts for which *as an individual,* he does not care to be responsible." [26] Thus the abuses of power may be traced not only to the psychological needs and anxieties of the leaders but also to those of the led. It has often been observed, somewhat misleadingly, that men get the leaders they deserve. Indifference and apathy, the incapacity to criticize, and a tendency to turn leaders into idols may make the masses as "responsible" for a despotic leadership as the propensities of the leaders themselves. Superior knowledge and the cult of gratitude increase the leaders' conviction of their own infallibility as well as their contempt for the rank and file so that they "proclaim both the sovereignty of the masses and the incompetence of the people." [27] Thus, the oligarchy inherent in organization is perpetuated by the psychological reactions of leaders and led. "The development of the democratic oligarchy is accelerated by the general characteristics of human nature. What was initiated by the need for organization, administration, and strategy is completed by psychological determinism." [28]

Social distance: Excessive social distance between leaders and led, especially when accompanied by gross material inequalities, is another source of despotism. When a minority monopolizes material and intellectual resources, the majority is left too poor or too ignorant to safeguard its rights, which is why many persons argue that equality is the first step toward freedom. In fact, however, these two phenomena are distinct. For, as Michels rightly insisted, the rise of leading minorities is a result of social expansion and the organization which this necessitates. As long as these structural requirements persist, the concentration of responsibilities, skills, and power in a few hands will also persist. In the modern world such minorities are therefore here to stay, even if material and moral inequalities are lessened. But while the concentration of responsibility will necessarily make for a concentration of power, it does not automatically make for its abuse. Indeed, minorities may represent and act for the majority, although they cannot do so for all equally. De Tocqueville insisted, in fact, that where the interests of the majority are defended those of the minority must suffer. This is a fundamental source of injustice even in the most enlightened democracies.

Finally, despotism stems in part from the interests of the small coterie of admirers, advisers, and intimates that all leaders attract and depend upon. Those who have access to the court, who have the master's ear, who "know someone who knows"—whether they be close to political figures, artists, actors, or priests—have a vested interest in power without commensurate responsibility. They can urge actions and measures which will benefit themselves without being called into account. Since their social position rests on the leader, if it is to be maintained his power must be secure. Hence the pressure from in-groups around all leaders for permanence. Writing of the presidential campaign of 1960, White observes: "All these campaigns—those of Humphrey, of Symington, of Johnson—were thus, by the end of 1959, organizations in being, shapeless perhaps, yet captained by men who meant to be President of the United States and staffed by in-groups of three, five or ten men, whose lives and ambitions were now devoted to no other purpose." [29] Concerning a very different situation, Djilas notes: "Today I am able to conclude that the deification of Stalin, or the 'cult of personality,' as it is now called, was at least as much the work of Stalin's circle and the bureaucracy, who required such a leader, as it was his own doing." [30] In more general terms: "There is an axiom in politics that a candidacy for any office is not simply the expression of individual ambition—any great candidacy is the gathering place of many men's ambitions." [31]

The dangers of despotism are still with us, and may even have increased with the rise of techniques of mass persuasion and destruction. But today despotism also faces greater limitations, including the following four circumstances: (1) *Increased public control over the leaders, limiting the caprice and arbitrariness of those in power.* This was Aristotle's reason for favoring the rule of the majority, which he considered inferior on other grounds. This control may be informal, as in the case of consumers and audiences rejecting or selecting products and programs; or it may be formal, illustrated by the election of public officials. (2) *Free and open discussion of timely public issues concerning politics, economics, art, morality, and taste.* Freedom consists of choices among available alternatives, and these rest on competition and conflict of opinions, interests, and ideas and on partisan review and argument. Such discourse is widespread today, enlisting a variety of groups formerly excluded, though it is neither quantitatively nor qualitatively all it might be.[32] (3) *The specialization of authority, constricting the range of power.* In modern industrial societies, no single strategic elite, group, or individual, has absolute or total power. Where the politician may tread, the general may not; where the artist holds sway, the civil servant does not. In this variety, too, there is freedom. (4) *The narrowing of the gap between leaders and led with respect to education, standard of living, and general well-being.* This development makes it less possible for leaders to assume unwarranted notions of absolute superiority, and for the led, unwarranted notions of absolute inferiority. It also facilitates the relinquishing of power, for just as individuals do not gain everything merely by assuming positions of leadership, so they do not lose everything merely by surrendering them.[33] At the same time, however, though opportunities should be equalized, absolute equality is not desirable. As Simmel pointed out, the existence of a hierarchy of responsibilities and authority in a society is a cushion against the emergence of centralized despotism—when everyone can be legitimately superior to someone, no one can be superior to all.[34]

In highly industrialized societies, then, power has become less arbitrary and personal and is increasingly shared among various groups and institutions. The differentiation of elites into specialized and partly autonomous entities has shattered the image of a single, homogeneous power center. A "center" still exists, of course, but it is internally divided. The current strategic elites are not as free to exercise their powers as were the aristocracies and ruling classes of the past because in being functionally specialized they are themselves subordinate in spheres not relating to their specialty, and because they are now far more dependent on the good will of the public. Seen in this light, the claims of Pareto, Michels, and others that history is a continual cycle of tyranny, rebellion, triumph of the new, and a return to the old tyranny appear distorted. They have noted certain surface similarities among elites but have ignored the deep differences between various forms and contexts of power and the abuses associated with them.

Today, no single strategic elite has absolute power or priority, none can hold power forever, and none determines the patterns of selection and recruitment for the rest. Moreover, their more varied skills and experiences result in the formation of a more complex and many-sided social core, one in which a number of personalities must coexist. This makes the core group a more diversified and less monotonous model for the members of society, more of whom can see themselves partly reflected in it. At best, strategic elites are temporary aristocracies over whom the public, in its various roles as voter, audience, and consumer exercises considerably more control than it did in the past. The possibilities of choice are greater than ever before—in the paths to the top, in the types of responsibilities and rewards attached to different elite positions, and in the types of challenges confronting these elites. The victory of variety and spontaneity, old enemies of despotism, signals the defeat of monolithic tendencies in manners, morals, and styles of life. The one-track society, indispensable perhaps at certain stages of social development, is being replaced by a social order moving toward different destinations at different speeds.

Saint-Simon's dream of a society governed not by force but by ability, with people submitting not out of fear but out of respect for skill and knowledge, is gradually being realized.[35] But while this realization has vastly extended moral equality among men, it has by no means eliminated the seeds of despotism. The tyranny of the expert over the unenlightened, though different from that of the haves over the have-nots, is nevertheless a tyranny. Any exercise of superiority, however justified, contains the possibilities of personal and social abuse. For this reason Saint-Simon advocated the rise of a new Christianity supervised by priests to be chosen from among the most compassionate of men. The unifying faculty of social life, he realized, is not alone technical excellence but requires human sympathy. In reaching this conclusion, he isolated the two themes at the heart of the problem of despotism and exploitation: incapacity among those in superior position, as when those born to such status lack the desire or talent for it; and a lack of sympathy among leaders for human problems, as when those superior to the common man in one respect consider themselves superior in all.[36]

The first problem is well on the way to being solved, for strategic elites are increasingly composed of individuals of proven capacity in specialized spheres. The second problem is still very much with us: the danger of arrogance, snobbery, and insensitivity to the problems of human life. This danger, hopefully, will be offset by greater understanding of the complex social order by all men—and especially by the occupants of key positions in modern society. If the chief task of earlier societies was the creation of a common life, the chief task of current societies is the creation of a better life. In very large measure this depends on the skills and vision—and humanity—of the strategic elites.

Notes

1. Edward Hallett Carr, *The New Society* (1951), p. 77.
2. *Ibid.*
3. In a recently published book the characteristics of the "meritocracy" of the future are effectively portrayed in the broad strokes of caricature. The society described by Michael Young is Great Britain after the year 2000, where measured intelligence reigns as the supreme value. The goal to which all aspire is to get as high an I.Q. as possible because the highest social positions go to those who do. Intelligence, tapped at an early age, thus determines an individual's destiny. The strongest point of the book also proves to be its weakest. For while there is no doubt that the society described by Young would be ludicrous and as inequitable and unsatisfactory as the class system out of which it arose, the significant point is that such a society could not exist for long. For one thing, intelligence as measured by intelligence tests is not identical with talent as needed by the movie actor, the politician, or the general. The intelligence of the politician is a particular kind of intelligence, representing an amalgam of interest, capacity, and accident. It can hardly be measured by current intelligence tests. Also, the politician who needs to be intelligent about politics may not and indeed cannot be intelligent about all things.

   Young also fails to distinguish between social classes and elites. He speaks of lower and of upper classes, but he fails to indicate in which respects they will be designated as such or what their role will be in a society organized along quite different lines. And when he refers to the most intelligent class breeding superior offspring, he neglects to take into account the nature of the intelligence needed in a dynamic industrial society. Intelligence is one quality that is least reliably transmitted within families, and everyone knows that brilliant parents may have average children, and quite ordinary parents brilliant ones. At any rate, there is no evidence to support a view that artists, writers, statesmen, and inventors have been able to pass their unique talents on to their offspring. But without this no true aristocracy can arise. See, Michael Young, *The Rise of Meritocracy, 1870-2033* (1959).

4. Max Gluckman, "The Frailty in Authority," in *Custom and Conflict in Africa* (1959), pp. 27-53.
5. The struggle for existence is still accepted as inevitable, though it can be mitigated. One way of mitigating it is to equalize opportunities—or, in Durkheim's phrase—to "equalize the internal conditions of conflict."

   A recent study of the attitudes of a random sample of students attending institutions of higher learning in Warsaw showed that whereas exploitation was repugnant to them, the idea of inequalities of rewards was not. For example, 93 per cent thought the abolition of exploitation of some men by others an important matter, but fully 55 per cent did not consider income and salary differentials a form of economic exploitation. In addition, 98 per cent of the students felt that jobs requiring higher education should be financially more profitable than jobs which did not. There was some feeling that the existing salary range in Poland should be reduced "right now," but only one fifth of the students were definite in their stand. Finally, it was found that egalitarianism differs within each social class—among the students from manual workers' families, the better off were more egalitarian; among the students from professional and white collar families, the higher the income of the parents the less egalitarian the children. Thus egalitarianism was found among the wealthier manual workers and among the poorer professionals and white collar workers. Stefan Nowak, "Egalitarian Attitudes of Warsaw Students," *American Sociological Review,* 25 (April 1960), No. 2, 219-32.
6. Durkheim, *The Division of Labor in Society* (1947), p. 375.
7. Harold J. Laski, *The American Democracy* (1948), pp. 35, 39-40.
8. Recently it has been suggested that the rate of mobility has been no higher during this century here than in Europe, but the findings are in part an artifact of the broad classifications—manual to nonmanual—used. See S. M. Lipset and Natalie Rogoff, "Class and Opportunity in Europe and in the United States," *Commentary,* XVIII (1954), 562-8.

   Downward mobility is still relatively low in the United States, though not as low as in the USSR. See S. M. Miller, "Social Mobility and Economic Change: A Typology," Preliminary Paper delivered at the Annual Meeting of the Eastern Sociological Society, Boston, April 23-24, 1960, and the same author's "Comparative Social Mobility," *Current Sociology,* IX (1960), No. 1.
9. S. M. Lipset and Hans L. Zetterberg, "A Theory of Social Mobility," *Bureau of Applied Social Research,* Reprint No. 185, p. 161.
10. Robert W. Smuts, *European Impressions of the American Worker* (1953), p. 2. He adds: "Whether they liked what they saw or not, most foreign observers did not doubt that America was a democratic society and that the circumstances of workers and the attitudes towards work and towards working people were very near the heart of American democracy. They did not mean, in any literal sense, that there was even approximate equality of wealth, social status, or power in the United States. They meant, first, that most jobs were almost equally respectable" (p. 3).
11. It is this aspect that Orwell selected to reveal the rise of inequality on

Animal Farm after the revolution. "Milk and apples soon went disproportionately to the pigs. . . . It was about this time that the pigs suddenly moved into the farmhouse and took up their residence there . . . some of the animals were disturbed when they heard that the pigs not only took their meals in the kitchen and used the drawing room as a recreation room, but also slept in their beds. . . ." When at the last only a single one of the seven commandments remained, it had been altered to read: "All Animals Are Equal but Some Are More Equal Than Others." George Orwell, *Animal Farm* (1956), pp. 42, 69, 90.

12. "Civil troubles arise," Aristotle warned, "not only out of the inequality of property, but out of the inequality of honor, though in opposite ways. For the common people quarrel about the inequality of property, the higher class about the equality of honor." Aristotle, *Politics,* p. 1159. He goes on to say that in oligarchies the masses make revolution because they are equals without an equal share, whereas in democracies the notables revolt because they are not equals and yet have only an equal share. *Ibid.,* p. 1237.
13. De Tocqueville, *Democracy in America,* II, 189.
14. Equality in the sense of compensation is an idea of long standing. It receives prominence in the writings of Aristotle who seems to like the idea of a balance of forces, an equilibrium of compensations. Instead of punishing individuals for the unequal distribution of talents and desires, he would want to compensate them for it. So he suggests that groups deprived of office holding (that is, the rich in a democracy, and the poor in an oligarchy) should be especially privileged or favored in other aspects of life. See Aristotle, *Politics,* p. 1248. Similarly, Tawney suggests that even if some men are inferior in specific abilities such as intelligence it does not follow that they should receive less consideration than others. "It is not at all certain," he writes, "that slavery is the most suitable penalty for lack of intelligence." R. H. Tawney, *Equality* (1929), p. 41.
15. Inequality according to some, is considered indispensable, for when individuals are not moved to improve their situations they will fall into laziness and despair; thus, "full social equality would be the end of society." Gustav Schmoller, *Die Soziale Frage, Klassenbildung, Arbeiterfrage, Klassenkampf* (1918), p. 185.
16. Durkheim, *Socialism and Saint-Simon* (1958), p. 200.
17. See esp. de Tocqueville, *Democracy in America,* I, 340 ff.; II, *passim,* but esp. Chaps. 1-4.
18. See Max Weber, "National Character and the Junkers," in Gerth and Mills (eds.), *Essays,* p. 393.

    Leadership is the crux of James Reston's essay, "Our History Suggests a Remedy," in *The National Purpose* (1960), pp. 109-124. He suggests that "the great political crises of the American past have been resolved not by the zeal and purpose of the people, but usually by the will power or obstinacy of their leaders" (p. 109). "Thus criticism of the American people for lack of purpose is not new. What is new is that leaders now seem to think they must follow the nation instead of leading it."

    "Of all the resources required for economic development," it has been discovered the hard way, "high-level manpower requires the longest 'lead-time' for creation. Modern dams, power stations, textile factories or steel mills can be constructed within a few years. But it takes between 10 and 15 years to develop the managers, the administrators, and the engineers to operate them. Schools and college buildings can be erected in a matter of months; but it requires decades to develop high-level teachers and professors. . . ." Quoted in Melvin J. Lasky, "Africa for Beginners," *Encounter* (July 1961), pp. 32-48, esp. p. 44.

19. In this connection, White's observations on the Humphrey campaign are instructive. Apparently too little social distance between political leaders and the voters is just as damaging as too much. "What spoiled the Humphrey campaign . . . was the very simplicity, the clarity, the homely sparkle he could bring to any issue. He could talk on almost any subject under the sun—to farmers, to workers, to university intellectuals. And when he finished there were no mysteries left; nor was he a mystery either. He was someone just like the listeners. There was no distance about him, no separation of intrigue, none of the majesty that must surround a king. Humphrey in a druggist's jacket explaining the problems of druggists in small towns and their inventories (which he could, spectacularly), or Humphrey, joining a picket line to sing 'Solidarity Forever,' was just like everyone else; and a President, unfortunately for Humphrey, must be different from everyone else." T. H. White, *The Making of the President, 1960* (1961), p. 88.
20. Tawney's incomparable book still contains the best discussion of the matter. See, *Equality, op. cit.*, p. 37.
21. Quoted by T. H. Marshall in his admirable essay "Citizenship and Social Class," in the book by the same name (p. 4), in which he traces the development of civil, political, and social equality from the seventeenth century to the present.
22. Michael Harrington estimates that from 20 to 25 per cent of the American people are poor. *The Other America* (1962), p. 182. See also Gabriel Kolko, *Wealth and Power in America* (1962).
23. Michels, *Political Parties* (1959), p. 205 ff.
24. In fact, this has been interpreted as a potential source of despotism under modern conditions. In the past, power holders had economic and social position to fall back on. Today, power is their one and only possession. "For most of those who must depart from the citadel, there is no other place to go. The ex-power holder is swallowed up by the crowd from which he came, a man without status and without a shelter against the slings of social anxiety." Robert Strausz-Hupe, *Power and Community* (1956), pp. 34-35.
25. Michels, *op. cit.*, p. 229.
26. Georg Simmel, in Wolff (ed.), *The Sociology of Georg Simmel*, pp. 133-134.
27. Michels, *op. cit.*
28. *Ibid.*, p. 205.
29. T. H. White, *op. cit.*, p. 46.
30. Milovan Djilas, *Conversations with Stalin* (1962), pp. 105-6.
31. T. H. White, *op. cit.*, p. 47.
32. Mosca, *The Ruling Class* (1939), pp. 171 ff. refers to this as the "juridical defense" of civilizations, and would judge the extent of liberty by the extent of "juridical defense" or freedom of speech, belief, and insurances against arbitrary arrests in a society.
33. See, Lipset *et al.*, *Union Democracy* (1956), pp. 406 ff. for a discussion

of this aspect as it relates to trade union leadership. See, also, Nicolai Bukharin, *Historical Materialism* (1925), p. 309.

Michels, too, realized that the despotic tendencies of leaders could be controlled and minimized. If leaders are paid adequately, he said, they will be less likely to use their positions for their own economic ends, and if the masses are educated adequately, they will be less likely to idolize and passively submit to their leaders. Michels, *op. cit.*, p. 205.

34. Simmel, in Wolff (ed.), *The Sociology of Georg Simmel, op. cit.*, p. 198. See also, De Tocqueville, *Democracy in America,* II, 336.
35. "One can say," he wrote, "that in such a society there are no longer inequalities, for there no longer are privileges. Those who direct are not above those who are directed; they are not their superiors. They fulfill a different function—that is all. And as each has the role which fits his capacity, all are equally treated." Quoted in Durkheim, *Socialism and Saint-Simon, op. cit.*, p. 151. This development is reflected in forms of address. Since the nineteenth century, "power" pronouns have been displaced by "solidarity" pronouns. See Roger Brown and Albert Gilman, "The Pronouns of Power and Solidarity," in *Style in Language* (1960), ed. Thomas A. Sebeok.
36. "The curse of aristocracy," Charles Merriam observed, "is not that great men fill great places, but that small men fill great places and piece out their inferiority with arrogance." Charles Merriam, "The Assumptions of Aristocracy," *American Journal of Sociology,* XLIII, No. 6 (May 1938), 857-77, esp. 876.

APPENDIXES

I. Moral differentiation among elites

▲

In the following pages, we will briefly discuss the impact of functional differentiation and specialization of strategic elites on the moral order by noting the specific contribution of each to the culture. We shall focus here on the military, scientific, religious, and cultural elites.

The military elite: In the United States this elite has only recently become possessor of sufficient power, independence, and scope to influence the shaping of high-level policies. And its newly won prominence in America, where the professional military has been traditionally distrusted, has raised old anxieties concerning the nature and duration of military influence on national life. Apart from the traditional reservations, the special habits and traditions of the military elite in and of themselves have apparently fanned antimilitary sentiments. What has been called the "military mind" is chiefly responsible for this. Its characteristics have been summarized as follows:

> a) rigidity in thought and problem-analysis—the rejection of new ideas and reliance on tradition rather than lessons learned from recent experience; b) inadequate weighing of non-military factors in military problems, and inability to understand complex politico-military relationships; c) an authoritarian approach to most social issues and situations, accompanied by disrespect for and disregard of civilian authority; d) insulation from non-military knowledge and

anything beyond what is narrowly defined as militarily relevant; and e) judgment of policy goals and techniques primarily in terms of military force and military strategy.[1]

Friends and foes alike of the military generally agree that its public role cannot be reversed but must be accepted and integrated into the over-all framework. The military, even when they wish to adhere to a narrow definition of their functions, apparently no longer find it possible to give advice unobtrusively to decision-makers. Indeed they have become decision-makers themselves, and have ceased to be immune to political pressures. Generals and admirals are politically active, make public speeches, and have a public following. The cold war and the tensions of waging peace have increased not only the decision-making capacity of the military elite but also its public prestige. This plus the ambivalence toward "nouveaux arrivistes" underlie the apprehensions about a military grown more powerful in recent years.[2] According to one observer, the organization of the military establishment has come to resemble that of business and political establishments. "The consequences of the new tasks of military management imply that the professional soldier is required more and more to acquire skills and orientations common to civilian administrators and even political leaders." [3]

[1] Burton M. Sapin and Richard C. Snyder, "The Role of the Military in American Foreign Policy," *Short Studies in Political Science* (1954), p. 20.

[2] In his farewell message to the American people in January 1961, Eisenhower warned against the "acquisition of unwarranted influence whether sought or unsought by the military-industrial complex." "Surely," writes Walter Lippmann, "it is impressive that the old soldier should make this warning the main theme of his farewell address." But how is this warning to be heeded? Only "by making civilian influence greater, not by reducing military power," says Lippmann. He therefore advocates the appointment of civilians with some military experience to the various high civilian posts dealing with military matters, who will be able to work with rather than defer to the professional soldiers. Walter Lippmann, "Eisenhower's Farewell Warning," *New York Herald Tribune,* January 19, 1961.

[3] Morris Janowitz, "Military Elites and the Study of War," *Journal of Conflict Resolution,* I (1957), 9-18, esp. 16. A similar point is made by C. Wright Mills, *The Power Elite* (1956), Chap. 8. Both authors seem to agree that the transferability of skills as between the military and civilian establishments has been increased, resulting in a greater uniformity and coalescence. But these elites may resemble each other organizationally without doing so functionally or morally.

Yet the difference between the military and the political elites as regards moral values and functional responsibilities have, by all accounts, increased. An extensive study of American military life during wartime found the three most distinctive characteristics differentiating military from civilian institutions to be authoritarianism, inequality, and traditionalism, in the service of its function of protection and defense of society.[4] The military elite must be prepared to kill and to die—a fate that is uniquely its own. "Military life is more serious than civilian life because it is more deadly and because soldiers are required both to die for the community as a whole and to kill in the interests of its preservation." [5] Thus the range of moral duties and the expectations surrounding the military elite differ from those of other strategic elites even though they are oriented to the preservation of the same society.

The scientific elite: The spectacular growth of science in the last century has been mirrored in the corresponding growth of influence of its leaders and spokesmen. To paraphrase one observer, modern society cannot "live reasonably without science nor gracefully without arts and letters." [6] It is the culmination of a process begun long ago when men began to search for the type of truth that scientific knowledge can provide. Francis Bacon in his reconstructions of the rational meaning behind ancient myths portrayed Science as the Sphinx, a monster with the face and voice of a virgin, the wings of a bird, and the claws of a griffin lying in ambush for travellers near Thebes with a series of riddles. Those who failed to solve them had to forfeit their lives. The parallel between the Sphinx and Science concludes that "the riddles of the Sphinx have always a twofold condition attached to them: Distraction and laceration of mind, if you fail to dissolve them; if you succeed, a kingdom." [7] The values of this kingdom are rationalism, specialization, and empiricism. Science implies faith in the possibility of solving

[4] Samuel Stauffer *et al., The American Soldier,* I (1949), 55.
[5] Hans Speier, "The 'American Soldier' and the Sociology of Military Organization," in Robert K. Merton and Paul F. Lazarsfeld, eds., *Continuities in Social Research* (1950), p. 113.
[6] The complete phrase is: "It occurred to me very early that one could not live reasonably without science nor gracefully without arts and letters." George Sarton, *A History of Science, Hellenistic Science and Culture in the Last Three Centuries B.C.* (1959), p. ix.
[7] Francis Bacon, "Sphinx or Science," in Hugh H. Dick, ed., *Selected Writings of Francis Bacon* (1955), pp. 418-19.

problems, belief that there are discoverable truths, and confidence in the application of human reason to human problems. Max Weber observes that science does not, in effect, signify an increased knowledge of the conditions of life but rather a change in basic attitudes toward life—particularly in the conviction that one can discover more about these conditions if one wishes. It implies a belief in the principle that all things can be mastered by calculation.[8]

The scientific elite, representing a particular component of the value system, is only one among several strategic elites. To those who would like to see this elite become *the* policy-makers of society, Weber, citing Tolstoy, would argue that "science is meaningless because it gives no answer to our question, the only question important for us: 'What shall we do and how shall we live?' "[9]

From this fact stems one dilemma, increasing as the role of science in public life increases, of the scientific elite. Unlike the political leader who must exhort and plead the common cause, the scientific leader must be guided not by his wishes or by the passions of the public he confronts but by the results of his laboriously collected findings. His duty is to search for the truth, to reveal what Weber calls "inconvenient facts," and to ask to be "surpassed and outdated." To plead in the name of science for this or that particular cause is to abdicate the scientific role.[10] For, the essence of science is a love of truth, but truth is only one of many possible values, and scientific truth is but one of several kinds. The scientist face to face with the problems of his community will have to resist the temptation, fostered by a humanity eager for quick and ready solutions, to become a demigod. If he is to articulate—for the other elites and for the community as a whole—a set of special principles and objectives, he will have to adhere to the basic, though partial, values which underwrite the rise and success of scientific endeavor. Among these are a devotion to log-

[8] Max Weber, "Science as a Vocation," in Gerth and Mills, eds., *From Max Weber: Essays in Sociology* (1946), pp. 129-56. Weber is not especially concerned here with great scientists but with scientists as distinct from other professional men.

[9] *Ibid.*, p. 143.

[10] According to Merton, loyalty to the canons of science involves commitment to four institutional imperatives: universalism, "communism," disinterestedness, and organized skepticism. Robert K. Merton, "Science and Democratic Social Structure," in Merton, *Social Theory and Social Structure*, rev. ed. (1957), p. 522.

ical clarity, empirical validity, and the desire to discover and know things for their own sake. This will not necessarily meet with the approval of the members of other strategic elites with different ideologies, values, and programs—the practical man who must act whether or not he has enough knowledge, the religious man who opposes tampering with the sacred mysteries, and the artist who prefers empathy and intuition to inexorable logic and rationality.

The religious elite: Historically, the most difficult adjustment to changing circumstances has been demanded of the religious elite—once the supreme arbiter of the thoughts and actions of men. Even today its influence, though circumscribed, has not ceased. The role of the religious elite in modern industrial societies has all too often been underestimated as a survival of a bygone era. But closer examination suggests that such problems as undeserved good fortune, unmerited disaster, and death underwrite the continued survival of religion, and hence of its elite spokesmen.[11] The high priests of today no longer claim supremacy as the guardians of knowledge, art, and the laws, but they do retain power as the caretakers of the souls of men, as the mediators between frail and vulnerable human beings and the mysterious powers that pull the strings of their destinies. Death, injustice, and evil persist and men must account for and come to terms with them. The religious elite still belongs to the strategic elites because it shares with them responsibility for collective survival.

Today, however, this elite must coordinate its activities and programs with those of the other elites, and its leading representatives must confront the facts of power, knowledge, art, and wealth and come to terms with them. They may hold to theodicy and theology but only when they will not conflict with the discoveries of the scientific elite. They may continue to exert social control but within a framework that grants their other colleagues, the political leaders, the ultimate resort to the legitimate use of force in society. They may preach an ethic of poverty and humility but not to the ex-

[11] Max Weber, in "The Social Psychology of World Religions," develops the point in some detail that religion supplies a rationale for undeserved good fortune as well as for misfortune. See Gerth and Mills, *op. cit.*, pp. 267-302. Talcott Parsons continues this line of thought in "Religious Perspectives in Sociology and Social Psychology," in William A. Lessa and Evon Z. Vogt, eds., *Reader in Comparative Religion* (1958), pp. 118-24.

tent that they fail to appreciate the wealth made possible by the economic elite. They may continue to orient the collectivity to a supernatural world, but they must expect to encounter as a rival conception a belief in the future of this world.

Religion survives because frustration is built into the very structure of society: there is no absolute coincidence between moral behavior and reward. This is especially true in societies with highly consistent and institutionalized value systems, where the moral order exhorts all to the same moral behavior but cannot guarantee the same rewards to all. The frustration stemming from this source must therefore be far greater in simpler societies with their precarious and uncertain existence than in societies more diversified and skilled in the struggle with nature. This may be one reason for the coercive, not to say despotic, powers assumed by many primitive priests. In industrial societies where a plurality of moral ideals coexist, individuals have more justifications and rationalizations to explain misfortune. The moral complexity and pluralism of modern industrial societies may actually protect men from oppression and so reduce the level of frustration caused by the capriciousness of fate. The modern moral dilemma seems to be what to believe, whereas the ancient one was how to go on believing. The role of the religious elite is less coercive now than in the past, but its place is no less secure. It has retained its link with the unseen and the unknowable, but it has yielded its place as supreme authority of the known. The tension and inconsistency between these two roles—the claim to ultimate authority and wisdom, and the helplessness before inscrutable divinities—led in the past to the exercise of an arbitrary and oppressive authority on the part of this elite. This tension lessens as the division of labor among strategic elites increases.

Men today are less ready to consider themselves pawns in some cruel sport of the gods, but they are nevertheless still preoccupied with the very questions that first gave priests such extraordinary power. The growth in the size of churches and the rise in church attendance testify to the enormous resiliency of an institution whose decline was prematurely mourned or heralded more than a century ago. The role of this elite today is mainly moral, affecting the emotional and ethical life of man. In this it joins forces with other spiritual healers—the artists and physicians of the mind—

and thus reconstitutes the original unity of ancient times between priest, healer, and artist.

The cultural elites: Societies cannot afford to ignore their poets, painters, and actors. These men renew the latent psychic energies of a people by providing outlets for private perspectives in a public existence. To neglect these elites in societies preoccupied with external dangers or internal comfort would be extremely damaging. Karl Mannheim was among the first to stress the equal importance of what he called the "integrative" and the "sublimative" elites, the latter referring to the artistic and intellectual elites. Whatever the internal organization of these elites, it is clear that their functions have been similar throughout the ages: to create means for social self-perception, for new and unconventional forms of beauty, and for highly individual signatures on the pages of collective life. Art is a yearning for completion, an indirect mode of self-knowledge, a symbolic bridge to be unexpressed and inexpressible—all of which are needed by organized society to stimulate and to calm the imagination of men living with, for, and against others.[12]

The role of the intellectual elites is to criticize, debate, challenge, and teach; to question established opinions, to explore new ideas, and to widen the experience and limited knowledge of men. "In every society," Mannheim has written, "there are social groups whose special task it is to provide an interpretation of the world for that society. We call them the 'intelligentsia.'"[13] In elaborating their ideas they provide models and standards for others, and in creating symbols they guide opinion as well as taste. Their reworking of the past in the light of present and future aims helps define and establish categories of experience. "By means of preaching, teaching, and writing, intellectuals infuse into sections of the population which are intellectual neither by inner vocation nor by social role, a perceptiveness and an imagery which they would otherwise lack."[14] Intellectuals have been the counselors of

[12] See Arnold Hauser, *The Social History of Art* (1957), and Leonard Adam, *Primitive Art* (1949).

[13] Karl Mannheim, *Ideology and Utopia* (1949), p. 9. The term *intelligentsia* was introduced into the Russian language by Boborykin in the latter part of the nineteenth century. It has since gained world-wide currency. See Martin Malia, "What is the Intelligentsia?" *Daedalus* (Summer 1960), 441-458.

[14] Edward Shils, "The Intellectuals and the Powers: Some Perspectives for

kings, the fathers of revolutions, the creators of utopias, and the guardians as well as the attackers of traditions. Their careers have been fluid. They have been hired by states, political parties, and churches, have eked out a living through the sale of polemical writings, or have followed academic careers. Wherever they are, they seek to influence the minds of men and to heighten the consciousness of the age in which they live.

In commercial and industrial societies, these elites often feel neglected. They resent the power of money and the cult of comfort, but they need money and comfort themselves to make an impression, to be members in good standing among the strategic elites. Realizing that their outlook and values cannot be carbon copies of the attitudes and values of businessmen, generals, or scientists, they feel a latent or overt hostility toward these groups. Yet, lacking a room at the top of their own, they often fail to construct a view of their own. At times they think the world owes them something, and the world does—it owes them their own place in center stage along with the other elites, a place in which they can find the stimulus to creativity and the means to communicate it to other parts of society. Only the best of them live there, but this may encourage the best in the rest. In turn, the artistic, literary, and intellectual elites must succeed in solving certain cultural problems, either by making apparent and articulating what was obscure or by exposing unpleasant truths or by providing entirely new forms of experience. They must arouse interest, controversy, sympathy, opposition, or be ignored—which amounts to their death sentence.

As a result of moral diversity and functional differentiation, each strategic elite is more closely associated with some moral values than with others. Hence the members of the different elites internalize one set of moral beliefs more firmly than others, and both their self-images and the public's image of them are affected by how well they live up to these standards and cultivate a public style appropriate to these tacit judgments and expectations. The moral value principally associated with the political elite is loyalty, with the economic elite, wealth, with the cultural elites, originality,

---

Comparative Analysis," *Comparative Studies in Society and History,* Vol. I (October, 1958), No. 1, 5-22.

with the military elite, safety; the scientific elite represents the value of truth, the recreational elite, pleasure and amusement.

I. Social class origins of various elites

Political: According to Donald R. Matthews' study of 180 men and women who served in the United States Senate between 1947 and 1957, the majority came from business and professional families, enjoying material advantages denied to the majority of Americans. Born and raised in small towns, their early attitudes reflect Main Street rather than the metropolis. But it is the Main Street of the well-to-do, for few of these men and women ever knew poverty. Only 7 per cent came from the homes of industrial wage earners and low-salaried workers; one third, from farm families. (*U.S. Senators and Their World* (1960), esp. Chap. 2.)

C. Wright Mills reports roughly the same pattern for the 513 men who occupied the following political offices between 1789 and 1953: President, Vice President, Speaker of the House, Cabinet members, and Supreme Court Justice. Most of these office holders came from prosperous professional and business families. At the same time, a sizeable minority, nearly one fifth, were described as lower class, although Mills includes small businessmen, farmers, and wage earners in this category. (*The Power Elite* (1956), Chap. 10.)

The predominance of middle-class individuals among the members of political elites has been remarked for other countries, in particular England, France, Italy, and Israel. Whether this is because "Voters show a tendency to prefer candidates of higher level than themselves," or because middle-class parents are more likely than parents in other classes to encourage political aspirations in their children, or because nominating committees prefer middle-class candidates, is still an open question. (Jean Meynaud, "Introduction: General Study of Parliamentarians," *International Social Science Journal,* XIII (1961), No. 4, 513-545.) For additional bibliography, see: "The Parliamentary Profession," *International Social Science Journal,* XIII (1961), No. 4, esp. the following articles: Leon Hamon, "Members of the French Parliament," pp. 545-567; Benjamin Akzin, "The Knesset," pp. 567-583; G. Sartori, "Parliamentarians in Italy," pp. 583-600; H. B. Berrington and S. E. Finer, "The British House of Commons," pp. 600-620; K. Gubin, "The Supreme Soviet of the USSR and Its Members," pp. 635-640. See also Donald R. Matthews, *The Social Backgrounds of Political Decision Makers* (1954); Dwaine Marvick (ed.), *Political Decision Makers* (1961); F. M. G. Willson, "The Ranks of Entry of New Members of the British Cabinet 1868-1958," *Political Studies,* VII (1959), No. 3, 222-232; Heinz Eulau and David Koff, "Occupational Mobility and Political Career," *The Western Political Quarterly* (September, 1962), 507-522.

The future Senators also enjoyed a middle-class education. More than eight tenths attended college (one eighth at an Ivy League school) at a time when only one sixth of the adult white population had done so, and fully three fifths had gone on to law school. Party affiliation affects all of these variables considerably, with the more conservative parties in France, Italy, England, and the United States selecting the more conservative candidates as regards lineage, ethnicity, social class background, and type of schooling.

For studies of the psychological characteristics and personal perspectives of politicians, see: Harold D. Lasswell, "The Selective Effect of Personality on Political Participation," in Richard Christie and Marie Jahoda, *Studies in the Scope and Method of "The Authoritarian Personality"* (1954), pp. 197-226. See also other writings by the same author, notably *Psychopathology and Politics* (1930); *Power and Personality* (1948).

The ideal type attributes of a politician are described by Max Weber in "Politics as a Vocation," in Gerth and Mills (eds.), *From Max Weber,* pp. 77-129. See also Heinz Eulau *et al.,* "Career Perspectives of American State Legislators," in Dwaine Marvick (ed.), *Political Decision Makers* (1961), pp. 218-263, esp. p. 247.

Business: Recent studies of the American business elite, variously defined as the leading officers in the leading corporations, have agreed substantially in their findings on the social class origins of the members. Warner, analyzing 8,562 returns out of more than 17,000 questionnaires, found that the majority came from business and professional families; less than one third—15 per cent from the homes of manual laborers, 9 per cent from the homes of farmers, and 8 per cent from the homes of clerks or salesmen—from the lower social classes. Keller, reporting the findings for more than 1,000 business leaders representing three historical periods (1870, 1900, and 1950) indicates that 57 per cent of the business leaders in 1950 had fathers who were businessmen (owners or managers). She found only one fourth of the 1950 generation to have originated in lower-class homes, perhaps because she included only the largest corporations whereas Warner's 1952 study also included medium-sized firms. See W. L. Warner and James C. Abegglen, *Occupational Mobility in Business and Industry, 1928-1952,* 2 vols.; Suzanne Keller, *The Social Origins and Career Lines of Three Generations of American Business Leaders* (1953). Unpublished doctoral dissertation, Columbia University; W. L. Warner and J. C. Abegglen, *Big Business Leaders in America* (1955), Chaps. 4, 5, 8; Mabel Newcomer, *The Big Business Executive* (1955); Editors of *Fortune, The Executive Life* (1956); Osborn Elliott, *Men at the Top* (1959); David Granick, *The Red Executive* (1961); Fritz Redlich, *History of American Business Leaders* (1940).

According to Keller, six tenths of the 1950 generation of business leaders were college graduates, and almost one half had postgraduate training in either law (15 per cent), engineering (15 per cent), or other professions (15 per cent). Warner's figures closely parallel Keller's—57 per cent of the 1952 business elite were college graduates (*Big Business Leaders in America,* p. 47). Similar findings are reported for British business magnates who tend to be born to business families and attend the public schools. See Rosemary G. Stewart and Paul Duncan-Jones, "Educational Background and Career History of British Managers, with some American Comparisons," *Explorations in Entrepreneurial History,* IX, No. 2, pp. 61-71; and Roy Lewis and Rosemary Stewart, *The Managers* (1961), p. 96.

Military: The most recent comprehensive study of the military elite—760 United States generals and admirals appointed since 1910, 550 staff officers on duty at the Pentagon (113 of whom were intensively interviewed)—showed the majority to come from professional, managerial, and business backgrounds. Only 5 per cent of the latest generation leadership in each of the main branches of the service came from workers' families, and an additional tenth—10 per cent of the 1950 Army generals, 7 per cent of the Navy admirals, and 15 per cent of the Air Force generals—came from farm families (Morris Janowitz, *The Professional Soldier* (1960), p. 91). Classification by income, occupation, and status (although no specific evidence is provided) permitted Janowitz to infer the social class origins of the three groups of officers as lower middle and upper middle class (*Ibid.,* p. 90). Members of the military elite in the recent generation have had extensive formal education—85 per cent of the Army officers, 95 per cent of the Navy officers, and 73 per cent of the Air Force officers were college graduates, most of them from the service academies of West Point and Annapolis (*Ibid.,* Chaps. 5 and 6 contain specific evidence).

The Higher Civil Service: Two main studies, both more than twenty years old, provide our main data. *Higher Civil Servants in America,* by Reinhard Bendix, is based on 192 questionnaire returns sent to higher government officials in 1940. It showed that only 10 per cent came from the homes of manual laborers; the majority were middle-class individuals from professional homes. Eight tenths were college graduates, and six tenths had had post-college training. The other study, by MacMahon and Millet, notes a "marked prevalence of college graduates" among the Under Secretaries and Assistant Secretaries of ten Federal departments. Further, of 62 bureau chiefs, 85 per cent were college graduates and about one half had had post-college training. (See Arthur MacMahon and John D. Millet, *Federal Administrators* (1939), p. 294; Chap. xvii.)

The middle-class character of this elite is also prevalent in other industrial societies. In fact, it was anticipated as part of a broader historical trend by a French observer who noted more than two decades ago that government posts "that had once been the exclusive preserve of the upper bourgeoisie began to be filled increasingly from the middle and lower bourgeoisie." (See Walter Rice Sharp, "Historical Changes in Recruitment," in Robert K. Merton *et al., Reader in Bureaucracy* (1952), pp. 299-303, and other articles in this collection.) More recent data, on the other hand, suggest that "French, German, Dutch, British, and Swedish civil servants come from families of higher social status than their American peers, a finding that probably reflects national variation in the status of civil service positions" (S. M. Lipset and Reinhard Bendix, *Social Mobility in Industrial Society* (1962), p. 39). One study found that three fifths of the candidates who presented themselves for entry into the Ecole Nationale d'Administration in France were from upper middle-class backgrounds, whereas the proportion among the successful entrants was more than three fourths (Thomas Bottomore, "La Mobilité Sociale dans la Haute Administration Française," *Cahiers Internationaux de Sociologie,* XIII (1952), 165-178).

Scientific: Studies of the scientific elite suggest that it, too, is largely recruited from business and professional families. Knapp and Goodrich—after examining two samples of scientists listed in *American Men of Science* for 1881-1890 and 1931-1940, who were either starred or who had received their doctorates in selected scientific fields—concluded that scientists "most frequently seem to be recruited from middle and lower middle-class families" (R. H. Knapp and H. B. Goodrich, *Origins of American Scientists* (1952), esp. pp. 1-24; 259-97). Earlier studies suggested that scientists are generally drawn from families of teachers, clergymen, and other scientists. (See, for example, Stephen Sargent Visher, "Environmental Backgrounds of Leading American Scientists," *American Sociological Review* 13 (February, 1948), No. 1, pp. 65-72. A summary of such studies is contained in Barber, *Science and the Social Order* (1952), pp. 134-38.) Anne Roe in her intensive interviews with 64 eminent physical, biological, and social scientists found more than half of them to have come from professional families in the upper middle class (Anne Roe, *The Making of a Scientist* (1952), esp. Chaps. 5-7). A study of Nobel Prize winners in physics, chemistry, and medicine, while lacking information on the social backgrounds of two thirds of the 214 prize winners included, stated that the "social origins of the Nobel Prize winners are never 'humble' and that the fathers almost always are of very high social position" (Leo Moulin, "The Nobel Prizes for the Sciences from 1901-1950—An Essay in Sociological Analysis," *British Journal of Sociology* VI (September, 1955),

No. 3, pp. 246-63). See also George W. Gray, "Which Scientists Win Nobel Prizes?" in Bernard Barber and Walter Hirsch (eds.), *The Sociology of Science* (1962), pp. 557-65. Presumably most scientists were college graduates. Detailed information about the scientific elite is obviously lacking.

Diplomatic: In countries with a feudal past, diplomats are often drawn from the upper classes of society. The United States, lacking such a past, has generally drawn its ambassadors or ministers from circles of wealthy businessmen or from old New England or Southern plantation families. Keller collected information about the backgrounds of 120 American ambassadors (and ministers, where no embassies existed) sent to the following ten countries between 1900 and 1953: Great Britain, France, the USSR, Germany, Italy, Spain, Turkey, Iran, Japan, and China. (See "Twentieth Century Ambassadors." Unpublished manuscript.) One third of the 120 men could be classified as members of a native aristocracy of old landed wealth; another third, as members of a native plutocracy of financial and commercial wealth. The former was particularly prevalent among career diplomats (one third of all), whereas the latter prevailed among political appointees (two thirds of all). The majority of this elite came from families engaged in business or the professions. Ties of home and school linked them to the Northeastern United States and, to a lesser extent, to the South. Four fifths held college degrees; one half, graduate degrees mostly in law. One third of the group had attended private preparatory schools, and two fifths had received their degrees from Ivy League colleges—a figure twice that found among Republican Senators (Matthews, *U.S. Senators and Their World,* p. 28) and four times that of all Senators; but it equals the figure given by Warner for the American business elite in 1952 (Warner and Abegglen, *Big Business Leaders in America,* p. 51) and that for Supreme Court justices (John R. Schmidhauser, *The Supreme Court—Its Politics, Personalities, and Procedures* (1960), p. 43).

The clergy: Virtually no studies exist of leading Protestant ministers in the United States for the period under review. It has been said that although the clergy enjoys considerable prestige, its current status is not comparable with that accorded it at an earlier period—from Colonial times to the mid-nineteenth century, when ministers were "largely recruited from 'good' families," and when "entering the ministry itself conferred a measure of prestige in a community." (Ministers were ranked fourteenth by a 1947 cross-sectional sample of the American public, according to C. C. North and Paul K. Hatt, "Jobs and Occupations: A Popular Evaluation," *Opinion News* (September 1, 1947), pp. 3-13.) After 1800, ministers were "recruited more and more from the lower social and economic strata of the society," a trend that has apparently continued into the twentieth century.

Two early 1930's studies reached roughly the same conclusion regarding the less favorable socioeconomic backgrounds of seminary students. Mark A. May, *The Education of American Ministers,* Vol. III (1934), studied the patterns of recruitment involving students at 224 institutions that trained men for the ministry. He concentrated on the largest seminaries and on those with a three-year professional course for the ministry. Maynard L. Cassady, *A Comparative Study of Two Generations of Theological Graduates* (1934), studied two groups of graduates from Union Theological Seminary for the periods 1888-1900, and 1919-1929. May estimated that the majority of the students came from the homes of manual laborers, farmers, and small tradesmen, and only one fifth from professional families. He judged that only 30 per cent of the students originated in poor homes. Cassady, comparing first-year divinity, law, and medical students at Yale from 1904-1928, found that nine times as many divinity students as medical students were sons of unskilled laborers and twice as many divinity students as law students; six to eight times as many divinity students were sons of farmers. A recent set of interviews with more than one hundred students at eight leading theological schools presents a somewhat different pattern, which may reflect a genuine change or be only an artifact of the method used. Seven tenths of these students came from business and professional families; only 5 per cent were ministers' sons. A high of one fourth, however—including farmers, laborers, or factory workers—had fathers who were manual workers. (See Jhan and June Robbins, "The Surprising Beliefs of Our Future Ministers," *Redbook,* August, 1961.) See also: Sidney E. Mead, "The Rise of the Evangelical Conception of the Ministry in America, 1607-1850," and Robert S. Michaelsen, "The Protestant Ministry in America: 1850 to the Present," in H. Richard Niebuhr and Daniel D. Williams (eds.), *The Ministry in Historical Perspective* (1956). In 1926, according to Michaelsen, only one third of the ministers of the seventeen largest white Protestant denominations in the United Sates were graduates of colleges or theological seminaries. These figures may be artifically inflated by a too liberal interpretation of college or seminary training. Beverly Davis, "Eminence and Level of Social Origins," *American Journal of Sociology,* LIX (July, 1953), No. 1, p. 15. This analysis of a sample of 803 males listed in *Who's Who in the East* for 1942-1943 showed that "twice the expected number of individuals of the clerical and labor strata attained eminence in the clergy."

Unfortunately, material is scanty concerning the elite element among Jewish rabbis and Roman Catholic priests. Interestingly, although the Roman Catholic Church has been a church of the poor, its leadership has come from the wealthy strata. Sorokin states that three fifths of the Roman Catholic Popes throughout history were of the "noble and wealthy" classes, adding that recruitment from the lower classes was greater in the past than in more recent centuries. The late Pope John, of humble peasant stock, reversed the trend. (See Pitirim A. Sorokin, *Social Mobility* (1927), p. 158.) The death, in 1961, of Cardinal Canali removed the last nobleman from the ranks of the College of Cardinals (*New York Times,* August 4, 1961, p. 21).

In 1958, the Roman Catholic hierarchy in the United States consisted of 2 cardinals, 57 archbishops, 230 bishops, and 50,813 priests. A questionnaire sent to the total membership listed in the official Catholic directory—113 individuals—was returned by three fourths, representing 56 per cent of the archbishops and 75 per cent of the bishops. The men, largely second and third generation Americans of Irish descent and secondarily of German and Polish, were clearly from lower socioeconomic backgrounds. Only 5 per cent had fathers classified as professionals; only 10 per cent had fathers classified as minor business executives. The cardinals and other members of the Roman Catholic hierarchy have been described as "drawn from the more upwardly mobile Catholic families in the United States." They were all highly educated at parochial schools and seminaries. Three fourths possessed higher degrees. (See John D. Donovan, "The American Catholic Hierarchy: A Social Profile," *The American Catholic Sociological Re-*

view, XIX (June, 1958), No. 2, 98-113.) Specific figures were: 17 per cent of the American Roman Catholic hierarchy in 1957 came from unskilled or semiskilled laborers, 11 per cent from skilled, 27 per cent from owners of small business, 8 per cent from clerks or salesmen, 7 per cent from foremen, 9 per cent from farmers (owners and tenants), and 5 per cent from other types of backgrounds. *Ibid.,* p. 105. See also Gerhard Lenski, *The Religious Factor* (1963), Chap. 7. A study of the social origins of Roman Catholic saints showed the majority had been born into the upper classes, although there was some variation by century. However, the data are subject to distortion because the sample of 2,494 saints were those "for whom we possessed sufficient data to enable us to catalogue them by the century in which they had died and by the social class into which they had been born." The upper class, it is well known, is far more apt to keep extensive records of its activities than the lower classes; it is also more likely to have its activities recorded by others. Moreover, as the authors point out, there may have been a tendency to upgrade the social backgrounds of the saints by later churchmen—which would increase the upper class total. See, Katherine and Charles H. George, "Roman Catholic Sainthood and Social Status: A Statistical and Analytical Study," *The Journal of Religion,* XXXV (April, 1955), No. 2, pp. 85-98. No systematic study of leading Jewish rabbis could be located. However, a number of special studies do exist. See Robert J. Marx, "Changing Patterns of Leadership in the American Reform Rabbinate, 1890-1957," Unpublished doctoral dissertation, Yale University, 1957.

Supreme Court: The 92 Supreme Court justices between 1789 and 1959 came overwhelmingly "from socially advantaged families. . . . In the earlier history of the Court, he very likely was born in the aristocratic gentry class, although later he tended to come from the professionalized upper middle-class. . . . It seems reasonable to assume that very few sons of families outside the upper, or upper-middle, social and economic classes have been able to acquire the particular type of education and the subsequent professional, and especially political, associations which appear to be unwritten prerequisites for appointment to the nation's highest tribunal" (Schmidhauser, *The Supreme Court—Its Politics, Personalities, and Procedures* (1960), p. 55).

Journalists: Part of the intellectual elite of the United States is found among its leading journalists. In the 1930's, Leo Rosten interviewed 127 members of the Washington press corps, constituting a crucial portion of leading journalists and thus of American opinion creators at that time. As political correspondents and columnists for the six major press associations, the news and feature syndicates, and 186 daily general newspapers, they reached an enormous audience. Rosten reports that most of them came from favorable economic backgrounds and from professional rather than from business families. Only one tenth came from the ranks of manual workers. More than one half were college graduates. See Leo Rosten, *The Washington Correspondents* (1927).

Intellectuals: A study of the social backgrounds of 1956 National Merit Scholars showed that certain occupational groups produced more scholars than did others. The five subgroups highest in productivity were: librarians, college presidents, professors and instructors, architects, lawyers, judges and clergymen. There was only one National Merit Scholar out of 3.5 million laborers (excluding farmers and miners), but 234 scholars out of nearly 3 million professional, technical, and kindred workers. (Horace Mann Bond, "The Producticity of National Merit Scholars by Occupational Class," *School and Society,* Vol. 85 (September 28, 1957), No. 2116, pp. 267-268.)

In their study of the American academic profession, Lazarsfeld and Thielens give some evidence on the social backgrounds of their 2,451 social science college teachers, but not of the elite of their sample—that is, the 881 who were full professors. For the sample as a whole, 25 per cent came from managerial backgrounds and 31 per cent from professional, 8 per cent of these having ex-teachers as fathers. White collar and business backgrounds made up 15 per cent of the sample; farmers, 13 per cent; and manual laborers, 15 per cent. The academic profession as a whole consists of a high proportion of upwardly mobile men, but we do not know whether this also characterizes the academic elite. The authors constructed a productivity index for each professor, based on the number of publications and other professional activities, and found that the professors from higher socioeconomic backgrounds were more productive than those from lower socioeconomic backgrounds. However, this is primarily true for younger men, and while the figures are consistent they are also small. After age fifty, there is hardly any difference in the productivity of professors, either from higher or lower socioeconomic backgrounds. (See Paul F. Lazarsfeld and Wagner Thielens, Jr., *The Academic Mind* (1958), pp. 7, 10.) A more detailed breakdown of the occupational backgrounds of the 2,451 respondents shows that 111 of the fathers were college or university teachers; 565, professionals; and 617, proprietors, managers, and officials. It would be most interesting to see how full professors differ from lower-ranking academic men on apprehensiveness, caution, and conservatism, controlling for age, socioeconomic backgrounds, and productivity.

By and large, these sparse studies of portions of the American intelligentsia show them to be sons of professional men, highly educated, and socially and regionally mobile. What, then, of the "classlessness" of the intelligentsia postulated by Karl Mannheim in *Ideology and Utopia?* By "classless" Mannheim did not of course mean that intellectuals have no group affiliations, but only that they have a great variety of them, and that they are not predominantly recruited from any single social stratum. In particular, he was contrasting the intellectuals not connected with any fixed estate with such groups as military officers (in Germany) who were bound to an estate. Existing evidence seems to support his suggestion.

It is important to interpret what material we have on intellectual elites with caution, for it is both limited and dated. The professional backgrounds of American intellectuals contrast sharply with the social backgrounds of the British intellectual aristocracy described by Annan as regards specific occupational milieus. Yet both groups were middle class in backgrounds and in styles of life. The British group, consisting of professors, professional civil servants, and journalists regarded themselves as gentlemen, although only a few came from the gentry. Many of them were of merchant families of the eighteenth century, others sprang from poor country parsons, dissenting ministers, or prosperous artisans. They never confused themselves with the nobility, however. Unlike the Russian intelligentsia they were not cut adrift and revolutionary in attitude. Rather, they favored gradual reform, although this did not soften the sting of their criticism or temper the ardor of their spiritual passions. See N. G. Annan, "The Intellectual Aristocracy," in J. H. Plumb (ed.), *Studies in Social History* (1955), pp. 243-287.

Clearly, there is noticeable lack of systematic and comprehensive information about the various components of the elites of thinkers, moralists, intellectuals, and writers. For additional evidence, see Joseph Schneider, "The Definition of Eminence and the Social Origins of Famous English Men of Genius," *American Sociological Review,* 3 (December, 1938), No. 6, pp. 834-849. The author found that "the lower classes produced relatively more poets, dissenting clergymen, and artists"; Joseph Schneider, "Social Class, Historical Circumstances and Fame," *American Journal of Sociology,* XLIII (July, 1937), No. 1, pp. 37-56. Here the author points out that we do not know as yet "why the largest classes in a population produce at all times relatively so few eminent men of genius"; Pitirim A. Sorokin, *Social and Cultural Dynamics,* Vol. IV (1941). Sorokin tries to account for variations in choice of fields by "the best brains" of a society during different periods; Karl Mannheim, "The Problem of the Intelligentsia: An Inquiry into Its Past and Present Role," in *Essays on the Sociology of Culture* (1956); George B. de Huszar (ed.), *The Intellectuals* (1960).

Sporadic bits of systematic and impressionistic evidence suggest that working class descendants are more prevalent among the elites of the cinema, the arts, journalism, and academic life than in other elites. Certainly the popular image of stage, screen, sports, religion, and art as channels of upward mobility would support such an inference, but popular impressions are subject to error. The pattern may not be characteristic at all.

Film stars: Leo Rosten, describing the backgrounds of the leading film stars between 1938-1941, noted the predominance of professional and business backgrounds for this elite. He found no individuals who had come from the homes of unskilled or semiskilled laborers. Only 5 per cent came from the homes of skilled laborers, and 4 per cent from those of farmers. The educational attainments of the stars, however, were modest—only one fifth were college graduates (this was in the 1930's). Unfortunately, no recent studies exist of the elites of stage, screen, television, the arts, or sports.

Rosten's findings may reflect the nature of his sample. Of the 309 interviewed, two thirds were male actors, who may come from more favorable social backgrounds than actresses. (See Leo C. Rosten, *Hollywood* (1941), and Hortense Powdermaker, *Holly-*

wood, The Dream Factory (1950).) This conclusion is suggested by a small exploratory study of some members of the cinema elite during two five-year periods—1932-1937 and 1952-1957. It was found that the female stars tended to come from the homes of unskilled laborers and migratory workers, whereas the male stars came from substantial middle-class homes—those of lawyers, chemists, and surgeons. The pattern is suggestive, but the numbers, just fourteen stars, are too small to be reliable. Few of these stars went to college and none had been graduated. The males were better educated than the females—this agrees with Rosten—and the stars of the fifties were better educated than those of the thirties. This material was presented by Rhoda Gluck in my seminar on elites at Brandeis University, May, 1958.

A recent study of 156 American entertainers, who were either native-born or who came to the United States before their tenth birthdays, and who were prominently featured in certain magazines with a wide circulation, found that at least 30 per cent of them came from the homes of laborers of all kinds. The difference between Rosten's and this study may stem from the nature of this sample which included entertainers in general and not only the brightest stars of the screen. It may also differ because of the time periods covered, the later study referring to the years 1950-1956. (See Sidney Willhelm and Gideon Sjoberg, "The Social Characteristics of Entertainers," *Social Forces,* October, 1958).

High society: The elite of first families among all strategic elites in industrial societies is virtually alone in its emphasis on birth and breeding, and constitutes the last remnants of a traditionalist, aristocratic outlook. However, even here the growth in the size, organization, and centralization of national life has had an impact. The original list of "The Four Hundred," compiled by Ward McAllister in 1887, had grown by 1960 to over 75,000. It has also had to become more formally organized. One landmark in this organization is the publication of the annual "Social Register," begun by Louis Keller in 1887, which now appears winter and summer in eleven American cities. See also E. Digby Baltzell, *Philadelphia Gentlemen* (1958); Cleveland Amory, *The Proper Bostonians* (1947), and *Who Killed Society?* (1960); Lucy Kavaler, *The Private World of High Society* (1960); and C. Wright Mills, *The Power Elite,* Chap. ii. Among the many novels describing the life of the upper classes, when high society still performed social, economic, and political functions, those of Edith Wharton, F. Scott Fitzgerald, Henry James, and John P. Marquand are outstanding.

The members listed in the Social Register constitute a modern version of a social caste. They are born to wealth amassed by ancestors who made their fortunes in shipping, fur trading, or industry and finance. Money is not an automatic entrance ticket into the inner ranks, but it is indispensable for starting a family on the road to eventual entry. The members have long roots in their local communities, and family and community history are considered inseparable. They are largely, if not exclusively, of Anglo-Saxon stock and the Protestant faiths. They attend old private preparatory schools and go to the "right college" where they belong to the "right" clubs. Informal socialization is rigidly augmented by formal training among the young—riding, dancing school, and some modern version of the grand tour, climaxed by annual coming-out parties and debuts that signify the maturing of a new generation. They intermarry and frequent the same clubs, the same shops, and the same friends. They wear their badge of membership as clearly as the general his uniform or the diplomat his attaché case. They are taught the values of self-control, subordination to the rules of the caste, good manners, and noblesse oblige towards those less fortunate than themselves. There is also stress on conspicuous nonconsumption, subdued elegance and understatement, and excellence of quality. Outsiders may not always recognize them but they always recognize each other, able to tell at a glance whether a particular style is the result of the effortless assumption of a status held from birth, or the hard-won shell acquired and maintained only by incessant vigilance. Living in the best houses in the best parts of their cities, they know about poverty and material insecurity mainly through their charitable activities and philanthropic work.

Conclusion: The scanty information on the social class backgrounds of the members of various strategic elites suggests that the majority are middle-class individuals, raised in the homes of business or professional men in comfortable economic circumstances. Earlier studies, more general in scope, found a similar pattern, despite their different methodologies and definitions. According to a study of ten occupational groups represented in *Who's Who in*

America in 1938-1939, the highest proportion of individuals without a college degree occurred among businessmen, editors, and writers. (J. R. Shannon and Maxine Shaw, "Education of Business and Professional Leaders," *American Sociological Review,* Vol. 5 (June, 1940), No. 3, pp. 381-383.) A later study showed that business and professional families predominated in the backgrounds of 803 men listed in *Who's Who* of 1942-1943 (Beverly Davis, "Eminence and Level of Social Origin," *American Journal of Sociology,* Vol. LIV (July, 1953), No. 1, pp. 11-18). Davis found the field of eminence to be closely related to the social origins of individuals—religion and education being the chief fields where the clerical, labor, and agricultural strata are likely to have the best chance for success. Joseph Schneider arrived at a similar conclusion, although his study covers a rather wide time span, from 1400-1850. (See Joseph Schneider, "The Definition of Eminence and the Social Origins of Famous English Men of Genius," *American Sociological Review,* Vol. III (December, 1938), No. 6, pp. 834-849.) He also wondered why "the largest class in the population produces at all times relatively so few eminent men of genius" (Schneider, "Social Class, Historical Circumstances and Fame," *American Journal of Sociology,* Vol. XLIII (July, 1937), No. 1, pp. 37-56). Schneider examined more than ten thousand biographies listed in the *English Dictionary of National Biography,* but these listings may not be representative of all great and eminent men from all classes. Sorokin, reporting on the 2,171 biographies of *RUS,* the dictionary of rural leaders in 1925, found that nearly nine tenths of this group, those with biographies of twelve lines or more, had college degrees. Presumably this was due to the fact that the largest proportion of rural leaders were teachers and deans. (See Pitirim A. Sorokin and Carl C. Zimmerman, "Farmer Leaders in the United States," *Social Forces,* Vol. VII (September, 1928), No. 1, pp. 33-45.) For summaries of other studies of elite groups up to 1927, see Pitirim A. Sorokin, *Social Mobility,* Part III, pp. 215-316.*

* This discussion has expressly omitted the elite of American labor leaders because, in my opinion, this elite is still too dependent on the business elite whose actions trigger its own reactions. Currently, the labor elite has the power to criticize and oppose rather than to initiate economic policies. Potentially one of the strategic elites, it is currently a segmental elite.

III. Trends in social class origins of elites

All of the elites with available information on social backgrounds of their members show an increase in the proportions coming from lower-class backgrounds. Keller found more sons of wage earners and office workers in the 1950 generation of business leaders than in the two earlier generations (*The Social Origins and Career Lines of Three Generations of American Business Leaders,* pp. 183-183a). Warner concluded that "there is confirmation of the long term, continuing trend to greater realization of opportunity in American business and to an increase in the proportion of men from the 'bottom' who make their way to the 'top' " (Warner and Abegglen, *Big Business Leaders,* p. 32). As regards the military elite, Janowitz states that "these elites have been shifting their recruitment from a narrow, relatively high, social status base to a broader base, more representative of the population as a whole" (*The Professional Soldier,* p. 10). More than 30 per cent of the 1960 West Point graduates were offspring of white collar and working classes. "Of those with working-class backgrounds, the majority came from skilled trades, such as the sons of machinists and printers, but some are from the very bottom of the social pyramid" (*Ibid.,* p. 92). The elite of the newest branch of the service, the Air Force, had the highest proportion of men from the lesser educated, poorer elements of society (*Ibid.,* p. 91).

The highest proportion of diplomats from lower-class homes was found in the most recent decade studied by Keller, mainly among the politically appointed envoys. Career diplomats differ substantially from politically appointed diplomats. The proportion of envoys coming from lower-class homes was 18 per cent for political appointees, but only 4 per cent for career men. Similarly, 60 per cent of the career men were graduates of one of the Big Three colleges, compared to 33 per cent of the political appointees. Keeping in mind the small size of the samples—25 career diplomats and 73 political appointees—and the limited scope of Keller's study, which included only ten countries, the suggestion nevertheless emerges that career diplomats come from more restricted social backgrounds than do political envoys. (See "Twentieth Century Ambassadors.")

A number of European studies of political, business, and civil service elites show a similar trend toward increased recruitment of lower-class men. Kingsley, discussing the British Civil Service, believed that the prevalent pattern of recruitment "from a narrow social stratum closely identified with the historic ruling class" may change, "for a smaller proportion of those entering the Administrative class in the 1930's had public school backgrounds." This suggests, he writes, "that the old order is slowly giving way." (See J. Donald Kingsley, *Representative Bureaucracy, An Interpretation of the British Civil Service* (1944), Esp. Chap. vii, pp. 448, 151.) For changes in parliamentary recruitment in England, France, and Italy, see the collection of articles, "The Parliamentary Profession," in the *International Social Science Journal,* Vol. XIII (1961), No. 4, pp. 523, 550, 588, 601, 602.)

IV. Lineage, ethnic, and religious backgrounds

The majority of the 1950 business elite, as well as earlier generations were of native-born fathers (76 per cent), of British descent (65 per cent) and of the Protestant faiths (85 per cent), especially Presbyterian and Episcopalian (47 per cent). An increase in the proportions of "second generation, Jewish, Roman Catholic, and South Irish and Southeastern European descendants from the 1870 to the 1950 generation" was also noted. (All figures are from Suzanne Keller, *The Social Origins and Career Lines of Three*

Generations of American Business Leaders, pp. 41, 44, 63, 66.) For corroborative evidence, see Warner and Abegglen, *Big Business Leaders,* p. 190; and S. M. Lipset and R. Bendix, *Social Mobility in Industrial Society,* Chap. iv.

According to Matthews, the majority of postwar Senators were native-born, third-generation, white, Protestants, and of Northwest European descent (Donald Matthews, *U.S. Senators and Their World,* pp. 22-25).

The majority of diplomatic envoys to ten selected countries between 1900-1955 were likewise old native stock (88 per cent), Protestant (60 per cent), especially Presbyterian and Episcopalian (45 per cent), and of British and Northwest European descent. (See Suzanne Keller, "Twentieth Century Ambassadors.")

The majority of admirals and generals had "many generations of native born parents," and were Protestant (84 to 90 per cent), especially Presbyterian and Episcopalian—66 per cent of the Army elite of 1950, 56 per cent of the Navy, and 43 per cent of the Air Force. Janowitz concludes that although there has been a general trend toward "greater and greater representativeness," a strong emphasis on "second and third generation, native born" backgrounds persists. (See Janowitz, *The Professional Soldier,* pp. 83, 99, 100.)

Some suggestions exist but no precise information on the status characteristics of the intellectual and recreational elites to the effect that they may exhibit greater variation as regards religion, ethnicity, and religious and national backgrounds. Rosten found that the proportion of foreign-born among the cinema elite of the 1930's was as high as 25 per cent. (See Rosten, *Hollywood,* p. 391.)

V. Trends in ascribed attributes

An increase in men possessing less-favored social attributes has been noted for the business, political, military, and diplomatic elites. Janowitz found for example, that the proportion of Roman Catholics among current West Point cadets (1961) was almost three times greater (29 per cent) than that of the Army and Navy elite of 1950. While there were no Jews at all in the 1950 elite, 2 per cent of the West Point class of 1961 were of the Jewish faith (*The Professional Soldier,* p. 99). Keller also found "more second-generation Americans, more Jews, and more descendants of South Irish and of Southeastern European immigrants in the 1950 generation of the business elite than in the 1870 and the 1900 generations" (*The Social Origins and Career Lines of Three Generations of American Business Leaders,* p. 66).

The following tables summarize some of the evidence on the social backgrounds of various elites based on the studies discussed earlier.

TABLE I: NATIVITY

Strategic Elite:	*Percentage of Foreign-Born**	*Percentage of Second Generation**
Political	2%	15%
Military	2%	9% (West Point Class of 1960)
Diplomatic	4%	8%
Business	6%	18%
Film	25%	No information

* As for the national origins of the foreign-born and the second generation, the majority in each case came from Northwest Europe.

TABLE II: RURAL-URBAN ORIGINS

Strategic Elite:	*Percentage of Urban-Born* (in towns of 2,500 or more)
Military	30-40% (taking Army, Navy, and Air Force separately)
Political	48% *
Journalistic ‡	61%
Diplomatic	66%
Business	65% †

* These were concentrated in small towns rather than in large cities.
† Warner's figure is 75%.
‡ Based on Washington Correspondents.

TABLE III: RELIGIOUS AFFILIATION

Strategic Elite:	*Percentage of Protestant*
Diplomatic	60%
Journalistic	70%
Political	81%
Business	85%
Military	90%

TABLE IV: FATHER'S OCCUPATION

Strategic Elite:	*Percentage of Professional*
Business	15%
Political	24%
Higher Civil Servants	28%
Diplomatic	32%
Journalistic	43%
Military	38-45%*
Film	50%

Strategic Elite:	*Percentage of Proprietary and Official*
Journalistic	24%
Military	29%
Higher Civil Servants	26%
Political	35%
Diplomatic	36%
Business	57%
Film	33%

Strategic Elite:	*Percentage of Farmers*
Film	4%
Journalistic	9%
Diplomatic	6%
Military	10%
Business	15%
Higher Civil Servants	29%
Political	32%

* This indicates the range for all three branches of the service—Air Force elite, 38%; Army elite, 45%; and Navy elite, 45%.

Strategic Elite:	*Percentage of Wage Earners*
Diplomatic	3%
Military	5%
Political	5%
Film	5%
Higher Civil Servants	10%
Journalistic	11%
Business	15%*

* Warner's figure is used here because Keller combined wage and office workers into one category. Of the 1950 generation of the business elite, 12% came from families in both categories. Thus Warner's figure is higher than Keller's. C. W. Mills arrived at a figure of 18%, but he combined small businessmen, farmers, and wage earners into one category. See C. W. Mills, *The American Business Elite: A Collective Portrait, op. cit.*

TABLE V: EDUCATIONAL ATTAINMENTS

Strategic Elite:	*Percentage of College Graduates**
Film (1930's)	18%
Journalistic	52%
Business	61%
Higher Civil Servants	80%
Diplomatic	81%
Military	73-98% †
Political	91%

* The proportion graduating from one of the Big Three colleges—Harvard, Yale, and Princeton—could be ascertained for only three strategic elites: 10% of the political elite, 40% of the business, and 40% of the diplomatic.
† 73% Air Force, 85% Army, 98% Navy.

VI. Types of ascent for the disadvantaged

Given the inadequate data currently available, it is impossible to indicate precisely how social class and social status are directly related to modes of ascent. The suggestion emerges, however, that individuals lacking status attributes succeeded via different paths from those lacking class attributes. Several studies suggest that the careers of aspirants reflect the sort of obstacles they must overcome. Thus it is not at all self-evident that "upward mobility into the top echelons of the business elite more typically involves a successful fight against social discrimination than a 'rags to riches' story" (S. M. Lipset and R. Bendix, *Social Mobility in Industrial Society,* p. 138). First we would have to know whether the two types of upward mobility involve the same or different groups of men.

Of the twenty-nine business leaders in 1950 (out of 422) who were descended from South Irish and Southeastern European stock, three tenths were self-made men, a proportion ten times that of business leaders of British descent. And one half had risen to business leadership via the bureaucratic hierarchies of their corporations. Further investigation revealed that the self-made men were largely Jewish; the bureaucratic career men, largely Roman Catholics.

The three religious groups were investigated separately, and the results show that the paths of the minority groups are quite divergent from those of the majority. The nineteen Jewish business leaders in 1950, for example, show very different patterns of social background and career than do either the Protestant or Roman Catholic business leaders. Three fourths of them had fathers who were businessmen, as against less than three fifths of the Protestants and two fifths of the Roman Catholics. In addition, and in line with the hypothesis, the proportion of Jewish business leaders coming from lower-class homes was only 5 per cent, as against 12 per cent among Protestants and 33 per cent among Roman Catholics. Of those business leaders with farmer and wage-earner backgrounds, only 16 per cent were Jewish, as compared to 25 per cent Protestant, and 62 per cent Roman Catholic. The Jewish business leaders also had the least amount of higher formal education (18 per cent did not even attend high school). Among both Jewish and Roman Catholic business leaders, the majority did not have college degrees (only 35 per cent were college graduates as against 65 per cent of the Protestants). The Roman Catholics, like the Protestants, achieved elite status in business mainly via ascent through the corporate bureaucracies (70 per cent); this path was taken by only 12 per cent of the Jews. Apparently, the Jews had to be middle class before succeeding to top business positions, and Roman

Catholics could climb upward mainly within the large corporations. (These data are taken from Suzanne Keller, *The Social Origins and Career Lines of Three Generations of American Business Leaders,* Chap. vii.)

Matthews' analysis of postwar Senators likewise suggests different career paths for those of lower class as against lower status backgrounds. First of all, there is a distinct difference between the two major parties—the Democrats being more accessible to lower-class and lower-status candidates than the Republicans. This is only partly due to the social composition of the Democratic constituencies—especially the Northern and Western Democrats—as Matthews shows in a series of tables (*U.S. Senators and Their World,* pp. 35 ff.). Sixty per cent of these, as against only 14 per cent of the Republican Senators and 4 per cent of the Southern and Border Democrats, were born into some kind of religious or national minority group (*Ibid.,* p. 36). Unfortunately, Matthews cites no specific figures on the extent of lower-class representation among the Northwestern Democrats and the Southern and Border Democrats. Interestingly, the group containing the largest proportion originating in racial or religious minorities has the smallest proportion of manual laborers.

Matthews concludes: "The Democrats were elected at an earlier age and were born and live in larger towns and cities than the Republicans. Their fathers, as a group, possess somewhat higher occupational class positions but were also more often immigrants, Catholics, Jews, and members of relatively low prestige Protestant denominations. The Democrats obtained more education than the Republicans, but less often at the well-known schools. They were more often lawyers, but they practiced in smaller towns and as members of smaller law firms than the Republicans. The Republicans were more often businessmen and came from industries different from those of the Democratic businessmen in the Senate" (*Ibid.,* p. 46).

A study of the ninety-two members of the United States Supreme Court since 1789 showed nine of the justices to have come from humble origins. Of these, eight were Protestant, old family, native-born, British and Northwest European descendants (Schmidhauser, *The Supreme Court,* Chap. iii).

In discussing the "elite nucleus" of the military elite, Janowitz notes that of the officers who entered the top half of 1 per cent of the hierarchy, one group could be classified as "military managers," the other, as "heroic leaders." He also notes, although gives no further evidence, that the "military managers were characterized by a social background at variance with the traditional pattern of recruitment from upper-middle class rural and old family stock. They tended to come from the families of lower social status or more marginal circumstances." Heroic leaders, however, reflected service-connected backgrounds and, often, aristocratic traditions (Janowitz, *The Professional Soldier,* Chap. viii, p. 160).

A recent study of the top lawyers in eminent law firms, which did control separately for parental socioeconomic status and for religion, found lower-class Protestants more likely to be in a large law firm than upper-class Jews, suggesting that if a choice must be made, ascriptive criteria are more important than criteria of achievement. "In fact" notes Jerome Carlin, "Jewish lawyers from full-time university law schools are even less likely to be located in a large firm than Protestant lawyers from the lower quality night law schools. It is only among lawyers who graduated both from Ivy League colleges *and* full-time university law schools that we find Jewish lawyers as likely to be in large firms as Catholics and Protestants" (Jerome E. Carlin, "Current Research in the Sociology of the Legal Profession," *Bureau of Applied Social Research,* Columbia University, August, 1962). In a series of tables, starting with Table 32 in the Appendix to his monograph, Carlin shows how different groups managed to succeed in the legal profession. (1). As regards attendance of prestige schools, ascribed status seems to be more important than social class status: 42 per cent of the top lawyers of lower-class Protestant background attended a prestige college, as against 17 per cent of lower-class Roman Catholics and only 9 per cent of lower-class Jews. (2). One third of full-time university law graduates of the Protestant and Roman Catholic faiths are now in a large law firm, but only 8 per cent of the full-time university Jewish law graduates. (3). Nearly half the Protestants who started in a large law firm are still in a large law firm, but this is true for only 35 per cent of the Roman Catholics and only 17 per cent of the Jews.

Similar patterns may be observed among a sample of diplomatic envoys in the twentieth century. Those who achieved diplomatic eminence despite apparent social class disadvantages exhibit quite distinctive characteristics from those who lacked desirable status attributes. For example, of the eleven lower-class Protestants who eventually became ambassadors or ministers to one of the world powers, all were of British descent, six from old Colonial settler stock. All started at or near the bottom of the economic ladder—five were sons of small farmers, two of railroad men, one of a skilled laborer, two were known to have been very poor in childhood, and one was raised in an orphan asylum. Seven of the eleven men had no college education. Of the four who did, none went to an Ivy League school. A number of the men read law and started a law practice without formal law school education. Nine of them were political appointees, one was an admiral who assumed his diplomatic assignment at a critical period, and one was a career diplomat. The most striking fact about their careers is the extent of political involvement—most of them had run for office at some point in their lives. Four of the men had been Senators; two, governors of their states; and several had run for national political office and been defeated.

Turning now to the men of the diplomatic elite who represented minority religions, a very different pattern emerges. Out of the sample of 120 ambassadors and ministers sent to ten selected countries of the world between 1900 and 1953, seven were Roman Catholic and seven were Jewish. (There may have been more, but these were the only ones for whom definite information was available.) Of the Roman Catholics, only one was of old American stock, five were of Irish descent, and several were poor. All were college graduates, but only one held a college degree from a Big Three college, Harvard. Two were law school graduates, and two had higher degrees in other fields, one a Ph.D. from Columbia University. Notably, only two of the seven were political appointees; the rest were career diplomats.

Of the seven Jews, three were born abroad—in Germany or Austria-Hungary. All had fathers who were either founders or prosperous owners of business firms. Not one came from Southeastern Europe, tracing their origins instead to Germany or Austria-Hungary. All attended college, five receiving their diplomas at one of the Big Three colleges. Six of the seven went on to graduate schools, four receiving law degrees from Columbia Law

School. All were political appointees, and of the seven, five went to the minor posts.

Comparing the ascent to elite diplomatic status for the three "underprivileged" groups—Roman Catholics, Jews, and lower-class Protestants—we find none of the last-named group and only one Roman Catholic to have been family-made men in the sense of being aided by their fathers in business, politics, or the professions. Five of the seven Jewish envoys, however, could be so classified. The lower-class Protestants succeeded via politics; the Roman Catholics, via corporate bureaucracies; and the Jews, via family businesses (Keller, "Twentieth Century Ambassadors").

These data, though sparse, are very suggestive: apparently, the least-favored status group, the Jews, must first achieve economic or social position to achieve elite position, whereas the least-favored class group is able to succeed via politics and the law. The group lacking status and class—as did half of the Roman Catholics—have their best chances for success in the corporate business hierarchies, in the army, or in the foreign service. The lower-class Protestant ambassadors, in contrast to the lower-status ambassadors, seem to need less higher formal education, for only two thirds of them compared to all among the others had college degrees. In summation, those possessing proper ancestry but little wealth succeed via politics and the bureaucracies. Those who possess wealth but lack proper ancestors succeed via family businesses and prestigeful schooling. The "proper" poor do not need as much higher formal education as the "less desirable" rich.

VII. Elites narrowly defined

If one defines each elite fairly narrowly, there emerges what might be called an elite of elites—an elite of class, of status, and of function.

Matthews, for example, located a small number of postwar Senators—7 per cent of 180—whom he termed "Patricians," men who clearly formed a social, economic, and educational, as well as a political elite. Their families—America's old families of wealth in the Northeast or the South—were also ones with extensive political experience. Soon after finishing college or law school, they entered the political arena, 85 per cent of them holding public office before they were forty. Despite their small numbers, these Senators predominated in the leading Senate committees. "Thus the caste system tends to feed on and perpetuate itself; the most influential committees tend to be composed of the most esteemed senators, which lends the committee even more prestige" (Matthews, *U. S. Senators and Their World,* p. 151). Specifically, they were prominent in the Appropriations, Foreign Relations, and Armed Services Committees (*Ibid.,* p. 159). They also were "heavily overrepresented among the chairmen," notes Matthews, and had the greatest staying power in the Senate—few being defeated for re-election (*Ibid.,* pp. 163, 240).

In her study of the business elite of 1950, Keller also located such a core elite of British, old family, upper middle and upper class Protestant business leaders who were concentrated in the older established business fields of manufacturing, transportation, and finance. In a summary table, comparing the simultaneous impact of social class and educational attainments on business careers, she found the incidence of most rapid success among business leaders of high achieved and ascribed status. One half of the well-educated sons of businessmen attained top positions in business before age thirty-six; this was true of less than one third of all the business leaders. Social class in fact, was apparently more important than educational attainment: one third of the poorly educated sons of businessmen succeeding at such a young age as compared to only one fourth of the well-educated sons of wage earners. Not surprisingly, the poorly educated sons of wage earners had the least meteoric careers, only 18 per cent succeeding before age thirty-six, principally in the marginal business fields. Warner and Abegglen also found such a core elite in the leaders of the more stable companies and among brokers, dealers, and investment bankers. (See Keller, *The Social Origins and Career Lines of Three Gener-*

ations of American Business Leaders, pp. 131, 199; Warner and Abegglen, *Big Business Leaders,* pp. 204, 207-210.)

According to Keller, the ambassadors who were sent to the big European powers—Germany, Great Britain, France, and Italy—were largely of British, old family, Protestant stock, and graduates from Ivy League colleges. Of the thirty diplomats so classified, sixteen were descendants of Colonial settlers; and sixteen were Protestant, all but three Episcopalian and Presbyterian. Sixteen had attended private preparatory schools, and twenty-six of the thirty had college degrees, twenty of them from an Ivy League college (Harvard, eight; Yale, five). Fifteen had had formal law school training. Twenty of the thirty diplomats were political appointees, and eighteen of these had achieved the very top status in business prior to their appointments. The group as a whole included three men from lower-class backgrounds, and twenty from the homes of businessmen and financiers (nine of these from the highest financial and business circles). The group included two Jews and three Roman Catholics (Keller, "Twentieth Century Ambassadors").

When elites are narrowly defined, the pull of class and of ascribed status is obviously very powerful.

VIII. Career lines of various elites

Perhaps the most significant finding regarding the careers of various elite members was that their social and economic backgrounds did not noticeably affect their career paths, except insofar as social and material advantages smooth the way. Today, all elites work hard and accept the uncertainty of success as part of the game. This is true not only in the United States but in other countries as well.

The "bureaucratic pattern of success" characterized the majority of the business elite of 1950. Increasingly, the road upward involved a commitment to a single industry—often to a single company—and long years of endeavor. Three fourths of the 1950 business elite in America was promoted to the topmost position from within the company (Keller, *Business Leaders,* p. 112). The professionalization of the business elite has been noted throughout the industrial world. It is chiefly reflected in the rise of extensive graduate education in business or in law for potential elite members, and in the growing apprenticeship in particular industries and firms. The majority of the business leaders of 1950 were college graduates, but they all were subject to the requirements of bureaucratic organizations (*Ibid.,* p. 173). Moreover, the majority of these men had to work their way up through several levels of their companies' hierarchies. The American experience in this regard is paralleled by similar tendencies in other industrial societies. In the Soviet Union, for example, the maintenance by the Soviet manager of his managerial position is "very much dependent upon quality of performance . . . he must continually demonstrate and redemonstrate his competence. Mobility within the ranks of Soviet management is notoriously great—both upward and downward." (F. Harbison and C. A. Myers, *Management in the Industrial World*, pp. 329-30. See also, Joseph S. Berliner, "The Situation of Plant Managers," in Alex Inkeles and Kent Geiger (eds.), *Soviet Society,* pp. 361-381.)

A recent study of Soviet business executives, although not expressly of the business elite, shows them to be surprisingly similar to their American counterparts. They are drawn from white collar families, are largely college educated, and are trained engineers. They live relatively well, but they work extremely hard. And though most of them are party members, they do not have direct access to the highest political agency, the Central Committee. In the Soviet Union as in the United States, the business elite is a highly specialized, differentiated, and partly autonomous member of the leadership core of society. (See David Granick, *The Red Executive.*)

As the business elite is increasingly becoming a co-opted elite, members must appear to be the same kinds of men as their predecessors. As Dalton noted, merit is indispensable for access to this elite, but so are moral and ideological qualifications—ethnicity, religion, family, and club membership. Current executives, he concludes, are likely to look for and choose "good men like themselves," if only because loyalty to the institution of business is closely tied to loyalty toward other basic institutions of American society. (Melville Dalton, *Men Who Manage,* esp. Chap. 6, "The Managerial Career Ladder.") The British business elite appears to be less professionalized and more family-oriented. In Great Britain engineering training is not strongly associated with business success. And only 40 per cent of the British business elite had been in the same company all their lives (Lewis and Stewart, *The Managers,* pp. 97-100, 184-185).

It has been suggested that the shift from owner-operated to manager-dominated business firms has resulted in a diminution of the actual power wielded by big business executives—accentuated by the rise of "counter-vailing" power, to use Galbraith's phrase. Daniel Bell has argued that this situation has caused a feeling of helplessness among the older members of this elite ("The Dispossessed—1962," *Columbia University Forum,* V (Fall, 1962), No. 4).

However, aside from the increasing specialization of the business elite and its growing concern with specifically economic rather than moral and political issues, the power of big business seems to have suffered no such decline as regards economic decision-making. To be sure, the new managers have learned their public relations lesson well and no longer damn the public but seek to "serve" it. But this should not obscure the equally important fact that it is they, not the public or the stockholders as a whole, who set their companies' objectives and over-all policies, making or approving decisions that "significantly affect profits and future plans." A study of 1,100 individuals consisting of members of top management, their subordinates, and their professional consultants, carried out by the magazine *Fortune,* revealed little disagreement over the functions of the executive however he might be defined. In any company "only a few at the top" were considered to function as executives, and the making of profits for the company was one of their major concerns. (See *Fortune,* "The Executive Life," pp. 17-19. For a contrary view, see, Lawrence A. Kratz, "The Motivation of the Business Manager," *Behavioral Science,* Vol. 5

(October, 1960), No. 4, pp. 313-316.) Kratz hypothesizes that whereas the maximization of profits was a dominant objective in owner-operated firms, in management-dominated firms it is in the interests of the managerial staff to "lift physical output up to but not above the Break-Even Point in a manager-dominated, straight salary firm."

The professionalization of life is reflected in the career paths of most members of most strategic elites. Among postwar Senators, for example, Matthews found the most prevalent type to be the "professional politician" (55 per cent). Most of them had been trained as lawyers, entered politics early in life, and had a "slow but steady rise to the Senate," usually coming up via the House of Representatives or of state governorships. More than one half were over fifty years old upon being elected Senator (*U. S. Senators and Their World,* p. 63).

Similarly, entrance "into the military elite comes only after many years of professional education, training, and experience" (Janowitz, *The Professional Soldier*, p. 125). The education of generals and admirals in the past decade, writes Janowitz, "was basically a technical and engineering education." At the same time, however, an "elite nucleus" composed of men with highly individualistic careers exists within this broader framework of specialized technical training. Janowitz distinguished also between heroic leaders and military managers, each of whom had different career paths. The latter reflect the emphasis on "the scientific and rational conduct of war," and their increase implies an increase in technical specialists among the military elite. Top posts, it is felt, should be assigned to the graduates of the service academies, and indeed this seems to be the case in all branches except the Air Force (*Ibid.,* p. 59). In short, members of the military elite are "successful men by the standards of their organization, and organizational realities force them to be continuously concerned with managerial skill and achievement" (*Ibid.,* p. 64). See also: Walter Millis, "Puzzle of the 'Military Mind,'" *New York Times Magazine,* November 18, 1962. Similar trends apparently prevail in other countries. For comparative evidence, see Janowitz, *op. cit.*

For Supreme Court justices, professional experience with the law has increased as part of a long-term historical trend. All of the justices have had legal training of some kind, and 97 per cent practiced law as their principal nonpolitical occupation. The chief change, though inconsistent, has been an increase in justices after 1862 who had primarily judicial careers (Schmidhauser, *The Supreme Court, Its Politics, Personality, and Procedure,* p. 47).

Similar tendencies toward apprenticeship and specialization are evident for other elites as well. Ambassadors are increasingly selected from among those who elect to make the foreign service a lifetime commitment, having passed the required examinations and survived the bureaucratic ascent within the service.

The clergy, too, has felt the impact of specialization, but we do not know the extent to which this has altered the careers of its top leadership. Adams argues that the minister's status has suffered "because of the diffused, generalized character of his responsibilities," in face of the more specialized professions. (See James Luther Adams, "The Social Import of the Professions," Address given at the Twenty-First Biennial Meeting of the American Association of Theological Schools, Boston University School of Theology, June 17-20, 1958, p. 13. He also considers the minister's function to be mainly "integrative.") An increasing involvement with the community has paralleled a decreasing preoccupation with doctrinal controversies and theological problems. This may, as Laski has argued, herald the minister's succumbing to the moral standards of the secular order instead of rising above them. Conversely, it may simply reflect the changing social functions of the ministry and a shift of its major responsibilities from "goal-attainment" to "integration." (See, Harold J. Laski, *The American Democracy,* Chap. 7, pp. 303, 315.) A recent survey of theological students shows a lack of concern for the burning doctrinal issues of the past. Only 2 per cent were seriously interested in the subject of "original sin," and only 1 per cent convinced of the second coming of Christ. The inroads of science are evident in the division of opinion on the virgin birth of Christ (in which only 44 per cent believed) and on the physical ascension of Jesus into heaven after his crucifixion (in which only 46 per cent believed). In this age of space travel, only one out of four future ministers believe in a real heaven and hell. There was, instead, a deep interest in contemporary social problems and in the potential role that the Church should play in avoiding war, in hastening racial integration, in eradicating slums, and in disarmament. (Jhan and June Robbins, "The Surprising Beliefs of our Future Ministers," *Redbook,* p. 107.) A study of the clergy of the ninth largest "individual religious organization in the United States," the Lutheran Church Missouri Synod, found an increase in professionalization and specialization among seminary students. (See, Ross P. Scherer, "Career Patterns in the Ministry: The Lutheran Church-Missouri Synod," Paper presented at the American Sociological Association, Annual Meeting, Washington, D.C., August 30-September 2, 1962.)

Specialization and apprenticeship in the arts and the theater, more informally organized perhaps, have long characterized these fields, but there is no systematic recent evidence on length of time and type of training most typical for the elites in these fields.

Concomitant with increased professionalization has been the increase of professional inbreeding. For those elites having information on the matter, it ranged from a low of 2 per cent to a high of 25 per cent. The precise figures on these elites—whose members had fathers in the same field—were as follows: 2 per cent of the diplomatic elite, 3 per cent of the Civil Service elite, 11 per cent of the Washington correspondents, 15 per cent of the political elite, 25 per cent of the military elite, and 23 per cent of the business elite. Whether their fathers were also members of the elites of these fields is not known. (The figures are taken from: Matthews, *op. cit.,* p. 49, and Janowitz, *op. cit.,* p. 96—this figure for the military refers to the 1960 class at West Point. Of the 1950 Army elite, only 11 per cent were recruited from military families, but in 1935, fully 23 per cent had been. World War II apparently disrupted whatever trend existed toward professional inbreeding. The figure for the business elite is from Warner and Abegglen, *Big Business Leaders in America,* p. 15.)

Professionalization and lengthened career spans have also resulted in the older age of those achieving elite status. The oldest members occur among the most highly specialized and formally organized elites. The proportion of members who were fifty or older upon first achieving elite status was as follows: Washington correspondents, 3 per cent; film elite, 35 per cent; business elite, 59 per cent; political elite, 60 per cent; diplomatic elite, 63 per cent; military elite—average age, in the fifties.

IX. The prevalence of lawyers

Specialized performance requires not only specialized education and apprenticeship but also a familiarity with rules and regulations, with organization and formal procedures. This may be why lawyers are highly prominent among the business, diplomatic, and civil service elites. In these areas, law is without doubt the most frequent stepping stone to the top positions. Within the business elite of 1950, one sixth were trained as lawyers; within the diplomatic elite for the century, two fifths; and within the political elite, one half. (As to the Supreme Court justices, all, of course, were lawyers.)

The predominance of lawyers in the political elite has usually been accounted for because of the kinship between the two fields, but this would not account for the predominance of lawyers in diplomacy and business. Among several attempts to explain the high esteem in which lawyers are held in the United States, de Tocqueville's is most intriguing. As early as 1832 he commented on the importance of lawyers in America. In his view they were a necessary countervailing force in the democracy that was then being established. He saw the lawyers and the public involved in a complementary relationship that balanced excess enthusiasm with sobriety, and aristocratic propensities with democratic impulse:

> When the American people are intoxicated by passion or carried away by the impetuosity of their ideas, they are checked and stopped by the almost invisible influence of their legal counselors. These secretly oppose their aristocratic propensities to the nation's democratic instincts, their superstitious attachment to what is old to their love of novelty, their narrow views to its immense designs, and the habitual procrastination to its ardent impatience.

(De Tocqueville, *Democracy in America,* I, 289.) Harold J. Laski traces the high esteem of lawyers to the "grateful recognition of the part played by the lawyer in defining the American case in the Revolution, and . . . [to] the increasing need of his services, with the growth of industry and commerce, after independence had been won" (*The American Democracy,* p. 567).

As de Tocqueville proposes, lawyers enjoy such high public esteem as to be able to exercise their moderating influence, because they possess superior information which, though necessary to all, is not available to all.

Moreover, although they are "of the people," they are aristocratic by nature and can thus act as a link between the people and their sacred traditions. The conservatism of lawyers is thus attributed to their "natural" aristocratic tendencies. De Tocqueville, however, does not account for these tendencies.

The dual role played by lawyers in a rapidly changing society goes a long way to explain their public importance. Not only must they keep informed about the past—for this is what a knowledge of the law entails—they must also keep abreast of changing conditions—for this is what they are typically called upon to do in their professional capacities. In a dynamic society, therefore, lawyers are both guardians of the old order and creators of the new.

The social backgrounds of the most influential lawyers appear to be more restricted than those of the business and political elites whom they serve. William Miller found the lawyers among the business leaders of 1900 to be better educated and more restricted as to ancestry, religion, and national origins than the rest of the business elite ("American Lawyers in Business and Politics," *The Yale Law Journal,* January, 1951, 65-76). The legal elite is clearly an elite of achievement and also, apparently, of ascription, but not of social function (as distinct from professional)—hence it is an auxiliary of the strategic elites it serves. The reasons why the legal elite should be less socially accessible than the elites it serves need to be investigated further. For other evidence on the social backgrounds of the members of twenty-one large law firms, see Erwin O. Smigel, "The Impact of Recruitment on the Organization of the Large Law Firm," *American Sociological Review,* XXV (February, 1960), No. 1, pp. 56-66.

BIBLIOGRAPHY

AJS—American Journal of Sociology.
ASQ—Administrative Science Quarterly.
ASR—American Sociological Review.
BJS—The British Journal of Sociology.
POQ—Public Opinion Quarterly.

AARONOVITCH, SAM. *The Ruling Class: A Study of British Finance Capital.* London: Lawrence and Wishart, 1961.

ADAM, LEONHARD. *Primitive Art.* London: Pelican Books, 1949.

ADAMS, BROOKS. *The Law of Civilization and Decay.* New York: Vintage Books, 1959.

ADAMS, JAMES LUTHER. "The Social Import of the Professions." Address given at the Twenty-First Biennial Meeting of the American Association of Theological Schools, Boston University School of Theology, June 17-20, 1958.

AKZIN, BENJAMIN. "The Knesset," *International Social Science Journal* XIII, No. 4 (1961), 567-83.

ALMOND, GABRIEL A., and JAMES S. COLEMAN (eds.). *The Politics of the Developing Areas.* Princeton, N.J.: Princeton University Press, 1960.

AMMON, OTTO. *Die Gesellschaftsordnung und Ihre Natürlichen Grundlagen.* Jena: Gustav Fischer, 1895.

AMORY, CLEVELAND. *The Proper Bostonians.* New York: E. P. Dutton, 1947.

———. *Who Killed Society?* New York: Harper, 1961.

ANDERSON, C. ARNOLD. "A Sceptical Note on the Relation of Vertical Mobility to Education," *AJS,* LXVI, No. 6 (May, 1961), 560-70.

ANDERSON, THEODORE R., and SEYMOUR WARKOV. "Organizational Size and Functional Complexity," *ASR,* XXVI, No. 1 (February, 1961), 23-8.

ANNAN, N. G. "The Intellectual Aristocracy," in *Studies in Social History.* Ed. J. H. PLUMB. London: Longmans Green, 1955.

ARENDT, HANNAH. *The Origins of Totalitarianism.* New York: Harcourt, Brace, 1951.

ARISTOTLE. *Politics,* in *The Basic Works of Aristotle.* Ed. RICHARD MCKEON. New York: Random House, 1941.

ARON, RAYMOND. "Social Structure and the Ruling Class," *BJS,* I, No. 1 (March, 1950) 1-17; I, No. 2 (June, 1950) 126-144.

———. "Classe sociale, classe politique, classe dirigeante," *Archives Européennes de Sociologie,* I (1960), No. 2, 260-82.

———. *The Opium of the Intellectuals.* Trans. TERENCE KILMARTIN. New York: W. W. Norton, 1962.

ASHLEY-MONTAGU, M. F. (ed.). *Toynbee and History.* Boston: Porter Sargent, 1956.

BACON, FRANCIS. *The Selected Writings of Francis Bacon.* Ed. HUGH H. DICK. New York: Modern Library, 1955.

BAGEHOT, WALTER. *The English Constitution.* New York and London: M. Walter Dunne, 1901.

BALTZELL, E. DIGBY. "Social Mobility and Fertility Within an Elite Group," *Milbank Memorial Fund Quarterly,* XXXI, No. 4 (October, 1953), 411-420.

———. *Philadelphia Gentlemen.* New York: The Free Press of Glencoe, 1958.

———. "The American Aristocrat and Other-Direction," in *Culture and Social Character.* Ed. S. M. LIPSET and LEO LOWENTHAL. New York: The Free Press of Glencoe, 1961.

BARBER, BERNARD. *Science and the Social Order.* New York: The Free Press of Glencoe, 1952.

———. *Social Stratification.* New York: Harcourt, Brace & World, 1957.

———, and WALTER HIRSCH (eds.). *The Sociology of Science.* New York: The Free Press of Glencoe, 1962.

BARNARD, CHESTER I. *Organization and Management.* Cambridge, Mass.: Harvard University Press, 1958.

———. *The Functions of the Executive.* Cambridge, Mass.: Harvard University Press, 1950.

BASCOMB, WILLIAM R., and MELVILLE J. HERSKOVITS (eds.). *Continuity and Change in African Cultures.* Chicago: The University of Chicago Press, 1959.

BAUER, A. *Les Classes Sociales.* Paris: 1902.

BAUER, RAYMOND A., ALEX INKELES, and CLYDE KLUCKHOHN. *How the Soviet System Works.* New York: Vintage Books, 1960.

BELL, DANIEL. *The End of Ideology.* New York: The Free Press of Glencoe, 1960.

———. "The Dispossessed—1962," *Columbia University Forum,* V, No. 4 (Fall, 1962).

BENDIX, REINHARD. *Higher Civil Servants in American Society.* University of Colorado Studies, "Series in Sociology," No. 1, July, 1949.

———. *Max Weber, An Intellectual Portrait.* New York: Doubleday, 1960.

———, and FRANK W. HOWTON, "Social Mobility and the American Business Elite," *BJS,* IX, No. 1 (March, 1958). 1-14.

———, and S. M. LIPSET (eds.). *Class, Status and Power.* New York: The Free Press of Glencoe, 1953.

BERENT, JERZY. "Fertility and Social Mobility," *Population Studies,* V, No. 3 (March, 1952), 244-60.

BERGER, MORROE. *The Arab World Today.* New York: Doubleday, 1962.

BERLINER, JOSEPH. "The Situation of Plant Managers," in *Soviet Society: A Book of Readings.* Ed. ALEX INKELES and KENT GEIGER. Boston: Houghton Mifflin, 1961.

BERRINGTON, H. B., and S. E. FINER. "The British House of Commons," *International Social Science Journal,* XIII, No. 4 (1961), 600-20.

BIERSTEDT, ROBERT. "The Problem of Authority," in *Freedom and Control in Modern Society*. Eds. MORROE BERGER, THEODORE ABEL, and CHARLES H. PAGE. New York: D. Van Nostrand, 1954.

BIRD, CAROLINE. "How To Get Ahead in Russia," *Esquire* (February, 1959).

BIRNBAUM, N. "Monarchs and Sociologists: A Reply to Professor Shils and Mr. Young," *Sociological Review,* III, New Series (July, 1955), 5-22.

BONILLA, FRANK. "Elites and Public Opinion in Areas of High Social Stratification," *POQ,* XXII, No. 3 (Fall, 1958), 349-56.

BOTTOMORE, THOMAS. "La Mobilité Sociale dans la Haute Administration Française," *Cahiers Internationaux de Sociologie,* XIII (1952), 167-78.

BRECHT, BERTOLT. *Chansons et Poèmes*. Trans. ALAIN BOSQUET. Paris: Pierre Seghers, n.d.

BROWN, ROGER, and ALBERT GILMAN. "The Pronouns of Power and Solidarity" in *Style in Language*. Ed. THOMAS A. SEBEOK. New York: John Wiley and the Technology Press of M.I.T., 1960.

BROWN, WILLIAM BURLIE. *The People's Choice, The Presidential Image in the Campaign Biography*. Baton Rouge: Louisiana State University Press, 1960.

BRYANT, ARTHUR. "Camelot's King: Man and Myth," *New York Times Magazine,* December 11, 1960.

BUCKLEY, WALTER. "Rejoinder to Davis and Levy," *ASR,* XXIV, No. 1 (February, 1959), 84-6.

BUKHARIN, NICOLAI. *Historical Materialism*. New York: International Publishers, 1925.

BURNHAM, JAMES M. *The Managerial Revolution*. New York: John Day, 1941.

———. *The Machiavellians: Defenders of Freedom*. New York: John Day, 1943.

CAPLOW, THEODORE. "Organizational Size," *ASQ,* (March, 1957), 484-505.

CARLIN, JEROME E. *Current Research in the Sociology of the Legal Profession,* Bureau of Applied Social Research, Columbia University, August, 1962.

CARR, EDWARD HALLETT. *The New Society*. Boston: Beacon Press, 1951.

CASSADY, MAYNARD L. *A Comparative Study of Two Generations of Theological Graduates*. Rochester, New York: 1934.

CHILDE, V. GORDON. *Man Makes Himself*. New York: New American Library, Mentor, 1951.

CHOWDHRY, KAMLA, and THEODORE M. NEWCOMB. "The Relative Abilities of Leaders and Non-Leaders to Estimate Opinions of Their Own Groups," in *Small Groups: Studies in Social Interaction*. Ed. A. PAUL HARE, E. F. BORGATTA, and R. F. BALES. New York: Knopf, 1955.

CHUNG-LI CHANG. *The Chinese Gentry*. Seattle: University of Washington Press, 1955.

CLIFFORD-VAUGHAN, MICHALINA. "Some French Concepts of Elites," *BJS,* XI, No. 4 (December, 1960), 319-32.

CODERE, HELEN. "Power in Ruanda," *Anthropologica,* IV, No. 1 (1962), 42-85.

COLE, G. D. H. "Elites in British Society," *Studies in Class Structure*. London: Routledge & Kegan Paul, 1955.

COLEMAN, JAMES S. *Nigeria: Background to Nationalism*. Berkeley: University of California Press, 1958.

CONANT, JAMES B. *Modern Science and Modern Man*. NewYork: Doubleday, Anchor Book, 1952.

COOLEY, CHARLES H. *Human Nature and the Social Order*. New York: Scribner's Sons, 1902.

CRANKSHAW, EDWARD. *Khrushchev's Russia*. London: Penguin Books, 1959.

CROSBY, JOHN. "If Socrates Had Lived in Scarsdale," *New York Herald Tribune,* November 18, 1960.

DAHL, ROBERT A. "Critique of the Ruling Elite Model," *American Political Science Review,* LII, No. 2 (June, 1958), 463-70.

DAHRENDORF, RALF. *Class and Class Conflict in Industrial Society*. Stanford, California: Stanford University Press, 1959.

———. "Aspekte der Ungleicheit in der Gesellschaft," *Archives Européennes de Sociologie,* I, No. 2 (1960), 213-33.

DALTON, MELVILLE. *Men Who Manage*. New York: Wiley, 1959.

D'ANTONIO, WILLIAM V., and EUGENE C. ERICKSON. "The Reputational Technique as a Measure of Community Power," *ASR,* XXVII, No. 3 (June, 1962), 262-76.

———, HOWARD J. EHRLICH, and EUGENE C. ERICKSON. "Further Notes on the Study of Community Power," *ASR,* XXVII, No. 6 (December, 1962), 848-54.

DAVIS, BEVERLY. "Eminence and Level of Social Origin," *AJS,* LIX, No. 1 (July, 1953), 11-18.

DAVIS, KINGSLEY. *Human Society*. New York: Macmillan, 1949.

———, and WILBERT MOORE. "Some Principles of Stratification," *ASR,* X (April, 1945), 242-9.

DE COULANGES, FUSTEL. *The Ancient City*. New York: Doubleday, Anchor Book, 1956.

DE GRAZIA, SEBASTIAN. *The Political Community*. Chicago: The University of Chicago Press, 1948.

DE HUSZAR, GEORGE B. *The Intellectuals*. New York: The Free Press of Glencoe, 1960.

DE TOCQUEVILLE, ALEXIS. *The Old Regime and the French Revolution*. New York: Doubleday, 1955.

———. *Democracy in America,* Vols. 1 and 2. Ed. PHILLIPS BRADLEY. New York: Vintage, 1956.

DEUTSCH, KARL W., and LEWIS J. EDINGER. *Germany Rejoins the Powers*. Stanford, California: Stanford University Press, 1959.

DONOVAN, JOHN D. "The American Catholic Hierarchy: A Social Profile," *The American Catholic Sociological Review,* XIX, No. 2 (June, 1958), 98-113.

DREITZEL, HANS P. *Elitebegriff und Sozialstruktur*. Stuttgart: Ferdinand Enke Verlag, 1962.

DRUCKER, PETER F. *The New Society*. New York: Harper, 1950.

———. "The Employee Society," *AJS,* LVIII, No. 4 (January, 1953), 358-63.

———. "The Tasks of Management," in *Industrial Man,* ed. WILLIAM L. WARNER and NORMAN H. MARTIN. New York: Harper, 1959.

DURKHEIM, EMILE. *The Division of Labor in Society*. New York: The Free Press of Glencoe, 1947.

———. *The Rules of Sociological Method*. New York: The Free Press of Glencoe, 1950.

———. *The Elementary Forms of the Religious Life.* Trans. J. W. SWAIN. London: George Allen & Unwin, 1954.

———. *Socialism and Saint-Simon.* Yellow Springs, Ohio: The Antioch Press, 1958.

EISENSTADT, S. N. "The Place of Elites and Primary Groups in the Absorption of New Immigrants in Israel," *AJS,* LVIIX, No. 3 (November, 1951), 222-31.

———. *From Generation to Generation.* New York: The Free Press of Glencoe, 1956.

ELLIOTT, OSBORN. *Men at the Top.* New York: Harper, 1959.

ELLIS, HAVELOCK. *A Study of British Genius.* London: Hurst and Blackett, 1904.

ETZIONI, AMITAI. "Functional Differentiation of Elites in the Kibbutz," *AJS,* LXIV (March, 1959), 476-87.

———. *A Comparative Analysis of Complex Organizations.* New York: The Free Press of Glencoe, 1961.

EULAU, HEINZ, and DAVID KOFF. "Occupational Mobility and Political Career," *The Western Political Quarterly* (September, 1962), 507-22.

———, WILLIAM BUCHANAN, LEROY C. FERGUSON, and JOHN C. WAHLKE, "Career Perspectives of American State Legislators" in *Political Decision Makers.* Ed. DWAINE MARVICK. Baltimore: The Johns Hopkins Press, 1961.

FAHLBECK, PONTUS E. *Der Adel Schwedens (und Finlands): Eine Demographische Studie.* Jena: Gustav Fischer, 1903.

———. *Die Klassen und die Gesellschaft.* Jena: Gustav Fischer, 1923.

FAINSOD, MERLE. *How Russia Is Ruled.* Cambridge, Mass.: Harvard University Press, 1953.

FEUER, KATHRYN. "The Book That Became 'War and Peace.' " *The Reporter* (May 14, 1959).

FINDLAY, J. N. *Hegel: A Re-Examination.* New York: Collier, 1962.

FIRTH, RAYMOND. "Religion and Social Reality" in *Reader in Comparative Religion.* Ed. WILLIAM A. LESSA and EVON Z. VOGT. New York: Row, Peterson, 1958.

FORD, CLELLAN S. "The Role of the Fijian Chief," *ASR,* III (August, 1938), 542-50.

FORM, WILLIAM H., and WILLIAM V. D'ANTONIO. "Integration and Cleavage Among Community Influentials in Two Border Cities," *ASR,* Sec. 1950, XXIV, No. 6, 804-14.

FORTES, M., and E. E. EVANS-PRITCHARD (eds.). *African Political Systems.* London: Oxford University Press, 1940.

The Editors of FORTUNE. *The Executive Life.* New York: Doubleday, Dolphin Book, 1956.

FRANKEL, MAX. "The 8,708,000 Elite of Russia," *New York Times Magazine,* May 29, 1960.

FRANKFORT, HENRI. *The Birth of Civilization in the Near East.* New York: Doubleday, Anchor Book, 1956.

FRAZER, SIR JAMES GEORGE. *The New Golden Bough.* Ed. and with notes and foreword by T. H. GASTER. New York: Criterion, 1959.

FREUND, MICHAEL. "Das Elitenproblem in der Modernen Politik," in *Politische Bildung,* Heft 46 (1954), 235-52.

GALBRAITH, JOHN KENNETH. *The Affluent Society*. Boston: Houghton Mifflin, 1958.

GALTON, FRANCIS. *Hereditary Genius, An Inquiry into Its Laws and Consequences*. New York: Appleton, 1871.

———, and EDGAR SCHUSTER. *Noteworthy Families*. London: John Murray, 1906.

GEORGE, KATHARINE, and CHARLES H. "Roman Catholic Sainthood and Social Status: A Statistical and Analytical Study," *The Journal of Religion*, XXXV, No. 2 (April, 1955).

GERTH, H. H., and C. WRIGHT MILLS. *From Max Weber: Essays in Sociology*. New York: Oxford University Press, 1946.

GIBB, CECIL A. "The Principles and Traits of Leadership," in *Small Groups: Studies in Social Interaction*. Ed. A. PAUL HARE, E. F. BORGATTA, and R. F. BALES. New York: Alfred A. Knopf, 1955.

GINGER, RAY (ed.). *American Social Thought*. New York: Hill and Wang, American Century Series, 1961.

GINI, CORRADO. "Real and Apparent Exceptions to the Uniformity of a Lower Natural Increase of the Upper Classes," *Rural Sociology*, I, No. 3 (September, 1936).

GLOVER, T. R. *The Ancient World*. London: A Pelican Book, 1957.

GLUCKMAN, MAX. *Custom and Conflict in Africa*. New York: The Free Press of Glencoe, 1959.

———. "The Origins of Social Organization" in *Readings in Anthropology*, Vol. II. Ed. MORTON H. FRIED. New York: Crowell, 1959.

GOERLITZ, WALTER. *History of the German General Staff, 1657-1945*. Trans. BRIAN BATTERSHAW. New York: Praeger, 1953.

GOODMAN, PAUL. *Growing Up Absurd*. New York: Vintage Books, 1962.

GOULDNER, ALVIN W. *Patterns of Industrial Bureaucracy*. New York: The Free Press of Glencoe, 1954.

———. "Organizational Analysis," in *Sociology Today*. Ed. R. K. MERTON, *et al.* New York: Basic Books, 1959.

GRANICK, DAVID. *The Red Executive*. New York: Doubleday, Anchor Book, 1961.

GRAY, GEORGE W. "Which Scientists Win Nobel Prizes?" in *Sociology of Science: A Reader*. Ed. BERNARD BARBER and WALTER HIRSCH. New York: The Free Press of Glencoe, 1962.

GUBIN, K. "The Supreme Soviet of the USSR and Its Members," *International Social Science Journal*, XIII, No. 4 (1961), 635-40.

HABAKKUK, H. J. "England," in *The European Nobility in the Eighteenth Century*. Ed. A. GOODWIN. London: A. & C. Black, 1953.

HALBWACHS, MAURICE. *The Psychology of Social Class*. Trans. CLAIRE DELAVENAY. New York: The Free Press of Glencoe, 1958.

HAMON, LEON. "The Members of the French Parliament," *International Social Science Journal*, XIII, No. 4 (1961), 545-67.

HARBISON, F., and C. A. MYERS. *Management in the Industrial World*. New York: McGraw-Hill, 1959.

HARE, A. PAUL, E. F. BORGATTA, and R. F. BALES (eds.). *Small Groups: Studies in Social Interaction*. New York: Alfred A. Knopf, 1955.

HARRINGTON, MICHAEL. *The Other America*. New York: Macmillan, 1962.

HAUSER, ARNOLD. *The Social History of Art*. 4 vols. New York: Vintage Books, 1957.

HAVEMAN, ERNEST, and PATRICIA S. WEST. *They Went to College.* New York: Harcourt Brace, 1952.
HEMPEL, CARL. "The Logic of Functional Analysis," in *Symposium on Sociological Theory.* Ed. LLEWELLYN GROSS. New York: Row, Peterson, 1959.
HERSKOVITS, MELVILLE J. *The Human Factor in Changing Africa.* New York: Alfred A. Knopf, 1962.
HOCART, A. M. Kingship. London: Oxford University Press, 1927.
HODGKIN, THOMAS. *Nationalism in Colonial Africa.* New York: New York University Press, 1957.
HOMANS, GEORGE C. *The Human Group.* New York: Harcourt Brace, 1950.
HSIAO-TUNG FEI. "Peasantry and Gentry: An Interpretation of Chinese Social Structure and Its Changes," in *Class, Status, and Power.* Ed. REINHARD BENDIX and S. M. LIPSET. New York: The Free Press of Glencoe, 1953.
HUNTER, FLOYD. *Community Power Structure.* Chapel Hill: University of North Carolina Press, 1953.
———. *Top Leadership, U.S.A.* Chapel Hill: The University of North Carolina Press, 1959.
HUXLEY, JULIAN. "World Population," *Scientific American,* CXCIV, No. 3, 64-7.

IBSEN, HENRIK. *Enemy of the People,* in *Seven Plays by Henrik Ibsen.* New York: Walter J. Black, 1942.

JAEGGI, URS. *Die Gesellschaftliche Elite.* Bern/Stuttgart: Verlag Paul Haupt, 1960.
JANOWITZ, MORRIS. "Military Elites and the Study of War," *Journal of Conflict Resolution,* I (1957), 9-18.
———. *The Professional Soldier.* New York: The Free Press of Glencoe, 1960.

KAVALER, LUCY. *The Private World of High Society.* New York: David McKay, 1960.
KELLER, SUZANNE. "The Social Origins and Career Lines of Three Generations of American Business Leaders." Unpublished Ph.D. dissertation, Department of Sociology, Columbia University, 1953.
———. "Twentieth Century Ambassadors." Unpublished ms., 1956.
KELLY, AMY. *Eleanor of Aquitaine.* New York: Vintage Books, 1957.
KELLY, SIR DAVID. *The Ruling Few.* London: Hollis & Carter, 1952.
KERR, CLARK, *et al. Industrialism and Industrial Man.* Cambridge, Mass.: Harvard University Press, 1960.
KINGSLEY, DONALD J. *Representative Bureaucracy: An Interpretation of the British Civil Service.* Yellow Springs, Ohio: The Antioch Press, 1944.
KIRCHOFF, PAUL. "The Principles of Clanship in Human Society," in *Readings in Anthropology.* Ed. MORTON H. FRIED, Vol. II. New York: Crowell, 1959.
KITTO, H. D. F. *The Greeks.* London: Penguin Books, 1960.
KNAPP, ROBERT H., and HUBERT B. GOODRICH. "The Origins of American Scientists," in *Studies in Motivation.* Ed. DAVID C. MCCLELLAND. New York: Appleton-Century-Crofts, 1955.
KOLABINSKA, MARIA. *La Circulation des Elites en France.* Lausanne: 1912.
KOLKO, GABRIEL. *Wealth and Power in America.* New York: Praeger, 1962.

KORNHAUSER, ARTHUR (ed.). *Problems of Power in American Democracy.* Detroit, Mich.: Wayne State University Press, 1957.

KORNHAUSER, WILLIAM. *Politics in Mass Society.* New York: The Free Press of Glencoe, 1959.

KRATZ, LAWRENCE A. "The Motivation of the Business Manager," *Behavioral Science,* V, No. 4 (October, 1960), 313-16.

LAMPEDUSA, GUISEPPE DI. *The Leopard.* Trans. ARCHIBALD COLQUHOUN. New York: Pantheon Books, 1960.

LANE, ROBERT E. "The Fear of Equality," *The American Political Science Review,* LIII, No. 1 (March, 1959), 35-51.

LASKI, HAROLD J. *The American Democracy.* New York: The Viking Press, 1948.

LASKY, MELVIN J. "Africa for Beginners," *Encounter* (July, 1961), 32-48.

LASSWELL, HAROLD D. *Psychopathology and Politics.* Chicago: University of Chicago Press, 1930.

———. *Politics, Who Gets What, When, and How.* New York: McGraw-Hill, 1936.

———. *Power and Personality.* New York: W. W. Norton, 1948.

———. "The Selective Effect of Personality on Political Participation," in *Studies in the Scope and Method of "The Authoritarian Personality."* Ed. R. CHRISTIE and M. JAHODA. New York: The Free Press of Glencoe, 1954.

———, and ABRAHAM KAPLAN. *Power and Society, A Framework for Political Inquiry.* New Haven: Yale University Press, 1950.

———, DANIEL LERNER, and C. E. ROTHWELL. *The Comparative Study of Elites, an Introduction and Bibliography.* Stanford, California: Hoover Institute Series, Stanford University Press, 1952.

LAVINE, ROBERT A. "The Role of the Family in Authority Systems: A Cross-Cultural Application of Stimulus-Generalization," *Behavioral Science,* V, No. 4 (October, 1960), 290-5.

LAZARSFELD, PAUL F., and WAGNER THIELENS, JR. *The Academic Mind.* New York: The Free Press of Glencoe, 1958.

LENSKI, GERHARD. *The Religious Factor.* New York: Doubleday, Anchor Book, 1963.

LERNER, DANIEL. *The Passing of Traditional Society.* New York: The Free Press of Glencoe, 1958.

LEVI-STRAUSS, CLAUDE. "Social Structure," in *Anthropology Today,* pp. 524-4. Chicago: The University of Chicago Press, 1953.

———. "Tristes Tropiques," *Encounter* (April, 1961), 28-41.

LEWIS, ANTHONY. "The Justices' Supreme Job," *New York Times Magazine,* June 11, 1961.

LEWIS, ROY, and ROSEMARY STEWART. *The Managers.* New York: The New American Library, Mentor Books, 1961.

LINZ, JUAN, in *Le Elites Politiche.* Ed. R. TRAVES, pp. 165-8. Atti. del Quarto Congresso Mondiale di Sociologia. Bari: Editori Laterza, 1961.

LIPPMANN, WALTER. "Eisenhower's Farewell Warning," *New York Herald Tribune,* January 19, 1961.

LIPSET, S. M. "Political Sociology," in *Sociology Today.* Ed. ROBERT K. MERTON, *et al.* New York: Basic Books, 1959.

———, and REINHARD BENDIX. *Social Mobility in Industrial Society.* Berkeley and Los Angeles: University of California Press, 1962.

———, and NATALIE ROGOFF. "Class and Opportunity in Europe and America," *Commentary,* XVIII (1954), 562-8.

———, and HANS L. ZETTERBERG. "A Theory of Social Mobility." Bureau of Applied Social Research, Reprint No. 185.

———, M. A. TROW, and J. S. COLEMAN. *Union Democracy.* New York: The Free Press of Glencoe, 1956.

LIVI, LIVIO. "Considerations theoretiques et pratiques sur les concept de 'minimum de population,' " *Population,* IV, No. 4, 754-6.

LUKACS, GEORG. *Geschichte und Klassensbewusstsein.* Berlin: Der Malig Verlag, 1923.

LYND, ROBERT S. "Power in American Society as Resource and Problem," in *Problems of Power in American Democracy.* Ed. ARTHUR KORNHAUSER. Detroit, Mich.: Wayne State University Press, 1957.

———, and H. M. LYND. *Middletown in Transition.* New York: Harcourt Brace, 1937.

MACCOBY, E. E., T. M. NEWCOMB, and E. G. HARTLEY (eds.). *Readings in Social Psychology.* New York: Henry Holt, 1958.

MCGRORY, MARY. "The Optimist." *New York Post,* August 2, 1961.

MACIVER, ROBERT M. *The Modern State.* London: Oxford University Press, 1926.

———. *Society.* New York: Rinehart, 1937.

———. *The Web of Government.* New York: Macmillan, 1947.

MCKEE, JAMES B. "Status and Power in the Industrial Community: A Comment on Drucker's Thesis," *AJS,* LVIII, No. 4 (January, 1953), 364-70.

MACMAHON, ARTHUR, and JOHN D. MILLET. *Federal Administrators.* New York: Columbia University Press, 1939.

MADISON, JAMES. "The Federalist, No. 10, 1787," in *A Documentary History of the United States,* by RICHARD D. HEFFNER. New York: The New American Library, Mentor Book, 1952.

MAIR, LUCY. *Primitive Government.* London: Penguin Books, 1962.

MALIA, MARTIN. "What Is the Intelligentsia?" *Daedalus* (Summer, 1960), 441-59.

MALINOWSKI, BRONISLAW. *Crime and Custom in Savage Society.* New York: The Humanities Press, 1951.

MANNHEIM, KARL. "Das Problem der Generationen," *Kölner Vierteljahrshefte für Soziologie,* VII (1928), 157-85.

———. *Man and Society in an Age of Reconstruction.* London: Kegan Paul, 1946.

———. *Ideology and Utopia.* New York: Harcourt Brace, 1949.

———. *Freedom, Power, and Democratic Planning.* New York: Oxford University Press, 1950.

———. "The Problem of the Intelligentsia: An Inquiry into Its Past and Present Role," in his *Essays on the Sociology of Culture.* New York: Oxford University Press, 1956.

MANUEL, F. E. *The New World of H. Saint-Simon.* Cambridge, Mass.: Harvard University Press, 1956.

MARSH, ROBERT M. *The Mandarins.* New York: The Free Press of Glencoe, 1961.

MARSHALL, T. H. "Citizenship and Social Class," in his *Citizenship and Social Class.* Cambridge, England: Cambridge University Press, 1950.

MARVICK, DWAINE (ed.). *Political Decision-Makers*. New York: The Free Press of Glencoe, 1961.

MARX, KARL. *The Poverty of Philosophy*. New York: International Publishers, n.d.

———, and FRIEDRICH ENGELS. *Manifesto of the Communist Party*. New York: International Publishers, n.d.

———, and FRIEDRICH ENGELS. *Selected Correspondence, 1846-1895*. Trans. DONA TORR. New York: International Publishers, 1942.

———, and FRIEDRICH ENGELS. *The German Ideology*. New York: International Publishers, 1947.

———, and FRIEDRICH ENGELS. "Socialism: Utopian and Scientific," in *Selected Works,* Vol. II. Moscow: Foreign Language Publishing House, 1958.

MARX, ROBERT J. "Changing Patterns of Leadership in the American Reform Rabbinate, 1890-1957." Abstract of Doctoral Dissertation, Yale University, 1957.

MATTHEWS, DONALD R. *The Social Background of Political Decision Makers.* New York: Random House, 1954.

———. *U. S. Senators and Their World.* Chapel Hill: The University of North Carolina Press, 1960.

MAY, MARK A. *The Education of American Ministers,* Vol. III. New York: Institute of Social and Religious Research, 1934.

MEAD, SIDNEY E. "The Rise of the Evangelical Conception of the Ministry in America (1607-1850)," in *The Ministry in Historical Perspective.* Ed. H. RICHARD NIEBUHR and DANIEL D. WILLIAMS. New York: Harper, 1956.

MEISEL, JAMES H. *The Myth of the Ruling Class: Gaetano Mosca and the Elite.* Michigan: The University of Michigan Press, Ann Arbor Paperbacks, 1962.

MEREI, FERENC. "Group Leadership and Institutionalization," in *Readings in Social Psychology.* Ed. E. E. MACCOBY, T. M. NEWCOMB, and E. G. HARTLEY. New York: Henry Holt, 1958.

MERRIAM, CHARLES. "The Curse of Aristocracy," *AJS,* XLIII, No. 6 (May, 1938), 857-77.

MERTON, ROBERT K. "Science and Democratic Social Structure," in *Social Theory and Social Structure.* New York: The Free Press of Glencoe, 1957.

———, *et al. Reader in Bureaucracy.* New York: The Free Press of Glencoe, 1952.

———, LEONARD BROOM, and LEONARD S. COTTRELL, JR. *Sociology Today.* New York: Basic Books, 1959.

MEYNAUD, JEAN. "The Parliamentary Profession," *International Social Science Journal,* XIII, No. 4 (1961).

MICHAELSON, ROBERT S. "The Protestant Ministry in America: 1850 to the Present," in *The Ministry in Historical Perspective.* Ed. H. R. NIEBUHR and D. D. WILLIAMS. New York: Harper, 1956.

MICHELS, ROBERT. *Political Parties.* Trans. EDEN and CEDAR PAUL. New York: Dover, 1959.

MILLER, S. M. "Comparative Social Mobility," *Current Sociology,* IX, No. 1 (1960). Oxford, England: Basil Blackwell, 1960.

MILLER, WILLIAM. "American Lawyers in Business and Politics," *The Yale Law Journal* (January, 1951), 65-76.

MILLIS, WALTER. "Puzzle of the Military Mind," *New York Times Magazine,* November 18, 1962.

MILLS, C. WRIGHT. "The American Business Elite: A Collective Portrait," *The Tasks of Economic History,* supplement to the *Journal of Economic History,* V (December, 1945), 20-44.

———. *The New Men of Power.* New York: Harcourt Brace, 1948.

———. *The Power Elite.* New York: Oxford University Press, 1956.

MOORE, WILBERT E. *Industrial Relations and the Social Order.* New York: Macmillan, 1947.

———. "But Some Are More Equal Than Others," *ASR,* XXVIII, No. 1 (February, 1963), 13-18.

———. "Rejoinder," *ASR,* XXVIII, No. 1 (February, 1963), 26-8.

MORRIS, RICHARD T., and MELVIN SEEMAN. "The Problem of Leadership: An Interdisciplinary Approach," *AJS,* LVI, No. 2 (September, 1950), 149-56.

MOSCA, GAETANO. *The Ruling Class.* New York: McGraw-Hill, 1939.

MOSELY, PHILIP E. (ed.). *Social Change in Latin America Today: Its Implications for United States Policy.* New York: Vintage, 1960.

MOULIN, LEO. "The Nobel Prizes for the Sciences from 1901-1950—An Essay in Sociological Analysis," *BJS,* VI, No. 3 (September, 1955), 246-63.

NEUMANN, FRANZ. *Behemoth.* London: Victor Gollancz, 1943.

NEWCOMER, MABEL. *The Big Business Executive: The Factors That Made Him.* New York: Columbia University Press, 1955.

NIEBUHR, H. RICHARD, and D. D. WILLIAMS (eds.). *The Ministry in Historical Perspective.* New York: Harper, 1956.

NORTH, C. C., and PAUL K. HATT. "Jobs and Occupations: A Popular Evaluation," *Opinion News,* IX (September 1, 1947), 3-13.

NOWAK, STEFAN. "Egalitarian Attitudes of Warsaw Students," *ASR,* XXV, No. 2 (April, 1960), 219-32.

ODIN, A., *Genèse des Grands Hommes.* Paris: H. Welber, 1895.

OLMSTED, MICHAEL. *The Small Group.* New York: Random House, 1959.

ORWELL, GEORGE. *Animal Farm.* New York: New American Library, Signet, 1956.

OSSOWSKA, MARIA. "Changes in the Ethics of Fighting in the Course of the Last Century," *Transactions, Third World Congress of Sociology* (1956), 81-6.

OTTENBERG, SIMON, and PHOEBE (eds.). *Cultures and Societies of Africa.* New York: Random House, 1960.

PAGE, CHARLES H. *Class and American Sociology: from Ward to Ross.* New York: The Dial Press, 1940.

PARETO, VILFREDO. *Les Systèmes Socialistes,* Vols. I and II. Paris: V. Girard and F. Brière, 1902.

———. The Mind and Society. Trans. A. BONGIORNO and A. LIVINGSTON, ed. ARTHUR LIVINGSTON. 4 Vols. New York: Harcourt Brace, 1935.

"The Parliamentary Profession," *International Social Science Journal,* XIII, No. 4 (1961), entire issue.

PARSONS, TALCOTT. "A Revised Analytical Approach to the Theory of Social Stratification," in *Class, Status and Power.* Eds. REINHARD BENDIX and S. M. LIPSET. New York: The Free Press of Glencoe, 1953.

———. *The Structure of Social Action.* New York: McGraw-Hill, 1937.

———. *The Social System.* New York: The Free Press of Glencoe, 1951.

———. "Religious Perspectives in Sociology and Social Psychology," in *Reader in Comparative Religion*. Eds. WILLIAM A. LESSA and EVON Z. VOGT. New York: Row, Peterson, 1958.

———. "An Approach to Psychological Theory in Terms of the Theory of Action," in *Psychology: A Study of a Science*, Vol. III, ed. SIGMUND KOCH. New York: McGraw-Hill, 1959.

———. *Structure and Process in Modern Societies*. New York: The Free Press of Glencoe, 1960.

———, and NEIL SMELSER. *Economy and Society*. New York: The Free Press of Glencoe, 1956.

———, R. F. BALES, and EDWARD SHILS. *Working Papers in the Theory of Action*. New York: The Free Press of Glencoe, 1952.

PERISTIANY, J. G. "Law," in *The Institutions of Primitive Society*. New York: The Free Press of Glencoe, 1956.

PIRENNE, HENRI. "The Stages in the Social History of Capitalism." Address delivered at the International Congress of Historical Studies, London, 1913.

PLATO. *The Laws*, in *The Dialogues of Plato*, Vol. II. Trans. B. JOWETT. New York: Random House, 1937.

POLSBY, NELSON W. "Three Problems in the Analysis of Community Power," *ASR*, XXIV, No. 6 (December, 1959), 796-803.

———. "Community Power: Some Reflections on the Recent Literature," *ASR*, XXVII, No. 6 (December, 1962), 838-41.

PORTERFIELD, AUSTIN L., and JACK P. GIBBS. "Occupational Prestige and Social Mobility of Suicides in New Zealand," *AJS*, LXVI, No. 2 (September, 1960), 147-52.

POWDERMAKER, HORTENSE. *Hollywood, The Dream Factory*, New York: Grosset and Dunlap, The Universal Library, 1950.

POWELL, ELWIN H. "Occupation, Status, and Suicide: Toward a Redefinition of Anomie," *ASR*, XXIII, No. 2 (April, 1958), 131-40.

PRITCHETT, V. S. "The Man Who Snubbed Himself," *New Statesman*, March 14, 1959, p. 371.

Prospect for America. (The Rockefeller Panel Reports.) New York: Doubleday, 1961.

RADIN, PAUL. *Primitive Religion*. New York: Dover, 1957.

RAYMOND, JACK. "The Military-Industrial Complex: An Analysis," *New York Times*, January 22, 1961, p. 4E.

REDL, FRITZ. "Group Emotion and Leadership," in *Small Groups*. Ed. A. PAUL HARE, E. F. BORGATTA, and R. F. BALES. New York: Alfred A. Knopf, 1955, pp. 71-87.

REDLICH, FRITZ. *History of American Business Leaders*. Ann Arbor, Mich.: Edwards Bros., 1940.

RESTON, JAMES. "Our History Suggests a Remedy," in *The National Purpose*. New York: Holt, Rinehart and Winston, 1960.

———. "The Eisenhower Era," *New York Times*, January 19, 1961.

———. "To the Great Men's Ladies, God Help Them," *New York Times*, January 20, 1961.

———. "Kennedy Can Beat 'Em but Can He Convince 'Em?" *New York Times*, April 15, 1962.

RIESMAN, DAVID. *The Lonely Crowd*. New York: Doubleday, 1953.

ROBBINS, JHAN, and JUNE. "The Surprising Beliefs of Our Future Ministers," *Redbook* (August, 1961).

ROE, ANNE. *The Making of a Scientist.* New York: Dodd Mead, 1952.
ROSENBERG, HANS. *Bureaucracy, Aristocracy and Autocracy: The Prussian Experience 1660-1815.* Cambridge, Mass.: Harvard University Press, 1958.
ROSS, RALPH GILBERT. "Elites and the Methodology of Politics," *POQ,* XV (Spring, 1952), 27-32.
ROSSI, PETER H. "Community Decision Making," *ASQ,* I (March, 1957), 415-43.
ROSSITER, CLINTON. *The American Presidency.* New York: The New American Library, Mentor Book, 1959.
ROSTEN, LEO C. *The Washington Correspondents.* New York: Harcourt Brace, 1937.
———. *Hollywood.* New York: Harcourt Brace, 1941.
ROVERE, RICHARD H. "The American Establishment," *Esquire* (May, 1962).

SAINT-SIMON, COUNT HENRI DE. *Oeuvres Choisis,* Tome Premier. Bruxelles: Fr. Van Meened et Cie, 1839.
SAMPSON, ANTHONY. "What's in a Title," *New York Times Magazine,* January 15, 1961.
SANTILLANA, G. DE. "Galileo and J. Robert Oppenheimer," *The Reporter,* December 26, 1957.
SAPIN, BURTON M., and RICHARD C. SNYDER. *The Role of the Military in American Foreign Policy.* New York: Doubleday Short Studies in Political Science, 1954.
SARTON, GEORGE. *A History of Science: Hellenistic Science and Culture in the Last Three Centuries B.C.* Cambridge, Mass.: Harvard University Press, 1959.
SARTORI, G. "Parliamentarians in Italy," *International Social Science Journal,* XIII, No. 4 (1961), 583-600.
SCHERER, ROSS P. "Career Patterns in the Ministry: The Lutheran Church-Missouri Synod." Paper presented at the American Sociological Association Annual Meetings, Washington, D.C., August 30-September 2, 1962.
SCHLESINGER, ARTHUR, JR. "On Heroic Leadership," *Encounter* (December, 1960).
SCHMIDHAUSER, JOHN R. *The Supreme Court. Its Politics, Personalities, and Procedures.* New York: Holt, Rinehart and Winston, 1960.
SCHMOLLER, GUSTAV. *Die Soziale Frage, Klassenbildung, Arbeiterfrage, Klassenkampf.* Munich and Leipzig: Duncker and Humboldt, 1918.
SCHNEIDER, JOSEPH. "Social Class, Historical Circumstances and Fame." *AJS* XLIII, No. 1 (July, 1937), 37-56.
———. "The Definition of Eminence and the Social Origins of Famous English Men of Genius." *ASR,* III, No. 6 (December, 1938), 834-49.
SCHULZE, ROBERT O. "The Role of Economic Dominants in Community Power Structure," *ASR,* XXIII, No. 1 (February, 1958), 3-9.
———, and LEONARD U. BLUMENBERG. "The Determinants of Local Power Elites." *AJS,* LXIII, No. 3 (November, 1957), 290-6.
SCHUMPETER, JOSEPH. *Imperialism and Social Classes.* New York: Meridian, 1955.
SELZNICK, PHILIP. *TVA and the Grass Roots.* Berkeley, California: The University of California Press, 1949.
SERENO, RENZO. *The Rulers.* New York: Praeger, 1962.
SEVAREID, ERIC. "To the Victor," *New York Post,* November 14, 1960.

SHANNON, J. R., and MAXINE SHAW. "Education of Business and Professional Leaders." *ASR,* V, No. 3 (June, 1940), 381-3.

SHARP, WALTER RICE. "Historical Changes in Recruitment," in *Reader in Bureaucracy,* ed. ROBERT K. MERTON, *et al.*

SHILS, EDWARD. "The Intellectuals and the Powers: Some Perspectives for Comparative Analysis," in *Comparative Studies in Society and History,* I, No. 1 (October, 1958), 5-22.

———, and MICHAEL YOUNG. "The Meaning of the Coronation," *Sociological Review,* I (December, 1953), 63-81.

SJOBERG, GIDEON. "Contradictory Functional Requirements and Social Systems," *Journal of Conflict Resolution,* IV, No. 2 (1960), 198-208.

SMIGEL, ERWIN O. "The Impact of Recruitment on the Organization of the Large Law Firm," *ASR,* XXV, No. 1 (February, 1960), 55-66.

SMUTS, ROBERT W. *European Impressions of the American Worker.* New York: King's Crown Press, Columbia University, 1953.

SMYTHE, HUGH H., and MABEL M. *The New Nigerian Elite.* Stanford, California: Stanford University Press, 1960.

SOROKIN, PITIRIM A. *Social Mobility.* New York: Harper, 1927.

———. *Social and Cultural Dynamics.* Vol. IV, *Basic Principles and Methods.* New York: American Book Company, 1941.

———. *Society, Culture and Personality.* New York: Harper, 1947.

———, and CARLE C. ZIMMERMAN. "Farmer Leaders in the United States," *Social Forces,* VII, No. 1 (September, 1928), 33-45.

SPEIER, HANS. "The American Soldier and the Sociology of Military Organization," in *Continuities in Social Research.* Ed. ROBERT K. MERTON and PAUL F. LAZARSFELD. New York: The Free Press of Glencoe, 1950.

SPENCER, HERBERT. *The Principles of Sociology.* New York: D. Appleton, 1896.

STEWART, ROSEMARY G., and PAUL DUNCAN-JONES. "Educational Background and Career History of British Managers, with some American Comparisons," *Explorations in Entrepreneurial History,* IX, No. 2 (n.d.), 61-71.

STRAUSZ-HUPE, ROBERT. *Power and Community,* New York: Praeger, 1956.

SUTTER, JEAN, and LEON TABAH. "Les Notions d'isolat de Population Minimum," *Population,* VI, No. 3 (July-September, 1951), 480-98.

SUTTON, FRANCIS X., SEYMOUR E. HARRIS, CARL KAYSEN, and JAMES TOBIN. *The American Business Creed.* Cambridge, Mass.: Harvard University Press, 1957.

SYME, RONALD. *Colonial Elites, Rome, Spain, and the Americas.* London: Oxford University Press, 1958.

TAUSSIG, F. W., and C. S. JOSLYN. *American Business Leaders.* New York: Macmillan, 1932.

TAWNEY, R. H. *Equality.* New York: Harcourt Brace, 1929.

TERRIEN, FREDERICK W., and DONALD L. MILLS. "The Effect of Changing Size upon the Internal Structure of Organizations," *ASR,* XX, No. 1 (February, 1955), 11-14.

"Text of the Encyclical by Pope John XXIII on Social Problems of the Modern World," Rome, May 15, 1961. *New York Times,* July 15, 1961.

"Text of the Soviet Party's Draft Program," Moscow, July 30, 1961. *New York Times,* August 1, 1961.

THOMAS, HUGH (ed.). *The Establishment, A Symposium*. New York: Clarkson N. Potter, 1959.

THOMPSON, LAURENCE. *The Challenge of Change*. London: Oxford University Press, 1956.

THRUPP, SYLVIA L. *The Merchant Class of Medieval London, 1300-1500*. Chicago: University of Chicago Press, 1948.

TOYNBEE, ARNOLD J. *A Study of History*. 12 vols. London: Oxford University Press, 1934-1959.

———. "Spiritual Freedom as the Great Difference," *New York Times Magazine*, January 15, 1961.

TROTSKY, LEON. *The History of the Russian Revolution*. 3 vols. Trans. MAX EASTMAN. Ann Arbor: The University of Michigan Press, 1960.

TUMIN, MELVIN. "Some Principles of Stratification: A Critical Analysis," *ASR*, XVIII, No. 4 (August, 1953), 387-97.

———. *Social Class and Social Change in Puerto Rico*. Princeton, New Jersey: Princeton University Press, 1961.

———. "On Equality," *ASR*, XXVIII, No. 1 (February, 1963), 19-26.

TURNER, RALPH H. "Sponsored and Contest Mobility," *ASR*, XXV, No. 6 (December, 1960), 855-67.

VICTOR, PAUL EMILE. *The Great Hunger*. London: Hutchinson, 1955.

VISHER, STEPHEN SARGENT. "Environmental Backgrounds of Leading American Scientists," *ASR*, XIII, No. 1 (February, 1948), 65-72.

WALLACE, SIR DONALD MACKENZIE. *Russia on the Eve of War and Revolution*. New York: Vintage, 1961.

WARNER, W. LLOYD. "The Study of Social Stratification," in *Review of Sociology*, ed. JOSEPH B. GITTLER. New York: Wiley, 1957.

———, and J. O. LOW. *The Social System of a Modern Factory*. New Haven: Yale University Press, 1947.

———, and JAMES C. ABEGGLEN. *Big Business Leaders in America*. New York: Harper, 1955.

———, ———. *Occupational Mobility in American Business and Industry, 1928-1952*. Minneapolis: University of Minnesota, 1955.

———, and NORMAN H. MARTIN (eds.) *Industrial Man*. New York: Harper, 1959.

WEBER, MAX. "Die Sozialen Gruende des Untergangs der Antiken Kultur," in *Gesammelte Aufsaetze zur Sozial und Wirtschaftsgeschichte*. Tuebingen: J. C. B. Mohr, 1924.

———. *From Max Weber: Essays in Sociology*, ed. HANS H. GERTH and C. WRIGHT MILLS. New York: Oxford University Press, 1946.

———. *The Theory of Social and Economic Organization*. Trans. and ed. A. M. HENDERSON and TALCOTT PARSONS. New York: Oxford University Press, 1947.

———. *The Protestant Ethic and the Spirit of Capitalism*. New York: Scribner's, 1950.

———. *Ancient Judaism*. Trans. H. H. GERTH. New York: The Free Press of Glencoe, 1951.

———. *The Religion of China*. Trans. and ed. H. H. GERTH. New York: The Free Press of Glencoe, 1951.

———. *The Religion of India: The Sociology of Hinduism and Buddhism*. New York: The Free Press of Glencoe, 1958.

WEDGWOOD, JOSIAH. *The Economics of Inheritance.* London: Routledge & Sons, 1929.

WESTON, J. *From Ritual to Romance.* New York: Doubleday, 1957.

WHELPTON, P. K. "A Generation of Demographic Change," in *The Population Ahead,* ed. ROY G. FRANCIS. Minneapolis: The University of Minnesota Press, 1958.

WHITE, T. H. *The Making of the President.* New York: Atheneum, 1961.

WIESE, LEOPOLD VON. *Gesellschaftliche Stände und Klassen.* Bern: A. Francke AG Verlag, 1950.

WILLHELM, SIDNEY, and GIDEON SJOBERG. "The Social Characteristics of Entertainers," *Social Forces,* XXXVII, No. 1 (October, 1958), 72-6.

WILLSON, F. M. G. "The Ranks of Entry of New Members of the British Cabinet, 1868-1958," *Political Studies,* VII, No. 3 (1959), 222-32.

WITTFOGEL, KARL A. *Oriental Despotism.* New Haven: Yale University Press, 1957.

WOLFF, KURT H. (ed.). *The Sociology of Georg Simmel.* New York: The Free Press of Glencoe, 1950.

——— (ed.). *Emile Durkheim, 1858-1917.* Columbus: Ohio State University Press, 1960.

WOLFINGER, RAYMOND E. "Reputation and Reality in the Study of Community Power," *ASR,* XXV, No. 5 (October, 1960), 636-44.

———. "A Plea for a Decent Burial," *ASR,* XXVII, No. 6 (December, 1962), 841-7.

WRONG, DENNIS H. "The Functional Theory of Stratification," *ASR,* XXIV, No. 6 (December, 1959), 772-83.

YOUNG, MICHAEL. *The Rise of Meritocracy.* New York: Random House, 1959.

ZAHRNT, HEINZ. *Probleme der Elitebildung.* Hamburg: Furche-Verlag, 1955.

INDEX

ABOUT THE AUTHOR

Born in Vienna, Suzanne Keller completed her undergraduate work at Hunter College and received her M.A. and Ph.D from Columbia University. In 1953-54 she was a post-doctoral fellow at the Center of International Studies of Princeton University, and in 1960 a Research Associate at the Center of International Studies of the Massachusetts Institute of Technology. She was awarded a Fulbright Fellowship covering the academic year 1963-64 for research and teaching in Greece at the Athens Technological Institute. Professor Keller has also done extensive research in Paris and Munich, and has taught at Hunter College, Brandeis University, New York University, Vassar College, Princeton University, and New York Medical College.

A NOTE ON THE TYPE

The text of this book was set on the Linotype in a face called TIMES ROMAN, designed by Stanley Morison for The Times (London), and first introduced by that newspaper in 1932.

Among typographers and designers of the twentieth century, Stanley Morison has been a strong forming influence, as typographical advisor to the English Monotype Corporation, as a director of two distinguished English publishing houses, and as a writer of sensibility, erudition, and keen practical sense.